CW01510224

The Most Dangerous Detective:

The Outrageous Glen Patrick Hallahan and the Rat Pack

By Steve Bishop

ISBN-13: 978-1480253797

ISBN-10:1480253790

Dedicated to all those who were brave or foolish enough to find the courage to stand up, speak out and risk ostracism, job loss and even their lives in acting against oppression and corruption.

Introduction

Was Glen Patrick Hallahan, who became famous as the ace detective who 'solved' the Sundown Murders and won the George Medal for bravery, a callous murderer who killed at least twice and sent an innocent man to the gallows?

The Most Dangerous Detective provides the evidence to help answer these questions but this is also a multi-layered story covering nearly 25 years of corruption in Australia's Sunshine State of Queensland, together with murders most foul on the Northern Territory-South Australia border, courtroom drama in Adelaide and police protection of a sex empire in Sydney.

Two state premiers, three judges and a crime reporter who rose to be an editor are shown to have made decisions or reached conclusions which were at least perverse.

The book calls for a posthumous pardon in one murder case and for another murder case to be re-opened.

Holding the stage through this story of murders, organised crime, perjury, planted evidence, invented confessions, protection from on high, a major heroin importation, a bank robbery, political corruption, protection rackets and other appalling behaviour is the man who struck fear into even a federal political leader – Glen Patrick Hallahan, the most dangerous detective.

It contains the key elements of a whodunnit and a thriller, with complex plots to disentangle, clues to analyse and false leads which lead to tension as the hunt closes in on the villain. Will the hunters catch their man? Or will the prey somehow manage to escape?

The devious and cunning political plotting could stand alone as a tale of intrigue as two crooked police officers are selected as commissioners, supposedly independent inquiries produce the results desired by government and the leading anti-corruption campaigner has his parliamentary career killed off.

Meet some memorable characters, such as:

Shirley Brifman, who wore the cast-offs from 12 brothers and sisters growing up in country Queensland before becoming Sydney's richest madame;

Col Bennett, a 43-year-old bespectacled barrister who's prepared to fight with his fists as well as with words;

John Shobbrook, a keen young Narcotics Bureau officer who builds his own surveillance van complete with roof-mounted video camera utilising sophisticated equipment such as bits of old vacuum cleaner;

John Milligan, a slightly effeminate former judge's associate with the IQ of a genius who gets his kicks by becoming a criminal;

Gunther Bahnemann, double Iron Cross winner and crocodile wrestler, who becomes a successful author from a prison cell.

The book also provides a fascinating journey through time, starting from the innocent days of the late 50s when police officers were bracketed with doctors, bank managers, the judiciary and government leaders as part of an establishment which was trusted to always do the right thing. The journey finishes in an era of disillusionment with the knowledge that some of these people and institutions can be deeply flawed.

And there's some travelling to do – from the dusty, scorched, red heart of the outback and Alice Springs to the prim and proper city of Adelaide in the days before its corner churches were converted to night clubs; to Sydney's seedy Kings Cross in the swinging sixties; to Queensland's isolated towns of Mount Isa and Charleville, separated by 1200 lonely kilometres; and there's even a side trip to sedate, genteel Eastbourne, on England's south coast where a serial lady killer is on the loose. But we'll be spending most of our time in sub-tropical Brisbane with its veranda'd wooden houses on quarter-acre blocks, palms and poincianas, hilltop views and shady valleys, its broad convoluted river and its laid back lifestyle.

Why would you worry about corruption when the sun comes up each morning, there's a blue sky all day, the cost of living is low and life is easy?

The Fitzgerald Inquiry into corruption, between 1987 and 1989, finally exposed much of the endemic corruption which had riddled Queensland but this book reveals many untold stories and throws new light on previous revelations.

Foreword by the Hon Mike Ahern AO,

Premier of Queensland 1987-89

There is an old saying my father used to use: *"Those who don't learn from history usually relive it"*.

During my life I have seen many examples of people doing just that.

However, a good question is "Who will write the history? And further, what are their qualifications to write it anyway?

During my time in politics in Queensland, there was operating in the State a system of police corruption operating "under the radar" called "The Joke". It operated for many years unknown by some including myself and denied by others. The Joke grew in influence and reached its zenith with the appointment of Terry Lewis as Police Commissioner. There came a time however, when The Joke became too arrogant and obvious and media publicity forced a Royal Commission on the Government and the Fitzgerald Inquiry was appointed. It was a real game changer for Queensland.

I gave a public undertaking at the time that Tony Fitzgerald's Report would be implemented *"Lock, Stock and Barrel"*. *238* people were charged as a result of the Inquiry, some with multiple offences. 148 were found guilty. Lewis was identified as part of a so called "rat pack" of three members: Tony Murphy, Glen Hallahan and Terry Lewis. These three wielded enormous power and influence in the Queensland Police Force over the years. This ended abruptly with the Fitzgerald Inquiry and the Police Commissioner Lewis was jailed

The lead up to this watershed inquiry was an important time. Just how such a cancer could develop in a police force is a vital study for public administrators here and in other jurisdictions. This book gives some opinions as to how The Joke's supporters grew the process.

Prior to this Steve Bishop was a respected ethical journalist who, from his position, was able to see The Joke unfold and grow. He made notes at length on the various developments he could see occurring over the years. He determined to write a book about it all some day. I met him at various intervals over the years. I always found him fair and professional.

His central character Glendon Patrick Hallahan was characterized in the Brisbane media at the time as an "Ace Detective". Steve Bishop finds him as one who let an innocent man go to the gallows, in the process let a murderer go free, was a notorious verballer, a possible murderer and one of the architects of the Asian drug import business into Australia. I am grateful

I didn't meet Hallahan. It is truly amazing that Hallahan and others were able to act as they did.

I was appalled to read this book. As one who was in Parliament from 1968 to 2000 in various roles, it was not comfortable reading. My ministerial positions were in economic portfolios so I suppose it is not surprising that I had little knowledge or contact with the major characters mentioned in this book. I am also consoled by the fact that things are much better now that the recommendations of the Fitzgerald Inquiry are implemented.

I am very grateful that Steve Bishop has had the courage and conviction to write as he has. He is well qualified to write it. He has carried out a lot of research to confirm his assertions. I hope many read it. It would be so easy to forget and simply move on.

It must be emphasized that if we are not to have a "*Joke Mark2*" some day, as many people as possible should learn the lessons of history well described in this book.

Hon Mike Ahern AO
Former Premier of Queensland

Preface

Queensland: beautiful one day, perfect the next but constantly riddled with corruption. That was the situation I discovered when I arrived in Brisbane in 1982 fresh from Fleet Street to start a new life with my wife and two young children. I had been attracted by the outdoor lifestyle in an eternal summer and an egalitarian society. I was looking forward to writing positive and uplifting stories for the state's Sunday Sun instead of the weekly diet of exposés and revelations of the News of the World where I had worked as an investigative reporter for the previous nine years – a time when the paper was still principled and ethical in dealing with people and information. But it didn't take long to realise something was rotten in the state of Queensland and that the weeds of corruption were actually being propagated and nurtured by the most senior levels of government, with a crooked police commissioner acting as head gardener.

At one level innocent people were framed, demonstrators bashed by police, political opponents spied on, honest police bullied and vilified, and efficient companies failed to gain government contracts despite submitting the best tenders.

More extremely, lives were ruined or extinguished. There was a lack of action in tackling the growing illegal drug trade, with some victims becoming criminals to support their habits and others dying from overdoses. Families fell apart when gamblers at the illegal casinos lost vast amounts, even their homes. Young girls were allowed to become enslaved as prostitutes. There were suspicious deaths and unsolved murders – prostitutes who perhaps threatened to rock the boat and were found dead from overdoses, drug dealers who became a problem, and men who were involved with illegal gambling.

The media had largely failed to expose this regime and its effects. The state's daily newspaper, The Courier-Mail, was a sedate, old-fashioned daily newspaper which, until 1982, suffered from a lack of competition. There were other media outlets but many journalists were in thrall to some of the biggest villains, gambling regularly with illegal starting price bookies and drinking after hours at an illegal gambling den associated with a brothel, where police were paid for protection. There was also an attitude among some journalists that this was the way it had always been and there wasn't much point in trying to change it.

As an example, I came across a flagrant abuse of power by the officer in charge of a small country town. He avoided any risk of local youngsters getting drunk and disorderly on Friday nights by locking them up early in the evening, with no charges but with a beating when he considered it necessary, and then releasing them in the early hours of the next morning. The chief of staff told me: "Look, there's nothing wrong with that. I was kicked down the back steps of my local police station when I misbehaved at that age and it taught me a lesson." I had to take time off work and visit the town in my own time, take statutory declarations and then give my story to the Opposition police spokesman to expose the brutality. For my trouble I was 'named and shamed' in Parliament as a lousy no-good journalist by the government MP representing the town.

I made it my business to discover why Queensland had reached this appalling position. In addition to asking pointed questions of people in a position to know, I read every copy of the Sunday Sun for 30 years and then examined Hansard for a similar period, photocopying anything and everything which I felt had a bearing on the corruption. Later, I analysed the Sunday Sun's coverage of the 1963-64 National Hotel Inquiry as part of a master's degree and wrote an 85,000 word thesis on why it was that the media had failed to expose corruption over a 30-year period.

In February 1986 I compiled an in-depth article for the Sunday Sun naming and exposing the criminals who ran Brisbane's prostitution rackets in the guise of massage parlours. I used as a basis for the story a government report by Director of Prosecutions Des Sturgess who had hidden the identities of the Mr Bigs. The newspaper refused to name the men on legal grounds. It was another year before The Courier-Mail got round to printing a similar story and then running a brilliant, sustained campaign by reporter Phil Dickie which led ultimately, with an explosive ABC documentary by Chris Masters, to the establishment of the two-year Fitzgerald inquiry and the end of the corrupt systems.

The inquiry and its revelations about corruption by senior police and politicians was one of the most important chapters in the history of Queensland but on several occasions executives attempted to prevent me covering it, including one occasion when I was called out from the inquiry's press benches and sent on an urgent assignment to write a story about cattle in Rockhampton. There were occasions when the Sunday Sun refused to print exclusive stories I had researched. One of the possible reasons for the newspaper's attitude will become clear in this book.

Over the years since then I have interviewed men and women who played a major role in fighting corruption. For a long time I had difficulty in working out how to tell a complicated story spanning three decades and involving criminals, a network of crooked police and the involvement of two state premiers and some of their ministers. I took inspiration from Joseph Wambaugh and John Berendt and decided that I wanted a narrative that knitted a myriad of events together into a compulsive storyline that brought personalities and the culture that had shaped them to the fore.

And then former detective Glen Patrick Hallahan came to my rescue. I realised Hallahan had been at the centre of major criminal and corruption activities for the best part of three decades. More importantly, there was a detailed paper trail of statements, court cases, inquiries and newspaper stories. Through him I could tell a story on many levels – murders most foul, who dunnits, the tension of manhunts, rewriting a section of Queensland's political history, and the changing character of Queenslanders from the naïve innocence of the late 50s through to the cynicism of the 80s.

Peter James, a trailblazer in dissecting and exposing the activities of the Rat Pack of corrupt Queensland police officers, wrote books about the Sundown Murders and the National Hotel Inquiry. I include a detailed examination of both events from source material but have a very different focus and therefore reach a set of different conclusions.

I was fortunate in being granted long interviews by barrister Col Bennett and former Assistant Commissioner Norm Gulbransen, two men who spent many years fighting corruption. They believed that, while not always accurate, the vast majority of what 'vice queen' Shirley Brifman said in her long interviews with police was credible, while former detective Basil Hicks is on the record saying he had no doubt she was telling the truth. John Shobbrook deserves the same recognition as Bennett and Gulbransen and I thank him for providing me with his gritty story. There are many more people who have helped me with information, including Joe Moore, who told me of Shirley's early life, Ken Blanch, who has written extensively about crime and corruption in Queensland, David Young, who bravely volunteered to give evidence against corrupt police and had his reputation unjustly savaged, former Democrats leader Senator Don Chipp, former Queensland Premier Mike Ahern, former Queensland Deputy Premier Bill Gunn, Kevin Hooper MP, Ron Royes, long-serving police officer Arthur Pitts, Gerald Stone, Bob Gordon, Des Sturgess and many others. I thank Charles Hopkins and the South Australian Police Historical Society for permission to use passages from his articles on the Sundown murders; and Sandra Smith of the Macquarie Regional Library, Dubbo, for going beyond her normal duties to help me.

All words placed in quotation marks are taken from interviews, official documents and newspaper articles. Most indirect speech is my summary of longer quotes from interviews, official documents and newspaper articles. Shirley Brifman was interviewed at length 21 times by police and the transcripts later tabled in the South Australian Parliament. I have taken sentences from answers scattered through these interviews dealing with particular events and people and placed them in what I have assessed to be logical sequences. I have changed the name of a rape victim.

I have converted most imperial measurements to metric to aid comprehension but have left unchanged those measurements referred to in quotations. The Australian pound comprised 20 shillings, each of which comprised 12 pence. A guinea was 1 pound and 1 shilling. On metrication 10 shillings became 1 dollar and 1 shilling became 10 cents.

Steve Bishop
September 28, 2012.

Contents

Chapter 1 - The Bowmans Are Missing

News that the space age had arrived with Sputnik circling the earth and that Jailhouse Rock was top of the charts may have reached the Bowmans via their pedal-powered radio connecting them to the operator at the Royal Flying Doctor Service. It would have depended on how much time the operator had for gossip between dealing with the health of a few hundred people scattered across thousands of square kilometres of a land with no mains electricity, phones or sealed roads. News was as scarce as water. And the people of the red heart seldom made news. But as Christmas approached, millions of people would become deeply concerned about the fate of the Bowmans.

In his mid-40s, Pete Bowman had a rural background but for years had lived in South Australia's capital city of Adelaide and worked as the chief recording engineer of Radio 5AD. Home in Adelaide was a pleasant, modern single-storey home in suburban Davenport Terrace, opposite a wooded park in the eastern suburbs. He was a big-boned man, with a face dominated by a large nose and ears, connected by large, round-rimmed glasses. His wife Thyra, also known as Sally, was 43, wore floral frocks and, as was expected in middle-class Australia, spent each day on "home duties". They had two daughters. Marian, aged 16, had suffered from encephalitis when she was six and had suffered severe neurological after-effects. Wendy, 14, was blue-eyed, fair-haired, excelled at sport and was deeply religious. She was very close to her father and adored two pet dogs, a brown corgi mix and a black and white sheepdog. The family's lives changed dramatically in 1957 when Pete's brother Brian, owner of Mount Helen Station, a vast cattle property four hours on a dirt track west of Alice Springs, bought the property on its northern boundary, Coniston Station. The 2,000 square kilometre property bordering the Tanami Desert looked waterless with its dried-up river beds and creeks but Coniston had a hidden lake, a huge and sustainable underground water basin. Brian's problem was that although Coniston's homestead was only 150 kilometres to the north of Mount Helen the Western MacDonnell Ranges barred his way and there was no road between the two stations. To drive the 140 kilometres into Alice, 100 kilometres up the main Alice-Darwin road and 150 kilometres along a dirt track to the Coniston homestead took eight or nine hours. Brian needed someone to look after Mount Helen while he sought to develop Coniston so he invited Pete to come out to manage Mt Helen with a view to eventually forming a partnership.

Pete moved his family from suburbia to the lonely Mount Helen homestead in May 1957 as winter approached. Not that winter meant much in central Australia: it was like turning a grill half off during the day, but the nights were blissfully cooler. They moved into the prefabricated homestead which Brian had built in 1955. Pete was up at dawn most days with the dawn chorus to take advantage of the cooler temperatures of the early mornings, giving his aboriginal stockmen instructions on what he wanted from them each day.

The closest neighbours were several kilometres away and the main road through this vast landscape, north to Darwin and south to Port Augusta in South Australia, was still a dirt track.

The landscape is spectacular but this beauty can be a killer. You can die of thirst if you don't know where the water holes are. In summer the oven-heat can dehydrate you, burn you and send you into delirious sunstroke in an afternoon. To make things worse, a drought had started the previous year and there were no signs of it easing. Cattle were dying as the pasture dried and died and the red dirt turned to dust. It's a land so harsh that the spinifex grass has to send its roots down three metres to survive. Stations were forced to de-stock and the future looked increasingly uncertain. Pete Bowman was finding it tough going.

So he was delighted in November when one of his former colleagues at Radio 5AD, Tom Whelan, arrived at Mount Helen for a three-week holiday. The copper-haired 22-year-old had joined 5AD in 1953 as assistant recording technician and Bowman had trained him to take over his job when he left for Glen Helen. In the process they had become close friends. Tom provided male company, a listening ear, an extra hand. His plan was to return to Adelaide with the Bowmans when they left for their Christmas holiday on December 4.

Wednesday the fourth was a day of great excitement. For the girls it meant they would shortly be enjoying the company of other youngsters for the first time in six months. Thyra was also looking forward to spending time with her housewife friends in Adelaide and enjoying the conveniences of a modern kitchen with running water and an electric stove instead of the wood-burning range at the back of the homestead. She would have shops round the corner instead of having to depend on a monthly trip to Alice Springs which took an entire day to accomplish. Pete was looking forward to a few weeks without the worry of the drought.

Being young and single, Tom had splashed out on a return flight from Adelaide to Alice. The Bowmans decided that with Tom as a chaperone it would make sense to send Marian, with her disabilities, with him instead of her having to suffer a three-day car journey. So Pete, Thyra and Wendy would make the long drive, along with the two dogs in the family car, a 1954 Standard Vanguard, one of the last of the big, tall, rounded cars that stood about 150 centimetres high and you sat up high. Already the newer models were lower and sleeker.

Most of the 1,700 kilometre drive would be over sand, rocks, roots and gravel. They would spend the first night at a hotel in Alice Springs 200 kilometres away but that still left at least one night camping at the side of the track for there were no towns in the 680 kilometres between Alice and Coober Pedy, the opal-mining capital of the world where many miners live underground to avoid the temperature extremes. The most crucial item to pack was a four-gallon (18-litre) drum of water to keep them alive through the dusty, empty plains. Next came a tucker box with enough food for four days and a two-gallon can of petrol. There were a few clean clothes, bed rolls and tarpaulins. To deal with snakes, any kangaroos or wallabies injured on the road and the chance of shooting a rabbit for the pot they carried a Sportmaster Remington rifle. They just had to remember not to place more than six cartridges in it because it would jam. They took two boxes of cartridges – 50 solid-nosed bullets and 50 hollow-nosed bullets.

Pete noted that they left the homestead at 4.40pm and arrived at Alice Springs about 9pm. Thyra took the wheel for about half of the journey. That night they stayed at the historic Stuart Arms Hotel, built in 1889 when less than a dozen Europeans lived in the town. The dogs were not allowed in the hotel so Wendy insisted on sleeping in the car with them. Thyra and Marian shared one room while Pete and Tom shared another. Like Wendy, Tom was deeply religious and knelt at his bed praying for a safe journey. Next morning Pete woke with a piercing headache and told the others he was not sure if he was going to be able to drive. Tom came up with a solution – Pete should take his place on the plane with Marian. Tom would share the driving with Thyra. They checked their supply of cash, with Thyra having about 40 pounds and Tom well over 20 pounds. Pete would have the rest of that day and night in Alice with Marian before they caught their plane at 3.30 on the Friday afternoon.

All this took time and instead of getting away soon after dawn it was 10.56am on Thursday, December 5 and already well on its way towards 40 degrees centigrade when Pete and Marian waved goodbye to Thyra, Wendy and Tom, all sitting on the front bench seat of the car, with the two dogs in the back.

The drive was very different to the previous evening when the tilted, exposed, jagged sandstone strata of the Western MacDonnell Ranges soared over them on their left all the way to the Heavitree Gap in the range where they turned north and into Alice. Today they drove south out of Alice, through the gap and into a land which for most of the journey consisted of vast flat horizons with not a building in sight. The dirt road south to Port Augusta had been graded two years before and now as many as a dozen cars a day travelled the 1,200 kilometre route between the two towns.

They had covered about 300 townless kilometres when they pulled off the track for the night. There were still another 900 kilometres to Port Augusta and a further 300 on better roads from there to Adelaide. They stopped in an area of scrub where the bushes were just high enough to block any view of the surrounding country but they could still see the track. There they lit a camp fire to cook their evening meal and brew tea. They went to sleep under the stars still wearing the clothes they had been wearing during the day, Thyra in a floral dress, Wendy in a cream blouse and blue-grey shorts and Tom in a dark shirt and khaki military-type trousers but minus shoes and socks. They had blankets to keep them warm if the temperature dipped much below the usual 20 degrees centigrade. Thyra would probably have joined Wendy and Tom in prayer, no doubt continuing to ask God for a safe journey.

In far off Adelaide Pete was opening up the Adelaide house after it had been shut up for so long. He went shopping on the Saturday and planned a family meal for that night. When his wife and Wendy failed to arrive he wasn't over-alarmed, after all, it was a massive drive in wearying conditions. But when they still hadn't arrived on Sunday afternoon Pete raised the alarm with police.

The Royal Flying Doctor Service at Port Augusta contacted pastoral properties en route without success. A road block was set up at Port Augusta, so that police could seek information from travellers who had come from Alice Springs. On Tuesday December 10 South Australia's morning newspaper, The Advertiser, carried a front page story about the disappearance under the headline "Overdue on NT Trip". From then on the story of the search was front page news throughout Australia every day.

On Friday 13th a Royal Australian Air Force Lincoln bomber was despatched from Adelaide to fly up the Alice track. Just after noon one of the officers in the plane spotted a car stationary in small bushes about 30 kilometres south of the border between South Australia and the Northern Territory. It hadn't been seen before by searchers because it was about 50 metres to the west of the track and although the bushes here were fairly sparse, there were enough to completely screen it from passing drivers. But was it the car they were looking for? The pilot found a blue Austin A40 driving down the Alice-Adelaide track about 25 kilometres away and buzzed it several times until the driver, no doubt terrified, stopped the car. The pilot then used his bombing practice to drop a container with a message on to the road. The driver drove to it and picked it up. It read: "A car similar to that reported missing is stopped four miles south of Sundown Station and 50 yards to the right of the main road. If you identify the car as the missing blue Vanguard and in need of assistance please wave something white." The pilot flew back south and circled the car in the bush. The A40 pulled over on the road, two men ran through the bush and opened doors in the Vanguard and almost immediately began waving handkerchiefs. The pilot gained height to establish good radio contact with police at Alice Springs.

At the same time Eddie Connellan, a bloke who'd started his own airline out of Alice, had joined the hunt and was piloting a Cessna with Roy Coulthard, a 73-year-old with leather skin who ran Kulgera Station, and Patrick Davis, of Hamilton Downs Station, as passengers. Eddie was an Aussie who was usually ahead of the pack. Nevil Shute had met him and taken a shine to him when he was researching the background for the novel which eventually became A Town Like Alice and had incorporated him into the novel as Eddie Maclean. Shute had his heroine Jean Paget spend some time with Mrs Maclean at her "lovely swimming pool just out by the aerodrome". Eddie, Roy and Pat watched as the handkerchiefs were waved and flew back to the air strip in a paddock at Kulgera where they found local Constable Jim Conmee who was checking who had been through the store and fuel station at Kulgera since Thursday. Roy told his 22-year-old son Noel, a stockman on the property, what had happened while Constable Conmee quickly grabbed a couple of aboriginal trackers for the flight back to Sundown.

Meanwhile, down in far-off Adelaide Detective Inspector Gil Gully, acting head of the Criminal Investigation Branch, was about to take action. Despite being sartorially naive, wearing his tie out in front of a gaudy pullover with a sports jacket that hadn't a hope of ever buttoning, he was a smart copper. He started gathering an experienced team to take on what appeared to be developing into a murder investigation.

Also in Adelaide Detective Charles Hopkins, after having been on night patrol until 7.30 am on December 13, spent some time in the city with a friend who was visiting from the country. He recalls: "I returned to my car, which was parked adjacent to Police Headquarters, and was about to go home for some much needed sleep. Inspector Gully, who was in charge of the Homicide Squad, spotted me. He came out and asked me to take charge of the investigation and go to Port Augusta immediately. After making the necessary preparations, I set out at about 3.30 pm with an associate, Detective Kevin Moran, and a police photographer (Frank O'Neill)."

Hopkins and his colleagues were given an old Holden sedan for the drive.

At Sundown the Cessna circled the Vanguard once again to get bearings on just where it was in relation to the road. As the plane landed on the rudimentary, abandoned airstrip at Sundown Station the occupants were assailed by the heat. The shade temperature was now about 40 degrees centigrade. The trouble was, there was very little shade. The sun scorched them from above and the superheated bare earth and sand threw up more heat. The light was dazzling. They were in a vast red plain dotted with woody bushes. The noise of the engine was replaced by absolute silence: it was too hot for birds to sing. They set off down the dirt road with trepidation. What would they discover when they reached the car? What had happened to the occupants? They reached a tripod of dead branches placed by the side of the road by the driver and passenger of the A40 and turned into the scrub. Suddenly, it was there, looking so incongruous, parked amid pristine wilderness. The doors had been closed by the earlier visitors and with the metal too hot to rest a hand on and the temperature in the parked car approaching 80 degrees centigrade it shimmered.

Constable Conmee warned the men not to disturb any tracks but they all approached the car and, as Eddie, Roy and Pat watched with great apprehension, Constable Conmee opened the driver's door. A rush of oven-heat hit the men with an appalling smell and they instinctively stepped back. They opened other doors to dissipate the heat. They checked the boot. The car was empty. But they were horrified to find a pool of blood on the floor in the back of the car and smears of blood on the inside of the rear nearside door. They also noticed that the area around the driver's seat appeared to have been hurriedly washed. Nearby was an empty four-gallon drum. The two trackers started scouting round the car to learn more.

Next to arrive were Noel Coulthard and his mate and fellow stockman Neville Read who had ridden down from Kulgera on a motor cycle. Conmee didn't stop Noel from approaching the car and opening a door to inspect the interior.

Roy, who had spent 55 of his 73 years in central Australia, would later say: "Near the car, the first track I noticed was a woman's track leading from the car, it would be about a size 4 shoe, I would say. That was leading from the car back to the main road. There was also a man's track walking to the car and out again. And a man's track leading from the front of the car, walking out in the scrub in a southerly direction."

Noel agreed: "Only one track of a woman's footprint, about size 4, was found. It was a single set of tracks from the abandoned Vanguard car back to the roadway."

Neville Read wandered around by himself and found the tracks left by the car. He jumped on to the motor cycle and followed the tracks. They meandered through the scrub for about 250 metres and then joined the main road. Dozens of cars had left tracks in the dust since the Vanguard had passed but Read kept going, examining both sides of the road. A kilometre back down the road he saw what he was looking for, the same tyre pattern going off into the scrub on the other side of the road, to the east. About 600 metres into the bush he saw a low mound covered by a green tarpaulin under a mulga tree. He realised that this was no time for amateur sleuthing and raced back to alert PC Conmee to the discovery. They walked back. An appalling stench assailed them as they approached the tarpaulin and Constable Conmee started lifting a corner of it. Under it were the decomposing bodies of Thyra, Wendy and Tom.

Chapter 2 - The Sundown Murders

The first thing to do was let the rest of the police force know that this was no longer a hunt for three missing people. It was now a manhunt for the murderer of three people. In Adelaide an officer was sent to break the news to Pete Bowman. And another was sent to tell brother Brian – and to ask him to drive down to Sundown to officially identify the bodies.

The murder scene was under the control of Jim Conmee. He was stationed at Finke, a tiny huddle of homes in the middle of vast, empty red plains where the most serious crimes he would normally have to contend with were domestic incidents involving local Aboriginals. As the first police officer on the scene it was his job to secure the murder scene. But he wasn't up to the job. It was bad enough when there were just Eddie, Roy and Pat blundering through the area. Within hours more than a dozen cars and at least 20 people from local stations had congregated at the scene, with people walking through the area as they sought to piece together what had happened. This wasn't the sticky-beak mentality which results in motorways slowing to walking pace as drivers slow down to gaze at carnage on the opposite carriageway. It was an example of the way life is lived in the Outback where, because of the isolation and hardship, people are ever ready to drop what they're doing and help a neighbour. As news of the discovery spread it was natural for men to down tools, turn up and join in.

Just after 5.30pm at Sundown, the constantly growing number of sleuths heard the sound of a light plane coming towards them. It circled them and then headed for the nearby strip. A little later Constable Bruce Evans from the tiny South Australian hamlet of Oodnadatta arrived and, as senior officer, took control of the crime scene. The biggest crimes he usually had to deal with were outbreaks of drunken domestic violence in an Oodnadatta population of about 150 but his one-man station was responsible for about 338,000 square kilometres with one other tiny permanent settlement and an unknown number of nomadic Aboriginals. The Outback had weathered this tall, lean man so that he appeared to be in his 40s despite being only 32. He was a man who was content to spend his life in a small community rather than in the city. He now joined Conmee in examining the horror under the tarpaulin.

Under the tarpaulin, bloodstained blankets covered three bodies. All were clothed. Thyra Bowman's body was face-up in a floral dress. She was wearing a silver watch and there were two rings on her left hand. Whelan was on his stomach in a dark shirt and khaki military-type trousers. Wendy was on her back in a cream blouse and blue-grey shorts. None of them had shoes or socks on but Whelan's shoes had been placed on either side of his body. Between and beneath Whelan and Wendy was a rifle with its barrel broken from the stock. There were also two pieces of hessian bag tied with wire.

Back at the car Evans examined some wheel tracks and decided they were from a second car which had been towing a trailer of some sort.

Eddie Connellan flew back from the murder scene to his Alice office and was quick to tell reporters it was clear from tracks and blood in the car that the occupants had been murdered in the car. He then told of a suspicious character who had been seen twice in the past week on the north-south track. On one occasion he dashed off and tried to hide when a car passed, which "was a bit unusual because people don't footwalk in this country". The man had been seen by Mr and Mrs Frank Wilkinson, of Kulgera Station, on Wednesday. On the previous day he had been given a meal at Erldunda Station. Later on Wednesday he had been picked up and given a ride to Alice Springs.

That night, as on following nights, Evans, Conmee, the trackers and others camped at the murder scene, keeping vigil in the moonlight over the three bodies.

Australians were horrified and outraged by news of the murder. The whole of the front page of Saturday's Adelaide News was devoted to the murders:

"Wendy Bowman, 14-year-old victim in the missing Outback car case, was bashed to death. Her mother, Mrs Sally Bowman, and Mr Tom Whelan, who were also in the car, were shot. Wendy was shockingly injured, apparently with the butt of the rifle found under her body. The solid wooden butt had been smashed. Police are now seeking to interview, among others, a migrant who was driving a Ford Zephyr car with a woman passenger, in the area last weekend. The hunt, which was first focused on an elderly hitchhiker who was dressed in unusual clothes, dramatically switched when he was questioned at Tennant Creek. He was able to satisfy police he was not in the Sundown area at the time of the tragedy. The car in which the migrant and the woman were travelling was drawing a trailer when it called at Kulgera Station on Sunday for petrol. Police blacktrackers have pieced together from footprints a picture of a man and a woman walking from the main road to the missing car. The footsteps appear to wander around the car, then return to the car parked on the road. The footsteps could not have been those of any of the Bowman party because the mother and daughter are considered to have been dead at this stage. Trackers have linked the Ford Zephyr with these footsteps because signs indicate the car which drew away from near the parked Vanguard was drawing a trailer – or at least a heavy load on the rear wheels. Pedal wireless is being used from station to station to relay messages forward. It has now been established that the car filled up with petrol at Kulgera on Friday about 4pm and not on Saturday as previously reported."

On Saturday Evans, Conmee, Roy and Noel Coulthard and aboriginal trackers concentrated on finding more tracks. Eventually, they found the spot close to the road where Tom, Thyra and Wendy had camped. There were patches of blood but the ground surrounding the camp fire had been pawed and turned over by bullocks. Evans followed drag marks from the camp area to a pile of fresh earth. Wendy's dogs had been killed and buried here.

It was completely dark before 8pm. Men sat around the campfire discussing what they had found, the sort of man who might have committed the murders and why. Most of them were asleep by 10pm, ready to rise again before dawn but they were awoken at midnight by the sound and headlights of two cars driving off the main track and into the camp. The South Australian police had arrived red-eyed after their exhausting 30-hour drive over 1,200 kilometres.

Hopkins recalled: "We were able to snatch a few hours' sleep, lying on a stretch of sand adjacent to the road. At about 4.00 am we were awakened to find the place alive with activity. It was explained to us that the sand would heat up very quickly, and that we would suffer badly if we overslept. Everyone was eager to get on with the job. We were treated to a "real bush breakfast" comprising a thick slice of fritz (large pork sausage) and a cup of tea, which, given the circumstances, we greatly appreciated. After breakfast we were told that tyre marks showed where the offender's vehicle had parked and we went to the site, which was just off the highway. The tyre marks were clearly visible in the soft sand. We also saw that a two-wheeled trailer had been towed; there were three pairs of wheel marks. However, we could not tell which pair was made by the caravan and which by the car, and consequently did not know whether the car was going south towards Adelaide or north to Alice Springs. Near the site was a discarded piece of bagging, which was photographed and retained."

Sydney Stanes, a 37-year-old pastoralist, of Erldunda Station, South Australia, said he arrived at the scene on December 15 and had seen the tracks of a vehicle which had been towing something. He said the woman's tracks from the Vanguard back to the road followed those of a man, size 7 or 8. Her shoes would have been 3½ or 4. He hadn't seen any sign of a woman's tracks leading from the road into the Vanguard.

People pointed discreetly, murmured and fell silent when Brian Bowman arrived at Sundown to identify the bodies. A tall, fit, lean man with a big bush hat, he walked slowly with Evans and Conmee towards the stench and the flies. It was 41 degrees centigrade. The pervasive, debilitating heat enveloped and smothered them. A corner of the tarpaulin was once again lifted to expose the three bodies. Brian nodded. The remains were those of his sister-in-law, daughter-in-law and Tom Whelan. He stood for a while and then, cursing the murderer, joined in the search for tracks and clues.

The detectives from Adelaide then got on with the grisly task of moving the bodies into the coffins. Hopkins noted the canvas rifle case and the broken Remington Sportmaster rifle between the bodies of Wendy and Whelan. As the bodies were moved he saw an empty .22 calibre cartridge case. He put it in an exhibit bag. As the day wore on about 15 people combed the area looking for clues and adding to the tracks.

Monday's Advertiser ran a story from 'Our Police Reporters at the scene of the murder and at police headquarters. Hunt for Outback murderer. Theft may have been motive.'

"Police believe robbery was the motive for the brutal murder of three people whose bodies were discovered hidden under tarpaulins and scrub near the main Alice Springs-Adelaide road south of the NT border on Friday afternoon. Mrs H. N. Bowman, about 45, one of the victims, is known to have been carrying valuables, which are missing. Another development yesterday was the discovery of the bodies of Mrs Bowman's two dogs, which the murderer had evidently killed, some yards from a campfire at which the murders are believed to have taken place. Police have thrown road blocks across all roads leading from the centre into other states. However, an oyster grey or cream Ford Zephyr whose occupants the police are eager to interview has not been intercepted and is believed to have slipped across the border into Queensland. A description of the car has been flashed to all parts of Australia. Police are today investigating the discovery of burned clothing about 21 miles north of the murder scene and about one mile on the SA side of the NT border. The clothing was found at a campfire about 10 yards west of the Alice Springs-Adelaide road. It included portions of jeans, as well as buttons, brass eyelets and other fragments. Police have also been told that on the day of the murder a man noticed two or three people sitting around a campfire at the site where the clothing was found. The man said a car was standing nearby. Police believe the murderer's clothing must have become bloodstained while moving the bodies. Police have cordoned off the area around the murder scene for about 500 yards to avoid obliterating any tracks the killer may have made. The dogs, a brown half-corgi and a black and white sheepdog, were known to have been savage towards strangers and may have caused a quarrel when a stranger or strangers approached the party. It is thought that Mr Whelan may have attempted to have defended the party against the attack with the rifle. The rifle's wooden stock was broken off, probably with the force of the blows with which the murderer killed Wendy Bowman. One of the strangest clues found by the blacktrackers and Mr Sid Stanes, part-owner of Erldunda cattle station, who is an expert tracker himself, was that a woman wearing size 3 shoes with flat heels walked in a crescent from the victims' Vanguard car, which was found 50 yards from the road, and about a third of a mile from the murder scene. Blacktrackers also found prints of a man's shoe, about size 10. However, some of the man's and woman's tracks found may have been made by a couple who stopped and looked at the murder scene and the hidden Vanguard car without reporting their discovery to the police. Police throughout the NT and Queensland are still searching for "a surly-looking foreigner" and a woman with brown hair over her forehead,

travelling with a child aged about six years in an oyster-grey Ford Zephyr car, hauling a trailer with wooden sides."

The News on December 16 said: From staff reporters at the murder scene and at Adelaide CIB:

"An Alice Springs report today said it was understood that the Sundown Station killer stripped rings from the finger of one of his three victims and stole about 70 pounds in money. An armed policeman is driving along the lonely Tennant Creek-Camooweal road today searching for a migrant and a woman who, detectives think, can help solve the murder. Townsville-based Lincoln bombers have also been alerted to search trackless desert wastes for these two people who, with a girl, are travelling in a late model sedan. Police are convinced robbery was the motive for the murders. Police found that Mrs Bowman cashed two 25 pound cheques at Alice Springs shortly before she was murdered.

The News of the 16th headlined a story: NT clamour for swift action:

"As the stark brutality of the triple murder pattern is disclosed Alice Springs people are clamouring for swift retribution. Territorians say the crime is one of the most fiendish in Outback history."

The strong reaction was due to the fact that in the Outback trust, friendship and reliability were essential. If you were driving on a lonely road and saw someone by the side of the road you stopped and asked if they were all right. You would ask if they needed a lift. And you trusted that they were honest, straightforward people. When you saw another vehicle coming towards you, it was automatic to give a little wave of acknowledgment as you passed. If anyone turned up on your front doorstep, you automatically invited them in for a cup of tea. No one locked car doors, house doors or windows. Now there was a monster lurking out there. Life was going to be very different from now on.

Next day, newspaper readers were told that robbery was no longer a motive. The Advertiser reported Inspector Gully as saying no rings or other jewellery had been taken from the bodies. The focus now was on the hunt for the murderer.

"From Frank Kennedy at the scene of the murder. At dawn today Queensland and Northern Territory police will start to close in on the car which has been hunted throughout northern Australia. Last night police road blocks had completely hemmed in the car and trailer which was reported to have obtained petrol on Sunday night from Yelvercroft Station, 60 miles east of Camooweal. The vehicle was also sighted from an aircraft yesterday. The couple believed to be in the car – a surly-looking foreign man accompanied by a woman – evidently detoured over station tracks to by-pass police road blocks. Police believe the two people stopped and looked at both the scene of the triple murder and the hidden Vanguard car without reporting the discovery to the police. Further evidence disclosed yesterday points to the shrewdness of the murderer – he washed the Vanguard in a desperate attempt to remove fingerprints after it had been hidden behind trees; he wore makeshift Hessian gloves and used tools hurriedly made after the

murder to avoid leaving fingerprints or shoe tracks. As the murders probably took place early on the evening of December 5, it must have taken the killer much of the night and possibly a portion of the following day to complete his destruction or hiding of clues. A theory has been advanced that the murder may have taken place after a large savage black and white kangaroo dog owned by Mrs Bowman and her daughter Wendy bit a stranger when he approached the spot where they were camping. The theory is that the stranger hit the dog with a shovel which the victims had used to dig a hole for grilling meat, Territory style, over fire coals."

Hopkins and his colleagues set off south again, stopping on the way at a homestead for a few hours because of the intense heat. "In fact, it was so hot that native birds were flying in under the veranda and dropping dead from exhaustion," Hopkins recalled.

On the 18th the Advertiser still had a man at Sundown.

"From Frank Kennedy at the scene of the murder: The only tracks leading from the murder scene were those of a man moving towards the tracks of a parked vehicle. The only tracks leading from the victims' hidden Vanguard car were apparently those of the same man and of a woman wearing about size 3 shoes. The bodies of the three murder victims arrived in Adelaide late last night in a police truck."

South Australian Government pathologist Dr John Dwyer carried out post mortem examinations of the three bodies at Adelaide's city morgue, starting with Tom Whelan on January 18.

Dwyer noted Tom Whelan had been 175cm tall. The body had been carried face down in the coffin which carried it from Sundown. A bullet which had entered the back of the skull low down on the left had fallen out of the eye socket. And a second bullet fell out of a kidney during examination, again from a wound in the back. They were both .22s which Dwyer passed to Detective Constable Ivan Patterson, a ballistics expert who attended the post mortems. The left shoulder blade had been pierced by a bullet from the rear. In addition to the bullet wounds, Whelan's forehead had been fractured across the front. Dwyer noted: "It was very likely that Whelan was prone when he was shot in the back of the head. Looking at the broken rifle butt, the fractures on Whelan's skull were consistent with having been caused by a blow from this rifle butt."

Next day Dr Dwyer examined the body of Thyra Bowman and noted: "The clothing on the trunk and limbs had not been disturbed. A small purse containing money and jewellery was concealed in the clothes on the right side of the abdomen." The purse contained 24 pounds 1 shilling and a penny-halfpenny, a ring and three rings. He found she had been shot once in the back of the neck on the left, the bullet passing up through the roof of the mouth and through the brain. She had extensive fractures to the right of her skull which had not been caused by the bullet but by a blow from an object with rounded or smooth surface such as the rifle butt. Dr

Dwyer passed the flattened bullet to Constable Patterson who had already been given the cartridge case found by Hopkins with the bodies.

Finally, on the 20th Dr Dwyer examined the body of 14-year-old Wendy. She had suffered two massive blows to the left of her head, resulting in extensive fractures. She too had been shot. Dr Dwyer noted: "The only position I can envisage is that she was lying on the ground with the right side of the head downwards when she was shot through the head."

He concluded that all three had been alive when they were laid out on the ground where they were found. The fractured skulls had all resulted in extensive bleeding, showing that they had been alive when they were bashed. If the skulls had been fractured after death, there would have been no bleeding. For some reason the murderer had attacked the three at their camp ground. They had then been moved to the spot where their bodies had been found and each executed with a bullet to the head: put out of their misery just as a grazier would despatch a doomed animal.

The Advertiser reported that the Vanguard:

"is believed to have been washed by a woman to remove fingerprints. This is the theory of Mr Brian Bowman, brother-in-law of one of the victims, Mrs H. N. Bowman. Mr Bowman, an expert bushman, has come to this conclusion after discussion with black trackers at the murder scene. He believes the woman was wearing about size 3 shoes. Mr Bowman said yesterday: "My opinion is that after the bodies had been hidden a woman drove the Vanguard car into the roadside scrub and called out to her man companion for water to wash it. The man then got out of the Vanguard a four-gallon drum of water which the woman used. An empty drum similar to that habitually carried in the Vanguard was found some distance from it." Mr Bowman said the theory was confirmed by the fact that only a man's tracks led to the spot where the Vanguard was found but tracks of both a man and a woman led from the car back to the road. "My opinion is that the murderer is probably a city criminal with some bush knowledge. I base this on the enormous trouble to obliterate fingerprints while still leaving foot tracks."

Next day the Advertiser offered a 500 pound reward for information leading to the arrest of the murderer. The newspaper said:

"…diamond rings belonging to Mrs Bowman were found by police yesterday. The discovery of the rings, and the probability that money also thought stolen, is not missing, has prompted police to consider a possible motive for the crime other than robbery. Brian Bowman offered a 4,500 pound reward to add to the Advertiser's 500 pounds.

On Christmas Eve the Advertiser reported:

"Police said last night they were still unable to discover a motive. Robbery as a motive had been dismissed with the finding of the victims' possessions intact in their luggage and the fact that the murder weapon had not been located, police said. The earlier theory that the shattered rifle owned by the victims and found near their bodies was used by the murderer has been disproved by police ballistic experts."

It was Boxing Day, before the mystery was off the front pages for the first time since December 10. By January 3 The Courier-Mail in Queensland was reporting:

"After interviewing hundreds of people in the outback and relatives, Police today admit they are no nearer solving the triple murder. Police have dropped their search for the oyster grey Zephyr."

In Adelaide Gil Gully still had nothing to go on. He told Moran and Hopkins to bring in sleeping bags and enough clothes for an extended tour of the Outback. He wanted them to go back and speak to everyone living along the route the Bowman car had taken.

Police told the Advertiser that the detectives were equipped with all available information established by minute scientific tests of the victims' clothing, bullets and samples of sand found.

On January 9 Moran and Hopkins flew to Alice Springs and picked up an unmarked police car. First stop was a grocery store where they loaded the boot with tinned food. From now on they expected to be sleeping and eating beside their car if they couldn't find a homestead for the night.

Eventually, the police hunt resulted in Detective Inspector Gully announcing in typical police jargon that it had now been ascertained that a man, woman and child known to be travelling in a battered pre-war black car towing a caravan could assist police in their enquiries. They had been seen near the scene of the Sundown triple murder about 8pm on December 5, the same day the murders were believed to have been committed.

The wanted car was thought to be a 1938 black Dodge sedan. Police in Adelaide checked dozens of pre-war American sedans and started checking the registrations of 82,000 caravans in South Australia at the rate of 7,000 a day.

Inspector Gully told police that there was no doubt the occupants of the car and caravan could be of assistance. The car was towing a dilapidated light-to-cream-coloured small caravan believed to have a blue or grey door. The tow bar may have been oxy-welded. Descriptions of the people in the caravan were: Man – between 28 and 30 years old, clean appearance, about 170 centimetres tall, medium built, weighing about 70 kilograms. He had a long thin clean-shaven face with a medium to sallow complexionA woman with him was said to be attractive looking, 25 to 30, slim to average built, about 163 centimetres tall, fair to light brown hair recently permed They had a young boy with them, aged 2 to 5 hair inclined to be snowy, fair complexion, very active and talkative. The man had repaired the caravan at Wirraminna Station about 240 kilometres north of Port Augusta at the end of November. Inspector Gully appealed to anyone knowing of the car, caravan or the occupants to immediately communicate with the CIB or nearest police station. They were heading for Mount Isa or Darwin.

Chapter 3 - Hallahan Seizes His Chance

Mount Isa! It was a booming mining town with a population of about 8,000 in the middle of empty north-west Queensland, some 875 kilometres to the north-east of Alice Springs. It was the cuckoo in the nest of Cloncurry Shire which had a mining and settlement history going back to the 19th century. The capital of the 52,000-square-kilometre shire was Cloncurry, with a population of 3,052 if they were all at home. Mt Isa was the young upstart, founded in the 1930s around a fabulously rich silver, lead and copper mine 120 miles west of Cloncurry on the banks of the Leichhardt River. The police headquarters for north-west Queensland was still at Cloncurry but most of the action was now at Mt Isa with its cosmopolitan community of miners from all over the world.

This is where we meet Glen Patrick Hallahan. Aged only 25 but highly ambitious, he's in charge of Mt Isa Criminal Investigation Branch. He's a big man, more than 180 centimetres tall and broad shouldered, personable but not brash, self-contained but also self-assured, a man who has earned the nickname among some of his colleagues of Silent. One colleague went as far as to describe him as particularly charismatic, well spoken, with something of the manner of the actor Gregory Peck. He was born on March 10, 1932, at Charleville, in the Outback, a 17-hour train journey west of Brisbane. With a population of about 3,300 it boasted it was the largest town in south-west Queensland. It didn't have much to compete with. Morven, the next town along the line, 90 kilometres away, had a population of 250. Then the family moved to the big smoke of Toowoomba, Australia's second-largest inland town with a population of about 35,000 perched on the very edge of the Great Dividing Range. Hallahan gained 72 per cent in the State scholarship exam and was of above average intelligence and 'normal mentality'. On leaving school in June 1948 he was accepted for a commission in the RAAF and was posted to Wagga Wagga as an aircraft apprentice. But his father became ill and he applied for a discharge and left on May 24, 1950, to run his father's milk and ice run at Toowoomba for about six months until the business was sold. He then worked as a labourer with the Forestry Department at Cooran, a tiny community behind a beautiful hamlet on the coast called Noosa for another six months. Then he moved hundreds of kilometres up the coast to the tropics to take on one of the toughest jobs in the world, cutting sugar cane, for four months. It was then that he applied to join the police. An official, internal, police report on him said his home life, upbringing and environment had been good. He started as a probationary at the police depot, Brisbane, on November 23, 1951. After a posting to the tiny town of Tara he became the State's youngest detective, serving briefly in Brisbane before being transferred to Mt Isa. One of his biggest attributes was his memory. He had amazing recall.

On January 20 Hallahan and the other officers at Mt Isa were alerted by the South Australian police to the fact that the main – perhaps the only - suspect in the Sundown murders could be in their vicinity.

Next day a particular car was identified - a black 1938 DeSoto, registration SA 379-622 or SA 534-755, associated with a man, woman and a fair-haired boy. The hue and cry was spread to every police station in the country. Not only had the car been seen towing the small cream or beige caravan near the scene of the murders at about 8pm on the day of the murders, it had also been seen again on December 7 or 8 north of Tennant Creek, heading for Mount Isa or Darwin. Police were told to look for a dark-complexioned man, a carpenter from NSW, who was between 25 and 30 and 168 centimetres tall.

Hallahan took all this in. This was no vague alert for a middle-aged male of average height who could be any one of thousands of men anywhere in Australia. This was obviously a clearly-identified suspect. And Hallahan would have taken particular notice of the phrase that there 'was no doubt the occupants of the car and caravan could be of assistance'. This was an opportunity too good to be missed. Just over 24 hours later he could hardly contain himself. Miles Street had its beginnings as a dusty tree-lined street in a residential area of the town but it ended in the town centre, a street so wide that there was nose-in, angle parking on both sides and plenty of room in the middle for cars parked at right angles to the road. It was lined with one-storey shops and offices. And there, amid dozens of anonymous cars, utes and trucks was a black DeSoto. He walked up to the car with his offsider Reg Pfingst. The registration plate was 379-622.

Hallahan arranged for a call to be made to Inspector Norwin Bauer, the senior officer in the north-west of Queensland, who was stationed at Cloncurry. The car had been found. Bauer, a senior Freemason with the deportment to match, got through to the local exchange and asked the operator to phone an Adelaide number. The suspect was in reach.

Hallahan and Pfingst parked their car and stood in the shade of a shop awning and waited. 10 minutes. It was now the hottest part of the day. The temperature hovered around 40 degrees centigrade. Sweat ran down their faces and stickied their armpits and groins. 20 minutes. 30 minutes. They talked about whether the man might run or stand and fight, or even draw a gun on them. People did funny, unexpected things when they were cornered. 40 minutes. Had he seen them waiting and scarpered? 50 minutes. God, they would kill for a cold beer. An hour. How long would they wait before sending for someone else to relieve them? Not in this case. No chance. This was their moment of glory. 70 minutes. What sort of person would have killed three people in cold blood – and then killed the dogs as well? 80 minutes. A man walking down the street stopped at the car. This couldn't be him, surely? He was a mere wisp of a man, about 60 kilos and no taller than Hallahan's shoulders. He reached the car. And he reached for the door handle. It was him. It's him. He's the man. He's getting in. Quick.

Hallahan and Pfingst walked quickly up to the DeSoto and warned the man not to move.

Chapter 4 - Hallahan's Story in his Own Words

At this point, I'll hand over the narrative to the hero of the day and let Glen Hallahan tell his story in his own words in a statement which he swore was the truth, the whole truth and nothing but the truth. His story starts as he introduces himself to the suspect.

"I'm Detective Hallahan and this is Detective Pfingst, what's your name?"

"Ray Carter."

"How long have you been in Mt Isa?"

"About two weeks."

"Do you own this vehicle?"

"No, I don't own it but I am paying it off. I got it in South Australia a couple of months ago and I have still got a fair bit to pay."

"Have you the registration papers with you?"

"No."

"Will you come with me to the police station I would like to have a talk to you?"

"Yes."

Hallahan said he walked round to the passenger door of the big old black car and got in, giving the driver directions on how to reach the police station.

Hallahan: In the Criminal Investigation Branch interview room I asked him: "Do you own a caravan?"

"Yes, it's parked a couple of miles out. The wife and little fellow are out there now."

"What colour is it?"

"A light colour."

And then, said Hallahan, the man suddenly blurted out: "My right name is Bailey, Raymond Bailey. I have been using the name of Carter for tax reasons."

Hallahan said: "I have received information that you are in possession of a revolver, is that correct?"

"It's incorrect. I've got no guns at all."

"Can I have a look through your car?"

"Go ahead and look."

Hallahan: We walked out into the police station yard and I inspected the car. I saw that the seat covering on the back rest of the front seat was sewn with cotton. I examined inside the seat cover and I found a .32 calibre, five-chamber revolver. This revolver was contained in a leather holster. I showed the revolver to Bailey and said to him: "Where did you get this from?"

"A chap gave it to me in Adelaide."

Hallahan: I then took possession of the revolver and holster. Back in the Criminal Investigation Branch room I said to him: "Where is the caravan now?"

"Just off the camping reserve."

"I'd like to have a look at it"

"Yes, you're welcome."

Hallahan: We were accompanied by Detective Pfingst and other police and drove to a position on the Duchess Road, Mt Isa, about two miles from Mt Isa. On arrival at this position I saw a grey and pale blue coloured caravan, bearing registered number NSW TM5489. I said to the accused: "Where did you get this caravan from?"

"In Dubbo, I live there."

Hallahan: I then had a conversation with a woman named Patricia Merle Bailey. I then said: "Can I have a look through the caravan?"

"Go ahead."

Hallahan: With the accused I made an examination of the inside of the caravan and on a shelf in the caravan I found two packets containing Civic .22 calibre long rifle bullets. I indicated the bullets to the accused and said to him: "Where did you get these from?"

"They were in the caravan when I bought it, they are no good to me I haven't got a rifle."

Hallahan: I then took possession of these bullets. Also on a shelf in the caravan I found a cash invoice docket from McConville Motors, Todd St, Alice Springs dated 7 December 1957 for 5 pounds, seven shillings and sixpence. I then said to the accused: "I want to take your caravan to the police station."

They then all drove to the police station with the caravan. Hallahan says he continued to question Bailey until about 9.30pm, this time about the purchase of the DeSoto at Renmark, South Australia. At that stage Hallahan charged him with being in possession of an unlicensed revolver.

Detective Hopkins, still out in the red centre, recalled: "On 21st January we returned to Kulgera Station and were advised by radio to return to Alice Springs immediately, because the offender had been arrested at Mt Isa."

Someone at the police station, almost certainly either Hallahan or Bauer, made time to ring Queensland's daily paper The Courier-Mail to tip it off that Hallahan had arrested the man wanted in connection with the Sundown Murders. The tip enabled the paper to splash next day, the 22nd, with the headlines: Sundown Murders detectives fly to Mt Isa after three held – black car spotted:

"Two South Australian detectives investigating the Sundown triple murders will fly by specially chartered plane to Mt Isa this morning to question a man, woman and child. They believe the three may be able to help them in their investigations. A black

1938 DeSoto sedan towing a small light-coloured caravan was located in a Mt Isa main street at 5pm yesterday by two Mt Isa detectives. Later, a man, woman and child were detained. Police in all states, particularly Queensland and the Northern Territory, were alerted in the search for a car. Mt Isa police were alerted by Adelaide headquarters yesterday to watch for a black DeSoto sedan towing a light-coloured caravan. Detectives G. Hallahan and R. Pfingst stopped a car towing a trailer in Miles Street Mt Isa at 5pm. A young man, his wife and a child were in the car. They were questioned by the detectives and taken to the police station. Late last night a 26-year-old labourer, believed to be a native of New South Wales, was charged with being in possession of an unlicensed concealable firearm. He will appear in Mt Isa police court this morning. Police early this morning were still questioning a 22-year-old woman. A further charge of false pretences relating to the obtaining of a sedan car in South Australia may be preferred against the man. The man is believed to have been in Mt Isa for a month."

In Adelaide the Advertiser received similar information. It reported:

"...at midnight police were still questioning a 22-year-old woman, believed to be the man's wife. Lights in the Adelaide CIB building burned late last night as Mr McKinna and Det Insp Gully conferred on the new Mount Isa developments. They made lengthy telephone calls to Mount Isa and to Alice Springs."

At 9.50am on the 22nd Hallahan charged Bailey that he had been guilty of false pretences in obtaining the DeSoto at Renmark. At 10.00 Bailey was led triumphantly into Mt Isa's tiny wooden courtroom. The trophy was unveiled. The presence of 10 burly police officers signalled that here was a dangerous criminal as Bailey was remanded in custody.

Bailey's wife and child were not in the court. Bailey, slim, dark-haired and sunburnt, wore a dirty open-neck shirt, dirty shorts and sandals. He was self-possessed. He spoke only two words – "No questions" – when Inspector Norwin Bauer of Cloncurry, prosecuting, asked if he wanted to question the arresting police officers.

Hallahan takes up the story again with his sworn statement:

"Where did you camp on the Thursday night on 5th December? That's the night before you bought petrol at Kulgera."

"A couple of miles the other side of Kulgera."

"Do you know Sundown Station, it's about 20 miles south of the South Australia-Northern Territory border?"

"Yes, that's where those people were murdered. I saw the people when I came through but that's all I can tell you about it. I didn't hear about the murder until a couple of weeks ago. I thought it would have been the same people I saw on my way through. I was going to come up and tell you about it but I thought it was a bit late."

"Where did you see these people?"

"It would be about 30 miles south of Kulgera."

"When did you see them?"

"About 7o'clock on the Thursday, the sun had just gone down."

"That would be 5th December 1957."

"Yes."

"Can you describe these people to me?"

"Well, there was a middle-aged woman, a young girl and a chap about 20 I suppose."

"What were they doing when you saw them?"

"They had stopped on the side of the road and they were ready to have tea. They had a fire going."

"Did they have a car?"

"Yes, it was a blue or green Vanguard."

"Did you stop when you saw them?"

"Yes, I stopped the car and the young chap came over and the woman came over and they asked us if we wanted a cold drink of water and if we would stay for tea."

"What time was it when you left these three people?"

"I don't know the time but it wasn't quite dark."

"Do you own a .22 rifle?"

"No, I have never owned one."

"Did you have one with you in your car when you left Whyalla to come north?"

"No."

Hallahan says he left the office and that when he returned he said to Bailey: "I have been talking to your wife and she told me that you did own a .22 rifle. She says that you bought it from an Englishman when you were wheat lumping at Wirrulla."

The defendant said: "That's right, I forgot about that. I sold it just after I bought it."

"Whom did you buy it from?"

"He was a pommy, I think Dave was his name."

"What type of rifle was it?"

"A single shot .22, I think it was a Huntsman."

"Whom did you sell it to?"

"I had it with me when I left Whyalla to come north and a couple of days after we left I sold it to a blackfellow for some opal."

"Do you know the name of the blackfellow?"

"No."

"Where did this sale take place?"

"A place called Coober Pedy."

Hallahan says he left the office a second time for a couple of minutes and that when he returned he said to Bailey: "Your wife has told me that you did see a blackfellow at Coober Pedy and you gave him three cigarettes and he gave you some opal. She says you still had the gun when you left Coober Pedy and after you left Kulgera you walked away from the car towards a hill with your rifle and came back without it."

The defendant then lowered his head and supported his head with his hands and said: "I do know something about those people who were killed, can you give me a smoke?"

I then handed him a cigarette. The time was approximately 11.50am and I said: "What do you know about it?"

He said "I didn't do it, don't get that idea. After I was speaking to them on Thursday night I drove on and it got dark and I stopped the car and caravan about two miles from where they were camped. We had tea there and next morning we were ready to go on our way and I saw that my rifle was missing out of the front of the car. I had an idea that I heard shots through the night and I decided to walk back down to see if those people were all right. I saw there was no one around the camp fire and I walked a bit further and I saw their car in the bush off the road. I walked over to the car and I saw something under the tree, covered with a tarpaulin. I had a look and saw that it was the people I had been talking to the night before and they were all dead. I had a look in their car and I saw my rifle on the front seat. The wooden part of it was broken and it was covered in blood. I didn't want to get the blame for this so I drove the car back down where I had my caravan parked and I drove it into the bush and washed the car with water. When I was talking to the young chap the night before I was leaning on the front mudguard and I thought they would blame me for it. After I washed it I drove on and threw away the gun."

I said "Why did you throw the gun away?"

"My gun killed them and I didn't want to be blamed for it."

"Are you suggesting that some person stole your rifle from your car during the night and shot the people with your rifle?"

"That's the only thing that could have happened."

"What bullets did you have in the car?"

"Only the two packets which you got."

"Were any of the bullets taken?"

"No. The bullets were in the caravan and they couldn't get in there without waking me."

"It seems strange that someone would take your gun and not the bullets?"

He then said: "I will tell you. I shot the young chap but I want to tell you how it happened."

I said: "I am going to ask you some more questions about this but before I do I am going to tell you that you are not obliged to answer any questions or make any statement as anything you do say will be noted and may be used in evidence. Do you understand that?"

He said "Yes but I will tell you what happened."

When I cautioned the defendant, Inspector Bauer was there and he remained there thereafter. The time was then approximately 12.15pm. Throughout the time I was questioning the defendant he was quite composed and speaking rationally in his conversation. He displayed no emotion of any kind whatever.

Bailey continued: "After we left them that night I went further down the road and stopped the car. We camped there that night. We had tea and after tea I got a guts ache and I went outside and had a couple of shits. I went back to the car and got the gun. I had some bullets in my pocket and I decided to go for a walk back down to where the people were camped. I don't know why I walked back. I walked into the bush and down towards them and saw them sleeping under a tree. I was about 12 feet away from them and a dog jumped out and barked. I fired a shot at it. When I fired the shot the young fellow jumped up off the ground and screamed and fell over and I knew that I had shot him. I must have had a blackout. The next thing I remember was coming to beside the car which was on the other side of the road. I saw something covered by tarpaulins and blankets and I went over and had a look and I saw three bodies. One of them was the young fellow that I had shot. My rifle was in the front seat of the car and I saw that the wood was broken and covered with blood and I realised that I must have killed the others too. I left everything there and went back to the caravan and had a wash and came back early next morning and saw the rifle still in the car and I drove the car back down to where the caravan was parked and stopped near the caravan. I went into the caravan and got a pair of gloves and drove the car into the bush and washed it inside and outside with water and then went back to my car and drove towards Alice and threw the rifle away before I got there."

I said: "What side of the road did you stop your car and caravan that night?"

He said "The other side of the road to them. That's the eastern side."

"What time did you leave your caravan to go for a walk?"

"Just after 9."

"Why did you decide to go for a walk?"

"I was feeling upset in the guts."

"Did you intend to walk down to where the people were camped?"

"I just went for a walk."

"Why did you take your rifle with you?"

"I don't know."

"Where did you get the bullets from?"

"They were in my pocket."

"Are they the same bullets as those in these packets here?"

I then indicated the two packets I had taken possession of the previous night and he replied "Yes."

I said: "Where did you get them from?"

"Wirrulla."

"Did you walk down the road?"

"No, I walked into the bush on their side of the road and walked down towards them."

"Was the gun loaded?"

"I don't remember."

"How were the people lying?"

"They were under a tree and they seemed to be close together."

"Did the dog bite you?"

The defendant then indicated two small scars on his left wrist and said: "Yes. But I don't know whether it bit me then or later."

I said: "How far were you away from the place where they were lying when you noticed the dog?"

He replied "About 10 to 12 feet."

"Was the dog on a chain?"

"I don't know."

"What sort of dog was it?"

"I don't know."

"Where was the young chap when you fired the shot?"

"Lying on the ground."

"You said that when you fired the shot he jumped up in the air and screamed and fell over. Do you remember which way he fell?"

"I think he fell frontwards."

"What do you say happened after that?"

"I told you. I must have blacked out. I came to beside the car on the other side of the road and I saw that they were all dead."

"What time would this be?"

"I don't know the time but it would probably be about midnight."

"Have you ever had blackouts before?"

"No."

"How were you dressed that night?"

"Jeans and a tee shirt."

"Was there any blood on them when you say you came to?"

"I don't know."

"Did you notice how the other two people had been killed?"

"No, but I thought I must have shot them."

"What happened when you went back next morning?"

"I just drove the car down to the caravan and got gloves and drove the car into the bush and washed it inside and outside with water and drove off."

"Where are the gloves now?"

"They should be still in the caravan."

"Why did you wear gloves?"

"So there would be no fingerprints."

"What type of gloves were they?"

"Leather gauntlets."

"Where did you get the water from to wash the car?"

"There was a four gallon drum in the back seat of the car."

"Did you use rag to wash the car with?"

"Yes. I got some out of the caravan."

"What did you do with it?"

"I don't know what happened to it."

"Did your wife know about it?"

"No. But when I was washing the car she came over and asked me what I was doing and I told her that I had heard some shots during the night and went down and found the people were dead and I didn't want anyone to think that I did it."

"What happened then?"

"We drove to Kulgera and after we left there I got rid of the rifle before we got to Alice Springs."

Inspector Bauer was called away to a phone call and he returned to the office at this stage. That was approximately 1.30pm. I then left the office and Bailey was given lunch in his cell.

About 1.30pm Hallahan spoke to Mrs Bailey for about 1½ to 2 hours. Detectives Hopkins and Moran and Constable Evans arrived at about 3.30pm

Chapter 5 - "Sensational Developments"

That afternoon (22nd) The Adelaide News could hardly contain itself: CIB dash to Mt Isa as man remanded. Sensational turn in Sundown probe likely:

"Sensational developments are expected late today in the Sundown triple murder case. Two Adelaide detectives arrived at Mount Isa early this afternoon and immediately began interrogating Raymond John Bailey, 25, carpenter, who was earlier remanded on two minor charges. It is understood certain statements have been made to both the SA detectives and Mount Isa police. South Australian police are believed to have traced the weapon with which the crimes were allegedly committed. A warrant for Bailey's arrest on a false pretences charge was issued in Adelaide in August."

Here's Hallahan again, in his own words:

Bailey was given afternoon tea. Then, at 4.30pm, in company with Detectives Hopkins and Moran, I saw the accused at the CI Branch office. Detective Moran warned the accused. He said: "We are going to ask you some questions but I am going to tell you that you are not obliged to answer any questions or make any statement as anything you say will be taken down and used in evidence."

I then said to him: "These men are detectives from Adelaide. They are making inquiries about the murder at Sundown Station which is 20 miles south of the Northern Territory border where three persons were found murdered. This morning when I spoke to you, you told me that you had been working at Whyalla in a motorbike shop and you left there about the end of November last to go north looking for work. You headed in the direction of Alice Springs with your wife and child in a DeSoto sedan pulling a caravan. On Thursday, 5th of December 1957, you came across a party consisting of a middle-aged woman, a young man and a young girl camped on the western side of the road. You saw that they had a fire going and when you stopped the car and caravan the middle-aged woman and the man came over to your car and you stopped and spoke to the man about the roads and your wife had a conversation with the women. You saw the girl standing near where the fire was burning. The woman asked you if you would like to have a drink but you refused and she also asked you if you would stay to tea and you again refused and said that you would push on further. At this time it was nearly dark. You drove on about another mile and it was completely dark and you pulled up your car and caravan off the road and on the eastern side of the road with your car facing toward Alice Springs. You had tea with your wife and son and about an hour and a half after tea you got a stomach ache and you used your bowels twice near the caravan. You then decided to go for a walk and took your gun with you. You had bullets on you and then you walked into bush on the western side of the road towards the camp where you saw these people and when at the camp you heard a dog bark and you turned around and fired a shot in its direction and the young man who was lying down sleeping jumped into the air screaming, then fell down and from that time you had a blackout. The next thing you remember is coming to on the eastern side of the road near the deceased persons' car and you saw something covered by tarpaulins and blankets and you went over and you had a look under the tarpaulins and saw three bodies but only recognised the young man. You then walked up to your caravan and had a wash and went to bed. At the time you came to near the bodies it was still dark. Early next morning you went back to the car and bodies and found your rifle in the front seat of the car with some blood on – and the stock of the rifle was broken. You then drove the deceased's car back along the track to where your car and caravan was parked and you stopped the car there and went into your caravan and got a pair of gloves and you drove the car then into some scrub on the western side of the road and washed the car inside and outside to get rid of prints. After doing this you took your rifle back to your car and caravan and drove your wife and child towards Alice Springs. And between Kulgera Station and Alice Springs you stopped your car and threw your rifle away. Is that correct?"

He replied: "Yes. That is the whole story."

At this time I left the CIB office. The time was approximately 4.45pm. At about 10pm on the same date I again saw the defendant in company with his wife in the day room office of the Mount Isa Police Station. He said to his wife: "I would like to tell you what happened. Everybody will know about it sooner or later. I killed those people back along the road."

I then left him.

Later, Bailey signed this statement:

"I, Raymond John Bailey, a carpenter, residing at Mount Isa Queensland have been told that I need not make this statement unless I wish to and anything I do say will be taken down in writing and used in evidence.

"On Thursday the 5th December 1957, I was driving my DeSoto motor car pulling a caravan north along the main North-South Road towards Alice Springs. My wife Pat and my little lad Michael was in the car with me.

"When it was getting dark, I think it would be half past seven, we were about 20 miles south of the Northern Territory border, at Sundown Station.

"We were driving along and I saw a Vanguard sedan motor car parked on the left hand side of the road with its front facing west and the back of it was about seven yards from the road. There was a camp fire burning near the car, in front of it, to the side, but I think it was on the left hand side. I stopped my car on the road at the camp, and I saw a young man and a middle aged woman who walked over to me at the camp fire. A girl aged about 14 was there and she stayed at the camp fire. I asked the man and the woman what the roads north were like. The chap said, "Alright, but there is a bit of bull dust." He said, "What is the road like south." I said, "They aren't real good but you will get through alright."

"I told you before I got out of the car, but I did not. The woman asked my wife who was sitting alongside of me if she would like something to drink. The wife said that she would not like one. I said to the chap "How far is it to the next water." He said, "A fair way up the road."

"We left the camp and started to make for there and it got too dark and my light(sic) were not working too good, so I stopped about a quarter of a mile to half a mile north of the camp. I parked the car and caravan on the right hand side off the road facing towards Alice Springs. The car and caravan were on the eastern side of the road. We had tea there. I think it was spaghetti and a cup of tea. My wife went to bed. I was feeling sick so I sat on the bed. I got a stomach ache, so I went outside and had a shit, and soon after had another one in the scrub just near my caravan. I went back to the caravan, the time may have been about 10 o'clock. And got my Huntsman single shot rifle from out of the front seat of my motor car, and I went for a walk down the road towards the camp where the three people were, south of my car and caravan.

"I walked down until I got to near where they were, I went off the road into the scrub near the camp, which was on the western side, and when I got to the camp, I saw the three people lying down, that is the woman, girl and the chap. As I walked through the camp they were on my left. They were lying east of the fire.

"I heard a noise behind me, when I was passing through the camp, and was just about through it, and I turned around and fired. I did not see if it was, but it sounded like a dog growling.

"When I fired, and a chap jumped up and made a noise and fell down again I thought that I had killed him, and I just went mad after that. When I did this I thought I would have to kill the lot to cover up.

"The young girl and the woman rushed towards me, that was when I moved over to see if the chap was dead. They had been sleeping near him. I loaded my rifle again and aimed it at the older woman who was rushing towards me and fired. She fell down straight away. The young girl rushed at me too, so I loaded again, aimed it and shot her. She fell down too.

"Before I shot the older woman, when the young one and her were rushing at me, I used the butt of my rifle and hit her on the head, knocking her to the ground, and then I shot the older woman.

"After I shot the older woman, the younger girl was getting up off the ground so I shot her. When I shot these two women I was only about 3 yards from them. I shot from the waist. I aim that way generally.

"When I shot the chap that was an accident, I didn't mean to kill him, but when I shot the two women I meant to kill them to get them out of the way, because if they lived they would report me to the Police.

"I do not know how many times I shot them, I just went mad.

"I put the three bodies in the Vanguard Car together in the back and put all the canvas and blankets and other stuff that I could find around the camp with them.

"Then I drove the Vanguard car into scrub on the other side of the road, and went in a fair way, and emptied the back out of all the bodies and the blankets and canvas.

"I laid the bodies out, and put the canvas and blankets over them, as well as everything else that was there. I drove the car back, back onto the road, and went back towards the camp where these people were, I shot, but before getting that far down I turned right and left the car there overnight.

"I walked back to where my car and caravan was. I did not have any blood on me because I covered the bodies with the blankets when I carried them. I had a bath and went to bed. My wife was awake and she asked me where I had been and I told her I was out being sick.

"I got up next morning at about 5 o'clock, went along the road south to the camp where I killed the three people, and I saw the two dogs tied up against a tree south of the camp fire. One dog was bigger than the other, but I don't know what they were. I tried to let them off the chain but I could not get near them. One of the dogs bit me on the left wrist. I then shot them. I didn't use a shovel on them though. I dragged the dogs on their chain and strap to a place behind the camp. I left them there and took the chain and collars off them and also the strap and threw it more west.

"I went over to the eastern side where I left the Vanguard car the previous night, and drove back to where the bodies were covered to make sure that they were covered properly because I had covered them before when it was dark and I did not want the birds to see them or touch the bodies. I felt sorry for what I did and I did not want them to damage the bodies. Before leaving my caravan that morning I took a wheat bag from out of my car, this was before my wife was out of bed, and cut two squares from the bag and wrapped them around my feet and went to the camp where I killed the dogs and then went to the car, and drove to the bodies.

"I did this so I would not leave any tracks. When I drove back to the bodies I put these pieces of bag off my feet under the canvas with the bodies. I had wire through the bags on my feet. I knew that I had left a bag under the car and caravan but I did not worry about it.

"After I went back to the bodies the second time, I drove the car out onto the roadway again, travelled north and drove it into the scrub on the western side of the roadway just about opposite where my car and caravan were parked.

"There was a four gallon tin of water in the Vanguard car, so I used this to wipe finger prints from the inside of the car and also the outside where I thought I had touched it.

"My wife came over to me when I was washing the car and asked me what I was doing and I told her I was washing any marks off it, because the people had been killed down the road and I thought they might blame me, but I told her I did not do it.

"I then went back to the caravan and car and my wife packed up and we left and travelled to Alice Springs.

"On the way we went into Kulgera Station and bought some petrol. This was about 10 o'clock on the Friday morning 6th December 1957. On the way to Alice Springs I had trouble with the right rear spring of my caravan and I had to turn it around and it went alright then.

"Just before getting to Alice Springs, I threw my rifle away on the western side of the road, I went in about four or five paces and threw it in. The rifle I threw away was a Huntsman single shot rifle that I killed the three people with. The stock was cracked but it is not in two pieces. I got that rifle from an Englishman named Dave who is a wheat lumper at Wirrulla on the West Coast just before I left there.

"When I went back to where I left the bodies on Friday December 6 I took a wallet out of the hip pocket of the dead man while he was under the canvas. It was a light brown leather wallet and I took a number of fivers and single pound notes from it and later threw the wallet away between Tennant Creek and Mount Isa, but I cannot say when. I got about 20 to 25 pounds from him.

"I did not get the watch that you spoke to me about though.

"I am sorry for what I have done and it has been worrying me since. I have read it once in the paper but I did not want to read any more. My wife knew nothing about it.

I have never told her that I did it.

"If she knew I had ever done a thing like this I don't think she would live with me.

"I want to point out that I shot the man by accident when I shot at the dog, but I did mean to kill the two women because they would have reported it and I wanted to cover my tracks."

(signed by R J Bailey)

This was followed by typewritten questions and answers:

"Was this statement made by you of your own free will, without threat or promise held out to you?" (handwritten: YES)

"Have you read it and has it been read to you?" (handwritten: YES)

"Is this statement true in every detail to the best of your knowledge?" (handwritten: YES)

(In handwriting): "I wish to add following. When I threw my Huntsman rifle away I took the butt away from the barrel and threw it where I told you before. R J Bailey."

He was told he would later be charged with murder and no doubt taken back to South Australia.

He said "I expect that."

Hallahan says he was with Bailey at 10pm that night when he admitted to his wife that he had killed "those people."

Next day's Advertiser reported:

"A warrant for the arrest of Raymond John Bailey, 25, carpenter of no fixed abode, charging him with the murder, on or about December 5, at Sundown Station SA of Thyra Bowman, was issued in Adelaide last night. It is alleged that an amount of money in notes belonging to Mrs Bowman and Whelan's wrist watch were stolen. It is not yet known how police will travel from Mount Isa to Adelaide with Bailey but a search will probably be made in the vicinity of the crime for a .22 calibre rifle."

At noon on Thursday January 23 Hallahan executed a provisional warrant on Bailey, charging him with the murder of Thyra Bowman at Sundown Station in South Australia on or about the 5th of December 1957.

A conspicuous box on the front page of Mount Isa's local newspaper, the Mt Isa Mail, told readers under the headline of Youngest Detective:

"Detective Glen Hallahan is the youngest detective constable in the Queensland Police Force. He is just 25 years of age and during his time in Mt Isa has become respected as an efficient police officer."

His boss Norwin Bauer had been impressed by the way Hallahan had handled himself and the Sundown case. In February Hallahan gave evidence at the committal proceedings in Adelaide and in May was instrumental in Bailey being convicted of murder.

He had chosen the right moment to make an impact. At the end of January 1958 the Queensland Government appointed a new police commissioner, Frank Bischof, a farmer's son who had left school at 14.

Soon after Hallahan returned to Mount Isa after Bailey's trial in Adelaide, Commissioner Bischof announced he would be visiting this outpost of civilisation as part of a tour of the north-west. He was greeted like royalty when he arrived on a cold winter's day at the beginning of July, for not many important personages turned up in this corner of the state. He spent some time talking to Bauer and Hallahan about his plans for the force. It wasn't long before the result of this conversation became apparent. On July 10 Bischof announced that Hallahan would be transferred to the criminal investigation branch in Brisbane. He was followed almost immediately by Bauer, who was given charge of the capital's licensing branch which policed liquor laws, prostitution and illegal gambling – all so-called victimless crimes which led to police being offered bribes to ignore breaches of the law. After a succession of farewell parties in Mt Isa, Hallahan took a month's leave in Toowoomba before taking up his appointment in Brisbane.

He was hailed a hero.

Chapter 6 - Hallahan is a Hero Again

Come with me now to Brisbane, the sunny sub-tropical capital of Queensland, at the end of the fifties where three precocious schoolboys called Barry, Robin and Maurice Gibb are singing *Does Your Chewing Gum Lose Its Flavour On The Bedpost Overnight?* in youthful high-pitched voices around the dance halls and Returned and Service Clubs. It's not long before they're appearing on Radio 4BH, being paid 3 pounds 3 shillings a performance by shonky nightclub operator Tony Robinson and graduating to Channel 9, Queensland's first television station which had only recently started broadcasting – in August 1959. We're in a city of 600,000 where many of the wooden houses in tree-lined streets are on stilts, keeping them clear of flash flooding and voracious wood-eating white ants as well as letting air circulate under them on humid summer days. Even humble homes have a generous veranda where residents can sip a cold beer or a cup of tea, sleep out or store the junk. Most homes are surrounded by lawn with a sentry box-sized wooden building out in the backyard. It's the dunny, the outside loo, because nearly two-thirds of the city has not yet been sewered. You can see the dunnies from hilltops, standing in militarily straight lines behind the houses. The wooden-wharf-lined Brisbane River writhes in contortions through a city where the highest building is City Hall with its 91-metre clock tower. The central business district is a grid of straight streets where you can park anywhere you choose and where generous shop awnings protect walkers from sudden downpours and burning sun. Life is easy in the Sunshine State's capital city.

It is also Australia's Deep North. Sydney and Melbourne in the south have for a long time reigned as the industrial, cultural and spiritual capitals of the continent.

When Hallahan started serving in Brisbane in 1958 he formed a close relationship with another young copper determined to make a name for himself, Terry Lewis, who was four years older and had three more years' experience. Lewis, born on February 29, 1928, had left school before his 13th birthday to work in a shop. He had joined the force on November 8, 1948, starting to pound the beat from Brisbane's Roma St police station on January 17 the next year. Less than two years later he became a detective.

It was with Terry Lewis that Hallahan next hit the headlines. In the cold early hours of Saturday August 8, 1959, Lewis and Hallahan were working as a team when they were called to a domestic incident in a bungalow in Whites Road, in the bayside suburb of Lota.

Anna Bahnemann phoned Wynnum Police Station at 1.10 on Saturday morning. Come quick, she said, my husband's got a gun.

Two uniformed officers turned up and found Gunther Bahnemann in his home holding a .303 rifle but Bahnemann had no problem in letting one of the officers leave the house to phone Lewis and Hallahan. And the officer felt sufficiently confident to return to the house after making the call.

According to Hallahan and Lewis, when they arrived at 2.15am they found Bahnemann sitting on his bed wearing brown pyjamas with a .303 rifle pointing at the constables.

Terry Lewis said that he and Hallahan had identified themselves as they entered the room. Lewis said: "When I entered the room Bahnemann pointed the rifle at me and said 'Don't try any tricks Mr Lewis and stay where you are. This gun is loaded and if you move any closer I'll blow your guts out. I am not joking'. Lewis said he told Bahnemann: "Your wife says you threatened to kill her and she asked us to come here and talk with you."

Lewis said that when asked what his trouble was, Bahnemann replied: "'I was oberlieutenant in the Panzer Division of Rommel's Afrika Korps. This gun is to kill and if you try to trick me I will kill you. I fought Australians at Tobruk and I killed my share. I am going to kill my wife tonight and then die myself. She is no further use to me. I have killed before and another one, especially her, would be easy. Killing means nothing to me and I will kill again."

Not only had he written a biographical account of his part in the war in North Africa called 'Tonight I Desert', he said, but the starring role of Gunther Ernst Martin Bahnemann would be played by Marlon Brando.

Lewis said that after more conversation Bahnemann swung the rifle towards Hallahan who had moved closer and said: 'If you try another smart trick you are dead. Don't move any closer. I'm not joking. I'll die tonight but I'll not die alone.'

Lewis said: "Hallahan was about five feet from Bahnemann and I was about six feet away. Hallahan jumped towards Bahnemann and Bahnemann, who had the rifle pointed at my stomach, swung it towards Hallahan and fired. There was a deafening report. As Bahnemann fired I jumped on to the bed and sprang on Bahnemann. Hallahan dived and grabbed the rifle by the barrel and I grabbed Bahnemann's right hand to prevent him operating the bolt of the rifle. With the assistance of the two constables from Wynnum we overpowered Bahnemann, disarmed him and handcuffed him. Lewis said Bahnemann told Hallahan: "You are lucky. You should have died. I'm sorry I missed you. I am a German soldier and the man who jumps a man with a loaded rifle should be shot. I am not finished with you yet. I'll get you before I finish. I was a German officer and one of the best. I would have got you if Mr Lewis had not attracted my attention."

Later that morning, still in his pyjamas but with a jacket over them, Bahnemann was produced in the dock at the Police Court, charged with the attempted murder of Hallahan. A photograph of him wearing an officer's uniform and an Iron Cross was submitted. Lewis said the bullet had passed between Hallahan's legs, leaving a powder mark on his trousers.

Bahnemann told the magistrate: "I tried to commit suicide last night."

The magistrate would not have passed an audition as a counsellor with Lifeline. "I don't want to hear anything about that," he said abruptly.

"I was not in my own mind. I did not intend to kill him," said Bahnemann, who then asked for bail, saying: I have a wife and a few animals to look after." Bail was refused. Bahnemann was marched off to jail.

At the trial Mr Justice Stanley looked hard at Bahnemann as he told him: "It is my duty to prevent you and others who may be like minded from attempting to kill policemen. The policemen in this episode exhibited a very high degree of courage and devotion to duty. In particular, Hallahan, who attempted to disarm you by jumping upon you at point blank range, had an almost miraculous escape from your murderous intentions."

Bahnemann was sent to jail for seven years for attempting to murder Hallahan.

Hallahan was a hero again. Early next year he and Lewis drove through Brisbane's leafy inner western suburbs, up steep Fernberg Road, Bardon, where the homes become bigger in proportion to the expanding views, to arrive at the white Italianate, towered mansion that is Queensland's Government House. Amid appropriate pomp, ceremony and Champagne they were both awarded the George Medal, the highest medal for bravery after the George Cross.

Hallahan and Lewis knew the value of publicity and recognition in the battle to get ahead. Equally, reporters knew the value of establishing a relationship with coppers who could give them a yarn or two. As Don Lane, then a colleague of Hallahan in the consorting squad, put it: "He was good at attracting publicity and cultivated the press, in particular Ron Richards, then police roundsman of the Sunday Truth newspaper." Sunday Truth was the brasher, cheekier and more lurid of Queensland's two Sunday newspapers. A small man with a cheeky grin and a nose for a story, Richards became a close friend of Lewis and Hallahan.

A string of stories about the duo followed. Hallahan's title had grown. He was now invariably introduced in newspaper crime stories as "ace detective Glen Hallahan".

Chapter 7 - A Fraud on the Court

Let's move into the swinging sixties. Well, actually, it took a while to get the pendulum moving in Queensland which was still stuck in the mindset of the 50s. Vice squad detectives patrolled milk bars and hamburger joints of doubtful repute checking on "flashily-dressed" youths and girls. Sunday Truth reported: "Brisbane teenagers are dicing with vice in the gaudy atmosphere of a milk bar society which blatantly encourages defiance of the law. It is the heavily-rouged, tight-skirted teenage girl running with the larrikin packs who is causing police their concern. Jan, a petite, dark-haired girl who claimed to be 17 but looked not much more than 14, brazenly admitted her association with boys."

On a warm Saturday evening in October 1961 a 22-year-old short, plump dark-skinned Italian immigrant, Giulia Rossi, was picked up at a bus stop by Dutchman Hendrikus Plomp, a well-built, six-foot, boyish-looking 31-year-old Brisbane City Council bus driver. However, on this occasion Plomp was driving his car and he volunteered to take Giulia, who he had met once before, back to her hall of residence at Queensland University. He then proceeded to find his own route into the darkness of the extensive and mostly undeveloped campus which existed in a vast loop of the Brisbane River about seven kilometres from the city centre. At what was a particularly dark spot Plomp parked the car.

Next morning Giulia complained to police that she had been raped by Plomp.

Hallahan was instructed to take part in the interrogation of Plomp and to attend the interview with Giulia. She told Detective Sergeant Edward Dale and Hallahan that Plomp had stopped the car shortly after the alleged rape and she had talked to two men outside one of the halls of residence. She told them one of the men, named Zeldo Asinari, had been able to speak Italian. Dale interviewed Asinari and added his signed statement to the file. Plomp was eventually committed by a magistrate for trial.

Sergeant Dale was due to leave the force and asked Hallahan to take charge of the Plomp file, telling him he would find it in his locker. Hallahan emptied the locker, assisted Crown Prosecutor Lloyd George Martin to prepare the case for the Supreme Court trial and instructed him in court.

In the week before the trial, prosecutor Martin made available to M Nolan, the Public Defender who was handling the defence case, two statements from Giulia. In one of these she referred to meeting two men outside the hall of residence on the night of the alleged rape. Nolan came back to Martin and asked for any information the prosecution could give him on these two men. Prosecutor Lloyd Martin asked Hallahan if there was anything on file from either of the two men. As a result of what

Hallahan told him, Martin told the defence that the two men could not be located.

The jury found Plomp guilty on May 4. Justice Wanstall took a fortnight to decide on a suitable sentence and on May 18 sent Plomp to jail for six years. With hard labour.

Public Defender Nolan then started a Perry Mason hunt for the two men who he had been told the police could not find. When Nolan eventually tracked the Italian-speaking Asinari to Cairns in Far North Queensland where he had moved after leaving university, he was amazed to discover that Asinari had, in fact, not only been interviewed by police but had provided a signed statement.

The statement made it clear that the dark spot Plomp had chosen to park in with Giulia was actually outside one of the men's halls of residence. And as chance would have it Asinari, a 25-year-old sixth year medical student, who was of Italian heritage, pulled up shortly afterwards.

Asinari saw: "a woman standing beside the other car and I heard her say in Italian "Disgraceful" – in Italian "Disgraziato". She was yelling at the top of her voice in Italian and she walked over to where we were looking for a hamburger that I had lost in the car. She spoke in Italian and she spoke very quickly and loudly and I couldn't understand her because she spoke too quickly for me to understand her in Italian. She seemed upset. A man got out of the car and approached us and said to us in English: "Find out what this woman wants." I said to her in Italian "Che Vuole?" which means: What do you want? She replied: "All you men are the same," or words to that effect, in Italian. I then said to her: "This is private property" and the woman, after hearing this in Italian, walked away back to the car. I then continued to look for my hamburger and I then noticed that the car had gone after I found my hamburger."

But Giulia had alleged: "The defendant drove around for some time and after I started to get my strength back I said to him 'Take me home. I am going to get the police. Take me home.' The defendant drove around for some time and I was still feeling very faint. I then remember seeing two men near St Leo's College at the university and I called out to them 'Do you know this man? He has taken everything from me.' At this time I was crying and very distressed. When I called this out I spoke in Italian and one of the men replied 'This is private property. Get out.' He also spoke in Italian. I then said to the defendant 'You take me home or to the police'.

It was obvious that: 1. She had not told Asinari and his friend she had been raped nor asked them to call the police. 2. Instead of walking a short distance to her college or asking the men to take her home she had voluntarily got back into Plomp's car. 3. Surely if she had been crying and very distressed, one of the two men would have noticed and gone to her aid. All three points would have helped Plomp's case that he had not raped her.

Nolan lodged an appeal against the sentence, saying he wanted to call new evidence which had not been available at his trial, namely the evidence of Asinari and an assistant nightwatchman.

Justices Roslyn Philp, Edwin Stanley and William Mack overturned the finding of guilt on July 27 saying that possible witnesses had not been called to give evidence and that such evidence had not been brought to the attention of the defence case.

Justice Roslyn Philp pointed out: "The importance of this evidence is that it bears out Plomp's story and it contradicts the woman's story. It is hard to understand why these two witnesses were not called. The Crown had the evidence of one of them and must have known the name of the other. According to the woman's evidence she told these two men that Plomp had attacked her. She was within three minutes of where she lived at Duchesne College and she got back in the car."

The Court of Appeal was so appalled at what had happened that it refused to order a new trial.

Arnold Bennett QC was directed by the Minister for Justice to discover whether there had been a deliberate suppression of evidence.

Hallahan told the Arnold Bennett Inquiry that when he had told the Crown Prosecutor that Asinari and his friend were not known and that the police had nothing from them, he had qualified the statement by adding "to my knowledge". This was despite having been present when Giulia Rossi made her statement and having taken charge of the prosecution file containing Asinari's statement.

Arnold Bennett was generous in his finding that: "Hallahan apparently assumed that all matters were in order and all material evidence that could be secured was available in the depositions and exhibits tendered in the Police Court. If he had not made those assumptions, it was his clear duty to make inquiries.

"In this assumption Detective Senior Constable Hallahan was at fault. In my view the matter was not one which should have been left to assumption. From his knowledge of the long statement of the complainant he knew of the incident near St Leo's College and he knew in the early stages that an attempt was being made to locate the two men concerned. He knew that sometimes a prosecuting officer does not call all evidence in the Police Court. These considerations lead inevitably and, I believe, regrettably to a finding of lack of care on his part."

On August 30, 1962, Arnold Bennett found Hallahan had been negligent.

It was the first time that careful readers among the public would have realised that ace detective Hallahan was not the knight in shining armour he had appeared to be.

A month later Hallahan, along with close friend Detective Tony Murphy, was back before Justice Roslyn Philp in the Supreme Court prosecuting Roy Clifford Hart.

Murphy, a hard, determined man with cold eyes who stood no nonsense, made his own rules and was a natural leader. Murphy was slightly older than Hallahan's other close friend, Terry Lewis, but had joined the force at 16 in 1944 and become a detective in 1950

Hart, a 40-year-old timber getter, pleaded not guilty to the long-winded charge of "wilfully and unlawfully setting fire to a dwelling house" between January 10 and 21, 1962

The case involved a holiday house belonging to solicitor Vincent Macrossan, a member of Queensland's most prominent legal family. Two of Vincent's brothers had become chief justice of the State and his 31-year-old son John was a barrister on his way to emulating their achievement.

Situated in a mix of rainforest and bushland 600 metres above sea level on Mount Glorious nearly 40 kilometres from central Brisbane, the house was there on January 11 but by January 21 it was just a charred pile of embers. No one saw the smoke. A rueful Macrossan recalled that a handyman had lit a bonfire in the garden on the 11th but that had seemed to be well under control when everyone left the house. And a housewife living nearby didn't notice the house had gone until her husband mentioned it on the 20th.

Some time after the event, a couple of pictures and bookends and a pressure kerosene lamp were found in Hart's possession. They may have come from the house. They may not.

Now, what a feather in the cap it would be for a police officer if he could show that the cause of the fire which destroyed the home belonging to this illustrious legal family was arson and if he could track down the arsonist and bring him to justice.

According to Hallahan and Murphy, Hart had made a full confession to them when they spoke to him about a different matter at his home on March 19.

It was very much the sort of statement beloved of old-fashioned detectives, in which the criminal is overcome with remorse, finds God, or cracks under the weight of skilful and persistent questioning: All right Guv, I'll tell you everything you want to know. I done it.

Hallahan told the Supreme Court that he and Murphy had been interviewing Hart in his kitchen when he had suddenly interrupted the line of questioning and freely confessed to setting fire to the house.

In his record of interview with Hart, Hallahan was careful to include his interjection after Hart's confession: "Well, I have not heard anything about this fire at all. I have to contact Ashgrove Police to find out about it."

At the end of a long trial the court was ready to doze off. The prosecution had summed up. The defence had summed up. Now a third summing-up was about to be delivered by Justice Philp. It is usual for judges to be extremely long-winded and balanced in their comments. A wrong word here, a careless phrase there could result in grounds for appeal by the defence. The judge weighs his words as if he is placing his entire reputation and future on the delicate scales of justice. He is careful not to be seen favouring one side or the other, reminding the jury of what the prosecution said about an issue and then what the defence said, without giving his own opinion.

Judge Roslyn Philp, a man with matinee-idol good looks, delivered a devastating broadside. While regularly telling the jury that each issue was a matter for them to decide, he was brutal in his demolition of Hallahan and Murphy.

"Gentlemen, I should tell you that before you can find the prisoner guilty you must be satisfied beyond a reasonable doubt of his guilt.

"Gentlemen, this is a rather extraordinary case because the Crown relies on an alleged confession, not merely to prove that the prisoner committed the crime but also to prove that the crime was, in fact, committed. Apart from the confession, gentlemen, there is no evidence that any arson took place. Apart from the confession, there is no evidence that the prisoner took part in any arson. You see, the finding of the stolen articles in the possession of a man several weeks after the fire has occurred is not evidence of arson, gentlemen.

"As defence counsel Mr Cuthbert pointed out to you a few minutes ago, it is very unlikely that a man would steal a few inconsiderable things from a house, would burn it down just to cover his tracks – a man who has stolen what would be a lamp and a couple of bookends and a few pictures.

"However, it's a matter for you.

"What I want to stress to you is this: there is no evidence of the crime in this case and no evidence that the prisoner committed it except his alleged confession.

"If there were no confession in this case I would direct you to acquit and, indeed, the Crown Prosecutor would never have brought the case. So the whole thing depends upon whether his confession was made or whether it was not made.

"It has been pointed out to you that we do not know when this place burned down, apart from the confession, or the alleged confession. There is no proof that the house did not burn down on the 11th. The only proof as to when it was burned down – if you can call it proof – is contained in the alleged confession: the 14th.

"We have heard a somewhat alarming thing – alarming to me and I am sure to you – in this case. We have heard that it is to the interest of detectives to get convictions. We have heard – it was put this way – that the head of the criminal investigation branch, in an appeal, made it plain that a man's promotion in the criminal investigation branch depends on the number of arrests.

"Now, it would be no use a detective making an arrest unless he had evidence and unless it was real evidence or bogus evidence to support it, so the inference I draw from it is this: the head of the criminal investigation branch is saying that it is in the interest of a detective to have evidence. Well, gentlemen, that seems to me to be a very dangerous thing because if it is to the interest of a detective to have evidence then he will be inclined to manufacture evidence and so, as I say. That is an alarming thing.

"That may be only the head of the criminal investigation branch and both Mr Murphy and, I think, Mr Hallahan have repudiated that as being their conception of their duty. However, this fact remains that the head of the department thinks that promotion should depend partly upon the number of arrests a detective makes. Perhaps it is just as well that we, the public, have been made aware of this. It is just as well that you and I have been made aware of it because if there is an inducement to detectives to lie, then your liberty and my liberty are in jeopardy, let alone the liberty of people with a criminal record, against whom false evidence can be so easily brought and which is so difficult to refute.

"Normally, gentlemen, I would have said to you that a police officer has no interest in getting a conviction. I think judges have been saying that for years but things seem to be different now.

"There is another matter which has exercised the minds of judges for very, very many years and has exercised the minds of all thinking men. That is this: that one must always be suspicious of a case which depends solely upon a confession – an alleged confession. It is so easy for a policeman to say: Oh yes, he confessed to me.

"Gentlemen, this is nothing new. Let me read to you from a case that was described in 1893. It is the case of Q v Thompson. Mr Justice Cave said this:

> *"I would add that for my part I always suspect these confessions which are supposed to be the offspring of penitence and remorse and which, nevertheless, are repudiated by the prisoner at the trial. It is remarkable that it is a very rare occurrence for evidence of a confession to be given when the proof of the prisoner's guilt is otherwise clear and satisfactory; but when it is not clear and satisfactory, the prisoner is not infrequently alleged to have been seized with*

a desire born of penitence and remorse to supplement it with a confession – a desire which vanishes as soon as he appears in a court of justice."

"In other words, gentlemen, you should approach the confession with suspicion, particularly when the confession is the only evidence that a crime was committed – and is the only evidence, if a crime were committed, that the prisoner committed it.

"Even though you are satisfied that the bookends came from the house, or the lamp came from the house, that does not prove the arson. It is possible that this man or some other man stole these goods from this house. It may be that some other man handed the goods to the prisoner. It may be that he stole them. It may be that, because he had stolen them and the police found these goods in his possession, all the police needed to do was to go a little further and imagine a confession of arson in order to – to use the vernacular – to fit him with the arson.

"However, it is a matter for you.

"One thing which may cause you to accept the evidence of Murphy and Hallahan would be (as it seems to me) that they had no pre-knowledge of this fire until the prisoner told them of it on March 19. If they had no pre-knowledge then it would seem to me that that fact would go far to support their story that the prisoner told them of the fire.

"However, on that we have some peculiar evidence which Mr Cuthbert has put before you and which is for you to evaluate. I refer to the evidence of Constable O'Keefe. It is essential to the truth of the confession that Hallahan and Murphy had no pre-knowledge of the existence of the fire – no knowledge as at March 19."

"But at a preliminary hearing on a different matter at a Police Court several months earlier Constable O'Keefe had given evidence to the effect that "later that day" on January 22 he had told Hallahan something about the fire.

"If that were so," said the Judge, "then it is perfectly plain that O'Keefe did tell Hallahan on January 22 and, if that be so, the Crown case is gone. We bother no more about it.

"However, Hallahan says that is untrue. He says that it is not true. He was not told by O'Keefe on January 22.

"When O'Keefe appeared at a trial before Mr Justice Mack in May, O'Keefe's explanation, or rather his lack of an explanation as to why he said he saw Hallahan on January 22 was this: "I don't know how it came about that I said 'Later that day…' He did not know how it came about. But when he came here yesterday he was cross-examined about it and there was a discussion between him and Hallahan about this evidence given in the Police Court and his explanation given to us was that what he said in the Police Court was 'at a later date I saw Hallahan…' and he could not remember that explanation in May but he remembered it yesterday – and you may think from that that he was trying to give an explanation for the evidence given in the Police Court, which evidence was in fact true – that he had spoken to Hallahan that day.

"However, gentlemen, it is a matter for you.

"It is a matter for you whether you believe Hallahan and Murphy or not. If you do not believe them and if you are not satisfied about it, then you should acquit the prisoner because his confession cannot stand if Murphy and Hallahan knew of the fire before March 19.

"Gentlemen, the matter is entirely for you.

"Then there are other matters with regard to this confession which I think you should look at. There is the manner of its getting, in this sense: according to the evidence given to you by the detectives, they were questioning the prisoner Hart about something – we do not know what – and then, suddenly, out of a clear blue sky Hart said to them: 'I want to get the lot cleared up…take that light…we fucking well pinched that from the joint burned down at Mount Glorious.'

"Well, gentlemen, is it likely that a man not being questioned about a lamp – about this crime, at any rate; not being questioned about the crime of arson – should, out of a clear blue sky disclose that he was guilty of arson?

"The matter is for you.

"Then he went on and, according to the evidence of Mr Hallahan and Mr Murphy, he indicated this pressure light which was hanging in the kitchen of his residence. Apparently, he had not been asked about the light before he indicated it. He just said: 'There is that light…I want to get the lot cleared up. We pinched it from Macrossan's place, a joint we burned down at Mount Glorious.'"

Justice Philp must have had his tongue deeply in his cheek and been almost winking at the jury when he finished his summing up with one more: 'Gentlemen, the matter is entirely for you'.

The fact that Hart had not been charged with the theft of anything from the house must also have influenced the jury. Hart was supposed to have told Hallahan and Murphy that he doused the house with kerosene but there was no forensic evidence to show that the fire had been deliberately lit.

The jury didn't take long to decide that Hallahan and Murphy had fabricated the confession and lied to the court and that Hart was not guilty.

Another newspaper might have highlighted the fact that the sworn evidence of two detectives had been rejected by a jury but the Sunday Truth's story focussed entirely on the judge's warning about a danger posed to people's freedom by the existence of arrest targets in the police force. It was not until halfway through a massive story that there was the first and only mention of the names of the officers involved in the case in a paragraph in brackets which read: "Detectives A Murphy and G P Hallahan were the officers who charged the defendant in the case."

Worse was to come. On a cool Friday night in June 1963 Hallahan recognised a Sydney criminal standing in the doorway of a sleazy Elizabeth Street nightclub and promptly arrested him. The wheels of justice turned at lightning speed and as soon as the magistrates court opened next morning, Gary William Campbell was up before the beak. He pleaded guilty to a charge that "you were a vagrant within the meaning of the Vagrants, Gaming and Other Offences Act 1931-1962 for that you, on the said day in June 1963, had insufficient lawful means".

The duty prosecuting officer, a Detective Sergeant Rhead, read out the statement of evidence prepared by Hallahan: "On the night of the 28th instant the present defendant was located in the city area and questioned as to his means of living. He told detectives that he had no money and had been unemployed for a period of about two weeks. During that time he had received the sum of three pounds for a night's work as a bouncer at a city night spot. It was established that the offender has been occupying expensive flats for about two months and is currently occupying a flat, the rent for which is seven guineas a week. The defendant admitted that he has no legitimate source of income whatever nor had he made any effort to seek employment. The defendant is an active criminal and recently has been associating with similar types in Brisbane. He admits that he has been engaging in crime and living on the proceeds."

The magistrate asked Campbell: "Do you agree with the facts as related by the police prosecutor?" "Yes Your Worship."

The magistrate spent some time reading Campbell's criminal history. He raised his head: "You have a very bad record for a man of your age. Have you anything to say for yourself?" he asked Campbell.

"Your Worship, I've been going straight since I came out of prison a little less than three years ago. I was shot by Sydney police in 1960 and nearly died as a result. I've spent the last two years working on a station near Longreach and came to Brisbane two weeks ago and foolishly spent all the money I'd saved. If you give me a chance I'll go back to the country and get another job."

Faced with Hallahan's statement that Campbell had admitted to committing crimes and living on the proceeds, and Campbell's long record, the magistrate ignored his hard luck story and delivered a tough sentence: six months' imprisonment – with hard labour!

Campbell was shocked by the sentence and appealed to the Full Court of Queensland, making the point that he had a clean record after being released from prison in October 1961.

Hallahan knew Campbell would have a strong case for the appeal court. The detective would need some big, positive publicity quickly to counter the evidence that was likely to be given in the appeal court.

He told his Sunday Truth friend Ron Richards he had been involved in the hunt for the killer of Robert "Pretty Boy" Walker in Sydney. The result was a massive front-page story by Richards who reported: "Information obtained in a top-secret trip to Townsville by Detective G P Hallahan last weekend could finally crack open the vendetta killing of "Pretty Boy", a small-time hoodlum." And later in the story: "First break in solving the gangland war death came in Brisbane last week after lengthy questioning of a young man well known to police in Brisbane and Sydney. This followed a flying visit to Townsville last weekend by one of Queensland's most active crime investigators, Detective Hallahan, under the direction of CIB chief, Inspector N W Bauer. It is believed that Detective Hallahan obtained information in Townsville that could crack open the killing."

In fact, no-one was ever convicted of Australia's first machine gun slaying.

Hallahan wanted another major advertisement for himself before the appeal court sat. He arranged an exclusive story for Ron Richards of a raid on a gay party where it was expected that one of Brisbane's top television personalities would be attending. The raid would be on a Saturday night which meant that no one else would be able to beat Truth to the story. On Saturday August 10 Richards and a photographer were told to wait at a Herston address. The result was a Hallahan extravaganza across the whole of the front page and page 3. A quarter of the front page carried a photo of a besuited Hallahan, wearing a thick sweater under his jacket to keep out the cold, with "a firm grip on a male strip tease dancer being bundled from a weirdos' party at Herston". The dancer appeared to be naked apart from a tiny towel that might have been the final part of his act. The headlines were: Brisbane rocked by vice exposure; marijuana seized in swoop by police on weirdos; television personality questioned. The whole of page 3 was dedicated to the story, with four more photos of police leading "weirdos" away. The biggest photo featured another close friend of Hallahan and Richards, Detective Don Lane, who we will meet repeatedly across the years.

The following Friday Hallahan, with his defence paid for and backed by the Crown Solicitor, was in court when three of the state's most senior judges heard Campbell's appeal. They said they would deliver their verdicts at a later date.

This meant there was time for another pro-Hallahan story in the Sunday Truth before the verdict was delivered. This time it was a full page story on page 5: Dramatic sequel to city sex raid: Drug ring forced into "smoke". The story started: "Australia's top gangland drug traffickers have gone into hiding following weeks of undercover investigation by Brisbane and Sydney detectives. The first breakthrough in smashing the dope-running gangs follows directly on the dramatic police raids on a marijuana party in the Brisbane suburb of Herston on August 10." It went on to say: "Last week one of the guests at the Herston party was dramatically arrested at Eagle Farm airport by Detectives G P Hallahan and R Price as he was about to leave for Melbourne. He was fined 100 pounds after he told stipendiary magistrate Mr Baker that he had given Detective Hallahan valuable information on the source of the sex drug in Sydney."

The Full Court cared nothing for this spin. On September 26 it delivered a damning verdict on Hallahan. Justice Stanley, who had already studied Hallahan's behaviour in at least two cases, took the lead in reporting:

"Campbell alleges he was induced to plead guilty to vagrancy in these circumstances: Detectives took him away from the place where he was employed and searched his flat for blankets, sheets and pillow slips alleged by them to be missing from premises formerly occupied by him. Not finding any such articles, Hallahan said to him: "*If you haven't got them, you know who has got them and we will charge you with having house-breaking instruments. We'll load you right up and make sure you get put away.*" Campbell replied: "*I don't know where the blankets and other things are.*" Hallahan said: "*How much money have you got?*" Campbell replied: "*About four or five shillings.*" Hallahan said: "*We will charge you with vagrancy.*" Campbell alleges he then told Hallahan about his employment history.

"He had, in fact, obtained part-time employment at the Top Cat Sound Lounge, 74 Elizabeth Street, Brisbane. He was required to work each Friday and Saturday evening, being paid three pounds per night. He worked on Saturday, June 22, and he was at work at that address on Friday June 28 when taken away by Hallahan.

"Campbell alleges that having told Hallahan this, Hallahan said: "*If you don't plead guilty we will go to your flat with house-breaking instruments and then charge you with having possession of them. You'll get at least 12 months' imprisonment. But if you plead guilty, you will get out of the vagrancy charge.*" He alleges Hallahan also told him what to say in court and said: "*If you say what I tell you, I will not rubbish you in court. If I get you out of this charge I want you out of town by Tuesday.*"

"In truth, Campbell was in work and taken away by the police while on duty at his place of employment. Such a disparity between the truth and the statement cannot in my opinion be fairly reconciled with mere negligence or over-hasty generalisation.

"It is difficult to imagine a more unsatisfactory trial. I have come to the conclusion that whether by deliberate intention or mere recklessness the statement to the magistrate in this case amounted to a fraud on the court.

"The respondent should pay the appellant's costs."

Justice Hart reported:
"I agree with my brother Lucas that the manner in which this case was presented amounted to a fraud on the court."

And Justice Lucas decided:
"In my view what was done amounted, on Hallahan's own evidence, to a fraud on the court."

The conviction was quashed and Hallahan was ordered to pay Campbell's costs.

The three senior judges found Hallahan had behaved dishonestly, had invented a confession and committed a fraud on the court.

The Courier-Mail carried an extensive report on the judgement and named Hallahan several times. The Sunday Truth did not mention the judgement at all.

But the Hart and Campbell cases were not the first time Hallahan had lied to courts.

Chapter 8 - A History of Lying

Come with me back to a "guest appearance" Hallahan made on the streets of Brisbane before his official transfer from Mt Isa in 1958. In fact it was exactly a week after the end of Bailey's trial in Adelaide Supreme Court. It is May 27. It's a cool evening but there are plenty of men in the city centre, tumbling out of public bars. To protect them from unseemly swearing and coarse jokes, women are barred from entering these sanctuaries where men are men and often drunk. Bodgies, widgies and other youngsters with their disgraceful clothes and disgusting long hair are making for the sound lounges where they drink milkshakes and listen to the new number one, 'All I have to do is dream' by the Everly Brothers. There are the euphemistically-titled 'private hotels' and 'residentials' which are tolerated by the Queensland Government where a man can buy a woman for half an hour, and nearby dark streets where prostitutes operating outside this arrangement can be found. This is where Hallahan is checking who's who. He arrests one of the women and takes her back to the station - a young mother who says she lives on the Gold Coast and is selling herself to pay the rent because her rotten husband isn't good enough at selling vacuum cleaners door to door to make ends meet. Her name is Kryloff. Next morning at 7.30 Hallahan arrives at the couple's home on the Gold Coast to confront Mr Kryloff. At the station he is charged with knowingly living wholly on the earnings of prostitution.

Later, in court Magistrate J Gaffney took a dim view of Kryloff, a father of three young children admitting that he lived wholly on the money his wife earned as a prostitute. He sentenced Kryloff to six months' imprisonment.

This came as a hell of a jolt to Kryloff who had been expecting only a small fine that would have taken his wife only a short time to earn. Down in the cells he demanded to see a solicitor. What Kryloff told the solicitor resulted in an appeal to the Full Court against the sentence on the grounds that his plea had been the result of enticement or inducement.

Kryloff swore an affidavit saying Hallahan had advised him: "The best thing you can do is to come to court and plead guilty. The magistrate will only fine you and there will be no publicity. The best thing you can do then is get out of the state. Tell the magistrate that you're sorry and that you will leave the state straight away." So, said Kryloff, he had only pleaded guilty because he had been told it would provide the best result for him.

Hallahan denied the allegation on oath but the three judges constituting the appeal court, Stanley, Mack and Wanstall, obviously did not believe him and were so concerned by his behaviour that they laid down a course of action that all magistrates should follow if a defendant appeared before them without a legal representative and pleaded guilty.

They said: "The magistrate should not only inquire whether anyone connected with the police has made any suggestion that he should plead guilty and advise the accused to plead not guilty unless he receives from the accused a prompt and convincing disclaimer of any such suggestion but also he should intimate positively to the accused his right of putting everything he wishes to the court, provided it is relevant to the charge and then get down on the record that the accused as said all he wishes to say."

This was Justice Stanley's first experience of Hallahan's conniving. He would later experience further examples of Hallahan's dishonesty in the Campbell appeal and in the Plomp case. It's intriguing that when Justice Stanley presided at the Bahnemann trial it was Lewis who acted as the story teller rather than Hallahan.

The Kryloff case earned Hallahan new fame, this time in legal circles. The case went into the legal lexicon as 'Hallahan v Kryloff, ex-parte Kryloff' and has been frequently quoted in Queensland judgements ever since. It was the first black mark against Hallahan's name. But newspapers gave it no coverage.

On Saturday April 15 1961 the CIB received a call from Brisbane's poshest and most modern hotel, Lennons, with a frontage which occupied the whole of George Street between Anne and Adelaide Streets. Anyone who was anyone stayed at Lennons when they were visiting Brisbane. Famous guests included General Douglas MacArthur, who lived there while commanding the Allied Pacific offensive in World War Two, and Gary Cooper. Hallahan was met at the hotel by general manager Mr A J Watt who explained that the hotel's regular cashier was on holiday and the night porter, a man named Tony Cavanagh, had been looking after the cash overnight. When it came to the change of shifts, two bags containing a total of 10 pounds 9 shillings – equivalent to nearly half a week's wages - were missing. Hallahan wasted no time at all. A few hours later he had Cavanagh up in front of the police court pleading guilty to having stolen the money. There was even a written confession from him. The magistrate ordered him to repay all the money. If he failed, he would be sent to prison for 14 days. It may have been only a few pounds rather than three killings but it was an identical result to the one achieved in the Sundown Murders case – a signed admission of guilt and another triumph for Hallahan.

Worse was to follow for Cavanagh. At 31 he had a wife and 14-month-old daughter at home to support but the hotel sacked him from his 25 pounds-a-week job.

There was just one problem which surfaced the following week when the regular cashier returned from her holiday. She found the larger of the two bags, containing all but a few shillings of the money, still in the safe. It had not been stolen, nor even lost. Just overlooked.

So why had Cavanagh confessed to a crime that not only did he not commit, but which had never occurred in the first place? He told his solicitor that on the Saturday morning he had been threatened by Hallahan: You can either plead guilty, go before the court today and be home with your wife this afternoon or we'll throw you in jail until you come clean and your wife will be worried sick at home.

"I know I pleaded guilty but I challenge anyone else placed in similar circumstances to do anything different," said Cavanagh. "I'd been taken away by the police and faced with a weekend in the watchhouse if I pleaded not guilty. Let's put it bluntly, I was scared, scared for my wife and child, and with me they come first."

Police Commissioner Bischof took on the role of Blind Freddy and announced he was examining all the papers in the case to see if any miscarriage of justice had occurred. Cavanagh gave a detailed statement to his solicitor and to Bischof.

Bischof recommended that the Government should grant Cavanagh a pardon. It was late August before Cavanagh received a letter from Queensland Justice Minister Alan Munro clearing his name. It said: "We are satisfied that you are innocent of the charge for which you were convicted." He received a Royal Pardon.

And what decision was taken regarding Hallahan and his colleagues? The letter told Cavanagh: "As regards to your statements against police, they do not give sufficient details that are required."

The only reports of this case appeared in Sunday Truth, written by Ron Richards. Readers may have wondered about the identity of the police involved in the case because not once did Richards name the police who had perpetrated this dastardly deed. But Richards did tell his readers: "I do know that one of the police officers concerned – a detective with an excellent past record – has been seriously ill since the Cavanagh case was first brought to light."

It may well be that in an attempt to limit the fallout from his A-grade stuff-up Hallahan gave Richards the story on the condition he was not named.

For the second time Hallahan's dishonesty in a court case resulted in a change to judicial procedures. This time Police Minister Morris announced that it would be an offence for a police officer to advise anyone to plead guilty to an offence.

The Queensland Criminal Code states: "Any person who in any judicial proceeding, or for the purpose of instituting any judicial proceeding, knowingly gives false testimony touching any matter which is material to any question then depending in that proceeding, or intended to be raised in that proceeding, is guilty of a crime, which is called *perjury*. Any person who commits perjury is liable to imprisonment for 14 years." It also states:

"Any person who, with intent to mislead any tribunal in any judicial proceeding—
> (a) fabricates evidence by any means other than perjury or counselling or procuring the commission of perjury; or
> (b) knowingly makes use of such fabricated evidence;
> is guilty of a crime, and is liable to imprisonment for 7 years.

We have discovered that far from being an ace detective, Hallahan was a liar, perjurer, and cheat who had committed a fraud on the justice system. But at least he was a brave man who had won the George Medal. Wasn't he?

There was another side to that story as well.

Chapter 9 - Gunther Bahnemann's Story

We've heard the Hallahan-Lewis version of the arrest and charging of Gunther Bahnemann. What follows is the story from Bahnemann's point of view.

Gunther Bahnemann was a highly intelligent boy who was doomed by his birth in Hamburg, Germany, on November 29, 1920, to reach his teenage years in the Great Depression and to be called up to fight for the Nazi war machine. He left school at 15 to become an apprentice seaman on ships sailing out of Hamburg to all parts of the world, rising through the ranks to become a fully-qualified second mate by the time he was called up in 1939.

He started the war as an army driver but later became a parachutist and glider pilot. He fought in Poland, France, Belgium, Holland and Norway. By 1941 he claims to have won the Iron Cross First Class (EK1) and Iron Cross Second Class (EK2) and was a corporal fighting in Tripoli with Rommel's Afrika Korps. He was devastated when he received a letter from his mother telling him his father, who had been an officer in the German Army in World War One, had been hanged in a concentration camp. He wasn't going to fight for bastards who had killed his father. "I deserted straight off," he recalled. He was hunted for three months by German and Italian military police and was eventually picked up by a British long-range desert patrol and taken to Cairo. There he was incarcerated in a British detention centre. The result was a free passage on the Queen Mary to Fremantle, Western Australia, where he arrived in 1941 on his 21st birthday. For more than five years he learned English and wrote a book in English about his adventures in North Africa, giving it the title *"Tonight I Desert"*.

Released in 1947, he chose to base himself in and around Australia, working as a delivery skipper aboard small craft in the Far East and Pacific islands. But he wanted to own and run his own boat so in 1949 he worked for a year as a miner in Mt Isa, saving most of the big wage packets then on offer. That enabled him to build his own boat. He became a qualified aqualung diver and used the boat to go pearling and trochus shell diving, eventually forming his own company. When the pearling industry collapsed he lived with West Guinea tribes while crocodile poaching with a rifle. He lost his first boat in the crocodile and shark-infested Gulf of Carpentaria. With it went the only copy of *"Tonight I Desert"*.

Gunther Bahnemann was down but not out. He built another boat, the Blitz, and rewrote his book. His next adventures involved taking wealthy businessmen big game fishing off the Great Barrier Reef from north Queensland ports.

In February 1959 he sent his manuscript to Percy "Inky" Stephensen, a noted scholar and literary agent in Sydney. Inky, a Rhodes Scholar, had befriended him 17 years earlier after being arrested and interned without trial on 10 March 1942 on suspicion of collaboration with the Japanese and of planning sabotage and assassination. Evidence provided by an agent provocateur that he had been involved in such a plot, was later discredited but Inky spent the rest of the war interned. There he met and encouraged Gunner to become a writer.

By 1959 Bahnemann had earned enough to buy a plot of land in Whites Road, Lota, half a dozen streets back from Brisbane's Moreton Bay coast. There he built a brick bungalow and installed a beautiful blonde wife, Anna.

In April his yacht sank off Mackay in North Queensland. It was uninsured. Seemingly undeterred, he continued to operate fishing charters using other boats and in July even wrote to Marlon Brando, enclosing a copy of his manuscript and inviting him to star in the film of the book.

But then he learned that Anna was being unfaithful – many times a day. She was a prostitute. Despite his wartime adventures it seems that Gunther had been extremely naïve in choosing a bride. He was deeply in love with her and, with this revelation coming on top of the loss of his yacht, he returned home and sank into a deep depression. Anna was well known to Hallahan and Lewis from her activities as a prostitute but Hallahan – and probably Lewis – had never met Bahnemann.

His memory of the night he was arrested on August 8, 1959, in Lota started with his wife telling him she was going to leave him and return to Western Australia. He told her he loved her and that if she left him he would do himself in. Far from softening her stance, she walked out to spend the evening at the local pub. Distraught, he decided he would kill himself. He took dozens of tablets of various kinds and even bit chunks out of the glass of water he was using to wash down the tablets. He put a photograph of his wife by his bed so he could look at her as he died. And in case the tablets didn't work he had put one bullet in his .303 rifle so that he could finish himself off. But then he had decided to stay awake until his wife returned. To stop himself from falling unconscious he had slashed his stomach with the broken glass. When his wife returned she had become hysterical and started yelling. She then walked 600 metres down the road to phone the police because there was no phone in the house. She was hardly in fear of her life.

So when the police arrived, Bahnemann was alone in the bedroom.

Although it was Lewis who told the court that Hallahan had thrown himself so courageously at the armed killer, Bahnemann blamed Hallahan for concocting the story. The transcript of the Supreme Court case is missing from the State Archives so it is impossible to use this as a basis for telling Bahnemann's account of the incident. Fortunately, Bahnemann's agent, Inky Stephensen, kept all his correspondence. From these letters and from newspaper reports of the case it appears that in essence the rifle had discharged only because Hallahan had grabbed it. "I will never understand how any court could have believed a former soldier and crocodile hunter would miss a man from one metre if he really meant to murder him," Bahnemann said. "At that range there is no way I could have missed a target that big." Bahnemann's story is supported by the fact that the bullet travelled downward, through the bedroom wall, hitting the concrete floor of the room next door, fragmenting and making holes in the walls. If he had been aiming at Hallahan from his sitting position on the bed, the bullet would probably have travelled almost horizontally.

On September 8 Bahnemann wrote to Stephensen from his remand cell in Boggo Road Jail: "I am in prison on a charge of unlawful attempt to kill. I tried to commit suicide and in the act of that a shot was fired and now the charge is as you read. Anna played around and is the reason. She sold the house to realise money for my defence but is too scared to act and stays away. Dear Percy, I appeal to you with everything I have to try and arrange a defence for me. Percy, I am prepared to sign over outright my two books to you, if you can help me as I have a good chance to win if I can have a solicitor and barrister. Please Percy for all you remember and help me, because I am innocent on this charge. All I have is 10 pounds."

Stephensen arranged for Brisbane solicitor Colin Murphy to represent Bahnemann. Murphy said he would need 250 guineas as the fee for a barrister and himself to appear for Bahnemann in court and was prepared to gamble on Bahnemann's war memoirs selling enough copies to pay the fee. On September 23 Bahnemann signed an indenture, pledging to Murphy the first 250 guineas from any sales of the book which Inky had now retitled *'I Deserted Rommel'*.

In October Bahnemann told Stephensen: "I had my trial and I was found guilty by the jury but have not yet been sentenced. Whatever your verdict, Percy, I beg of you to believe me, I am innocent of the charge, that is the truth but I cannot elaborate on the matter here. Anna came once for the first three weeks in here, since then I had no word from her nor a line in writing, Percy. I would not be here if Anna had gone to court and answered three questions, it would have established the fact that I did not fire the shot but no one knows her whereabouts. I am battling hard with my mental capacity to remain sane. I hardly sleep because I still love Anna though she kicked me down. Anna sold the house and cleaned out. I have not even got a house any longer and no money. You are the only friend I have and a proved great."

Bahnemann worked to become a trusty in Brisbane's notorious Boggo Road Prison and earned the right to have a typewriter in his cell. He became a storeman during the working day and then developed a new manuscript, *Hoodlum Junior*, using stories given to him by bodgies who had committed crimes serious enough to be fellow inmates. Later he became the prison librarian.

Almost a year after his failed suicide attempt Bahnemann was given a letter from Inky Stephensen dated August 1, 1960 saying: "I am very happy to give you the news that your book *Tonight I Desert* has been accepted for publication by the London publishers Messrs Jarrolds Ltd." There was a 100 pound advance and a promise of 10% of the first 3,000 books sold, 12½% of the next 2,000 and 15% of all books sold after that. Bahnemann was, understandably, deliriously happy. The book was published in London on October 23, 1961.

In January 1962 Hutchinson, the parent company of Jarrolds, was about to publicise the book in Australia. Bahnemann was told the company's Sydney manager, a Mr O Hoffner, would be publicising the book. Bahnemann wrote to Inky Stephensen: "Tell Mr Hoffner I am very grateful. Tell him also remarks made with regards the shooting etc on frontline are far-fetched. Police used this sensational thrash in court to bias the jury, to ring themselves up the ladder of having battled it out with a dangerous character. They brought this out in court and paper, in conjunction with my holding high German decorations and therefore of course had me accepted as a real Nazi till I blocked this move of theirs by telling the court that I in effect fought the Nazis and deserted from same. I assure you I never swashbuckled such rubbish but it served the cops admirably to make a conviction stick solidly. Next, start thinking they admitted I had only one round in the rifle but produced 153 in court. As an ex-soldier, a professional crocodile shooter, it looks rather funny that I did not load the Boer War rifle fully, more funny even that I didn't hit anyone at about two feet distance. Go on Percy, think about that. It sticks out a mile."

According to Bahnemann, he never had the murderous intent of taking a police officer's life as the judge would have us believe. He was a drugged would-be suicide. It was Hallahan's lunge and grab that triggered the shot.

I Deserted Rommel went on sale on January 20, 1962, priced at 21 shillings and was then serialised in newspapers throughout Australia, appearing in Brisbane's evening Telegraph for 14 days starting on February 3.

But Ron Richards and Hallahan took every opportunity to remind readers of Hallahan's "heroism" against a Nazi menace, culminating on September 15 1963 the page 3 headline was: Get this fellow out of Australia

FAST – Maudlin approach to gun-crazy Nazi must stop. The article labelled him a "gun-happy Nazi" "unnaturalised, irrational and a ruthless husband", and "a would-be policeman killer". The story read: "German Afrika Corps deserter and would-be killer Gunther Bahnemann was hailed as a hero by some Brisbane people when our State Parole Board stunned Queensland by letting him out of jail last week. Bahnemann was treated to a conqueror's welcome in some newspaper and television interviews – but Bahnemann is no hero in the eyes of Sunday Truth…How extraordinary it is that Bahnemann, the German soldier who ran out on his own mates at the height of the fighting in North Africa in 1941 and spent the war years as a prisoner in Australia, should now be considered as a prospect for permanent residency in this country…Bahnemann went to prison because he deliberately tried to shoot Detective G P Hallahan while Hallahan and Detective T M Lewis were questioning him."

The article then retold in minute detail the story of heroism related by Lewis and Hallahan at the trial. And it ended by saying: "These are the real facts in the Bahnemann story."

Bahnemann told Inky of his feelings towards Hallahan and Lewis: "If George Crosses(sic) are handed out like they have been handed out, I'll say they're a dozen to one Iron Cross."

He alleged many years later that Lewis and Hallahan had threatened his wife "with dire consequences" unless she stayed away from his trial "thereby getting rid of a witness."

Chapter 10 - The Brown Paper Bag

in the Premier's Safe

Hallahan was a serial cheat, liar and perjurer. And yet for years he had got away with this appalling behaviour.

Why? How?

In 1957 the Australian Labor Party (ALP) had ruled Queensland for 39 of the previous 42 years. Entrenched power had led to entrenched corruption. The Government ensured it had a police commissioner who would do its bidding. A retired police officer described how: "The officers in charge of police stations or districts were directed by the government to allow the hotels to trade illegally and bookies to operate and in return each and every publican and bookmaker paid for those favours." Renegade MP Tom Aikens said: "I know that the bookmakers' organisations in various towns in Queensland regularly sent very substantial donations down to the ALP Government of the day." Money from corrupt sources was paid into the Special Premier's Fund run by Premier Vince Gair. He had produced 12,000 pounds in a dirty paper bag towards the 17,000 pounds it had cost to run the 1956 election campaign which resulted in Labor winning power yet again. A bank account in the fund's name was accessible only by Gair, who used the cash to support his proteges.

Sir Thomas Hiley, Treasurer in the future Liberal-Country coalition government, revealed how the money had been collected. Most, if not all of it had come from SP bookmakers and was collected by trusted ministerial private secretaries who were given rail passes, a list of names and addresses and an empty bag.

"Don Marsen who was private secretary to several of the ministers of the Labor government told me the details of how he would personally collect funds," recalled Sir Thomas. "When the bag started to get a bit heavy he would have a letter of authority to the nearest police station entitling him to be given a police escort for the rest of the journey. His journey would be completed in Brisbane by delivering the bag, which contained only cash, to the office of the premier of the day. From what I understood there were no police beneficiaries of the fund."

Despite prostitution being regarded as a sordid, unmentionable sin, several houses of ill repute known euphemistically as private hotels were discreetly tolerated in Brisbane by the Government. This enabled the prostitutes' sexual health to be checked on a weekly basis and the collection of payments from the brothels by selected police. Part of this filthy lucre, it was said, then found its way into the Special Premier's Fund with the rest going to corrupt police.

Licensing laws meant Brisbane pubs were closed on Sundays to everyone apart from people who were more than 40 miles (64 kilometres) from home. This led to a lot of men with time on their hands, pay-day money still in their pockets and a strong thirst on a hot day looking for an open back door at their local. Those pubs that provided this service paid detectives to look the other way. Don Lane denied evidence to the Fitzgerald Inquiry by Jack Herbert that he had accepted such payments. Licensing branch officers had been ordered to keep out of ministers' electorates. Even more ridiculous was Section 1661 of the Licensing Act which prohibited people from drinking beer, wine or spirits at a dance in a public hall. Police were employed to check on people entering dances and were frequently paid to turn a blind eye to alcoholic "tea" being poured from large teapots into large mugs at tables. The annual Police Ball in City Hall was always awash with booze. In fact, it had been a riotous, drunken police ball which had resulted in the section being added to the Act.

The final part of this corruption trifecta was betting. Australians' love of betting is universally known. But unless you could get to a racecourse on a Saturday, there was nowhere to place a bet – legitimately. Queensland is the only mainland state in which more than half the population live outside the capital city, which meant that most men who liked a bet were a long way from a licensed bookie. In fact, there was a well-organised illegal betting system throughout the state. Even the smallest town had its barber or grocer with a backroom where bets were taken throughout the week. Once again, an appointed copper would collect the rent for being blind to this activity and a proportion of the takings were sent up the line to Brisbane. In Cloncurry and Mount Isa, where Hallahan had been stationed, Inspector Norwin Bauer protected two illegal betting shops in Cloncurry, one a shopfront in the main street and the second a major operation beneath a house behind a billiard saloon. The instruction to all police from Bauer was to leave them alone, recalled Don Lane, who had served as a constable there. Illegal gambling clubs were also protected but on one occasion an unexpected police raid collared an MP, the former Speaker of Parliament, Johnno Mann.

Honest officers accepted that politicians and selected police were not only engaged in corruption but were beyond the law.

In 1957 the Queensland branch of the Australian Labor Party split into two warring factions in a bitter dispute, the party insisting that the Labor Government must introduce a minimum holiday entitlement of three weeks and the Government refusing to obey the party directive.

Premier Gair and all but one of his Ministers split from the Australian Labor Party and formed the Queensland Labor Party. The resulting two Labor parties split the working class vote and enabled a conservative coalition to win government in August 1957. But politics didn't just involve the working class versus the employing class. Most Roman Catholics voted Labor. Conservative politicians were predominantly Protestant, and Freemasons at that. Immigrants from Northern Ireland would have felt very much at home in the bigotry, hostility and stupidity which occurred as a result of what brand of Christianity you subscribed to. It would be many years before the coalition conservative Government appointed a Catholic as a Minister. Whole Government departments were no go areas if you were the 'wrong religion'. The Police Force had been dominated by the Green Mafia, Catholics of Irish descent, who largely controlled the corruption.

Now that the Protestants were in charge there was a priority to install their own police chief. On December 22, 1957, *The Sunday Mail* reported that a senior police officer was expected to retire in a major shake-up in the force. A shake-up was needed because, it was alleged, there was a State-wide "protection racket" to tip off illegal bookies about any police raids. Some of the bookies were openly displaying betting boards in some country towns. Police Commissioner Harold, aged 59, was retired immediately after going before a medical board on December 23. He had been Commissioner only since April 26. The following week Police Minister Morris told the newspaper: "We want to appoint a new Police Commissioner as quickly as possible...then get on with the job of cleaning up the Police Force."

The obvious choice came down to two officers. Deputy Commissioner Jim Donovan was the more senior officer. His honesty and integrity were beyond doubt. He was widely respected and was young enough to be considered for the top job. But he was a Catholic and, therefore, was regarded as certain to be a Labor voter. Frank Bischof, head of the Criminal Investigation Branch, was corrupt, a Protestant and a Mason.

Two honest detectives got wind of Bischof's impending appointment and blew the whistle on him. One of the whistleblowers was Charlie Corner, an officer so imbued with honesty and to upholding the law that he would probably have reported himself if he had driven one mile an hour over the speed limit.

Here's Charlie, who discovered when he joined the Licensing Branch in Brisbane many years earlier: "that enforcement action with respect to gambling, sly grog trading, prostitution and hotels could be taken only on the direct instructions of the Commissioner."

As a plain clothes detective, he accompanied Detective Inspector Frank Bischof on a raid of the Athenium Club in Charlotte Street.

In perfect policespeak Corner recalled: "No offences were being committed. Bischof accused the keeper of the club of keeping a disorderly house. Later that day the keeper of the house, one Jack Smith, attended at the police station and told me he was there in order to pay Bischof."

While on the consorting squad, Corner was told: "No prostitutes were to be breached without Bischof's prior consent. I don't know who issued these instructions but I didn't abide by them. I recall warning a prostitute who had a long criminal history and who was tied up with a Southern criminal to leave Queensland. When I later heard that the prostitute, named Leggatt, was still at a brothel at South Brisbane, I arrested her for vagrancy. I was subsequently called to Inspector Bischof's office where Bischof took me to task about arresting Leggatt. Later that day I was informed by Inspector Mahoney, the prosecutor in the matter, that Inspector Bischof had directed him to allow Leggatt to obtain bail. Leggatt was granted bail and she absconded."

When he got wind of the plan to install Bischof as Commissioner, Corner arranged an appointment with Solicitor-General Bill Ryan and provided a detailed list of Bischof's corrupt activities, with names, dates and places, for Cabinet to read. The other whistleblower was Bill Osborne. The Government denied to the media there was any sort of investigation into anyone. "That's a damned lie," Police Minister Morris said. No police officer had made any such allegation to him or approached him.

On January 28 the debate split the State Cabinet, resulting in one of its longest meetings. Sir Thomas Hiley, the Treasurer, said of Bischof: "He will either make an expert Commissioner or he should be behind iron bars." It was 7pm before the Bischof supporters triumphed. The joke on all law-abiding Queenslanders was that the new Premier responsible for appointing a corrupt commissioner was known as Honest Frank Nicklin.

Immediately after the decision, Premier Nicklin and Police Minister Morris had a long, secret meeting with Bischof in a Parliament House back room where he was briefed on the Government's attitudes and policies relating to police administration, and its desires for re-organisation of the force and its operation.

Bischof, born in Toowoomba, 135 kilometres west of Brisbane, was 53. Known as the Big Fella or Big Frank, he was a notorious verbal brawler. Corrupt or not, Bischof, married but with no children, made a show of going to his local Anglican church in the leafy western suburb of The Gap every Sunday from his modest lowset brick home in Barkala Street.

The appointment sent a message to honest police that it would be pointless complaining about corrupt colleagues to the commissioner. More than that, they knew it would be pointless complaining to the Government. There were no other avenues open to them. The message sent to corrupt officers was that they were above and beyond the law. They could behave with impunity.

The government received a compliant police force that would do its bidding. It meant traffic offences against friends and relatives could be dropped. Promotions to senior positions were closely vetted by Cabinet.

Former Deputy Premier Ted Walsh hit the nail on the head when he said: "One of the first...who found it necessary to model a police force so that it would be useful to him was Hitler. It was he who, having corrupted the top of the police force, found it so easy to corrupt the whole of the force and so do the damage that was eventually done to that country." The comment accurately predicted the fate of Queensland over the next 30 years.

The media? Many reporters and newspaper executives placed bets with illegal bookies, drank after hours in pubs and frequented illegal casinos. They were part of the problem. And police reporters often obtained their best stories from corrupt detectives.

It wasn't long before Bischof took advantage of the fact that the Nicklin Government had not continued the Special Premier's Fund and had abandoned collecting graft from SP bookies. Bischof put his own collection scheme in place, hence the need for bagmen such as Hallahan, Murphy and Lewis. But after a price had been fixed for each town, the bookies objected when they were asked for more.

Sir Thomas Hiley, Nicklin's Treasurer, takes up the story: "I received a deputation of western SP bookmakers who revealed the whole story of the Bischof-led SP racket in towns west of the Dividing Range. These SP bookmakers told me there was an organised ring operating under a direct arrangement with the police. An annual fee was set and collected from the SP operators. It was $80,000 for each major town and $40,000 for some lesser towns and then $20,000 for smaller towns again. In return the police were to leave the bookmakers alone. Surprisingly, the bookmakers had no complaint about the bargain which had been struck. Their complaint was they were being hit for a second bite.

"When I asked these bookmakers how the money was disbursed they all said half was split up among the local police and the other half went to Brisbane. Although they could not be certain, the bookmakers said that Brisbane meant Bischof.

"I asked these bookmakers whether they were prepared to give evidence. They looked me in the face and said "Mr Hiley, we'd be dead, we'd be dead". They just would not budge one inch.

"I set out to find what Bischof was doing with his share of the money. I could find no trace of property acquisitions and I felt I was at a dead end when I had a real stroke of luck. I discovered that Bischof was a compulsive gambler on the horse races. He'd go to the races and bet stupidly. On a salary of about 11,500 to 12,000 pounds a year, he would lay

2,000 pounds on a single race meeting. He would often back three horses in the one race with substantial amounts – hundreds of pounds at a time."

It was Bischof's pomposity that had resulted in the rest of the sceheme being revealed.

"He stood over a bookmaker," recalled Sir Thomas. "He used to go to the racecourse in his major-general's uniform, all silver braid and studs all over him and he'd go down to the betting ring and always try to cosy the odds. This chap said to him on this day: 800 to 500. 1000 to 500, said Bischof. No, 800 to 500 - and the ticket was issued at 800 to 500. It was one of the rare ones that Bischof picked that won. And when he went to the ring in front of all the assembled crowd for the payout he accused the bookmaker of cheating on him, said the bet was 1000 to 500. At any rate, to shut him up the bookmaker unwillingly, rather than have this continue in front of the ring, paid him it but he blurted out the story to a chap who was working for me as an inspector of totalisators."

This bookmaker told the inspector that Bischof placed all his bets as credit bets but the bookmakers were instructed to enter in their sheets all bets made by Bischof as Mr B. If Bischof won, the entry was to be completed "Bischof". If the bet lost the entry would be completed in another name starting with B, with the most common of those being Baystone."

A check of betting sheets which had to be lodegd with the Commissioner for Stamp Duties confirmed that Mr Baystone should have been nominated to the Guinness Book of Records for the title of the world's worst punter. Mr Baystone had lost every bet he'd made. On the other hand, there were never any losing bets in Bischof's name. The sceme meant that Bischof could launder his dirty money, being able, if necessary, to produce proof that he had won a lot of money at the races.

"I took my information to Mr Bill Ryan, the Solicitor-General. Ryan advised me that we would stand no chance of prosecuting Bischof because none of the bookmakers, either SP or paddock bookmakers, would give evidence. Therefore, I decided to seek a remedy other than by a public inquiry or risking court proceedings for wrongful dismissal. I went to the Premier, Frank Nicklin, and told him the story. I told him that we couldn't get any proof. I told him we would have to bluff Bischof and either get a written confession out of him or bluff him into remedying the situation. I asked Nicklin to send for Bischof on the next Wednesday together with the Minister in charge of the police, Alex Dewar. I chose a Wednesday afternoon because a race meeting would be in progress at that time.

"When Bischof arrived I told him of the Government's concern over SP betting and asked him what it was like in Western Queensland. We got assurances from him that SP bookmaking was almost non-existent in the West. As he crossed those bridges we burned them behind him.

"I asked him particularly about Mount Isa, and he said it was completely clean. I told that at that moment there was a large SP operation in progress in a specific room, a table was covered with bags of money and a uniformed policeman was at the door to guard against hijackers. There was, I told him, a regular check by a senior policeman at least twice during the afternoon to make sure the operation was not disturbed. Bischof said 'You amaze me, Mr Treasurer'. I said I would amaze him a lot more and went on to tell him what each town was paying for protection."

Hallahan had proved to have nerves of steel when facing down allegations of corruption but now Commissioner Bischof, despite being nicknamed The Big Fella, turned to jelly.

"As each figure was given, the bluster went out of him. Bischof caved in in front of us. I described to him that the graft collected by police from SP bookmakers in the west included amounts for police in Brisbane and I told him that Brisbane and himself were synonymous. He made no denials and offered no resistance and he simply said to me "What do you want me to do?" I said to him: "You started all this, you stop it."

"Bischof was forced to raid the very bookmakers from whom he had been accepting graft. Police activity against SP bookmakers increased significantly after my meeting with Bischof.

Sir Thomas said that at the time he believed the racket had been stopped. He realised later that this had only been a temporary hiccup and that Bischof had continued the scheme for many years.

It was worth hundreds of thousands of pounds a year at a time when a fully-furnished luxury home could be bought for 17,000 pounds.

One of the best opportunities to indulge in corruption was offered to the detectives on the licensing and consorting squads, who spent their time keeping a close eye on known criminals, mixing with prostitutes, checking on when and where alcohol was being sold and investigating illegal gambling, all of which entailed long hours drinking in pubs with pimps, prostitutes and other members of the criminal class as well as businessmen wanting to sell alcoholic drinks illegally, with the potential of milking them for protection money.

Commissioner Bischof needed a small, closely knit team to help run his corrupt regime. This led, as we have seen, to the appointment of Norwin Bauer, a fellow corrupt Mason, to take charge of the licensing squad, with its superintendence of the potentially lucrative graft from hotels, clubs and betting. And then it became accepted knowledge that Hallahan, his fellow George Medal-winning friend Terry Lewis and their mate Tony Murphy, all Catholics, were placed in the consorting squad as his bagmen to collect corrupt payments. The three of them became notorious as the Rat Pack.

Bauer described how "The duties of the licensing branch consist of policing hotels and seeing to the administration of the Liquor Acts, the Gaming Acts and the Vagrants and other Offences Acts. The consorting squad's activities consist more of being on the lookout for criminals. They go through hotels and they go to each and every place where they are likely to find criminals or information concerning criminals. They also look to the activities of prostitutes and that kind of activity."

Murphy's notebook for April 24, 1959, provides an example of these duties: "General consorting duties – visited city hotels, night clubs, lounges, etc. re criminals and most particularly southern safe blowers Campbell, Ryan and Schofield. Later took up with Dets Lewis and Hallahan to patrol lounge of Grand Hotel at closing time."

Having ensured that the top end of the corruption system is secured and that there is no way that honest cops have a means of having their complaints dealt with, the next part of the system that needs making watertight is at the entry level. The system here was to give new detectives in areas such as licensing and consorting an honesty test. And if they were honest, they were sent packing.

Another aspect of the corrupt system involved verballing, also known as bricking. This meant that corrupt detectives did not need to work too hard at collecting evidence, they just invented it. Hallahan rivalled Agatha Christie as a writer of crime fiction.

Former detectives provide a quick master class in bricking. A young constable would be told how to present evidence, starting with a simple case of being drunk in charge of a car. Suspects should always be portrayed as walking, talking and looking in ways which leave no doubt that they were drunk. In interviews with criminal suspects a dummy police notebook should always be used. If there are two detectives working on the case you should work together on transferring the details to official notebooks at your leisure, adding the required incriminating or confessional quotes. You have the suspect denying everything for the first couple of pages. Mix up his denials so he contradicts himself. That goes down well with juries. Then you have him saying enough to convict him. Because notes are often taken on the run, perhaps when a car has been stopped or at the scene of a robbery, the detectives should stand in awkward positions when compiling these official records so that any barrister who asks to inspect their notebooks could not suggest that all the entries had been made at a desk. Leave a few pages blank between cases so that additional incriminatory facts can be added if necessary. Before the case is brought to court, fill any remaining spaces with an imagined search for a stolen car, taken from the daily list of stolen cars. The same basic rules apply to creating an incriminating or confessional statement. If he won't sign, you have him say: "Well, it's all true but I'm not signing anything." And, of course, even though you've never warned him about not needing to say anything, you make sure you've included a line to say he was warned. If you have a suspect who is prepared to sign a statement which is not as strong as you need, you slip a new page in as he's signing the bottom of each page. If you refer in your evidence to a character you've invented as part of the story and you're asked in court to describe him you always describe the lawyer who's asking the question so that when your colleague gives evidence, he can give the same description.

When it came to Judges' Rules the Australian and New Zealand judges said they had no power to introduce them – and it was up to the police to solve the problem. "A police officer's sense of fair play in a given case is likely to be of much greater importance than mere compliance with a set of written rules," they wrote in a report.

There would have been much laughter among Queensland detectives at the suggestion of fair play. The scale of the problem was eventually laid bare a decade later in 1976 when lawyers who had become exasperated by the extent of police verballing managed to persuade the Queensland Government into holding an inquiry into the way criminal law was being enforced.

The inquiry was announced in the Government Gazette of November 19. Its terms of reference were clear – this was not to be an inquiry which sought to find out who the guilty police were. The main question was: How ought police interrogations of suspect people be carried out so as to ensure that the manufacture of confessional evidence will not take place or, at least, so as to make it a very hazardous undertaking?

Supreme Court judge Geoffrey Lucas, barrister Des Sturgess and police chief superintendent Dynes Becker formed the panel of inquiry and admitted that they knew "injustice has undoubtedly been done in the past. But it is with the future we have had to concern ourselves."

Some police were so bold that they lied to the inquiry. "The evidence they gave only did damage to the causes it attempted to support," said the report. "One detective, for instance, with many years of service claimed a 100 per cent success rate in having people go voluntarily with him to the police station."

Dropping bricks, verballing, cutting corners and giving presents were all identified as police practices.

"The sad truth is that 'verballing', as it has become known, is a device that is not uncommonly employed by certain members of the police force…some verbal persistently and without conscience," said the report.

In Federal Parliament it was alleged that Detective Don Lane had arrested a man in Brisbane on a charge of using obscene language but it had later been discovered that the man was deaf and dumb. At the Lucas Inquiry Lane put on his best sheep's clothing to tell the committee: "There are, unfortunately, a handful of kill-hungry police who will resort to any length, including blatant perjury, in order to get convictions, either because they get their kicks from it or because they believe it will advance their careers."

Lucas responded: "This part seemed to us to be generally accepted by a number of witnesses. They are generally fairly well known not only by other police but by judges, magistrates and the legal profession and their evidence has little credibility in the courts."

In his report Lucas told of an address given by an assistant commissioner to police about "a couple of pubs in Brisbane where you can hear anything and find out anything regarding the CIB. A couple of drinks and anyone can hear all they want to know. 'Giving of presents' can be heard openly discussed in public."

Lucas said: "What this policeman, who was then the second highest ranking officer in the force, was finding objectionable was the discussion of it in hotels."

The Inquiry decided action was necessary to deal with the problem, urging the Government: "The recommendation which we regard as most important is that which we make as to the mechanical recording of interrogations by the police; the adoption of this, we hope, will eliminate or greatly reduce the protracted inquiries which take place in so many trials and which are designed to establish the authenticity or otherwise of confessional material adduced in evidence by the prosecution.

"Such a procedure should present no difficulties to an honest and competent officer, although it would be anathema to one who prefers the reprehensible but perhaps easy course of fabricating confessions."

All of this would have come as a great shock to most Queenslanders but the government of Joh Bjelke-Petersen (of whom we will learn much more later) conspired with the police commissioner to keep the report and its recommendations secret, enabling the corrupt system to continue.

What is clear is that the Inquiry found that many police officers fabricated evidence, some persistently and without conscience. Perhaps the most fascinating point made by the judge, the eminent barrister and the senior police officer is that these rogue cops were generally fairly well known not only by other police but by judges, magistrates and the legal profession.

The panel reported that such evidence was given little credibility. But over the years Hallahan and others invented evidence which was given sufficient credence to gain them the court verdicts they were seeking.

Politicians and police knew how the system was being abused but the vast majority of Queenslanders were still living in a fairyland: they believed God would look after the righteous; the sanctity of Sunday, which meant closed shops, closed pubs and no sport; the monarchy; the white Australia policy; hard work bringing guaranteed rewards; a woman's place being at home; law and order; the honesty of the police force; and the government knowing best.

In addition, the cowboys in the white hats beat the cowboys in the black hats every week in the cinema. Crime films always ended with the police triumphing, the criminals either being killed or locked up. Good always overcame evil. The population was protected from "unsuitable" books and comics by The Literature Board of Review which even banned comics such as Real Love, Romance Story, New Romances and Popular Romance. The board justified its approach by saying it "should act in the main as wise and prudent parents would act in relation to their children to ensure that the literature at large on the bookstalls of this state should be such as the normal parent would be willing to have available for his children."

It would be 1962 before it became legal to play sport on Sundays. Three years into the swinging sixties the Police Minister was still able to reply "No" to the question in parliament: "Has the Police Department received any complaints about the sale of that soul-destroying drug marijuana in this city?"

In all walks of life there are leaders, participants, critics and people who just don't care.

In the world of police corruption there were plenty of participants who accepted that this was the way the system worked and they received their small share of the profits for doing what was expected of them. A small minority did complain but to no effect, apart from being sent to the back of beyond. The majority refused to join in the corrupt system, were privately critical of the corruption but decided there was nothing they could do and it was best to join the three wise monkeys. And then there were those, such as Hallahan, Murphy and Jack Herbert, who saw an opportunity to extend and improve the system.

Hallahan was a leader who was constantly seeking to push the boundaries. Fellow bagman Jack Herbert remembered seeing Hallahan drinking in Lennons Hotel "in the days when detectives had to wear 10-gallon hats and they stuck out like dogs' balls". They had a 10-centimetre brim "and that was the order of the day. You had to wear them, which was rather foolish, we thought, but we weren't allowed to go out without them and Glen Hallahan was the first in Queensland to disregard this rule and I can recall seeing him in a hotel and he didn't have a hat on."

If Hallahan had chosen to be a businessman he would have probably become a ruthless, millionaire entrepreneur. If he had been honest he certainly had the drive and intelligence to have become commissioner.

Instead, he decided that if it was possible to make money from gambling, vice and alcohol sales, why not extend activities to organising crime?

As long as the police chief and the Premier were either on the take or prepared to tolerate the SP betting and after-hours trading, there was nowhere for the honest officer to go – apart from people like pugnacious lawyer and MP Col Bennett, who we'll meet in chapter 13.

But first, we need to examine who should tell the rest of this story.

Chapter 11 - Putting Hallahan in the Dock

The modern history of law and order has been created daily by the winners of the battle between police and criminals, which ensured that in Queensland the public believed that, like the Mounties, the Queensland police always got their man. More than that, there is another powerful force at work when recording the battle between police and criminals in the courts: the prosecution always gets to put its case first, which establishes in the mind of the public what actually happened because the police are supposed to always tell the truth. The criminal's defence will often be regarded as a fabrication. In the media the prosecution case will usually gain most of the coverage with the defendant coming second and a very-distant last.

When we want to learn what has happened in the past and what has conspired to produce the shape of the society in which we live, we study documents such as government reports, newspaper cuttings and diaries which contribute to our recorded history. But whose story is it? Usually, the establishment's.

Hallahan has been exposed as a fabricator of confessions, a liar and a perjurer. He was adept at creating a believable weft of absolute fiction and weaving this into a warp of incontrovertible facts to produce stories that convinced juries they were viewing the seamless truth. His memory was another asset. He had the ability to learn several pages of invented evidence verbatim as quickly and convincingly as an actor.

Bill Lee, a revered barrister in north Queensland, had seen Hallahan in action early in his career at Mt Isa Court and commented: "This man could be the most dangerous detective in Queensland." He had been referring to Hallahan's ability to reel off a dozen and a half pages from a notebook word for word without consulting the book. He meant dangerous to defence lawyers. It was turning out that Hallahan was just plain dangerous.

So it seems a reasonable decision to examine events involving Hallahan from the perspective of people who had a different version of what happened when they were dealing with The Ace Detective.

For the next few chapters we'll put their stories first in the manner of the prosecution and put Hallahan in the position of defending himself with his version.

Chapter 12 - Belle of the Ball to Brisbane Brothel

Our first witness appears to be, would you believe, a big-hearted, garrulous, happy-go-lucky prostitute from a ragged background. It really is very difficult not to portray Shirley Brifman as the archetypal prostitute with a heart of gold. Here's how she was described to me.

She had grown up as Shirley Emerson in abject poverty, in small towns in remote Far Northern Queensland, with 12 brothers and sisters and a pisspot of a father who drank as much as he earned. He was a railway fettler who was seldom in town but when he was, he was invariably drunk. Mum was a big woman who turned them out as best she could.

A neighbour was later to recall: "I always admired the mother. She was a big old tough bush woman." It was a typical depression family, living in a series of rented homes in small towns on the Atherton Tableland high above Cairns and a two-day rail journey from Brisbane. Shirley was born after the family moved to Atherton from Malanda, and before they moved on to Mareeba two years later. The kids lived in hand-me-downs and as Shirley was the youngest she had to make do with the most threadbare, washed-out and mended clothes. She was a proper little Cinderella, a very good looking girl with a beautiful complexion, attracting admiring glances at the local State school even before she started her teens. She had fair hair and a lovely olive/golden tan. A former classmate recalled that none of the kids ever had much money but despite their background, they were all pretty intelligent.

Shirley threw herself into everything. She was captain of the school basketball and tunnelball teams and enjoyed swimming, hockey and tennis. She joined the Girl Guides and loved dancing. As she progressed through her teens she was going out to dances up to six nights a week, sometimes travelling more than 100 kilometres a night. At the Atherton Debutantes Ball she was thrilled but scared half to death when the brigadier who received the debs crowned her queen of the debs and belle of the ball.

"My girlhood was one of the happiest imaginable - I wish I could have it all over again," she was to recall. "I wouldn't change it." But after thinking about that statement, she added: "Or only a few things." She wouldn't even change her career given a second chance.

No doubt she always dreamed of getting away from this abject poverty and the threadbare clothes. With her looks there was an easy way of making money. She went on the game in Cairns and with the travelling shows while still in her teens, working also as a barmaid at the seedy Court House Hotel, Cairns. The hotel was notorious as a pick-up spot for prostitutes and was protected by the police who took free meals, grog and cash from the Polish-born proprietor, tin mine owner and pimp Szama 'Sonny' Brifman so that he could run his business unhindered.

Perhaps it appeared to her that Sonny could offer her the security which she had never had as a child and, despite the fact that at 42 he was twice her age, she married him on June 13, 1957. They had even bought a dog from a bagman cop. How did she know he was on the take? "You get to know the cops who take money," she said.

The bright lights and bigger wallets of Brisbane beckoned and once again she was on the move.

The Brifmans moved into rented accommodation in Brisbane and Shirley commuted to work in one of half a dozen semi-official brothels that had been allowed for decades by the Queensland Government and police to operate in the capital.

She worked in the Killarney Private Hotel, tucked away from most people's view in narrow Fish Lane, just across the Victoria Bridge from the city centre in South Brisbane. It may have been only a short stroll across the always-swirling Brisbane River from the bustling city centre but it was a stroll from modern shops and offices to what was often, behind the back-street facades, just a clutter of rotting, rickety buildings and rusty corrugated iron sheds where people set up precarious small businesses such as panel beating.

"In Killarney you never used your right name," she recalled. "You used a house name. The only time you used your correct name was when you went to the clinic. I used the name Marg Chapple."

The brothels were policed by the Consorting Squad, which included Hallahan, Lewis and Murphy.

"Bauer was connected with the brothels," said Shirley. "The payments would have been going from the collect boys to Bauer to Bischof. The collect boys were Lewis, Murphy and Hallahan. They were his trusted boys.

"Once he went on holidays and they decided that the fees would go up and collect a bit more for themselves. They went around to do their collecting and up went the fees. They hit for half of what they were collecting again. I was in the house at the time of this blow up."

It was probably not that simple. Using information from several sources, including Charlie Corner, the straight copper who remained fearless in his opposition to Bischof, the events might have unfolded something like this. Billie Dean, madame at the Ernest Street brothel, was so incensed about the increased fees that she walked up George Street to the CIB headquarters, a one-storey building of stone blocks with twin peaked roofs opened in 1897 as a church institute (known colloquially and for good reason as "the confessional") and demanded to speak to the officer in charge. She complained that Hallahan and Lewis had told her that she was going to have to pay them more if she wanted to stay in business and avoid prosecution. She had told them she couldn't pay at the time and arranged to meet them at her home. While Bischof was enjoying his holiday on the Gold Coast 80 kilometres to the south, his deputy Jim Donovan, the honest Catholic who had been passed over for the top job, was the Acting Police Commissioner. He must have believed all his Christmases had come at once when he was informed of the complaint. A quick investigation by two straight detectives discovered the extent of the pair's demands and Jim Donovan approved a plan to trap Hallahan and Lewis red-handed at Billie Dean's home when they turned up to collect the money. Detectives hid in a back room and waited for the pair but they never turned up. Luckily for them Murphy had seen Dean at CIB headquarters and it hadn't taken the three of them long to realise they were in strife. They may have avoided the trap but the investigation revealed several allegations about the extortionate demands. Hallahan and Lewis were told that they were finished as detectives and would be required to report as uniformed constables at 6am next day at the Roma Street headquarters.

The history of Queensland would have been very different had this decision been carried through but someone had got word to Bischof about what was happening to his boys. He came rushing in to his office in the old Police Barracks, a landmark red-brick building looking down on the city from its western edge, in casual holiday gear and told his deputy to put an immediate halt to the investigation and rescind the directive that Hallahan and Lewis were to be transferred. But the fallout continued.

Shirley's take was that: "Bischof came back. He couldn't charge them. The only thing he could do was to close them (the brothels) and shut his mouth. I was at the clinic myself when they came down and told us they had one day to close up..."

But Bischof also had to deal with the Police Minister, Premier and Cabinet. Police Minister Morris dropped a bombshell in Cabinet on Tuesday October 13 1959 when, without the usual notice given to any normal Cabinet proposal, he told Ministers it was proposed to close all the tolerated brothels and place the supervision of prostitution under the direct control of police. Bischof's strategy was to announce that the brothels had failed to meet the guidelines for their toleration, with some acting as clearing houses for stolen goods, and for failing to act as informants on the criminals who used their services. Several Ministers had doubts about this but it seems no one asked how it was that every single brothel had suddenly gone bad like this. It was Allen Munro, the Minister for Justice and Attorney-General, who drew attention to a dilemma: "If we refuse this recommendation and it comes out that after getting a recommendation from the Commissioner of Police that brothels be closed, this Cabinet intervened to keep them open, we would have some awkward explaining to do." That just about decided the matter. The brothels were to be closed.

Intriguingly, Murphy, who had been in the consorting squad since May 10, 1958, was switched to other duties next day before returning to the squad at a later date.

Shirley Brifman told her story many years later. So it is interesting to find that her account tallies on several points with a small story which appeared in Queensland's Sunday Truth on October 18, 1959, headlined "Shake-up in CIB vice team":

"Two detectives were taken off the Consorting Squad of the Brisbane Criminal Investigation Branch and transferred to other duties this week. This was a prelude to further overhaul of the squad which is now planned, and other action to be taken by the Police Commissioner, Mr Bischof. Another result of the moves was that the Government decided to direct the Commissioner to clamp down on certain serious vice activities in the city. As a result, a number of houses regarded as undesirable resorts were closed down during the week, without notice. The action is believed to have begun while Mr Bischof was taking a week's leave at the South Coast. The Commissioner endorsed certain action taken by the Deputy Commissioner, Mr J P Donovan, and decided to refer the matter to the Government while the departmental investigation continued. The Government then directed the action against the resorts, and further action will depend on the result of Inspector T. Donovan's inquiries."

Former defence barrister Des Sturgess QC, who defended Hallahan and Murphy in cases brought against them in later years and freely admits his friendship with them, reports in his book "A Tangled Web" that he interviewed Jim Donovan when he was 88. Donovan told Des that he had made the recommendation to the government that the brothels should be closed and Bischof had then backed his decision – thus supporting that aspect of the Sunday Truth story of 1959. Donovan had refuted a suggestion that he had closed the brothels following his discovery of corrupt conduct by two police officers and as a payback so as to deny Bischof the graft he'd been receiving from the brothels. But that doesn't explain the contemporaneous newspaper report that two detectives had been taken off the Consorting Squad in connection with the closure of the brothels.

Many years later Sir Thomas Hiley said: "With the wisdom of hindsight in the light of what happened in the field of SP betting I am completely persuaded that Bischof was deliberately forging a police-controlled empire of brothels to add to what was happening with SP bookmaking. Today I confess that I made a grave error in dealing with Bischof. We should have pressed home our advantage and retired him there and then. My confrontation with him caused him to be more careful and to perhaps even widen the field of malpractice. I believe the worst thing that Bischof did was sow the seeds of corruption with a host of junior officers."

Like many of the other prostitutes who found themselves without a handy room to use for their services after the closure of the brothels, Shirley took to picking up men in selected city centre hotels, such as the Grand Central and National, and paying police for protection from prosecution.

Murphy was the first of the trio to get to know Shirley and to obtain her professional services on a very personal, non-fee-paying basis as part of the protection, she said. He had been sent to Sydney by Bischof on June 1, 1960, on what was called interchange duty, a method of meeting fellow detectives in the similarly-corrupt New South Wales police force, learning about their methods and getting to know who the top crims were down there – the idea being that if they came to do a job in Queensland they would be recognised. He returned to Brisbane at the beginning of July and soon afterwards bumped into Shirley.

"Murphy got me about three days after he came back from exchange," said Shirley. "Murphy took a liking to me and when he was broke for this and that I paid him and he was never on the basis of weekly pays.

"There was always money with him. Something for the kids. You will find that all of his kids have been tutored as well as their school. You may as well say I paid for all their tutoring. I paid for his appeals. Anything wrong with the car - I would pay for that. He collected money for reasons. There was always something - I have to paint the house, it's going to cost me so much. Of course, those days Murphy drank very, very heavily. It nearly killed him."

Shirley recalled that Murphy would sit her on his desk in his office and then with Murphy still on duty they would go across the road for a few beers at the Treasury Hotel on the opposite side of George Street where he could keep an eye on his office window. He had a permanent arrangement with the desk clerk so that if a superior was asking where he was, the clerk would wave a piece of blotting paper. He had become friendly with the Roberts brothers, particularly Rolly Roberts, who ran the Treasury Hotel until about April 1960.

"On duty, when he should have been somewhere else, he was with me," said Shirley.

Then Murphy made the mistake of introducing her to the very personable, smartly dressed, blue-eyed, handsome Hallahan who became one of her lovers.

"He regretted the day he introduced me to Glen," recalled Shirley.

"Glen came into the picture and Terry was in the picture too. Murphy was higher than the others and he always had a driver. Terry – I hold a very high respect for him. As far as the money goes, I didn't pay Terry anything.

"Murphy wanted to one day be the police commissioner...They used to sit there trying to work it out. They had it so well worked out. They all wanted to be commissioners. They had the power. They had Bischof, Bauer... Bauer would always stick with me. I did know all of them. I even knew their wives."

Meanwhile, Detective Don Lane, who had served with Hallahan in Cloncurry, was reunited with him in 1962 when he was posted to the Consorting Squad. In turn, he became a close friend of Lewis and Murphy. Jack Herbert, another bagman, later gave evidence that Lane was involved in corruption by this time. Don, the son of a country store owner, had left school at 14 to become an apprentice fitter and turner but two years later, on February 11, 1952, had joined the police as a cadet. On being sent to Cloncurry as a constable in 1956 he became friendly with Hallahan. Or, as Lane put it: "I got to know him as well as anyone could, largely because of the fact that he was a notorious loner."

One of the hotels used by the prostitutes who had been turfed out of the tolerated houses in 1959 was the National Hotel, bought by Rolly Roberts, of the Treasury Hotel, and his brothers Max and John a year earlier. The National was a large rambling old corner pub on four floors at the wrong end of Queen St, which started as a thriving shopping centre and then fizzled out into a nondescript mixture of businesses. Over a four-year period the brothers refurbished the hotel from its run-down, old fashioned past into a thriving business, with more bars and lounges, a cabaret lounge seating 250 people, snack bar, a large function room for dinners and dances, a steak house restaurant on the fourth floor, several other function rooms and 20 bedrooms. The Roberts brothers estimated that by 1963 up to 1,600 people would be in the hotel on a busy night, being served by about 150 staff. Rolly Roberts left the Treasury in 1960 and was often at the National with brother Max. Bischof, Hallahan, Murphy and other detectives followed him down to the National.

In a city centre which was still largely a museum piece containing buildings erected in three booms from the 1880s, the early 1900s and the late 1920s, it was refreshingly modern.

The Roberts brothers had turned the National into one of Brisbane's brightest hotels and function centres. But there were prostitutes available to those in the know. Bischof, Hallahan and other crooked police were among the regulars flouting the law by drinking after hours. And takeaway booze was available at the back door after hours, especially on a Sunday when people holding backyard barbecues found they hadn't got sufficient grog and Brisbane pubs were closed.

Chapter 13 - Colin Bennett MP – Barrister and Battler

It's July 6, 1962, and time to introduce our second witness, a relatively small, thin, bespectacled, left-wing Roman Catholic barrister who was also a Labor Member of Parliament. Don't underestimate him. He's as tough as a fence post, with a big heart and a gritty determination to fight for the underdog and battle the dragons of the corrupt police force.

He is the first person we have met who is in an ideal position to damage Hallahan or even bring him down.

At 43, Colin Bennett was happily-married but here he was, sitting in his chambers, waiting for the arrival of a prostitute. Solicitor Col Murphy had engaged him on a rather unusual case. A detective called Merton Hopgood was allegedly harassing prostitute Shirley Brifman and her colleague Lily Ryan. What could he expect, he wondered.

Both women were well dressed. Shirley walked in with calm assurance, a 26-year-old attractive, intelligent woman with a pleasant personality. Four years after arriving in Brisbane, she was an experienced Brisbane hooker and a stunning looker as well as being mum to three daughters. "You'd never pick her for a prostitute," Bennett thought to himself.

The immaculately suited Bennett sitting opposite her had grown up in the canefields of the Lower Burdekin area of rural Queensland, the son of a man who once contested a State election for the conservative Country Party. The lawyer looked suitably bookish as he examined his clients through his specs but he had been an A grade rugby union player, a welterweight boxer and had also shone at athletics. He had wanted to be a lawyer for as long as he could remember. In the Second World War he had joined the RAAF, and become involved in highly technical radar work. Despite having become a successful barrister, he once boasted in Parliament: "I have no money invested in anything, nor have I ever invested in any undertaking in Queensland. My only investment is a wife and large family. I put all my money into their education and welfare. That is the only investment I possess and I am very proud of it." Being a good Catholic, he had invested heavily, having fathered eight children. With his background, he could not only dish out a tongue lashing but was also handy with his fists. When a neighbour indecently exposed himself to Bennett's wife and children Bennett didn't bother with eloquent words, criminal charges or injunctions. He just flattened the flasher.

He was involved in a marathon war against corruption, a war which had been sparked by frequent complaints at an after-hours 'surgery' he ran. There was no legal aid in those days and Bennett argued loud and long for its introduction. Unlike some, he was not content merely to pontificate. He opened up his chambers to those who could not afford to pay a lawyer's fees. The battlers queued for help with their problems between 4.30 and 6.00 each night. Frequently, he was there until 7.00, dispensing free advice. He said that when it came to complaints about corrupt police during these sessions, three names stood out - Detectives Tony Murphy, Glen Hallahan and Terry Lewis.

Bennett was well qualified to know what was going on around the traps. He had devoted 12 years of his life to being a Brisbane City Alderman, nine of them as Labor leader and three as vice-mayor. Two years before his meeting with Shirley he had decided to stand for Parliament and had been successful in the seat of South Brisbane, a largely working- class area. His target was to become attorney-general in a Labor government. Right from the start he had spoken out against the way the police force was being run by the Government and Commissioner Bischof. He had found that verballing was the norm rather than the exception with many detectives.

The first meeting between Bennett and Shirley did not last long. And the case would eventually fizzle out. But their meeting would have major repercussions. Shirley told Bennett how she was allowed to use the National Hotel to ply her trade in return for payments to the corrupt detectives and of her relationship with Hallahan and Murphy.

It was at the National in July 1963 that Hallahan met the New South Wales force's most notorious detective, Ray "The Gunner" Kelly. Nearly six feet tall and physically imposing, he was bespectacled and wore his dark hair plastered to his skull and parted in the middle like an evangelising preacher. He had shot dead two criminals and injured others. The Sydney media portrayed him as a one-man crime-fighting force. To those in the know he was the worst kind of pimp, taking a cut from all the miserable, sordid backstreet abortions, protecting murdering thugs who were his informants, sanctioning killings and lying to courts.

Kelly arrived in Brisbane in the hunt for Ray 'Ducky' O'Connor who New South Wales police were trying to frame for the machine-gun slaying of Robert 'Pretty Boy' Walker earlier that month. Shirley joined in the socialising at the National Hotel as Kelly and Hallahan told stories and sized up one another. She believed one of Hallahan's long-time informants set up O'Connor so that he could be arrested and extradited to New South Wales. Shirley said that Kelly had gone back to Sydney and told his protégé, Sergeant Fred Krahe, about Hallahan. Krahe then made frequent visits to Brisbane.

"Krahe could never pull that string in Queensland until I pulled it for him and then I put them together," said Shirley. "Krahe then grabbed Glen. He did everything with Glen."

Of Hallahan, she said: "Once he mixed with Krahe, he wanted big money. He had been on small money before."

It was at this time that Col Bennett, barrister, MP and corruption fighter, decided to shine a light on Hallahan, Bischof and the Sunday Truth.

The old church "confessional" had been demolished to make way for a pleasant park. The force now had a magnificent new five-storey headquarters overlooking the Brisbane River just to the west of the city centre where Bischof had a sumptuous office on the third floor. It may have been the most modern police HQ in Australia but nothing had changed when it came to corruption.

While making a speech in the Queensland Parliament Bennett told how the Full Court of Queensland had found "that the top glamour detective of Queensland was guilty of perpetrating a fraud on one of the courts". He said: "That is perhaps one of the most serious offences that anybody in Queensland could commit, and it is even more serious when it is committed by an allegedly trusted police officer. But, lo and behold, the Commissioner of Police does not accept the unanimous decision of the Full Court and will have the decision investigated departmentally. What a shocking impertinence from any public servant or any other person in the community. There have been many occasions when this Commissioner has suspended policemen and dismissed them. On this occasion…he does not even suspend the police officer concerned. What is more this particular officer glamourises himself by dragging some poor individual, draped only in a little towel, not arrested – he still has not been charged – yet this officer assaults him by dragging him from private premises. No action has been taken and I know none will be taken. He drags him out from private premises and either arranges or had pre-arranged for a weekend newspaper to make an incursion into this individual's privacy and dignity by having a photograph taken."

Shirley discovered she was pregnant and moved to Sydney where she could more easily obtain a back-street abortion. Having moved to Old South Head Road, which cuts through Sydney's affluent eastern suburbs to the coast, she started worrying about bleeding to death as a result of an abortion and decided that, after all, she would have the child. Her son was born on October 3, 1963. But Hallahan and Murphy were constantly in touch with her by phone and letter, including at least two letters from Murphy.

Meanwhile, the late night drinking at the National continued when Murphy organised a farewell bash for Lewis on October 2, 1963, starting at 10pm – the legal closing time. Bischof had created a special post for Lewis where he could be kept out of harm's way and create a career path towards becoming commissioner. He was to head the juvenile aid bureau – the larrikin squad, as Bahnemann called it.

Later that month Colin Bennett created another stir in Parliament.

Parliament House, a beautiful French Renaissance building completed in 1889, lies next to the extensive Botanic Gardens which push into a sharp bend of the broad Brisbane River. No expense had been spared on the decor of Parliament House, with lots of red cedar panelling, chandeliers, ornate plasterwork and sumptuous furnishings. It was just a five minute walk from where Bennett often appeared in the Supreme Court, halfway down George St.

On October 29, 1963, at 4.37pm Bennett rose from his well-padded green leather chair in the parliamentary chamber. The ornate public gallery running round all four walls was virtually empty. Few of the 78 MPs were there to listen as Bennett said: "I propose to concentrate my attention on the police department and the police force of Queensland." A few hundred words into a rather mundane dissertation he could not resist using a tidbit of information about the National that had come from Shirley. The few Government members in the chamber failed to react to the barbed sentence that he suddenly thrust stiletto-like deep into the reputation of the Commissioner and his friends: "I do not wish to dally too long on this subject, but I should say that the Commissioner and his colleagues who frequent the National Hotel, encouraging and condoning the callgirl service that operates there, would be better occupied in preventing such activities rather than tolerating them."

Sunday Truth commented on its front page: "The campaign Mr Colin Bennett MLA is waging against the police commissioner Mr Bischof is now completely out of control and in the public interest the State Government can move only one way. It must order an immediate Royal Commission."

But Sunday Truth hadn't changed sides. The reason it gave for needing an inquiry was: "The facts are that the honour and integrity of the Queensland police commissioner have been attacked. His name has got to be cleared."

Chapter 14 - David Confronts Goliath

Bennett might not have been naming names but a young man named David Young, an active ALP member, went to his local member and said he was prepared to name those names. He had been a night porter at the National Hotel.

On November 4 1963 he wrote a letter to ALP leader Duggan saying he had served Mr Bischof both liquor and food during and after trading hours for which no payment was received and that he had regularly served detectives, including Tony Murphy, on the same basis.

Would Young be the man to bring down Hallahan and his colleagues?

The 31-year-old salesman spoke with a distinct Yorkshire accent, having been born in Rotherham and grown up there in his parents' hotels until they decided on a complete change of life and bought a fruit farm at Woombye in Queensland in 1949. David spent the next five years working on the farm. When his father died he came to Brisbane and got a job as a fruit inspector. Then he went back to what he had learned in England and became a waiter in various hotels.

He had worked at the Grand Central Hotel and got to know the prostitutes who worked in the pub's lounge, widely known as the Passion Pit. Then the National Hotel opened a dining room and he moved there just before Christmas 1958.

But Bischof and his bagmen were hardly going to sit back and let this sort of attack undermine their empire. Bischof and Bauer put Tony Murphy in charge of the defence and counter-attack, with some help from Hallahan, Lewis and Don Lane. Despite being one of the officers accused of illegal behaviour, Murphy was given the task of investigating Young. Within four days of Young putting pen to paper and a day after Young had been interviewed about his statement by the Solicitor-General, they were working with Shirley in Sydney to smear him. A report in the evening Telegraph of November 8 said: "A top secret police investigation is going on today about Mr Young's allegations. High-ranking police personally are directing inquiries. The Chief Inspector of Police, Mr N. W. Bauer is said to be one of the top investigators. A Sydney message today said a top Sydney police investigator was making inquiries to try to provide information from someone who claims to have known Mr Young."

That day another former night porter decided to go public. John Geza Komlosy, a storeman-in-charge, had been born in Germany in 1927 of Hungarian parents and had lived in a prisoner of war camp in Russia from the latter part of the war until 1947. He had married in 1948 while working as a steward in a British Army camp in West Germany. Then, in his search for a decent way of life, he arrived in Australia with his wife and children in 1951 and had been taken to a migrant camp. He had been the full-time night porter of the National Hotel in 1959 and 1960 every night of the week apart from Sunday from 6pm to 7.30am. When he tried to contact the Premier to volunteer his information he felt fobbed off. So he took his story to Sunday Truth.

He said: "I met Mr Bischof personally and served him. On all occasions it was past midnight. Other detectives and high-ranking officers were in and out of the hotel day and night. On at least one occasion I had to let Mr Bischof out of the hotel in the early hours of the morning. He walked through the foyer and saw a number of people drinking illegally. Some of these people were prostitutes. When I started at the National Hotel there was a call-girl service in operation there. The man I took over from advised me of this situation and gave me several phone numbers. I spoke to Mr Max Roberts about this service several times. Many of the girls arrived with Mr Max Roberts and his friends. On a number of occasions Mr Max Roberts introduced girls to me. One girl was a red-haired waitress at the Gresham Hotel called Wilma, who Mr Roberts introduced me to in his private room and said that she could be reached at a certain number if any rich farmers asked for girls. She was used on a number of occasions to entertain country visitors staying at the hotel. I had about a dozen other phone numbers of girls who could be called if required. I understood that most of these girls were paid between 40 and 50 pounds a night for their services. Mr Roberts knew this service was operating, condoned and encouraged it. If you collected all the prostitutes in Brisbane most could not deny that they knew almost every room in the old National Hotel inside out. On many occasions detectives drinking at the hotel spoke on first name terms with prostitutes who were there entertaining clients."

He said Max Roberts introduced him to a priest attached to St Stephen's Cathedral named Father Grennon. Mr Roberts said he was a regular customer who had a permanent account with the hotel. This priest was a regular visitor to the National Hotel. Sometimes he would arrive at 10.30pm and sometimes 2am but always he would leave about 5am. One night he became involved in a fracas and took off his jacket to fight two men. Komlosy stopped this happening. "I rang up New Farm – the Archbishop's residence – and two senior priests arrived at the hotel. One of them was the Monsignor at present in charge of St Stephen's Cathedral. These two priests took Father Grennon away. This would be early in the morning – about 4am. I received the instruction never again to call the Archbishop's residence but to call Mr Roberts if there was any trouble."

Truth published the story on November 10 headlined: "Hotel scandal. New witness fobbed off; ready to tell." A second night porter, John Komlosy, had made a 'sensational statement involving prominent Queensland police officers'.

The paper's leading article was revealing. "Sunday Truth today offers its deepest sympathy to the Queensland Police Commissioner, Mr Bischof. He has been badly let down by the Queensland Government...the very people who put him into his important job and the very people who should be right behind him. For some odd reason, Mr Nicklin and a majority of his Cabinet will not countenance a Royal Commission or any sort of inquiry into the damning charge barrister-MLA Colin Bennett made in Parliament recently against the police commissioner. They want Mr Bennett to give them facts before they will move. It is difficult to imagine an attitude so unworldly and so lacking in Parliamentary sense. By deciding on a Royal Commission, with terms of reference limited to the existence of a call girl service and whether Mr Bischof had knowledge of it, they could put Mr Bennett on a spot."

Again, Sunday Truth had come up with a novel reason for holding a Royal Commission – nothing to do with discovering the truth of allegations now made by three people but simply to embarrass Col Bennett.

However, the pressure paid off. At 11.20 am on November 12 Frank Nicklin stood up in Parliament and announced a Royal Commission - with severely restricted terms of reference. In appointing a commissioner the Government avoided choosing a judge appointed by the previous government or one who had examined Hallahan's activities. It selected a judge it had appointed only two years earlier, Justice Harry Gibbs, aged 46. The judge had been accused by independent MP Tom Aikens in the House three months earlier of having been appointed as a judge for political services rendered to the governing Liberal Party. Col Bennett, although a Labor Member, had stood up for the judge, saying he had outstanding ability and had not dabbled in politics. But Aikens had insisted: "What nonsense. He was an active worker for the Liberal Party. He was campaign director for a Liberal Party candidate."

The terms of reference would restrict the inquiry to the policing of the National Hotel. Other corruption and problems of the police force which Bennett had attacked were untouchable. And because Bennett's information about the corruption had come through his relationship with a client it was of a confidential and privileged nature and could not be taken any further by Bennett.

Murphy and his team, including Hallahan, were central to the Inquiry, investigating Young and Komlosy, collating all the police evidence and liaising with the Inquiry staff. All requests from the Inquiry in relation to the police were channelled through him. It was rather like allowing the defendant to run the prosecution case. Another judge might have refused to accept this arrangement and might have insisted on having independent investigators but Gibbs was happy to allow Murphy to run things. As Bennett said later in Parliament, the evidence was 'gerrymandered by

Detective Sergeant Tony Murphy before witnesses even entered the witness box'.

Young received his first shock at 9.50pm on Tuesday November 19. The phone rang at his home in leafy Rosalie where he lived with his wife and two young children. He picked it up and was told: "I will not give you my name. You do not know me or know who I am but I am a friend of yours. I think that there are some facts that you should be acquainted with. I think that you should know that the police have investigated you and have certain affidavits signed by a girl in Sydney, witnessed by another girl by the name of Val. This affidavit relates to an unsuccessful abortion attempt by you on the girl who signed the affidavit at her flat in New Farm, which was witnessed by another girl who is still living in Brisbane. The name of the flats was Ugola. She has described the method and instruments used and says she paid you 10 pounds. She has medical evidence to show in that she gave your name to a Brisbane doctor. This is a pretty sticky charge and I can assure you that I obtained the facts from a very reliable source. I just want to let you know this is not all they have."

The allegation was completely untrue but it suggested the police were prepared to manufacture evidence to discredit him and even have him imprisoned if he went ahead with his testimony.

The threats and the list of allegations that would be lined up against him went on and on. Young listened, made notes and reported the call to his solicitor.

Shirley said that once the commission had been announced she was told by Hallahan and Murphy to stay in Sydney.

After a preliminary sitting on November 20, and with everyone still shocked by the assassination of President Kennedy, the inquiry got under way in earnest on Monday, December 2, in the Supreme Court, a two-storey Italianate building set in an acre of grounds high above the Brisbane River between the parallel streets of North Quay and George Streets, with Ann Street running alongside. The T-shaped building had its main façade along North Quay, so that approaching the central business district from across the river, visitors looked up to this shining palace of justice.

When it was built in 1879 the building's arches, arcades, colonnades, columns and balconies combined to give it a grandeur second only to Parliament House at the other end of George Street. Now it was considered too small and dingy. There were offices on the ground floor with four courts on the first floor, each of them only about 12 square metres, each with a public gallery above it on one side. About 150 people, including a woman with her knitting, climbed a spiral staircase of 58 steps from the ground floor to sit on steps and watch proceedings through a metal balustrade.

The headlines that day reported Prime Minister Menzies had been swept back into power. In Queensland the federal government had gained three opposition seats, with one going to Liberal candidate Dr Wyllie Gibbs, brother of the Inquiry Commissioner. On a typically hot and humid Queensland summer day, three rows of tables were needed to accommodate 11 of Queensland's highest-paid barristers and their instructing solicitors and support staff.

Speeches droned inside the court and the unmistakable whine, grind and rattle of trams occasionally filtered into the room. Counsel assisting the inquiry, Lindsay Byth, spent hours outlining what various witnesses would say.

Three Roberts brothers were associated with the running of the hotel, Max, William – who was known as Rolly – and John. Bischof had first met the Roberts's parents in the 1930s. Max Roberts would say he and Bischof were firm friends and Rolly Roberts and Bischof were 'very, very close acquaintances'. Bischof had attended Max's wedding reception in 1961 and four times had used John Roberts's seaside home for holidays when he was not expected to pay rent. Rolly Roberts would say he knew two-thirds of the CIB and was friendly with Murphy.

Byth told how David Young had received an anonymous, threatening phone call, warning him not to give evidence and saying if he did that allegations would be made that, among other things, he had aided an abortion.

On Tuesday December 3 David Young, slightly below average height, with sandy hair, neatly dressed in a suit and tie, stepped into the box. He was Daniel to the massed ranks of legal lions. Behind them, in plain view and often in deep conversation were Bischof and his lieutenant, Murphy.

Young was articulate but very softly spoken and even barristers strained to hear what he had to say in his unfamiliar Yorkshire accent. "I first saw Mr Bischof as Police Commissioner when I was at the National Hotel in 1958 to 1959. He was a frequent visitor. On several occasions I saw him behind what was known as the private bar. There is an area there where Mr Max Roberts and his friends used to drink. He was talking to Mr Rolly Roberts or Mr Max Roberts on any of these occasions. On the first occasion he had been drinking after trading hours."

When he acted as night porter on Sundays and operated the switchboard: "I received calls which were believed to be from police headquarters stating that a raid was about to proceed against the National Hotel. This information would come from Mr Max Roberts after he had taken the phone call that I would put through to him.

"I served Tony Murphy with jugs of beer from the servery of the Music Box. On practically every occasion I worked at the Music Box Mr

Murphy was up there. It was only open on Fridays and Saturdays. He usually had three or four other detectives with him."

Young, who was repeatedly asked to speak up, said he had no definite proof of any call girl service operating at the National. But: "I have booked men and prostitutes into rooms straight from the lounge of the National Hotel. People would just get up out of their chairs and come over and book a room, pay 3 pounds or whatever it was, depending on the size of the room, and then they would go upstairs. Most of the clients left before morning. This applied particularly to the men. As far as I was concerned it was not my business after that. I don't think I booked anybody into the National who had any luggage."

Sitting at the back of the court from day one had been two very stylish women, decked out in extravagant hats, white gloves, smart suits - the lot. Come Wednesday they were identified from the box by David Young as Shirley's mates Lily, with black hair and an olive complexion, and Val, with brown hair and angular features. Both were about 5' 2", both plumpish and both aged between 35 and 40. It was 'Marg' (Shirley's working identity) and Lil who had told him how they were protected at the National and gave their services to senior police. Shirley had told him she had been informed by detectives that she would be able to operate up at the National Hotel now that the Grand Central was closing down. And she had told him that Lil "gave favours of sexual kinds" to members of the police force.

Byth: "Would you know Lil if you saw her?"

Young: "Yes. She was here this morning. She's still here."

"Is 'Lil' the witness Lillian May Ryan?"

"That's right, yes."

"The other girl, Val, to whom you have referred – has she been present?"

"She's also present here. She's sitting on the back row, second from the right."

"That would be the witness Valerie Patricia Weidinger?"

"Yes."

Val had lived at the National Hotel for a period as a guest of the hotel, with her luggage and clothes in her bedroom.

Young gave the names of prostitutes he had seen operating at the National Hotel, including one who had a pimp there. But Don Lane and his colleagues said they were totally unable to find them and therefore they could not be called as witnesses. Then Young picked out six prostitutes from police files as being women who frequented the hotel. Once again Don Lane and his colleagues were unable to find them.

Next day Young said that he could identify two rooms at the National where he had served prostitutes and men. Justice Gibbs, bespectacled, round-faced and wearing a light grey suit, said Young would have to go and identify them. "I am not suggesting for a moment that you are forced to go during the luncheon adjournment. You may not get the time."

"I may not get out alive," replied Young.

As far as Young was concerned, the facts were self-evident.

But the combined forces of the crooked police and the assembled barristers had a vested interest in presenting a different picture and this now resulted in the unmerciful savaging of the naïve whistleblower for hour after hour by most of the barristers.

Then Val and Lil took the stand and demurely said they were certainly not prostitutes, had never seen any prostitutes at the National and had no information whatsoever that could possibly be of any help to the Inquiry.

After one barrister had turned them away as prospective clients, they had a counsel named Eddie Broad to look after them. Irene Dale, another prostitute, described herself as a caterer's assistant and told the same story as Lil and Val. But when Ambrose, the most junior barrister at the bar table, started asking her questions regarding her association with prostitutes he was stopped by the Commissioner.

Chapter 15 - John Komlosy Speaks Up

and is Shot Down

On the second Monday, the 9th, John Komlosy went, unprotected by legal representation, into the fray.

A solidly built man approaching middle age, with a square face and hair thinning at the temples, he nodded vigorously to emphasise his remarks. It didn't take him long to incriminate Hallahan and start nodding determinedly.

He was cross-examined by Byth, counsel assisting the commission, who asked: "When you first started at the National did you see any men there that you knew as detectives?"

"Yes, I just know Detective Murphy and Mr Hallahan," Komlosy replied. "These two gentlemen just came in, brushed past me, through the door as if they were home and they just said: 'It's all right' and just to ask Mr Roberts. I asked Mr Roberts and I was instructed that these gentlemen were friends of his and they were always to be served at the hotel."

"Would you tell us what time of the day or night that happened?"

"Mostly after midnight."

"While you were night porter at the National did any girls that you believed or knew to be prostitutes have any bedrooms at the National which they used?"

"Well, some of the prostitutes practically lived there. I could name some: for instance, Irene, Valerie, Christine, Mary and Lala. Her other name, I think, is Mrs Anderson. Sometimes they would ring me up on the telephone from the La Boheme and other night clubs – the El Morocco – and ordered their rooms with drink and food. We had a small night porters' book at the hotel where the instructions were in, and prices for rooms and prices for liquor, what we were supposed to charge and also in the back of this book we kept phone numbers for all those girls: the Christian names and where they could be reached, and what time. Certain ladies would not have to be called except certain times."

"Which police officers did you see talking to which girls?"

"I see Detective Murphy and Detective Hallahan there definitely, and about three others," he nodded vigorously.

Yes, he said, there had been a call girl service operating at the hotel. On a number of occasions owner Max Roberts had introduced girls to him. A red-haired waitress called Wilma had been in Max's private room and Max had said she could be reached on a certain phone number if any rich farmers asked for girls. Wilma had indeed been used on more than one occasion to entertain country visitors staying at the National. Max himself would ring prostitutes for his own enjoyment and that of his mates.

Wilma was never called to give evidence.

Importantly, Komlosy corroborated Young's evidence that two of the prostitutes who had permanent rooms at the hotel were Irene Dale, also known as Halliday, and Val Weidinger.

Komlosy said he had received threatening letters and phone calls since announcing he was prepared to give evidence and had been threatened with the sack. But, he said: "I lost my country and everything dear to me. There were so very few people who spoke up for the truth. I don't think that should happen in this country."

The refugee who had come to Australia looking for a fair go and had stood up for this principle was then torn apart by the pack of lawyers for the rest of the week.

When Ambrose objected to a line of questioning by the intimidating Douglas for the police union, the judge overruled him, saying it was important to allow Komlosy's credit to be tested. When the cross examination became intensely personal as barristers sought to destroy his credibility, Komlosy said he would refuse to answer questions about his background. The judge said he could jail him for contempt of court if he persisted in his refusal.

Douglas, for the police union, questioned Komlosy about a time when he had gone to the airport to see Prime Minister Menzies arrive. As far as Komlosy was concerned it had been a happy occasion when he had spotted his friend Murphy from the National Hotel and introduced his 10-year-old son to "a real copper".

Under Murphy's instructions, Douglas accused Komlosy of being there to harm or interfere with the Prime Minister who, suggested Douglas, Komlosy regarded as the biggest political gangster in Australia. The accusations hit the bemused Komlosy like a flurry of punches below the belt.

The Commissioner asked Douglas what he was getting at. Komlosy was asked to leave while Douglas explained: "We are going to seek to establish a pattern of lying behaviour by this witness of which many instances will be put to you. This is merely part of the instructions, Your Honour."

Commissioner: "Has anyone else any submissions on this point?"

Campbell, acting for Bischof: "There are certain claims he makes other than these. He is making claims in a wild and exaggerated manner as my learned friend Mr Douglas has just read out. I submit that cross-examination directed to this witness to show that on other occasions he made wild claims, seeking publicity, is relevant as to whether or not the claims he made on this occasion are also in the category."

Draney, a stocky and pugnacious barrister appearing for members of the police officers' union: "I will be pursuing similar lines to those stated by my learned friend Mr Douglas, not only in relation to an isolated occasion but over a period of years when these things have been going on."

McGill, for the National Hotel: "This man has come along and made a lot of allegations and if it can be established that he has made unbalanced and irrational statements on other occasions, I submit that all goes to the matter of weighing him up."

Ambrose, for Young: "I submit in this case again we are running the risk of having this turned into an inquiry, not into the National Hotel and the police in connection with it, but into Mr Komlosy. We started in 1951 and have spent most of the day tracing him up to the present time. Apparently, very little time has been spent so far in dealing with the allegations he makes in connection with the National Hotel."

Komlosy returned to the witness box and said determinedly: "Excuse me, I would like to ask Your Honour. It was a terrific blow to my character and my personal references what has been said here. I would like to state this very small fact, that in 1954 when Her Majesty was here in Australia, I was in charge of the complete railway station running lines and everything for the safety of her train. I was very proud to be at the station at the time. I received a letter from her secretary thanking me. I am very loyal and I have no political connection whatsoever."

Douglas: "I put it to you that you said to Murphy: 'He is the man that gets the political police to have me fired from every job I get in Australia'?"

"That's a lie," retorted Komlosy.

Next came Len Draney for the police officers' union. With the air of a hungry tiger approaching a tethered goat, he put it to Komlosy that he was carrying on a dirty business procuring girls for men. Komlosy lost his temper and fought back: "You are representing dirt." He later apologised. Towards the end, the questioning had reached such obscure, minute historical points that Komlosy was asked to bring in to the commission his junior public exam certificates in Latin, maths and English which he had gained at night school.

"I am objecting most sincerely," he said. "Not one gentleman has asked me anything about the National."

Later in the inquiry he let counsel assisting, Byth, know that he had another name to put forward as having drunk illegally at the National after closing time.

He was recalled and testified: "I would like to ask your honour at this stage the name of the gentleman assisting Mr Douglas, and that his name be put on the list amongst the other names of gentlemen drinking after hours in Mr Roberts' place."

There was uproar, with Justice Gibbs saying: "I must, of course, order that that piece of evidence be not published."

Douglas, for the police union: "Are you suggesting this gentleman here (indicating Mr Macrossan)?"

"Yes, a friend of Mr Roberts."

"When was he there?"

"With the other gentlemen – I already put their names down, from the Yacht Club."

"It has taken you till this time to see him?"

"He does not wear his glasses," said Komlosy in his stilted English.

"Was he wearing glasses when he went to the National?"

"No. He was wearing glasses this morning but he does not wear it now."

"When was he there?"

"He was there at nights with the other gentlemen whose names I already has given."

"What time of the year?"

"He could not possibly deny it. Even Mr Roberts was with him there a few minutes ago when I said this to him a few minutes ago."

Douglas: "I would like to say that we do not want the press to come out and say…"

Commissioner Gibbs: "I have already ordered that. To make it clear, it has been my steady practice throughout this inquiry to order that the names of any person alleged to have been drinking after hours at the hotel be not published until further orders. So that there shall be no mistake about it, I am ordering that none of the evidence or discussion in relation to the gentleman in the courtroom who is alleged to have been drinking after hours be published. It should be made perfectly clear to the press that that direction covers everything that has been said in relation to that topic, so that any remarks on the subject would contravene my order."

The characters of Young and Komlosy could be sacrificed to the results of false allegations but a barrister's reputation was sacrosanct.

John Murtagh Macrossan was called. "I have heard the evidence which the last witness has just given. It is completely false. I have never been to the National Hotel at night time that I can recall."

The Commissioner put it to Macrossan: "He said in evidence that you were a friend of Mr Roberts?"

"It is true that I do know Mr Max Roberts," he conceded. "I see him very rarely. I am not a member of the yacht club."

Commissioner Gibbs: "It puzzles me in this way – that no sane witness would dishonestly identify a member of the bar seated at the bar table in front of him, as one of the persons implicated in a matter of this kind, because it would be obvious to the witness in all the circumstances of the case that he would not be doing his own credit any good by doing that."

Mr McGill, for the National: "My answer is that he does not fit into that description. He is not a sane witness."

So, in the eyes of Commissioner Gibbs and the assembled barristers, Komlosy lost any credibility he might have retained. Fancy suggesting a barrister could possibly enjoy a beer after closing time! It was obviously laughable. It is fascinating that Gibbs accepted the fact that "respectable" people such as a priest, a radio announcer and a television personality drank illegally after hours at the National Hotel but when it came to Komlosy identifying barrister Macrossan as being a fellow after-hours drinker, Gibbs said: "Obviously Komlosy was completely mistaken in naming Mr Macrossan…"

It was Monday the 16th before Komlosy was allowed to step down after having done what he believed was his duty.

Then Murphy took the stand. It was already clear that Murphy had a conflict of interest in that he was accused in the evidence of behaving illegally at the hotel and was also in charge of police investigations on behalf of the inquiry. Now it became clear there was a further conflict of interest. Hallahan was also accused of behaving illegally at the hotel. Murphy told Ambrose: "I consider Mr Hallahan is one of my close friends."

And, even worse as a conflict of interest, Murphy told the Inquiry he became acquainted with Rolly Roberts when he took over the licence of the old Treasury Hotel which was directly opposite where the old CI Branch building used to be.

"After work, of the evening, it was a habit of mine and quite a number of other detectives to slip over there for a few beers on the way home," said Murphy shamelessly. "That is how I came to really know Mr Rolly Roberts."

Murphy then described his work: "In the consorting squad you are required to pay frequent attention to hotels, wine saloons which existed in those days, billiard saloons and other such places. Your duties, fundamentally, are based upon the detection and prevention of crime, the making of reliable contacts to assist you in that regard, the cultivation of informants and agents and also the establishing of the movements and consorting of criminals and prostitutes generally." In other words, befriending criminals in pubs.

Next, Byth asked Murphy about the leading prostitutes of the day. The Catch-22 here was that the police were accused of condoning prostitutes working at The National Hotel. But because the working girls were protected by corrupt police they were not listed as prostitutes on official police records. In answer to questioning he said he had investigated Lily Ryan and Val Weidinger but had found they were not prostitutes.

"What about Shirley Brifman?"

"Yes, I know a Shirley Brifman."

"Was she an associate of the other two?"

"Yes, I would say a close associate."

"Did she frequent the Grand Central Hotel?"

"Yes, she did."

"Have you any information as to whether she was at the National at all?"

"None whatever."

"Shirley Brifman has not been called as a witness. Could you assist me as to where she might be found?"

"No. All I know is I did hear she was in Sydney."

"Have you had any inquiries made to try and locate her whereabouts?"

"No."

"Is there any information you can get as to her whereabouts?"

"I may be able to do that."

"If she can be located, I would like her called. I would like you to assist in locating her if you can"

"I am only too willing to give you all my assistance."

"Can you say when it was that you last saw her?"

"It was prior to the closing of the Grand Central about 12 months ago."

"Have you any information about where she might have been since then?"

"No."

Instead of intimidating witnesses like Douglas, Ambrose had an air of taking them into his confidence, as if they were just having a confidential chat in which they had nothing to fear.

"The position is, you and Detective Hallahan and the Roberts Brothers are friendly?"

"And a lot of other police too. That is the position."

"Have you been acquainted with a woman named Brifman?"

"Yes."

"Was she a reputed prostitute?"

"She could have been classed as such but I endeavoured to get evidence to the effect that she was a prostitute and I was unable to do so."

Valerie Patricia Weidinger, plumpish and 35 to 40, was asked which police she had seen at the Grand Central where she frequently drank – any of the gentlemen who have been in court in the last few days?

"I wouldn't know them without their hats on," she said.

"They had their hats on in the hotel?"

"Yes."

But she knew Murphy and the detective who was always with him. She, Marg (Shirley) and Lily went about in a group – always in a group.

"Can you tell His Honour where Marg is now?"

"I wouldn't know. I think she may be in Sydney."

"When did you last see her?"

"About June this year."

Murphy had not been sitting idly while chatting with Bischof. Komlosy had included a priest as one of the characters he had seen drinking in the pub after hours. The evidence had also brought Brisbane's Catholic hierarchy into disrepute. Murphy was about to trump Komlosy's priest with one of his own. He called Father Stefan Miklos whose only reason for being at the inquiry was to answer one question.

Father Miklos said he had been born in Hungary, had come to Australia six years earlier, was the Catholic chaplain to the Hungarian community in Queensland and had met Komlosy six years earlier.

Byth asked: "From your knowledge of the witness John Geza Komlosy, would you believe him on his oath?"

"No," Father Miklos answered simply and devastatingly.

Byth had no further questions. None of the other barristers had questions.

Father Miklos volunteered: "I could explain why."

Commissioner: "No, you must only answer questions. You may go."

Father Miklos: "Very well."

It was a dreadful abuse of the justice system. The question had not even been about facts. The entire reason for calling him was to elicit an opinion, however vaguely or wrongly inspired. No-one asked him how well he knew Komlosy nor what he knew about him. Whether he had an axe to grind was never probed. The issue may have been as simple as Komlosy having expressed doubts about his faith in God. Further damage to Komlosy's reputation had been achieved.

At the close of evidence on Friday, December 20, the commission took a break over Christmas until January 13.

Chapter 16 - Hallahan is Fingered

and Shirley has a Working Lunch

There was a new development in the Police Department before the Inquiry returned. A three-month internal inquiry regarding the decision of the three senior judges of the Full Court that Hallahan had committed a fraud on the court by fitting up Gary Campbell had not produced any closure. Now there was another black mark against Hallahan which needed to be resolved. It transpired in evidence at the Inquiry that he had not entered a solitary word in his official police diary since June 27 1963.

On January 8 1964 Hallahan was somewhere out in the wilds of Cribb Island, the dilapidated area of smallholdings between Brisbane Airport and the coast where the Bee Gees had lived, when his car radio told him to return to headquarters. There, CIB chief Donovan suspended him from duty and charged him with three departmental offences, two of them involving dishonest, inaccurate and misleading behaviour in the Campbell case; the third that he had failed to keep his official diary up to date. Hallahan told reporters that he was completely shocked by the charges and had decided to take a holiday on the Sunshine Coast.

Could he survive both the National Hotel Inquiry and the three departmental charges?

The National Hotel Inquiry reconvened in the big Number One Civil Court on Monday January 13. Next day, as the tension mounted with the humidity, Detective Senior Constable Glen Patrick Hallahan went through the charade of taking the oath with his slow, soft, modulated, rather deep voice. He was very particular with his use of words. Not for him 'wouldn't' or 'didn't'. He chose: 'I would NOT know' and 'I did NOT know'.

Byth announced: "Mr Hallahan has been ill and that is why he is giving his evidence today."

Byth: "You have been to the premises of the National Hotel on duty at various times?"

"Yes, I have."

"Have you any information about any police drinking there after hours?"

"No, I have not."

"I take it that you have not been drinking after hours there yourself?"

"No, I most certainly have not."

"Do you know David Young?"

"No, I do not know him."

"Have you ever spoken to David Young?"

"Never in my life."

He denied the allegations made by Young and Komlosy.

Hallahan admitted: "I know Lillian May Ryan. She frequented the Grand Central Hotel quite a lot. She was a woman whom we tried to trap for prostitution, unsuccessfully. We tried on a number of occasions. I set up the hotel on at least half a dozen occasions but at no time did I get any evidence that she was engaged in prostitution. I have never ever seen her at the National Hotel. The same applies to Valerie Weidinger. Irene Halliday was a person who used to frequent the Australian Hotel lounge. She is a hopeless alcoholic. I have never sighted her at the National."

Byth: "Shirley Brifman?"

"Well, I know of Shirley Brifman. I do not know her very well."

"Is she a reputed prostitute or not?"

"No, she is not."

"Anything to connect her with the National?"

"No, I have never sighted her at the National, only at the Grand Central."

Barrister Ambrose received similar denials to his lengthy cross-examination of Hallahan and sat down but then jumped up again and said: "I omitted to put certain questions that I proposed to put to this witness."

Commissioner Gibbs: "What does it relate to?"

Ambrose: "It relates to a finding by the Full Court concerning this witness."

Commissioner Gibbs had allowed barristers to attack the reputations of Young and Komlosy but he had a different attitude when Ambrose sought to expose Hallahan's record.

"I do not propose to allow you to put that. I will not grant you leave to put that."

Ambrose then put Hallahan on the spot: "I put it to you that, in fact, you were the man who rang Mr Young on November 19, 1963, and advised him of the matters that would be put before the commission if he gave evidence."

"I didn't ring him at all."

Ambrose then recalled Young who was emphatic that Hallahan was the man with the soft, well-modulated voice who had made the threatening phone call. Under cross-examination by other barristers Young said he first suspected Hallahan when he heard him speak in the witness box. Then under further cross-examination he told of a second phone call, in which he had been told by someone else that the threatening call had come from a man called Halloran. Then Young changed his story yet again. The date of the second call was wrong. At the end of the day Mr T O Jones, for the National Hotel, almost yelled at Young: "Why did you tell lies?" The cross-examination went on for the rest of the afternoon and continued next morning. Young then admitted he had broken the oath because he "had hate and revenge for a man who has caused me anguish and heartache." The damage to his credibility was immeasurable.

At the end of the week Sunday Truth reported: "The most startling moment of the week, without question, was the fiction-like "fingering" of suspended ace Brisbane detective Glen Hallahan."

According to Shirley Brifman's statements to police seven years later, Hallahan and Murphy had rung her in Sydney every night of the commission to tell her what was being said at the inquiry. Eventually, they told her she must come up to Brisbane to lie for them and destroy Young. She would stay in Sydney over the Australia Day weekend of January 25, 26 and 27 and fly to Brisbane on Tuesday the 28th. All through the weekend they were on the phone coaching and cajoling her.

The day she hit town to swear on oath she was not a prostitute, she couldn't help herself. The plane landed at the airport at 9.35 am and an hour or so later she was in the city where she met Lily Ryan. Why not a couple of drinks at Lennons Hotel? While they were there a bit of business presented itself and who were they to turn down an opportunity? They took the client to Lily's tiny wooden worker's cottage that fronted straight on to the narrow pavement in Bradley St, Spring Hill, and were all well into the Scotch when the phone went. The inquiry had broken for lunch and it was Tony Murphy with a report on what had happened so far. But after a while he realised Shirley had been on the grog. He was furious and said: "Don't come to court, you're drunk."

In the witness box this day was the burly, ruddy-faced, imposing figure of Francis Erich Bischof, known for good reason as The Big Fella. He almost filled the witness box, his bulging barrel chest straining the buttoned-up suit jacket. Under cross-examination he would look down and absentmindedly study his fingernails as if he was just checking that no-one had made off with any of them while he hadn't been looking.

It appeared that Shirley was not the only person to have enjoyed a few drinks at lunch time. In the morning session Bischof had provided big yawns with his mundane answers. Now Byth, the barrister assisting the commission was knocked back on his heels as The Big Fella planted himself at centre stage with a bravura performance.

Byth: "Have you received any information at all that there was a call girl service at the National Hotel?"

"Never at any time."

"Did you receive any information that any members of the police force had been guilty of doing anything wrong at that hotel?"

"No."

"Did you receive any reports or complaints about a call girl service at the National?"

"Never. If I did I would crack the whip very hard."

Enlarging on the fact that he was often obliged to socialise, Bischof explained: "I have always made myself available, whether to princess, prostitute, poet or peasant".

Byth: "Do you recall certain newspaper reports of allegations made in Parliament concerning the goings on at the National Hotel and, as a result, did you order any inquiries to be made by police?"

"Not by the police. I *am* the police and I knew they were incorrect."

"But this was without consulting any of your subordinates?"

"I didn't have to because I knew they were spurious."

So the allegations by Colin Bennett in Parliament of wrongdoing and corruption had not been investigated by anyone. But it was a different story when it came to witnesses.

Ambrose: "You were aware that various allegations had been made against Detective Sergeant Murphy?"

"Yes."

"Were you aware that Chief Inspector Bauer was instructing Murphy to conduct inquiries into the background of Mr Young?"

"Yes."

"Did you think it proper that the job of inquiring into the background of Young, who made the allegations against Mr Murphy, should be given to Murphy?"

"I didn't give them to Mr Murphy. I instructed Chief Inspector Bauer to have certain inquiries made."

Bischof added: "I don't want to be unkind to Mr Young or Mr Komlosy and if they and others in high places desire to crucify me and members of the police force, I have no hard feelings. All I can say is this: forgive them, for they know not what they do," he declaimed, and added as if explanation was needed: "That was said about 2,000 years ago – with great emphasis, too."

At 3 pm, still flushed from Scotch and sex, Shirley walked immaculately into the inquiry, dressed for ladies day at Flemington in a virginally white suit and a floppy wide-brimmed white hat that for ever after would be the photo of Shirley featured every time a newspaper ran a story about her. Bischof was still performing as Shirley and Lily walked in and sat down at the back of the court.

She was going to lie to protect the police. And there was also the fact that she did not want her family to know what she did for a living. Murphy and Hallahan had briefed her about the questions she would be asked so that she could think about the answers and not be surprised by anything.

After her lunchtime of Scotch on the job it was late afternoon before she started giving evidence. She took the oath with absolutely no intention of telling the truth, part of the truth or anything like the truth.

She said she was Shirley Margaret Brifman, of 195 Bunnerong Road, Maroubra, sister of Mrs Marjorie Chapple and she was also known as Marg, with a hard G.

She did not like Young's allegations that she was one of the girls and intended to refute it, she told the commission in the short time she gave evidence that afternoon.

That night Hallahan and Murphy met her at Lily Ryan's flat and they analysed what she had said in evidence. "They discussed with me the questions that would be asked the next day and told me the answers to give," she recalled. "Most of the evidence that I gave on the second day was what they told me to say."

'Destroy Young' was the order. And they gave her the ammunition to shoot him down.

She and the other women who had given evidence may not have been on the guest list of Government House but they knew how to dress for an occasion. All of them had worn a different outfit, with suitable accessories, on each day that they had attended and Shirley was replete in a splendid new outfit for her second appearance. She was asked by McGill if she had spoken to any police officer between arriving in town and arriving in court.

"Definitely not," said an aggrieved Mrs Brifman.

And barrister McGill, desperate to protect the honour of his clients and the witness, noted Shirley's demure appearance and asked the judge rhetorically: "Does she look like a prostitute? - No!"

Shirley, who had drunk at the National just about every day for years, was asked: "Did you ever have a drink at the National Hotel?"

"About six times in four years," said Shirley solemnly.

"Did you tell David Young that you had been told by police that you could operate at the National with safety?"

"Definitely not."

"Did you tell David Young that you gave any favours to any police?"

"No."

"Do you know any members of the consorting squad?"

"Yes," she said, naming Murphy, Hallahan and two others.

"How did you come to know them?"

"Well, at different times they would pull me out of the hotel lounge at the Grand Central."

J. D. McGill, for the Roberts brothers, asked her if she had met David Young. Shirley replied triumphantly: "Yes. David Young done an abortion on me."

Shirley watched the effect of her verbal grenade on people around the room. There was pandemonium.

Commissioner: "Just a minute."

Ambrose. "It is quite improper."

Shirley heard the judge eventually say: "Strike it from the record."

But she noted that later the judge said: "Mr McGill, I think you have made your point."

In fact, Young had a completely clean record and wouldn't have known an abortionist from an arborist. But, as with the priest and Komlosy, the hit and run had succeeded.

Shirley had done her duty. She had a few drinks with the boys and flew back to Sydney.

It was a great let down for Col Bennett and his reputation. He had made the claim about prostitution. Now Shirley had sold him out.

Chapter 17 - Do you Want to be in the Works for Three Quid?

Despite the best efforts of Bischof's spoilers, there were snippets of damaging evidence which got through their net.

Former National night porter Alan Lucas said there were occasions between 1 and 3am when women who he believed to be prostitutes arrived with men and he booked them into rooms. Another night porter, James Mahan, saw women drinking in the lounge trying to meet men for immoral purposes – but he couldn't be sure that they were going to charge for their services, he admitted under cross-examination. Former casual waiter Lee Elliott said he believed two or three women who regularly sat in the lounge were prostitutes.

There were people reading the reports of the inquiry in The Courier-Mail and the Sunday papers with astonishment that a whitewash was taking place. They caught a dose of the sentiment which had motivated Komlosy and Young to stand up and speak out. They knew that there was late night drinking and strongly suspected that there was organised prostitution at the National. They must have realised that they risked being savaged but they had the benefit of the surprise factor. The police hadn't had the chance to prepare plans to demolish their reputations.

On January 29 Basil William Grove, a 24-year-old New Zealander who was working as a warehouseman, decided he had to come forward. He gave a statement to the Crown Solicitor's Office in the afternoon.

He said he frequently drank at the National Hotel after hours, sometimes as late as 3am.

"Did you see any plainclothes police in the lounge after 10?"

"There were people who were pointed out to me at the National and pointed out at the Treasury as being plainclothes detectives. I had seen them in the lounge after 10. Sometimes there would be one or two women sitting together at a table, previously unaccompanied, and then some of the chaps in the lounge would go over and talk to them and drink with them, and I have seen people, meeting in those circumstances, go up in the lift from the lounge."

Grove was attacked for the whole of the next morning and much of the afternoon in cross-examination.

Then William John Ignatius Ousley, tax consultant, company secretary and non-practising barrister also came forward with similar evidence.

And finally Glen Robert Allen, a 21-year-old draftsman came forward.

Here was another man with an impeccable reputation, captain of the Tugun Lifesavers Surfing Club and a good record after three years in the Army.

He'd attended a 21st birthday party. "I came across the lift and the door was open. I was about to walk into it and there was a couch outside the lift with a girl lying on it. As I was about to get into the lift she propped her head on her hand…and she said: 'Do you want to be in the works for three quid?' I just looked at her and said: 'No, too dear.' So then she came back at me again and she came down to two pounds 10 shillings. I said: 'No, too much.' Anyway, she came down 10 shillings a time to a pound and I said: 'No, I'm afraid you're out of luck here. I've only got 15 shillings and 9 pence on me. Bad luck.'"

Komlosy approached the Inquiry just once more. This example of the Australian justice system had totally demoralized him. The disillusioned witness announced he and his family were going back to Germany.

Lewis and Don Lane were not called to give evidence. Lane later admitted in a self-serving autobiography which made no mention at all of the National Hotel Inquiry, that drinking on duty was accepted among the detectives of the consorting squad and that they ignored illegal after-hours trading in pubs.

On February 3 the last witness walked out of the witness box.

Ambrose, summing up for Young, said: "The Commission, at its inception, started off as an inquiry into the background and history of Mr Young. Some considerable time was spent by all counsel engaged on that. Young came forward as a witness who had everything to lose and absolutely nothing to gain. He gained nothing. He suffered severe financial difficulty. He must have suffered this as regards his legal costs. I submit further that he has been subjected to character assassination by some of the parties represented before Your Honour. Every aspect of his life was raked up and there was absolutely no endeavour made to show that Young's evidence was worthy of credit.

"I submit that quite clearly, on the evidence, the hotel was used frequently and regularly by persons who were prostitutes. I submit that the evidence of Komlosy and Maher shows that. I submit the evidence of Grove shows it. Brifman was obviously subject to police pressure. Her occupation, although she denied she was a prostitute, was prostitution. She would have an interest to co-operate with the police so that she might pursue her chosen calling without undue police interference.

"One thing which is quite striking, I submit, which emerges from this inquiry is the inadequacy of the existing legal machinery to assist Your Honour in an inquiry of this type. An allegation has been made against the police force. The allegation is not made against the hotel as such. It is made against the police force. How do we get inquiries made into the police force? Apparently, by getting members of the police force to inquire into the police force. Your Honour has not had the assistance of an independent investigator to conduct impartial investigations into the police force. Your Honour is required to simply put police officers into the box and have them asked: Have you been guilty of impropriety? It is not very surprising that police officers put in that situation should say: No. I submit that the same thing applies to the evidence given by the Roberts brothers. One would not expect them to say that there has been an association between them and the Commissioner or between them and the police department and that they have had any preferential treatment because of any association. Well, who else is there to assist Your Honour? I submit for this reason Your Honour will pay very great regard to evidence given by persons who are not members of the police force. The attitude of the police department towards this inquiry is shown most clearly from the evidence of Mr Bischof who scoffed at the whole idea. He made absolutely no inquiries into the content of the allegations. No senior man in the police department was commissioned or directed to make inquiries into the allegations. The only inquiries that were made were those made into the background of these persons who had the temerity to make any suggestion of police impropriety. Mr Bischof pointed out himself that Mr Murphy was put on to inquire into Young and Komlosy, and I submit that this was most improper of the police department. Murphy was the man against whom allegations had been made, and yet the very man is given the duty or the instructions to go and inquire into the background of the men who made the allegations. I submit that it is quite laughable to assume that any police officer is going to get into the box and admit that he has been guilty of improper conduct."

The Commission of Inquiry ended at 3.50pm on February 4 1964 after sitting for 31 days and recording 2968 pages of evidence.

Bischof and his supporters were so sure of victory and were so emboldened that they held a victory party at The National Hotel that night. Sir Thomas Hiley says he was told by a police officer who attended the party: "Bischof, by this time was full as a kite and he's up on the mini stage – it was a band area where the bands used to get up about one step off the floor – and he's got these three fellows up on the stage and he's doing his best to put his arms around three necks at once, rather a hard task, and he said: 'I want you all to know that these are the boys who got me off this rap', and he said: 'I want you all to know I'm going to look after them'. He said: 'You won't stop till you go right to the top.'

"The three men were Tony Murphy, Glen Hallahan and Terry Lewis."

Anonymous calls then plagued Young. They came at all times of the day and night. "Your home is going to be blown up." "I'm going to blast you with a shot gun." It didn't seem to matter whether it was 2.30 am or 10 am. Sometimes there was a second voice which took over the threats. Once there was the sound of a woman laughing in the background. Young kept the caller talking one night and sent his wife next door to phone the exchange but she was told that tracing the call was not possible. Shirley later revealed that Hallahan had threatened to shoot Young.

Col Bennett knew all about nuisance phone calls. Every time he mentioned Murphy's name in Parliament he would receive phone calls on the hour every hour all through the night. In the small hours of one of these nights an ambulance raced up the steep driveway to Bennett's home. "I believe your husband is very ill," said the officer to Bennett's wife. Half an hour later the fire brigade, bells clanging, made the same trip and rushed into the house. Other opponents suffered in the same way for many years.

Retribution on Barbara Yanku, a prostitute who had opened up about her activities at the National, was more violent and permanent. Shirley recalled that one of Hallahan's contacts and two other men "drugged her one night, took her down the Gold Coast and tattooed every part of her body. There is hardly a space on her body which is not tattooed. That is how bad Glen is, he had that organised. That is what they did to her for the Royal Commission."

The integrity of Young and Komlosy had been violently assaulted but Hallahan, Lane, Murphy, Lewis and their crooked colleagues must have lived in fear that Gibbs would find against them in his report, despite the fact that Don Lane had succeeded magnificently in failing to find more than a dozen prostitutes who were alleged to have used the National. He'd failed to find former National Hotel waiter, pimp and procurer Max Levine. He'd failed to find five men who were alleged to have procured prostitutes at the National and used rooms at the National to enjoy their services. Lane had also managed to avoid finding people who had been named as drinking illegally at the hotel. There were at least 20 potential witnesses with evidence about the goings-on at the National who Lane couldn't find. This must have been some sort of world record for a detective.

And finally, the hotel registers had mysteriously but conveniently been lost.

Now came Hallahan's next big test – the three departmental charges. Or was it such a test?

Chapter 18 - His Honour Demonstrates

the Art of Whitewashing

If Bischof and the Government were to retain Hallahan in the force, they had to deal with the fact that three senior judges had found Hallahan guilty of a fraud on the court. They needed to find someone in a senior position to deal with the issue. Another judge was hardly going to find against his superiors and the justice system, so that was out of the question.

So a unique decision was made by Police Minister Dewar, acting on Bischof's advice, to appoint a QC to hear the charges against Hallahan in camera. Normally, the charges would be heard by a commissioned officer who would report to the police commissioner. Dewar said he had the power to open the court but had decided against it.

Just as an inept conjurer might perform his sleight of hand behind a cloak so that the audience cannot see the trick being performed or work out what happened, the inquiry would be held behind closed doors.

The Government needed someone reliable to deal with this situation and had appointed ambitious young QC, Mark Hoare, to handle the inquiry. He had recently been selected to prosecute Bennett on a summons alleging common assault, a summons which would usually only require a lowly police officer to prosecute.

That case had its roots in a bitter confrontation between Bennett and former Premier Vince Gair when the two former 'comrades' had stood against one another for the seat of South Brisbane in the 1960 state election which Bennett had won. Bennett, the father of eight children, lost his youngest son at that time, drowned in Davis Park swimming pool. The bitterness between the factions was so appalling that a woman on Gair's staff who had received her first communion with Bennett's wife, wrote to the Bennetts: "There you are, that's God's reprisal for Colin's activities in politics!"

Both Gair and another beaten MP from the same faction, Gregory Kehoe, had gained positions in the public service. As Bennett strode briskly to the Supreme Court for the afternoon session of the National Hotel Inquiry on its first day he came across Gair and Keogh on their way back from lunch at the boozer. Kehoe, vice-president of the breakaway Queensland Labor Party, called Bennett a bastard. Bennett carefully put his armful of books and papers into his other hand and wham! A tooth went flying and Keogh was off to a doctor for three stitches. The summons was issued and it was arranged, at considerable expense, for Hoare QC to prosecute. Despite the enthusiasm to discomfit Bennett, Kehoe turned out to be reluctant to give evidence and the case dragged on for adjournment after adjournment until Bennett successfully had the case dropped.

Bennett believed that Hallahan should have been charged and tried in an open court.

Where three of the top judges had found Hallahan 'guilty' in his evidence about Campbell, Hoare created a new verdict: the charges of having given a court inaccurate, dishonest and misleading information were "not proven". Just two years later Hoare would receive promotion to the bench.

Hallahan was given the news as he returned to Redcliffe after a day's fishing on the Bay. "This is wonderful," he told the media. "All I want to do now is get back on duty."

Sunday Truth said Hallahan, "one of the State's top investigators", had been 'cleared' after fresh evidence had been taken from sound lounge manager John Hannay.

Mr Justice Gibbs handed his report on the National Hotel Inquiry to the Premier on April 10 1964, just in time for the force's centenary. The Courier-Mail splashed on the inquiry's findings with headlines reading: "Police failed to detect late night National drinking - but no neglect by policemen". The whole of page five was given over to highlights from the report. The editorial said the findings had given the police and Bischof a "complete clearance". Two archbishops joined the whitewash by praising the force's integrity and record.

Whether the Government had provided the media with the full report or a sanitized summary is not clear. Newspapers provided no analysis of the report, no critical examination of how closely the report reflected the evidence and no evaluation of the findings. Bischof could dance tall at the Police Ball for 1000 at Cloudland where 21 debutantes were being presented to Governor Sir Henry Abel Smith.

At the end of the week Sunday Truth said in its leader: "Cost of the Police-National Hotel-Call Girl Royal Commission was around 50,000 pounds...but every penny of it was worthwhile to get its character clearance for the Police Commissioner Mr Bischof and his senior officers. Public reaction generally amounts almost to a relief that Mr Justice Gibbs found the way he did. The great body of law-abiding people would have been nauseated had the Gibbs Report branded our police as call girl condoners. Now all fair-minded people will hope that we have heard the last of unsubstantiated attacks on police from inside and outside Parliament. That hope is aimed specially at the Labor Member for South Brisbane, barrister Colin Bennett."

Nobody wrote a letter on the subject to the papers.

But how did Justice Gibbs manage the whitewash?

I learned early in my journalistic life that the head of an inquiry, if he or she is so minded, can bring in almost any verdict, however absurd it might seem to some of those familiar with the evidence, and support it with a logical argument and facts from the evidence so that the judgement can withstand criticism. The trick is that once the verdict has been selected, to cherry-pick any bits of evidence that support that verdict, starting with the most persuasive. Having done this, start dismissing the most controversial or weakest of the evidence which supported what would have been the correct decision. The trick then is to suggest that all the rest of the "correct" argument should also fall by the wayside. The biggest part of the deception, just like a conjurer performing the three card trick, is to divert the eye from what is happening by inserting lots of extraneous material so that the watcher is bemused and diverted from the object of the exercise. The final report is therefore replete with examinations of arguments from witnesses about points which are made to appear important but which really have no bearing on the main issue.

The other part of the trick takes advantage of the fact that very few people have the time or are prepared to plough through 300 pages or more of a report and then analyse the evidence for themselves.

In the case of the National Hotel, it was correct that there was little or no evidence of an organised "call-girl service" in the strict meaning of the term – whatever that might have been - operating at the hotel in 1963. However, there was much evidence of prostitutes openly using the hotel in the presence of senior police officers and another inquiry commissioner could have drawn very different conclusions and recommendations.

What Gibbs did first of all was to say that "the evidence of Young and Komlosy contained so many allegations of systematic illegalities by those conducting the hotel and of the grave misconduct on the part of various members of the Police Force that it was necessary to examine their evidence separately before proceeding to consider the whole of the evidence".

He could, of course, have taken an opposite approach by selecting evidence of wrongdoing given independently by other witnesses and then looking for confirmation in evidence from Young and Komlosy.

But he chose examples of inconsistencies exposed by cross-examination to determine: "I cannot regard him (Young) as a witness whose evidence may be believed or acted upon unless it is corroborated by the evidence of some other witness who is himself reliable."

Now – and this is a trick – Gibbs said in his very next sentence: "I find there is no evidence to corroborate that of Young in relation to the following allegations, and I reject Young's evidence in relation to them..." The list included Bischof drinking in the hotel after hours and Murphy and other detectives being supplied with free booze.

Gibbs then wrote off Komlosy's evidence along the same sort of lines and even had the temerity to say "there is a remarkable parallel between the two sets of allegations". His suggestion was that there was either a conspiracy or that for some strange reason Komlosy had invented his story and used Young's allegations as a prototype. He didn't accept that the reason for similarities was the fact that the two men were accurately describing the facts.

Of Komlosy he said: "His evidence…contained violent inconsistencies, was a curious compound of fact, hearsay, exaggeration, theory and invention and perhaps even hallucination….In my opinion, it was Young's allegation that suggested to him the name of Detective Sergeant Murphy as that of a police officer who habitually drank at the hotel…"

Gibbs gave no reason how he had reached this opinion nor why he did not believe that Murphy had been seen at the National.

And he summed up Komlosy's evidence with familiar words: "On the whole it is clear that it is impossible to accept and act on any of his evidence unless it is supported by other credible testimony." This ruled out evidence about Bischof, Murphy and Hallahan.

In his next sentence he made the quantum jump to this statement: "I find there is no evidence to corroborate that of Komlosy in respect of these matters and I reject Komlosy's evidence in relation to them."

Gibbs also said: "It is also convenient to give separate consideration to the evidence of two witnesses, Donna Anderson and Rona May Youse, which must be considered in connection with that of Komlosy."

He did not say why the evidence of Anderson and Youse had to be considered with that of Komlosy but he eliminated their evidence with very little justification, even puzzling himself by saying: "The evidence did not reveal any reason why she (Youse) should say that she had frequently used the hotel for purposes of prostitution if that was not true. However, having carefully considered her evidence I cannot regard it as reliable."

There is obviously no good reason for Gibbs to come to this conclusion and he was reduced to saying a little later: "Perhaps an explanation why Youse fabricated or exaggerated her testimony may be found in some association between herself and Komlosy that was not disclosed."

This is Alice in Wonderland rubbish. Gibbs failed to produce any evidence that Youse fabricated or exaggerated her evidence. He then wandered further into a world of make-believe, of 'perhaps' and 'maybe', by saying that his invented hypothesis could be explained by a relationship that was not even hinted at in evidence.

Having disposed of the necessity of having to take any notice of the testimony of four of the main witnesses, Gibbs went on to take the occasional pot shot at other witnesses. Prostitute Barbara Yanku? "…certainly not a witness who could be treated as completely reliable." And so on.

However, when it came to evidence that the Roberts brothers were guilty of serving alcohol after hours Gibbs found the case overwhelmingly proved. He found the Roberts brothers had lied on oath about this and that those managing the hotel must have known many offences against the Liquor Acts had been committed. Despite these frequent, flagrant breaches over the previous five years Gibbs found that no one in the police force was guilty of any misconduct or negligence.

Now, another judge assessing all the evidence might have started his report in a different manner. He might have used a finding that the Roberts brothers were lying on oath about the illegal drinking as a starting point for the rest of his findings and gone on to surmise, bearing in mind the weight of evidence that prostitutes frequented the hotel, that the brothers were also lying about prostitution. This "other" judge might then have gone on to look at how various witnesses, with nothing to gain, gave evidence about prostitution which tallied. This judge may also have adjourned the Inquiry until a few more witnesses had been found. And he may have asked what the hell was going on when Police Commissioner Bischof, who Gibbs acknowledged was a friend of Rolly Roberts, delegated Detective Murphy, who Gibbs acknowledged was a friend of Rolly Roberts, to investigate whether Rolly Roberts had behaved illegally.

The joke in pubs and city office corridors was that Harry Gibbs was the only man in Brisbane who couldn't find a hooker at the National Hotel.

Hallahan and his crooked colleagues breathed a collective sigh of relief. But Hallahan was angry with his mate Ron Richards for having demanded an Inquiry into Col Bennett's allegations about the National Hotel. Former Gold Coast Bulletin editor Bob Gordon recalled in a memoir many years later: "One of the cops, at a barbecue on the roof of the National Hotel a few months later, suddenly picked Ron up and dangled him by his ankles over the edge." Queen Street lay four storeys below. One slip or a loosened grip and Richards was dead. Gordon recalled: "The detective made a joke and hauled him back but told him he'd drop him the next time the force had to endure such an inquiry." Who had the cop been? Bob racked his brain and came up with two possibilities. One of them was Glen Patrick Hallahan.

In the pomp and ceremony of the opening of Parliament on August 18, 1964, the National Hotel Inquiry Report was quietly laid on the table. It was the first time Parliament had sat since the report had been publicised in the media in April. But the world had moved on. The Rolling Stones had released their first album, the Great Train Robbers had been sentenced, Nelson Mandela had been sentenced to life imprisonment, the Bank of New South Wales had allowed a woman to become a teller for the first time since World War Two, Rupert Murdoch had launched The

Australian newspaper, the first Australian serviceman had been killed in Vietnam, the first BASIC computer program had been written and the Beatles had caused mayhem on their two-day visit to Brisbane at the end of June. The National Hotel Inquiry was old news. There was absolutely no debate at all on the report. And in front of the usual rubber stamp which read "ordered to be printed" someone had written with a pen in forbidding capital letters 'NOT'. Bennett believed that most members did not bother to attempt to read the report. Very few copies were available and it was a considerable time before one was provided for the Parliamentary Library.

And Hallahan? Over the last few years he had featured in too many negative stories. Worse, he had been groomd to be a police prosecutor but he was now virtually useless in that role, thanks to Justice Philp. He had recommended that Hallahan be prosecuted for perjury for his evidence in the Hart arson prosecution. He was appalled when no action was taken but word had soon spread about Philp's condemnation of Hallahan's perjured evidence. Now, as soon as a case started defence counsel would just beam at him: "Are you the Detective Hallahan who Mr Justice Philp castigated for perjury?"

Hallahan quietly disappeared from Queensland for a year on May 18, 1964, volunteering for a tour of duty with the United Nations' police on strife-torn Cyprus.

Murphy, Lewis and Lane were unscathed.

Chapter 19 - Lowlife 1965-70 –

the Vice Queen and the Crime Czar

Having been a leading prostitute in the Queensland capital, Shirley set about conquering Australia's largest city. She started off operating from the Hotel Rex in Macleay Street, Potts Point, which was handy for Sydney's biggest sleaze centre, Kings Cross.

Shirley recalled: "I'd done the right thing by the Queensland Police and I was trusted."

She said she received protection from Detective Sergeant Fred Krahe and other New South Wales police. The Rex was a modern three-storey building with a pleasant lounge and cocktail bar and a big tree outside as a welcome relief from all the concrete. The deal was that she could use the hotel as her pick-up base as long as she and her girls entertained clients there and they spent money on drinks but they had to use bedrooms in Earls Court. Tony Murphy would have caught up with her in June 1965 when he spent a month in Sydney on 'interchange duty'.

"After Glen came back from Cyprus (resuming duty on September 29, 1965) and I threw him into Freddy (Krahe), he was never away from Sydney: he was there at least once a month," said Shirley. This was despite the fact that Hallahan, now 32, was supposed to be working in Townsville, Queensland's second biggest city with a population of only 56,000, 1,350 kilometres north of Brisbane, rather than in Sydney, 1,000 kilometres south of Brisbane in another state's jurisdiction.

Shirley said: "Freddy knew I had Brisbane in the palm of my hand and he wanted Glen Hallahan. I had a hold on Glen. Glen would do what I wanted. Krahe then grabbed Glen. He did everything with Glen. They were two top men in different states. Glen knew what was happening in Queensland and Fred knew what was happening in Sydney and Glen trusted me. Once he mixed with Krahe he wanted big money. He had been on small money before."

In Brisbane Tony Murphy had been transferred to the corrupt licensing branch where Pommie Jack Herbert was running the corruption payments. Shirley recalled: "Tony had been trying very hard to get into the licensing branch. When he got into the licensing branch he said to me: 'Shirley, I'm sitting in the place where I've wanted to be for years - the place where I can make money'."

Bagman Jack Herbert paid Murphy from his first day in the branch and they became drinking pals. Murphy was not one to forget his Rat Pack mate Terry Lewis who was being groomed for the top in the juvenile aid bureau. He reminded Jack Herbert that Terry was a friend of Commissioner Bischof and should be paid as well.

Hallahan was spending an increasing amount of time in Sydney with Shirley and Krahe. "Sometimes Glen would be down in Sydney and back three days and back again," she recalled.

"Fred was always ringing Glen Hallahan from my place. It was always about this robbery or that robbery or what they were going to do about sending somebody up here or down there to do robberies. I heard the two of them discussing a tank man (safe blower) and I know they sent up a tank man here to Brisbane to do some tanks. He had been in Brisbane before and he did a couple of years here. Then he went to Sydney and Freddy sent him back up here.

"I have seen (them) split money at my place many times. It was just an everyday occurrence. Usually in the lounge. They were pieces of the furniture. Krahe bought land at Redcliffe. I often wonder whether Glen bought up land."

Hallahan spent Christmas Day 1967 in Sydney, having lunch with Gunner Kelly and dinner at Shirley's home before flying out to Melbourne "on business". "He was in Melbourne a couple of days," said Shirley." When he came back was when I saw the money.

"Glen had been overseas and he had a real good set of ports (portmanteaus). He opened his port and said: Have you ever seen the forged money Shirl? I had a look and he said: Do you want some? And I said: 'No'. He did point to me different things on the money. I said: 'It all looks alike to me'. The money was in a port bigger than a brief case. The money was stacked in the port. They were not done up with rubber bands. All tens. He said: 'With blokes I can't pinch, I'll load them with it.'"

Shirley said Hallahan had tried to arrest a man at the races in Brisbane. "An informant put the money on him. They were not quick enough so they went to Townsville and put it on him up there."

Hallahan boasted in an affidavit many years later: "With another detective I flew to Townsville and subsequently arrested a man and charged him with being in possession of forged $10 notes. This person pleaded guilty to the charge and was convicted and sentenced to imprisonment."

In May 1968 the Sydney Sunday Mirror reported that Commonwealth Police were investigating allegations that senior Queensland officers had been passing the forgeries. It was said to be the first time since Federation in 1901 that one force had investigated another. The Federal deputy commissioner himself was handling the investigation. The paper said the deputy commissioner had spent several days in Brisbane with his investigations being centred on a "well-known detective".

Col Bennett told the Queensland Parliament: "I have here a photocopy of a statutory declaration made by Francis Thomas Reid who claimed that in the course of the investigation he was stood over by the Commonwealth Police. However, he does say that when he was pressed to say who handed the notes to him, they endeavoured to shift the blame on to Detective Glen Hallahan. This is a serious matter, because this is a statutory declaration. No doubt the original is in the hands of the Commissioner of Police in Queensland. I do not know what kind of a character this man (Reid) is but he makes these allegations and he is coming in on the side of Detective Glen Hallahan. He claims that when he was closely interrogated by the Commonwealth police he said certain things. I propose to quote from a statutory declaration signed in the presence of a justice of the peace and dated May 1968 - his version of the investigation by the inspector of Commonwealth police.

"This is how the declaration reads:

Q. All you've got to say is that that money you got off Glen Hallahan.

A. I said: "I'd never got nothing off Glen Hallahan."

Q. He said: "Well say you got it off a police officer."

A. Well, at that time I was prepared to say I'd got it off Frank Bischof, providing I'd get off the hook. And that's what I've said and that's the amount of the conversation."

Unfortunately, that was when Bennett's time for speaking ran out. It would have been illuminating to have heard what Reid had said about Hallahan in the interview with the Commonwealth police. Francis Thomas Reid was known to police and the underworld as Tommy 'The Armourer' Reid, aged 50, a gunman and standover merchant who Shirley was later to allege was part of the mob of gunnies and crims who crooked police used to commit crimes up and down the East Coast. Murphy and Hallahan had busted him in 1961. In an aide memoir Bennett noted that Reid had been used to load up a criminal with the notes.

Meanwhile, Shirley had fallen out in a major way with the Rex Hotel and started her own brothel at Earls Court, Potts Point. She was becoming a wealthy woman.

Hallahan was also making plenty of (real) money. Shirley recalled a visit she made to Hallahan at his one-bedroom flat off Petrie Terrace in Brisbane. "I picked up a cent off the floor and I handed it to him and I said: 'Put it in your money box.' He opened his wardrobe and I saw a terrific amount of money there. There was bundles of it. It was just sitting in the wardrobe. It had bands around it and folded over. I said: 'Well, you don't need the cent piece.' He said: 'I have never been short of money since I went to Sydney.' The phone rang about half past eleven and Glen talked on the phone and Glen said to the other person on the phone: 'Forget about the bank robbery tonight – I've got a friend up from Sydney.' He talked for a while on the phone. When he got off the phone he told me about the bank at Capalaba. Glen said to me: 'The bank was going to be robbed tonight. I put it off because you're here. When it's done I will charge another couple of chaps with it.' I know the bank was robbed but not that night and I do believe Glen charged someone.

"We always ended up in Glen's flat at the Normanby. They were dirty on Bennett – he had been on TV and squealed his head off. This is the time they wanted a gunnie up here to shoot Bennett. Tony and Glen did a whole lot of things to Col Bennett. All they wanted was a cheap gunnie."

There had been a curious incident in 1967 when the Sunday Mail said it had received an anonymous letter saying that a vicious member of the Sydney underworld was threatening to kill Bennett. The author wrote that he was speaking for southern crims and "I have turned to you to try to stop this terrible thing. We all like Mr Bennett."

The gangster (unnamed in the newspaper) was Ducky O'Connor who had become known as Mad Dog in Sydney because of his violent attacks on other underworld heavies, often using an iron bar or a hammer on opponents. When Parliament sat two days after the Sunday Mail report Speaker Johnno Mann told Bennett that O'Connor was outside wanting to talk to him. Mann said he had known O'Connor's father for years and that Ducky had asked him to arrange a meeting with Bennett because he wanted to assure the MP that he meant him no harm. Of course, it could have been a ruse but Bennett was never one to take a backward step. He walked briskly outside to meet the notorious gunman fresh out of Sydney's Long Bay prison. There were no bullets just a fusillade of words from O'Connor.

"The letter was obviously sent to do me harm in the eyes of the police in Queensland," he told Bennett. "I can assure you and the police that I have no intention of tangling with anyone here."

Bennett said later: "It's hard, of course, to take these things lightly but I've accepted this man's word that the letter received by the newspaper was not true. Anyhow, if he'd wanted to get me he could have done it plenty of times."

Why O'Connor had made the 1,000 kilometre journey from Sydney was not explained. If he had been given orders by Hallahan he may have been dissuaded from carrying them out by his father who had only recently been successfully defended in a criminal case by Bennett. There is no doubt Ducky was in touch with Hallahan, who confirmed a meeting with him in Queensland which resulted in the detective sending O'Connor back to Sydney.

Two months later the notorious gunman was executed in a Sydney nightclub with a bullet to the brain. Two detectives were present but, unfortunately, by some chance, did not see what happened. And by the time they arrived at the table where O'Connor was slumped, two guns lying nearby had been wiped clean of fingerprints. The detectives would seem to have graduated from the same training college as Don Lane.

Newspapers called Gary Venamore 'a 35-year-old single playboy socialite'. Tall, well-built and a sharp dresser, he was also called 'Mr Immaculate'. He'd worked at the Australian Consulate in New York for two years and by November 1968 was working as a travel agent in Brisbane and living with his widowed mum. It was after 2am on November 6 when he left the Playboy Club in Brisbane's Petrie Bight as full as a butcher's dog. He caught a taxi with two other men at 2.20am and was taken to Maxwell Street, New Farm, close to the Brisbane River. Some residents were woken by screams but no one saw anything. At 6am a ferry master saw something floating in the water just downstream from Maxwell Street. Venamore had been viciously flogged with a wooden pole, his nose smashed and his liver ruptured, before being thrown into the river to drown. He would have been too drunk to resist, said the coroner, and if he hadn't drowned, he would have died from his injuries within 20 minutes.

Hallahan used the murder as a reason for one of his regular visits to Sydney, to interview the crew of a ship that had been moored in the Brisbane River the night Venamore was murdered. Shirley recalled that Hallahan had shown her photographs of the corpse. "I saw all the marks on his face. No motive of robbery. So they put, Glen told me, the television cameras on the Eagle Street toilets. He said: 'Shirley, the businessmen who are homosexual, you would not believe it. The businessmen would arrive at the Eagle Street toilets, meet different ones and leave with them. We pulled in the businessmen one by one. They would…be asked a terrific amount of questions'. They would deny it and so forth and to shock them all they would show the strip of them arriving and them leaving with so on and so forth. Naturally, they were shocked. I believe there was a terrific amount of businessmen they got there. So the murder to this day has never been solved but those big businessmen, the blackmail angle came into it – homosexuals – big businessmen happily married and their families and so forth – blackmail. Glen told me straight openly. After them all denying it, the blackmail angle came in. Tony said to me once, a good hobby was photography. Glen told it to me: wouldn't you pay rather than ruin your children's lives and your business?"

Early in 1969 she moved her brothel into a bigger, more exclusive suite in a block of luxury units in Elizabeth Bay known as The Reef, built in an arc to maximize views down the hill to Elizabeth Bay on the Harbour. Fred Krahe was so impressed by the luxurious nature of the brothel that he suggested Shirley should hold a house-warming party. Champagne flowed as big businessmen, senior police and criminals ogled and cuddled Shirley's stock in trade. And someone took a lot of photographs.

Hallahan was such a frequent visitor that Shirley would say: "Glen Hallahan lived in my brothel at 19 Ithaca Road, Elizabeth Bay."

Brisbane was now fast catching up with the rest of the world. Trams disappeared from the city in 1969, the new Victoria Bridge across the Brisbane River opened, and after two years of demolition and digging, King George Square emerged as a welcome open space in the city centre. It was also the year when, said honest detective Basil Hicks, Hallahan and Tony Murphy imported a notorious Sydney gunman named Donald Smith and his wife Linda to Brisbane to run prostitution from the Interlude Nightclub. Shirley recalled: "Freddy took Glen out to meet Donny and Linda at their place at Double Bay. Glen told me about the beautiful place. He said: Freddy wants them to go to Brisbane. Do you think it would be wise to let them go? Freddy rang from my place to Glen and asked about Donny and Linda coming up. He said: Glen is ringing me back to see if was alright for Donny and Linda to go up there. The phone call came back. It was alright. They went up."

The club became known as a hangout for some of Brisbane's worst criminals. Detective Basil Hicks wanted to take action to combat the robberies that were planned there and the fencing of stolen goods. Hallahan told him to stay away from the club - where he was allegedly involved in crimes such as sharing the proceeds of a $7,000 jewellery robbery.

But Hallahan found he couldn't control Donny and Linda, said Shirley. "Glen said 'Tell Freddy (Krahe) that I want to get rid of Donny and Linda'," she said. "Freddy was the actual handler of them. They went to Newcastle. They had done robberies and passed a few dud cheques. Glen was copping a lot of responsibility on these things. He gave them Newcastle. They went to Newcastle and from there to Western Australia and from there back to Sydney where Donnie got knocked off."

The Rat Pack had to appear to be doing something to combat crime and Murphy chalked up a world first for Queensland. He led a police raid on a music shop and seized 13 long-playing records of the Hair soundtrack. The magistrate declared the record obscene and banned it from sale.

Fred Krahe's whim to hold a house-warming party for Shirley's new brothel was about to cause a series of escalating problems. Two of Shirley's friends saw a way of making a quick buck and told Sydney's Sunday Mirror about the party, the photos and the scale of the business. The newspaper sent an undercover reporter to the brothel posing as a businessman. On June 8 the only story on the front page of the Sunday Mirror carried a massive headline: **SYDNEY'S RICHEST CALL-GIRL**. A smaller heading read: **$5000 a week from knights, pop stars, tycoons**. And at the bottom of the page in large type: **More Facts, Pictures – P2**. The story read: "She earns $5000 a week and her clients include wealthy businessmen, graziers, politicians - and a millionaire and his two sons." She also had a five-bedroom house on the North Shore, two homes in Brisbane and a flat at Surfers Paradise. Oil paintings adorned the walls, a chandelier lit the main room and guests sat in velvet arm chairs. Shirley wore a full-length silk robe while colleague Carol wore a see-through shortie negligee, brief black panties and a small brassiere as the reporter sipped on a Scotch. One night in the week the girls had entertained six businessmen, two comedians from the club circuit and later two politicians. On page 2 were two photos of Carol. Shirley refused to be photographed because she said she did not want her children to know what she was doing.

A week later she was again the main story in the paper. **'$5000 CALL-GIRL THREATS BY RICH CLIENTS'** ran the headline. The story said: "Sydney's highest paid call-girl is living in terror behind the locked doors of her luxurious Elizabeth Bay apartment. She is in fear because a number of her wealthy and powerful clients have made threats on her life." These men feared she could reveal their identities. The taxman had also called. On June 29 the Mirror again led the paper on Shirley: **'RICH LOVERS DUMPED GORGEOUS PLAYGIRL VANISHES'**, saying she had now vanished from her home. It was believed she could have gone to Brisbane where her name had been linked with politicians and senior public servants.

Shirley hated the publicity and was desperately trying to stop it. More newspaper exposes were threatened. A friend in publishing advised her to contact the ABC and put a stop to it by going public on television. She went to see Gerald Stone, later to produce 60 Minutes, who was the big name on the current affairs program This Day Tonight. He persuaded her to do a face-to-face interview which went to air on July 3, causing a nationwide stir. Shirley told how she had 'starred' in the National Hotel Inquiry.

Shirley reopened in a new brothel in two flats at 12 Wylde Street, Potts Point, a seven-story block of units which real estate blurb says is at the Parisian end of Potts Point with a leafy outlook and harbour glimpses. She used her contacts to have her old phone number transferred immediately.

Bennett was watching these developments with great interest and wondering what might come next when, on Thursday August 7, 1969, he answered the phone in his office to hear the voice of Shirley Brifman, ringing from Sydney 35-3837. It was the first contact they had had for six years. Shirley apologised to Bennett for what she had done to him and told him about the fallout from the publicity.

Hallahan and Murphy had dropped her as a result of the publicity and she was "dirty on them" after all she had done for them.

The main man I'm out to get is Hallahan," she said. "He told me the taxation men were in Brisbane investigating all the police I had been connected with." Clyde and Kerry Packer, who had been to the brothel with their father Sir Frank, were also causing her trouble, she told Bennett.

She said she realised she had done a great disservice by committing perjury at the National Hotel Commission, fibbing for 220 police. "I'm frightened of getting knocked," she told him. "Some coppers are saying to gunnies 'If you don't knock her, we'll get you a stretch'." But for the moment she planned to stay on in Sydney.

On October 9 Shirley was back in touch on the phone. "I'm frightened," she told Bennett. "I'm scared stiff." She said Hallahan was spending six weeks in Sydney, living in her brothel on 200 per cent penalty rates. "He never leaves me alone," she complained. Tony Murphy had told her: "If Glen comes undone we all go together."

According to Hallahan, who probably had an ulterior motive for telling the story, she had reason to be frightened. Many years later he told investigators in a statement: "As at this time she had made at least three attempts on her life by taking an overdose of sleeping tablets…she was admitted to the Wallsend Hospital near Newcastle suffering from an overdose of sleeping tablets. When she recovered she told the attending doctor that the tablets had been forced down her throat by Ron Lenton, a reporter with the Sydney Telegraph, and an ex boyfriend named Ron Williams. According to her, this was done at the instigation of Sir Frank Packer and the then commissioner of police in NSW, Mr Norman Allen. The doctor reported the matter to the police and investigations were made by the divisional inspector from Newcastle. When he interviewed Brifman she withdrew her allegations and maintained that she did not tell the doctor the allegations at all."

In November 1969 a Brisbane warehouse was broken into and tobacco worth $13,000 was stolen. Unfortunately, we only have Hallahan's version of what happened next. On November 20 Hallahan and Sid Currey raided the home of 28-year-old wharfie Carl Markert and found 26 cartons of tobacco and $6013 in cash. The reason why we don't have Markert's version of events will become apparent.

By the time Markert arrived at a magistrates court to plead guilty to the theft, the money had gone. The story told to the court by Hallahan and another officer was that Markert had convinced them that the money was not part of the ill-gotten gains from the robbery but was a case of that old standby of people found with more money than they earn – he had won the money at the races. They had given it all back to him (they said) but then Markert had lost it all at the next race meeting. Markert, a 28-year-old wharfie, broke down and wept as the story was told. The story was given more credence when Hallahan explained that Markert's only share from the proceeds had been $300. The magistrate decided that because of the seriousness of the charge he should send Markert to the District Court for sentencing.

Having learned what Hallahan was capable of, you may think that the $6013 was, indeed, the proceeds of crime and that Hallahan and his colleague may have pocketed the notes and invented the stories of the racing win and loss. It may also explain why Markert might have vowed to tell all when he appeared for sentencing. It would certainly explain why two men would have wanted to convince Markert not to say a word at his sentencing. On March 25 1970 two men armed with a .22 rifle called on him to take him for a ride to Victoria Park, a few acres of greenery with large dark areas on the northern edge of Spring Hill, the old working class suburb to the north of the central business district. At gunpoint they told him they had heard he was planning to talk. They would 'get' his wife and four young children if he talked, they said. To ram home their point the man with the rifle calmly and coldly shot him through his right shoulder.

Luckily, Victoria Park is right next to Royal Brisbane Hospital.

The bullet had cut nerves and limited the use of his arm for good, meaning that he would never work as a wharfie again. The prosecutor told the District Court judge that Markert had been shot by two accomplices who believed he was going to squeal about their identities. Markert had refused to identify them and they had not been caught. The judge said he considered the threats of violence to Markert and his family, Markert having been shot and having suffered a disability probably were a greater punishment than he could inflict. Markert was placed on probation but suffered one final slap in the face. He was banned from any form of gambling for two years.

At the beginning of February 1970, Shirley flew to Singapore with three other call girls at the invitation of a mining tycoon to entertain Asian businessmen. They were installed in a luxurious flat and guarded by a former Singapore police officer but Shirley became suspicious that this was just a front for a slavery racket. It didn't take her long to find out her suspicions were correct. "I know all their names and addresses because the first thing I did was get this ex-police guard into the cot to find out what he knew," she said. The prostitutes fled Singapore after a week but on February 19 she received a phone call from the Australian agent for the Singapore syndicate warning her: "If you talk, you're dead'. Six days later an Asian man had come to her Wylde Street brothel and attacked her with a hammer, giving her two black eyes and a badly bruised nose. Once again Shirley was front page news in the Sunday Mirror.

"Krahe came up to my place in a panic," said Shirley. A new superior had taken office and had taken a shot at Krahe about the white slaves report. It was too hot for Shirley to stay in Sydney. He suggested she should relocate to Western Australia. It was the last time Krahe took protection money from her. She was now by herself. Starting a new business in Brisbane would be impossible without the help of Hallahan and the Rat Pack.

It's February 15, 1970 and a desperate businessman is ringing Radio 4BH's Open Line forum.

"I'm ringing from Clayfield," he said. "I have a complex legal problem which I hope the panel can sort out for me. I am the subject of a blackmail attempt. For a number of months now I have been paying out $50 a month to an individual to keep my name out of the press for some wrongdoing of mine. I've been prepared to pay this because I don't want the publicity."

In answer to questions from the startled panel of media personalities, Don Secombe, Ivor Hancock and Wendy Mansfield, he enlarged on his problem: "It would mean loss of a job. Actually, I feel I'm being blackmailed by a policeman. I'm a homosexual. It's definitely a policeman. I know it's a policeman. He rings me at work and tells me where. I've been forced into the open because he's demanding an increase to $100 which I can't afford to pay."

The panel advised him to report his allegations to the police minister or police commissioner. Inspector Austin Kunst ordered an investigation, telling the media: "The allegation is most serious and it is true we want to bring the police concerned to book. But no complaint has been made to me and the difficulties of locating the caller are enormous."

The victim told The Sunday Mail that two detectives were involved in the blackmailing. The paper reported that the detectives had first questioned him at a "haunt in Brisbane of sexual deviates". Since then they had demanded $50 a month to keep him from being charged.

The businessman received a pointed phone call from the blackmailing policeman: "You are a very foolish man. You could end up like Gary Venamore." The victim was either very foolish or very brave. Without revealing his identity to the public he went on television to talk about the calls. Whether he survived or not is unknown.

The Venamore murder was never solved. The blackmailers were never brought to justice.

On March 10, 1970, Hallahan gave up his bachelorhood and married in Sydney. He contrived to stay in Sydney until April 22. By now, according to anti-corruption campaigner Dr Bertram Wainer, not only was there graft being paid to police for prostitution and marijuana but also for heroin being landed in Queensland before its journey south. After making the accusation Queensland police had put a contract out on his life, he said.

It's now that the image of a prostitute with a heart of gold is shattered. The enormous wealth and champagne parties created an illusion of success. But Shirley's daughter Mary Anne revealed to investigating lawyers in 1988 it had become a sordid life of excess and degradation: "She used to take, um, uppers and downers, sleepers, strong sleeping tablets, tuinal, um, when I was 13 she used to offer me purple hearts if I wanted any and pep pills and, um, she used to take tablets to wake up, tablets to go to sleep, um, and she used to have morphine.

"When I was 13 I was taken to a unit and held prisoner there, in a sense, and, um, I was forced to work as a call girl or prostitute and when the detectives finally came and I was so relieved to see them, not knowing that I would get my parents into so much trouble relating to that charge and my father did go to jail over it. My mother took me there. And I don't think she meant for anything to happen there but my father came up and I probably looked 16 and I was extremely pretty and just one of their wealthy clients wanted to see me and when I told him that I'd never done anything before he didn't realise I was their daughter he then offered to pay more and then that's how I ended up staying there and my father kept me there for 10 weeks I think, something like that until the police came. I wasn't streetwise enough to know how to run away. I tried to kill myself there and they took me to a private hospital and then I was taken back there."

What kept her there? "There was another lady that always lived there...and there were other girls that came in as well (it was) a brothel. They just knew that I wouldn't run away. And then my mother went to hospital because she had to have a couple of operations and that's when she taught me how all the business worked....and I resigned myself to the fact that I would be there till I was 18, until I thought I was old enough to run away. You know I just, sounds ridiculous but that's just how it was."

The detective who found her wasn't on the corrupt payroll and acted in a fatherly way. She was put in a home for about three or four weeks. "And, um, then finally I went into my aunt's custody in Queensland. My aunt was 20 years older than my mother. She was the very opposite. She was a Jehovah's Witness. And, um, extremely religious."

Sonny and Shirley were charged with introducing Mary Anne to prostitution. Shirley was at her lowest ebb. Her old mate Val Weidinger had died. "I got charged the same week as I buried Val. I buried her on the Monday and I got charged on the Friday."

Sonny went to prison but Shirley was remanded on bail week after week.

Chapter 20 - Strife at the Top 1965-70 –

Exit Bischof Muttering Madly

Queensland continued to be regarded as the Deep North. In 1965 Les Ballets Africains danced bare-breasted across Australia until they came to Brisbane where the dancers were ordered to wear ill-fitting bras. The man who led the protests against "the inherent lechery" of the ballet complained: "The frenzied oscillation of the breasts and buttocks – known as the bump and grind routine – is calculated to excite the sexual passion in the male." The following year Sunday Truth objected to the government forcing women to serve on juries. "Few men favour the idea of throwing their womenfolk into a cesspool of filth – and that is what a lot of our court actions involve. No woman of decent background could fail to be deeply shocked."

Bennett had been exposing corruption for six years when the State went to the polls on May 28, 1966. The result? Despite recording its lowest vote for a decade at 18.9 per cent, the Country Party actually picked up an extra seat to give it 27 while the Liberals stayed put on 20 seats and Labor remained with 26. The result meant that in coalition with the Liberals as junior partners, the Country Party continued to allow corruption to flourish.

Commissioner Bischof's double dealings with illegal SP bookies were preying on his nerves. He began to suffer from serious hypertension and paranoia. He was first admitted to hospital on October 11, 1965, for two weeks and needed a two-week cruise afterwards to convalesce. He was in hospital again in April 1967 and again in June, reportedly suffering from hypertension with newspapers suggesting he was so ill that he would not be returning to his desk.

Trasurer Sir Thomas Hiley recalled: "I am still convinced that Bischof's compulsive and stupid betting led him to seek the double dip from people who were paying him money for protection. I am convinced that this is what brought him down in the end. During one of Bischof's stays in hospital former Federal Treasurer Sir Arthur Fadden was also a patient. Fadden was a close friend of mine. He told me that Bischof was in a bad way and as soon as it got dark he became obsessed with the notion that he was being followed by people who wanted to harm him. He would go along the corridors of the hospital saying: 'They're after me.' As soon as the sun would go out of the sky he would become a victim of his own fears. He'd hide in the laundry rooms, he'd hide in the ironing rooms. He'd hide anywhere. He'd never stop in his own room at night. And there were search parties out at St Helen's and St Andrew's and the Holy Spirit trying to find

Bischof after dark, you see, and when they'd get him he'd be a quivering shaking morsel: 'They're after me, I can hear the voices, they're after me, they're after me.'"

This would tie in with psychiatric evidence given to a later court hearing that Bischof was suffering from a severe form of psychotic depression – an illness in which sufferers experience delusions and, occasionally, hallucinations.

In December 1968 it was announced that Norwin Bauer, the corrupt Freemason, would succeed Bischof in February 1969 but would only have a short time at the top before turning 65 in October 1970. Bischof was in such a bad state that he almost missed his own farewell, being hospitalized again in February 1969 with a gala testimonial dinner for him planned for March 3 at City Hall. He was discharged just in time to join 250 people at the dinner – 150 less than expected, despite regular editorial mentions from Sunday Truth, where Ron Richards was now deputy editor.

Lewis and Murphy were being pushed up the promotional ladder by Bischof as part of the succession plan. In 1966 they were both promoted to sergeant first class. In 1968 Lewis set off on a three-month world trip paid for by the Churchill Fellowship scheme to study foreign police methods. Shirley was there to see him off and welcome him home again. By the end of the year he was a senior sergeant. But Hallahan, being junior to the other two and having spent a year in Cyprus, was lagging behind. In July 1968 Bischof directed the Police Promotions Board to promote Hallahan to the rank of detective sergeant, ahead of others in the queue. When rivals appealed against the promotion, Hallahan brazenly claimed he was responsible for 90 per cent of the clean-up of crime in Queensland.

Bennett, representing one of the complainants, said that claim was a shocking indictment of the force because it meant every other detective was loafing. Inspector Abe Duncan appeared for the Commissioner and described Hallahan as an outstanding detective who possessed far greater knowledge of the duties expected for the position than the other applicants.

Don Lane was also lagging behind the others but he switched from the consorting squad to the special branch, spying on opponents of the government such as the Queensland Peace Committee, the Union of Australian Women and people opposed to the Vietnam War. The special branch also checked people selected to serve on juries for 'reliability' and 'attitude towards the Crown, law and justice'. It was the sort of spy agency which could easily be used by any unscrupulous member for the wrong reasons. Lane occupied an office next to Terry Lewis which made it easy to keep in touch each day.

The sudden death of Queensland Premier Jack Pizzey on July 31 1968 aged 57 after less than seven months in office, triggered a series of leadership changes that would prove to be the biggest challenge yet to Bischof, Bauer, Hallahan and their crooked cohorts.

Here we meet a country MP who appears at first glance to be Queensland's Jim Hacker. Truth reported on August 4 how the 'rather self-effacing' Johannes Bjelke-Petersen, probably one of the least known Cabinet Ministers, was about to challenge to become State Premier. "He has generally been content to go along quietly, rarely infusing overmuch spirit into his debates," said the paper. "Many of his own colleagues frankly have regarded him as the rather unworldly member of the team, a man happiest when he was throwing himself into church and Sunday school activities in the Kingaroy district."

Home was a peanut farm on 460 acres of land at Kingaroy, some 220 kilometres north-west of Brisbane, which his father, a Lutheran pastor, had named Bethany. Jo, as he was called at the time, still took the senior Sunday School class at the local Lutheran church hall.

He was grossly under-educated, having left the village primary school at Taabinga at the age of 13 and was barely articulate, often speaking in a succession of unfinished sentences but this hadn't prevented him from making a fortune through contract land clearing and aerial spraying companies.

He appeared to be a bumbling country bumpkin, as honest as the day was long, a committed Christian, a man who worked from dawn to midnight and was totally opposed to gambling, drinking and fornicating. At least, that was the widely-held, overwhelming perception! And having succeeded in his bid to become Premier, his first public appearance was to read the Bible in George St, in front of his office, for 30 minutes during a Bible readathon.

But a judge's decision in an income tax case discovered by Col Bennett revealed Bjelke-Petersen had been less than honest. The fiddle involved selling an oil prospecting authority obtained from his friend and Mines Minister Ernie Evans. Trafficking in these authorities was forbidden by the Mines Department. Because they were deemed to be assets of the state they could only be transferred for nominal sums. Bjelke-Petersen had declared in writing to the Government he was selling the authority for 2 pounds. In fact, he gained 12,650 pounds plus a 49 per cent interest in the company buying the authority. "The company was forced to accept this part of the deal even though it didn't regard the area as worth prospecting," said the Opposition. A new company called Exoil was floated with 16 million shares. One of its objectives was to acquire Bjelke-Petersen's company. For this Bjelke-Petersen's company was to receive 250,000 pounds plus royalties. His company had a million shares in Exoil and according to Bjelke-Petersen's own company report, the value of them was 360,000 pounds. Mr Justice Taylor found Bjelke-Petersen had perpetrated a fraud on the Minister for Mines.

And during six months as Police Minister he had made no public attempt to get rid of the corrupt Bischof or have an investigation made of the rot that had become endemic in the force. Nor did he do anything to have an illegal SP bookmaker who operated prominently in Kingaroy prosecuted or closed. So it seems he would have been aware of the importance of the police portfolio which was handy when it came to matters such as having minor traffic violations dropped for friends who could later be called on for a quid-pro-quo; such as using the special branch to gather information on opponents; and such as turning a blind eye to SP betting and after-hours drinking when required by colleagues. At any rate, on top of all his other duties, Jo retained the police portfolio under his wing. But four months later the workload was proving too much. There had been accusations in the House that the police department was virtually being allowed to run itself. Truth announced on December 15, 1968, that the Premier was finding the police portfolio too much for him, with the most junior Minister, Max Hodges, likely to be handed the portfolio.

Hodges, a short, tubby, quick, likeable, 52-year-old, was a self-educated man who, in the depression had taken jobs hewing sleepers, felling scrub, cutting cane and working on a dairy farm. He recalled that his working day on the farm was from 3am to 9pm, with the rest of the evening spent studying business and administration by correspondence course. He eventually became secretary-manager of his local fruit-growers' co-operative and was elected to Parliament in 1957.

Col Bennett and the Labor Party had publicised the way in which the Government was shoring up crooked police and had exposed Bjelke-Petersen's greed and disregard for public opinion. But at the 1969 general election the Country Party vote went up by three per cent. With only a fifth of the votes they gained a third of the seats and remained the senior party in the conservative coalition.

Bjelke-Petersen liked to have things his own way in Cabinet and might have expected that a junior minister could be bullied into being a 'yes' man, giving Bjelke-Petersen effective control over his police force. But Hodges would turn out to be his own man, a dynamo and honest.

Soon after assuming responsibility for the police portfolio Max Hodges started planning a total overhaul of the force and the installation of someone from outside Queensland who could provide Queensland with a modern, professional, clean police force.

What he couldn't do was provide Queensland with a modern outlook on life. As the swinging sixties loosened even more shackles elsewhere, respected actor Norman Staines was charged by police for using the phrase "fucking boongs" during a performance of Norm and Ahmed at the Twelfth Night Theatre. Country Party MP Russ Hinze (who would eventually be charged with bribery) launched a tirade in Parliament, suggesting that audiences at the theatre would comprise the sexually deprived or homosexuals, lesbians, wife-swappers or spivs. "To those who suggest we should emulate the United Kingdom, I refer to the latest importation from that country, the junkie Mick Jagger." Staines said he found the racially-derogative "boong" much more offensive than "fucking". He was convicted by a magistrate but the Full Court quashed the conviction. And in 1969 tourists on the Gold Coast were being arrested for drinking alcohol in night clubs. On the other hand, high-rise buildings were starting to appear on the Brisbane skyline and a new theatre opened.

Police Minister Hodges invited respected South Australian Police Commissioner Brigadier John McKinna, who had reformed and modernised his own force, to spend six weeks from October 26 investigating the organisation of the Queensland force and to make recommendations on what he believed was necessary to create an efficient force.

McKinna's report gave Bischof's police force an E minus. His main recommendation, made in private, was that Hodges should hire one of McKinna's protégés, Ray Whitrod, as commissioner.

The report also made Hodges realise that Queensland could not afford another year of Norwin Bauer as Commissioner. Bauer wasn't due to retire until October 1970 but Hodges persuaded him to leave early in 1970 by offering him an all-expenses world trip in the guise of a four-month fact-finding tour to discover what other countries were doing to improve policing. He would leave on April 30 to travel to 20 countries including Hong Kong, Israel, Greece, Italy, the United Kingdom and Ireland, France, Germany and the United States.

The Rat Pack could see that Bischof's succession plans were under threat. Lewis became aware of the Bauer trip as early as December 23, 1969, when Bauer asked him for a briefing on the overseas trip Lewis had taken as part of his Churchill Scholarship. Lewis knew that Hodges would be on holiday on the Gold Coast and on December 27 he arranged to meet him. No doubt he lobbied him about the need to ensure that a Queensland officer such as Bill Simpson was appointed to follow Bauer.

But in early January 1970 Hodges let the media know that he planned to tell Cabinet he wanted an outsider as police chief. The man he wanted was Ray Whitrod, McKinna's protégé.

Whitrod was interviewed by Cabinet and was up against local contenders, including Bill 'The Smoothie" Simpson. Whitrod remembered: "The Catholics had their man, the Irish had their man, and the Masons had their man, and they were nominating each of these very strongly. So in a sense I was a sort of ... sort of a half-way choice." But Minister for Local

Government and Electricity Wally Rae had been attached to the Royal Air Force with Whitrod in the Second World War and gave Max Hodges a lot of support for his appointment.

Whitrod was 54, a practising Baptist, who had been born and spent his childhood years in a tiny Adelaide home with just three rooms with a rent made smaller by its proximity to a carcass-rendering factory. As a teenager he cycled hundreds of miles looking for work before coming first in a test for police recruits and joining the South Australian force as a messenger at 18. He became a plainclothes constable at 21 and a fully-fledged detective at 23. When he caught an underage woman betting at the totalisator at the races he told her he would have to report her. Father was a prominent member of the Jockey Club committee who sought out the senior sergeant to see if the matter could be fixed. When the sergeant discovered the reporting officer was Whitrod he told the father: "No chance." The young detective rose rapidly through the ranks. After war service as an officer with the RAF he helped set up ASIO, of which he became assistant director. In 1960 he had been made Commonwealth Police Commissioner and had taken a degree in economics at the Australian National University. He also had a postgraduate diploma in criminology from Cambridge University.

We don't know whether Cabinet chose to do the right thing and clean up the force or if it couldn't agree on which local candidate to select and settled on Whitrod as a compromise, as Whitrod suspected. For whatever reason, Queenslanders were the winners when this scrupulously honest man was anointed. He may well have been Queensland's first honest police commissioner.

Hallahan and the Rat Pack could see the danger signs. If they could get rid of Hodges, there was a chance that a new police minister might reverse the decision on Whitrod. Even before January was out the police union lobbied other ministers to have the administration of the police force removed from Hodges' stewardship, citing the fact that deserving Queensland officers had been overlooked. Hodges stood firm and Truth reported that he had put down a rebellion.

Bauer was due to disappear on his retirement junket on April 30 but Hodges was so anxious to start the reform process that he couldn't even wait until Bauer was walking up the gangplank. He appointed Whitrod Acting Police Commissioner from Monday, April 13, 1970, three days before his 55th birthday. A couple of days later he received an informal royal commendation. During the Royal Tour of Queensland the Queen told Hodges: "Queensland is fortunate in having a man like Whitrod as Commissioner of Police."

Chapter 21 - The Rat Pack Attacks

an Honest Commissioner

Queensland now had an honest Police Minister and an honest Police Commissioner. It also had the Rat Pack which was backed by the Police Union.

Whitrod described the Rat Pack as very good operators, smart operators who were a very powerful group. In particular he discovered the way Hallahan almost commuted to and from Sydney on corrupt business. He "formed the opinion that Murphy clearly was the controller. In comparison, Glen Hallahan was a very bright, good-looking, active young man and a very capable operator. Murphy and Hallahan were, in my view, superior to Lewis. Terry Lewis had something about him that worried me. I never knew what it was but I thought he was not as robust as the other two."

Don Lane was also under close scrutiny.

But no-one told Whitrod the story of Bischof and the statewide SP bookie protection racket.

"I knew nothing about this," Whitrod recalled in an ABC interview. "Joh Bjelke-Petersen never told me that the whole of Queensland police force was operating on the understanding that SP bookmakers were not to be prosecuted. Now this meant a number of things. It meant that the police controlled most of the slush money, which was going to politicians, which meant that they, the police, really controlled votes in Parliament and also they were on very good speaking terms with politicians so that if the local sergeant of police of a country town didn't like one of my reforms, he would talk to the local politician, who owed him a lot of favours and so I had great difficulty in getting things through the Queensland Parliament."

Whitrod and Hodges might have been avuncular, balding, bespectacled, slightly tubby and unfashionable but when these two self-educated and self-made men donned their official mantles they became a dynamic duo in terms of a determination to stamp out corruption and modernise the police force.

Brigadier McKinna had made about 15 specific recommendations for the improvement of the force and Cabinet instructed Whitrod to carry them out. They included promotion by merit instead of seniority, greater delegation of authority down the ranks, the introduction of an operations centre and much improved education and training. These were all set out very clearly and handed to him by Hodges, who said, 'Ray, Cabinet would like you to bring these into effect'. In addition, Whitrod made it clear he would hold genuine inquiries into allegations of corruption, verballing and bashing, and get rid of guilty officers; and move officers from cushy jobs such as in the licensing and consorting squads.

He was soon under enormous pressure. "The media were very much in the pockets of the police roundsmen who were in the pockets of the detectives for information," said Whitrod. "We had a silent number at home, but I had to leave the number at police operational headquarters for them to contact me, and we would get calls at three o'clock in the morning inquiring about our health. In fact we had a heart specialist call, personally, at three o'clock in the morning because he'd been told by police headquarters that I was having a heart attack. We often had taxis coming, knocking at our door, at two o'clock, one o'clock, four o'clock in the morning, to take me to the airport. We had a load of gravel delivered on our front garden that we'd never ordered.

"My little team that were helping me were attacked through the media as turncoats and traitors to the cause of police. They had a very rough time and so did their families, and (my wife) Mavis had a very rough time. She - she really tried to shield me from this attack."

The Rat Pack and the Police Union fought the new regime from its inception. Hallahan, Murphy, Lewis and Don Lane met to formulate their tactics. Lane later described himself as the chairman of the Get Rid of Whitrod Committee and admitted publicly that opposition to the new Commissioner was generated from within the Criminal Investigation Branch where the men comprised the most cohesive group, had the best contacts in the media and had been taught to be flexible, "even to the extent of bending rules when necessary".

Hallahan was about to tear up the rules in a big way. He had established a close relationship with a small-time criminal by the name of Donald Ross Kelly.

We'll rely on Kelly's version of what the two of them got up to.

Kelly, aged 36, had experienced a troubled childhood in Sydney after moving there with his mother from the tiny township of St George in Queensland's far, rural south. At 10 he was so unruly his mother had him admitted to Boys Town in an attempt to bring him under care and control. He left at 15 to work in shearing sheds throughout the eastern states and became involved in opportunistic crimes. Somewhere along the way he had lost a finger. He first met Hallahan in 1958 after a fight in a hotel. They met again in 1959 when Kelly was charged with using obscene language and resisting arrest. He was jailed for a year in Victoria in 1962 for theft and a further three years in 1966. Hallahan had arrested him in Brisbane in July 1969 on a New South Wales charge that he had committed a $30,000 jewellery store burglary in Sydney. The arrest meant he would be extradited to Sydney. Kelly had been due to get married in Brisbane the following month and was distraught at the prospect of having to postpone or even

142 The Most Dangerous Detective

cancel the wedding. Hallahan told him that if he didn't fight the extradition he would arrange for him to get bail in Sydney. Hallahan even arranged to have Kelly's car taken to the water police yard and looked after while he was away. When Kelly returned to Brisbane to get married he rang Hallahan and arranged to pick up the car.

Hallahan ensured Kelly realised he was deeply in debt to him for being free to return to Brisbane for his wedding – it was a hold that Hallahan would never relinquish.

Now, the recently-married Kelly, with two newly-acquired step-children and a baby of his own, was trying to go straight and had bought a truck and started a haulage business. But he was still wanted in Sydney for not adhering to his bail conditions. Hallahan charged him $5,000 for ensuring his survival in Brisbane and told him he would have to carry out robberies and split the loot with Hallahan.

Kelly was constantly worried that he might be recognised by the police and rang Hallahan up to three times a week to check if anyone was on to him. In May 1970 he was indeed recognised in Fortitude Valley getting into a car but police lost him in the traffic. Hallahan told him: "They will have to circulate your number - they will have to put it down that they saw you in that car. It will be all right but it will cost you to get it pulled out." Hallahan's price was $700 which was paid at a meeting in New Farm Park.

Several weeks later Hallahan arranged for Kelly to rob an electrical store and to hand over the goods after dark at one of his favourite clandestine meeting points, the Newmarket Hotel's vast and unkempt car park where hummocks of earth and vast weeds obscured large areas. The car park was the size of several football fields, had no lighting and had long frontages to streets on opposite sides, making it ideal for such meetings. Hallahan turned up in his top-of-the-range light grey six-cylinder Holden Premier Sedan and told Kelly: "It's no good fooling around with these thin jobs - I have got a good bank lined up. I've got good mail on it. I've got word that there is $96,000 in the vault in the Bank of New South Wales at Kedron. The best time to do it is about one o'clock because they have only got a skeleton staff on in the lunch hour. It will have to go off on Thursday because that's when they have the money in there for the pay rolls. If you do it this Thursday I will be working 2 to 10. If you do it at one o'clock I will be around the corner in a police car with a siren on it. If a call comes through that you have come unstuck I will hit the siren to give you time to get out of the bank and away."

Kelly agreed: "All right, I'll do it." He had a friend, Charlie Fuller, up in Brisbane from Sydney who would do the job with him.

It was about 1.40 pm on August 6 when an alert teller at the Kedron branch of the Bank of New South Wales called Bill Glasson noticed a bearded man in a grey dust coat, Beatles wig and white towelling hat walking towards the back door of the bank with a man who pulled out a sawn off rifle. It was Kelly and Fuller. Kelly had a loaded automatic pistol in his hand and leapt over the counter shouting: "Don't move or I'll shoot." But he was too late. Glasson had run into the strong room and locked himself in with most of the bank's cash. Charlie Fuller pointed the rifle in the direction of the accountant's office where the bank staff had huddled. All Kelly could do was grab money from the drawers on the office side of the counter and then leap back on to the public side of the counter. Another teller, Vince Casey, activated the security camera. Kelly ordered staff in general 'Don't touch anything, don't be a hero' and made off through the front door with Fuller. Glasson dashed out of the front door and noticed the men going off in a white Valiant sedan PDE 625. Kelly and Fuller had only been able to grab about $3000 from the tellers' drawers. Police were handed 146 still photos.

Kelly rang Hallahan that night to be told: "You have no worries, Donny, they have only got five or six photos and they don't look like you. They won't be able to identify you."

Next day Hallahan drove into the vast car park at the Newmarket Hotel to collect his share of the booty. It was only after he had taken his cut of $900 that he told Kelly: "I've got a bit of bad news for you Donny. Your name got pulled out of the hat this morning by one of the young detectives. He's the same bloke that spotted you that time in the Valley in the Holden. He spotted your finger missing this morning in one of the photos and he says it just has to be you. The description the woman gave of the car fits the one he saw you in. He reckons the woman must have made a mistake with the middle letter. They have all been briefed to get you."

Kelly said: "He's no right to put the car number in because I paid the bastard to forget about that."

Hallahan said: "This is too big, Donny. No-one will risk his job to hush up this type of job for that amount of money. They have brought out a new batch of photos this morning."

Kelly moved house and made a point of not telling Hallahan about his new address.

Don Lane, still only a detective senior constable at the age of 35 after 19 years in the force, had made greater progress in the Liberal Party in which he was chairman of the Brisbane federal division and a member of the state executive. Having suffered for so long from the Parliamentary barbs of Col Bennett, the Rat Pack could see the value of political power and representation. When the Liberal MP for Merthyr announced on March 29, 1971, that he would retire on June 30 Lane grabbed the seat, which had been Liberal for 14 years, for himself, despite having been delegated to create a process of finding suitable candidates. To start his campaign he contacted his mate Ron Richards on the Sunday Truth, which reported on April 4 that it was tipped that Lane would be standing. When nominations for the Liberal candidature closed there was only one person, a newcomer to Queensland, who had failed to realise that Don's name was as good as printed on the ballot papers and he was easily beaten. The by-election was set for July 24. Lane's biggest problem seemed to be his police nickname which the Labor Party now seized on with great glee - Shady Lane!

Corruption conquered another bastion of the establishment in June when Norwin Bauer became grand master of the United Grand Lodge of Queensland, being deferred to and respected by Cabinet Ministers, judges and public service heads when they met in secret session.

Chapter 22 - Shirley Tips a Bucket

According to Mary Anne Brifman, Shirley expected Hallahan, Murphy or Lewis to intercede and arrange for her charge to be dropped.

"She was very determined because it was really her only hope," said Mary Anne. " That's why she was growing more and more depressed...and that's why she was growing more angry with them and it blotted her vision so that she couldn't realise that they weren't going to do anything with her and she was not about to let them get away with it. She was definitely going to um say a lot more, a lot of things about um Terry Lewis and Tony Murphy."

The final straw came at the beginning of June 1971 when Shirley was finally committed for trial. Bail was set at $400. This was no problem for her. She had plenty of cash. But the 'friend' who was supposed to deliver the $400 was advised by a senior police officer to take the money and run, leaving Shirley in the lurch. Now she was remanded in custody in Silverwater Prison. She was livid and vowed revenge on the police who had let her down. To keep herself occupied she asked to work and was kept busy scrubbing floors. Having weighed about 51 kilos when she was thrown in jail, she was down to 45 when her sister found out what had happened to her and bailed her out. She was released on Sunday June 13 determind to have her revenge.

On Tuesday June 15 she rang a friend in the publishing world who by chance had been contacted by Gerald Stone, the ABC journo. Stone had been looking for her while she had been inside. She rang him at the ABC and he asked her to come straight over. He would send a taxi for her. She arrived at the studios in late afternoon to find the whole place buzzing. She was rushed upstairs to see Gerald who told her the idea was to get her on the This Day Tonight current affairs show that night. There were less than two hours to go. A couple of beers helped her on her way. Suddenly, she was in the studio and talking to Gerald before a nationwide audience. And this time she let fly.

She told the country how she had committed perjury at the National Hotel Commission and why, although she did not name names. She had, indeed, worked as a prostitute at the hotel both before and at the time of the hearings. She had lied about the extent of her acquaintances among members of the Queensland force and about their knowledge of her activities. She said she had not received any immediate benefit for her evidence apart from having saved the lives of herself and her children and having been given immunity from prosecution. Since 1965 she had paid money every week to Sydney police so that she could work as a brothel keeper. But now she had been charged by Sydney police and would probably go to jail. Stone asked her why she had chosen now to make this statement. "Because I am now on charges and my children are suffering for this," she said. "My father brought me up the right way. He always told me to do the right thing and so, for the first time in my life, I'm doing it. Sometimes you've got to tell the truth sooner or later."

The story made only 19 paragraphs in Queensland's Courier-Mail next morning and for some reason was written in Melbourne rather than in Sydney, where the program originated, or Brisbane, where the commission had been held and where repercussions were most likely. It merited just 15 paragraphs in Brisbane's afternoon Telegraph. Nevertheless, it had more of a shock effect on the public than it did on the crooked police. It seemed the Rat Pack still felt completely invulnerable. Despite the appointment of Whitrod, the structure they had created under Bischof and Bauer was still largely in place. They had survived the National Hotel Inquiry unscathed. What had they to fear? They had the support of the union and there was still support at a political level. All they needed to do was frighten Shirley into keeping her mouth shut.

"Tony rang my sister the day after I was on TV," said Shirley. "He said: *She was on TV last night. Has she gone completely mad? There will never be another Royal Commission in this State. We won't allow it*. Tony went completely off with my sister. I haven't seen him since. He said to Terry Lewis: *One woman I could trust with my life – she has now brought me undone*.""

Shirley believed her life was now in danger. There were crooked cops who would stop at nothing to silence her if they thought she would carry out her threat to tell all. She went into hiding in a friend's flat above a shop in Victoria St, Potts Point, Sydney, with a beefy male friend to mind her. But someone was talking. Early on Friday June 18 a reporter from the Sunday Mail knocked on the door. "I'm supposed to be in hiding," she said. "No one should know where to find me." The guard was snoring on a nearby bed. "I think I'm doing a better job guarding him," she said with a wry grin. That was bad enough and she was still puzzling over who would have given her address away when at 4pm there was another knock. Johnny 'Shotgun' Regan, one of the most feared gunnies in town, ignored Sonny and her minder. "Don't talk," he warned her. "If you talk you are dead." He spent an hour telling her how short her life could be. It left her drained.

Regan was a notorious killer. At 26 he was also known as The Boy because of his good looks. Nearly 180 centimetres tall, he had brown hair and blue eyes under hooded eyebrows with a scar on his upper lip. In official police files he was listed as: "Assailant, robber, gunman, sexual offender, forger, utterer, false pretender and car thief. Commenced his criminal career in 1962 and has since developed into a most vicious and incorrigible offender with an unparalleled record of crime and violence. A standover man among Sydney criminals and prostitutes and will adopt any tactics in efforts to intimidate them. On one occasion, using knuckle dusters, viciously assaulted a member of the underworld who dared to challenge his authority. Although evidence is currently not strong enough to support the claim, is believed to have been involved in the murder and mysterious disappearance of several members of the underworld. An astute and cunning criminal who has an intimate knowledge of police procedure and has been found on occasions to have police publications in his possession."

He certainly frightened Shirley. But she now had her mind firmly made up. Even if it meant a jail sentence, she would come back to Brisbane and tell an inquiry exactly what had happened. She would also have realised that Regan would not suffer in any way if she confessed everything. He would have been working for one or more of the corrupt police – someone with the ability to gain knowledge of where she was hiding. Someone such as Glen Patrick Hallahan.

But her busy day was not over yet. Another knock on the door signalled the arrival of two local cops who asked her to accompany them to the station at Smith and Campbell Streets. She refused but had a chat to them and agreed to see them on June 23 as long as a barrister and a Member of Parliament were also present. But Shirley didn't feel safe in Sydney and failed to keep the appointment.

On Tuesday, June 29, Shirley and Sonny walked into barrister Colin Bennett's chambers in Brisbane. It was the first time he had seen her for eight years. Bennett looked her up and down and decided she hadn't changed much: she was just looking a trifle weatherbeaten after her exertions in Sydney. And she was full of remorse for what she had done to Bennett at the National Hotel Inquiry and for the effects of her perjury. She surprised him by telling him a contract had been taken out on his life at the time!

Sonny had a briefcase with him and from this emerged two 'prizes' - letters from Tony Murphy to Shirley – or Marg, as he called her. Shirley handed them over to Bennett and told him that in the new police climate that now existed in Queensland she was prepared to tell honest cops everything she knew.

A signed letter from Murphy dated August 28, 1963, included: "By the way Marg, I would like to reassure you that anything you tell me in confidence will always be kept that way by myself and so consequently you need have no fear of my repeating anything you tell me in your letters to anyone, for I am only too aware of the position that it would put you in. If you are worried over anything in that regard, you can leave it to me to see everything is always covered as I have in fact already done at all times. The first time I'm in Sydney, which I don't think will be that long, I'll give you a ring just to have a mag about what's going on down there. Wishing yourself and Sonny all the best, cheerio for the present."

The later letter, written just before the National Hotel Inquiry, read in part: "In particular I was pleased to learn what you knew concerning this person David Young... We waited at 8pm last night for your phone call. I do hope that you clearly understand that any information you give re Young etc will be used by myself most discreetly.

"But most important now to put your mind at ease if you are in fact thinking that some policeman either from NSW or Queensland will land on your doorstep any tick of the clock, such will not be the case. If any member of the force is to interview you it will be myself...In other words Marg, the same rule applies in this case as has applied with respect to all the other info you have given me over the years and I do hope you trust me in this regard. You are at liberty to ring me at my home, 40-3832, if you think fit, as it is most imperative that I know as much as possible re Young in order that I can protect myself. Should you think that there are other things which might occur to you if I were to talk to you personally in Sydney, I think that such could be arranged."

The police officer chosen to go along to Bennett's chambers at the Inns of Court in North Quay overlooking the Brisbane River for the first interview, on July 2, 1971, was Abe Duncan. This may have been a major error by Whitrod who was still learning who could be trusted and who was corrupt. Duncan, who had championed Hallahan when his promotion had been challenged, had received a swift rise through the ranks, having been appointed Bischof's troubleshooter as his first posting after becoming a commissioned officer in 1967. He arrived with Constable Greg Early to take shorthand notes. Shirley was there with Bennett and his daughter Judith who acted as his secretary. At 4.45 pm the official business began. Bennett formally told Shirley: "You are not obliged to answer any questions but you may do so if you wish." And then down to business. "I did lie at the commission," said Shirley. She had been to the National Hotel many times for work. And when she said 'work', she said, she meant prostitution. Then she started naming names, going right back to 1959 when, she said, she had dealings with Hallahan, Murphy and Lewis. The first interview finished at 5.35pm. She had specifically agreed to tell Duncan of her movements.

Shirley moved into her sister's home in Brindle St, Paddington, a steep, narrow road with overhanging trees, grass verges and no pavements, deep in suburbia. The illusion of being lost in the backstreets was smashed by a knock at the door. Johnny Shotgun Regan had arrived. It was another warning, a demonstration that she could not escape. "How did you find me?" she asked. "I've got ways and means," he replied enigmatically.

Hallahan and the rest had underestimated Shirley's resolve. She immediately started hunting for a house with no links to anyone and rented 57 Vardon St, Wilston, a two-storey wooden house with a deep veranda in a much wider, paved road closer to the city. She swore Bennett to secrecy and told him that if any address had to be given for her, he should say she was still living at Brindle St.

Bennett wrote to Police Minister Hodges about the meeting and of the background to what had happened before the Inquiry and of his knowledge of the corruption that existed. "I was not free to mention this at the National Hotel Commission because as a client it would have been unethical for me to have done so," he wrote. "I am now free, however, to mention that I did act on her behalf prior to the National Hotel Commission because she has widely advertised the fact that she has been a practising prostitute for many years." He forwarded copies of Murphy's letters and suggested they might have some relevance.

Premier Bjelke-Petersen now found a means of being seen as a tough leader and of winning extra support from conservatives and the religious right. The South African rugby union team was due to tour Australia and play one of its games in Brisbane. Despite many Western governments favouring pressure on South Africa's apartheid policy by banning sporting links, Bjelke-Petersen saw Nelson Mandela and the ANC as communist terrorists. He supported the apartheid government. When land in north Queensland and the Northern Territory was being returned to Aboriginal he said it raised important defence issues. "Worse still, it also raises the frightening and disgusting spectre of providing ideal training grounds for foreign black terrorist groups. We are set to become the world's centre of terrorist violence and murder. The Federal Government has paved the way for this possibility by opening Australia's door to the South West African People's Organisation. There is no doubt that this group, SWAPO, is a terrorist organisation. They and other groups like them such as the PLO are looking for safe and isolated areas to organise and train."

When thousands took to the streets to oppose the rugby tour, Bjelke-Petersen used the media and police to portray the marchers as communist ratbags who were stopping traffic and disrupting honest, hard-working people trying to go about their jobs in the city. These were the same unpatriotic communists who were marching and demonstrating against our involvement in the Vietnam war, said the Premier. Unfortunately, many otherwise honest police agreed with him and many demonstrators were roughly handled. These confrontations drew more people to demonstrate against such treatment. Joh, as he was now known, portrayed himself as the upholder of law and order – and Detective Senior Constable Don Lane was the Government candidate for the seat of New

Farm. He won the by-election on July 24 with an increased majority and acknowledged that the law and order campaign had been responsible.

But the interviews with Shirley were unstoppable. By the seventh interview with police on July 29, Shirley was showing a series of snaps that had been taken at her "brothel-warming" party about three weeks before the Sunday Mirror story on her being the richest call girl in the country.

"This one shows Fred Krahe, me and my husband," she explained. "And this one shows Dutchy Van Houten's father - he is an ex-gunman - dancing with Lily Ryan. It shows Fred Krahe in the background." There were many others, each one explained by Shirley just as other people would show their snaps of the holiday in Bali. There were big business leaders, including Sir Frank Packer, who, she said, had brought sons Clyde and Kerry to Shirley's brothel in the past. There was a birthday card from Krahe signed 'Claude' - his middle name.

"If the Sunday Mirror had not published the article it would have been all right. When it was published everyone panicked," she said ruefully.

The problem with interviewing Shirley was that she gave bagatelle answers. A detective would launch what was a straightforward question and Shirley would start by answering it, only to suddenly bounce off on to a fascinating fragment of a story about crooked cops, or prostitutes or safe blowers. And then, before the detective could get a word in, she would bounce on to yet another anecdote. It would need many interviews, over many weeks and much patience from detectives to try to piece together Shirley's life of paying Hallahan, Krahe and other police protection money, of Hallahan and Krahe organising crimes and of other illegal activities.

On the same day that Shirley was showing her photo collection, police officers angry at not having been given free rein by Whitrod to confront protestors passed a vote of no confidence in their commissioner. They claimed that Whitrod had subjected them to danger of grave physical injury from rock throwers for a prolonged period and he had not allowed them to deal promptly with demonstrators. The term 'promptly' was union jargon for chasing and bashing. But Whitrod pointed out there had not been one case of an officer being injured.

There was more than one way of bringing Whitrod down. On a Tuesday evening in Townsville the sedate members of Jubilee Ladies' Bowling Club were sitting in rapt attention as a figure under a spotlight invoked time-honoured rituals: two little ducks, 22; dirty Gertie, number 30; Heinz Varieties, 57 – when the doors were flung open and the illegal gambling joint was raided by the police. Money was seized; names were taken, summonses were issued. Many ladies were charged with having been found in a common gaming house without lawful excuse. The demeaning episode was raised in Parliament and probably did more damage to the image of Whitrod's police than many of the crime-based stunts of the Police Union.

When he took his oath of allegiance in Parliament House Don Lane was wished a long, happy and - somewhat prophetically - rewarding stay in Parliament. Becoming an MP opened a new opportunity to extort money from the police protection payments. According to Jack Herbert, the corruption paymaster, Lane demanded half of whatever was collected from every brothel in his electorate. Often cutting, supercilious and disdainful, Lane decided that politicians were not much different to criminals: they were devious and dishonest. For a poor policeman who had only risen to the rank of senior constable he had somehow managed to assemble enough wealth to move out of his suburban home in The Gap and buy a mansion on nob hill at Hamilton with magnificent views over the Teneriffe Reach of the Brisbane River to the city beyond. Rather than employ tradesmen to renovate it, he gathered a few blokes from St Vinnie's - the welfare organisation – and paid them a pittance. He was also destined to remain very much in the public eye. Like Lewis, Murphy and Hallahan, Lane was a close friend of Sunday Truth's Ron Richards. Both acquired holiday homes on Bribie Island, with its magnificent surf beach. When Ron Richards became editor of the paper he told his reporters he wanted at least one paragraph of news on Don Lane every week.

Now the Rat Pack had the advantage of a representative in the corridors of power. As unofficial chairman of the 'Get Rid of Whitrod Committee' Lane suggested it would be handy to have the Rat Pack meetings at the Cecil Arms Hotel, a mundane city pub, which had the advantage of being close to Parliament House.

Whitrod might have suffered continual attacks and harassment from the Rat Pack and the Union but the rest of the population liked what they saw and on August 12 1971 he was named Queenslander of the Year. That same day, in her 11th interview with police, Shirley blew up as a result of the pressure being placed on her by both the interviewers and the men she knew could kill her. "Fred Krahe will come after me," she told Col Bennett. "Glen Hallahan threatened me on Friday night." She felt she was a sitting target but didn't know who she could trust to protect her. She preferred to take her chances alone.

While Shirley was still naming names, Inspector Robert Campbell, newly stationed on the Gold Coast, blew the whistle by writing a letter to Whitrod on what he had learned about graft and corruption involving prostitution on the coast. More information on graft was sent to the Premier by a doctor who had visited a brothel on the Gold Coast.

News of Inspector Campbell's letter to Whitrod soon leaked, suggesting a source very close to the top of the force. Campbell was visited by Johnny Shotgun Regan who told him in no uncertain terms that he was a dead man if he said another word about corruption. Nevertheless, Campbell spent an entire day with Hodges and Whitrod telling them what he had learned about graft being paid to protect Gold Coast massage parlours.

The information resulted in Hodges announcing on Friday, September 3, an inquiry into massage parlour graft. Assistant Commissioner Val Barlow, Superintendent H. Low and Inspector Dynes Becker would conduct the inquiry and complete their report by the end of the following week. If the report revealed serious corruption a Royal Commission was an option.

Hallahan and Don Lane would have known from their time in Cloncurry that Becker, like Barlow, was implacably honest. Lane recalled that Becker was a detective with a reputation as the best white collar crime investigator in the business. He was so clean that when Commissioner Bischof had been organising corrupt payments in Brisbane he had put Becker back into uniform and sent him as far away from Brisbane as possible – to Cloncurry. On his first weekend in town Becker noticed two buildings doing enormous business. Lane, then a constable, told him they were the town's two illegal betting shops. They were blatant, one complete with shopfront and the other behind a billiard saloon, complete with boards for betting prices and seats for the punters. Lane had told Becker that all police had been told to ignore them because they were there with the approval of the department. Becker seized the operation's ledgers and announced charges would be laid. That night a furious Inspector Norwin Bauer demanded to know why he had taken this action and where the ledgers were. In a shouting match with Becker, Bauer, his superior, told him the betting shops were to be left alone. But Becker refused to hand over the ledgers and pressed charges.

The announcement of the inquiry sparked immediate reaction from corrupt cops. They did not want another royal commission. Messages would have to be sent to anyone thinking of talking to Whitrod's men that death was the ultimate silencer.

That same day, Assistant Commissioner Val Barlow picked up the phone in his office to hear a slurred voice. He realised it was Shirley, who managed to say simply: "Come quick". Barlow raced out to her address with Abe Duncan and a WPC Ryan. They found Shirley unconscious and close to death. There was no time to call an ambulance. They carried her out to the car and put her in the back seat with the WPC. They sped off with Barlow telling WPC Ryan how to hold her head so that she would not suffocate. The Courier-Mail reported next day in a two-paragraph story tucked away right at the bottom of a column on page 3: "Mrs Shirley Brifman, 35, of Brindle St, Paddington, was dangerously ill and unconscious in the respiratory ward of Royal Brisbane Hospital last night. She was admitted at 1 pm suffering from an alleged overdose of drugs." As far as the newspaper was concerned it apparently had nothing to do with the huge story on page one announcing the corruption inquiry.

Shirley had a long-time lover, millionaire stockbroker Robin Corrie, who knew all about Shirley's struggle with the corrupt police. Corrie was a flamboyant, famous stockbroker who revelled in publicity. During an oil boom he was known as Mr Oil. Despite worldwide forecasts of steady gold prices, he had told clients for months that a gold boom was on its way and to buy. When the boom arrived he painted his car gold and posed with it for Sunday Truth. The Stock Exchange promptly fined him $2000. The World War Two winner of a DFC, he had also driven a steamroller through the officers' mess in Darwin and had dipped the CO's pet dachshund into a pot of paint prior to encouraging it to jump on to its master's lap. More recently, he was reported to have been marooned on his boat out in the bay for half the week. Whether or not Shirley was also on board we don't know. He had told Shirley to keep fighting the parasites who had fed off her for so long. "Don't give up - fight 'em," he had said. He knew all there was to know about Shirley's 'protectors'.

As she lay in hospital that Sunday he would have been a welcome visitor. But he would never see her again, never talk about 'fighting them' again. He was last seen alive at 2pm that day at his Mermaid Beach holiday home after he had seen his daughter off on a flight south. Told he had committed suicide, Shirley said: "It is so hard to believe, it's not funny. He wasn't the type to kill himself. They knew I was linked with him completely."

Next day, Monday, Bennett received a phone call from a very frightened Inspector Campbell begging him to arrange protection, not so much for him but for his wife and children. Only he didn't say 'my wife'. He constantly referred to her as 'my widow'! He had been menaced into a state of terror by Johnny Shotgun Regan and had immediately taken leave and gone into hiding on the Sunshine Coast.

After being released from hospital Shirley said Johnny Shotgun Regan had been her visitor on Friday. And this time he had meant business. He had forced tablets down her throat.

Coincidentally, Corrie had been found with tablets close by and a post-mortem showed he had died from a drug overdose. Nearby were notes to his family. But his senior partner said the business was not in any financial trouble and Corrie's death had come as a totally unexpected shock.

Shirley recalled: "In fact, when I heard about him that was more of a shock than anything. He told me to fight back because they deserved everything they got. He was a nice man but very hard. I thought that somehow along the line that maybe Glen was blackmailing Robin because he knew that I used to fly up here for Robin. I thought that in the end he might have got stuck into him.

"People don't realise how close Corrie was to me. He was like the professor. He said 'You fight 'em, Shirley - I know all about them'. That man told me shortly before he died 'Don't give up - fight 'em. I will always stick by you...He told me to fight 'em back because they made me what I was. 'Take them with you' he said. If I am going to go, they are going to go with me. I am crooked on them because they had the power in both states. I will fight this one to every zack (sixpence) I have got. They knew I was linked with him completely. I am wondering if Glen got to him. I wouldn't overlook it. They tried him before on blackmail. I still reckon Robin Corrie was blackmailed. He (Glen) knew."

On Thursday the 8th Inspector Campbell turned up at the tiny police station at Eumundi in the Sunshine Coast hinterland and handed in his service revolver before driving down to Southport where he was stationed. He called a meeting of the police there and told them he had been suffering ill health for some time but felt he was recovering. He could not understand why he had made the allegations about corruption that he had. Next day he submitted himself to a medical test by the Government Medical Officer who placed him on sick leave with a case of "acute nervous disorder".

In her interviews Shirley said: "I know all about Inspector Campbell. I know he was telling the truth and that a threat was made on him – (by) Johnny Regan. Regan is tied up with everything. Regan decided he was going to be the collect man. I know Glen was in it."

Police Minister Hodges came under attack from both the Police Union and some fellow ministers who believed he had embarrassed the government by making allegations against police and announcing an inquiry. The union executive increased its pressure by gaining major publicity with a vote of no confidence in him. And in Parliament Shady Lane played his part by launching an attack on Whitrod's leadership, claiming that crime was rising so dramatically that he would have to start "boundary riding" his electorate to protect his constituents from the thieves who were plundering it. "The word is out among the criminal element in the southern states that Queensland is ripe for the picking," he said.

On September 18 Whitrod announced the formation of a corruption-busting team to be called the Criminal Intelligence Unit. Queensland's Elliot Ness in charge of this unit was to be Detective Superintendent Norm Gulbransen, a totally straight cop. Gulbransen had deservedly risen steadily through the ranks since joining the force in 1939 after having been a labourer, cane cutter and timber worker. A former cricketer, he was a lean, wiry man who still kept himself superbly fit at the age of 55. His hair was slicked straight back from the forehead and he wore heavy horn-rimmed spectacles. He was a man who had solved major crimes by gaining incontestable evidence and if ever a man should have been called an ace plainclothesman, it was Gulbransen. But he had not sought publicity. And newspapers had not courted him.

The CIU's first target was Glen Patrick Hallahan.

Whether or not Whitrod had suspicions that the top-level leaks may have been emanating from Duncan, he moved him off the Brifman inquiry and replaced him with Gulbransen.

The attacks on Gulbransen started immediately. "The phone calls were always on," he said. "They'd ring and then hang up. One night, I was very tired and in bed at 9.45 when my wife woke me up and said 'Quick! Quick! Somebody's breaking in'. I got up and I was just in time to stop a couple of young firemen from bashing a hole in the door. I said 'Where's the fire? Where's the fire? Can you see anything?' They said 'No'. I had Ambulance men turn up at the door. On the day I was going on holidays there was a Dutch fellow across the way. I told him I was going away and three days later he was just in time to stop some people from dumping a great load of sand and gravel on the footpath. And one morning I was on the lawn and a voice said 'Your ready mix is here Mr Gulbransen' and he was most upset and said it's going to cost so-and-so. Fellow was complaining about how much it was going to cost and I said it wouldn't have cost anything if they had have phoned to check. And lo and behold within a quarter of an hour another company phoned and said 'Do you still want that concrete?' The fellow who had taken the call said 'Hang on a minute while I check' and the caller had just hung up. There was no doubt they were police officers.

"But it was a challenge worth accepting - particularly in selecting my men. Max Hodges said 'You are going to finish up the most hated man in the job'. I set myself up at the police college at Chelmer. To get away from everybody."

Detective Sergeant Basil Hicks was a prominent and honest detective in Brisbane. The Rat Pack decided to try to recruit him before Whitrod did. According to Hicks, Tony Murphy arranged to meet him on the roof of police headquarters and told him: "There's no need for us always to be fighting. We want you to join us. Terry, Glen and I are the main three and there are another six." Hicks asked how they were going to deal with Whitrod.

"We'll surround him," replied Murphy.

They were wasting their time. Hicks reported the approach to Gulbransen and within a week Hicks was part of the CIU.

Shirley was certainly playing her part in furnishing reams of evidence, naming many of the consorting and licensing branch detectives as corrupt. "I am taking from your police force, if they do go, the best men in it," she said. "The best detectives because they are in the centre of everything. They have got the best informers." She would eventually take part in 21 interviews with NSW and Queensland police, starting on June 18 and not finishing until November 9. But the three-man inquiry eventually fizzled out because there was a lack of hard evidence to substantiate charges that would stand up in a court.

Chapter 23 - Execution

Hallahan and other corrupt coppers had continued to use the National Hotel, so secure did they believe themselves to be. Hotel manager Jack Cooper, more than 180 centimetres tall and weighing about 100 kilos, was known as Bingo because he kept his eyes down when talking to people. But that didn't mean he kept his ears closed. He had been manager at the National for about four years and would have been privy to many quiet conversations. It wasn't long before Whitrod's clean team asked him to have a chat about what he knew of the corrupt police. His wife Bea noticed that he was quieter than usual. He was never an extrovert but something seemed to be worrying him. She recalled that on Thursday September 23 1971 he "came home, and he was pretty full, and he said to me 'You don't think I've been a snitch, do you?'"

According to evidence given to a magistrate by Perry Vincent, a man who had skipped bail in the state of Victoria on a charge of armed bank robbery, Hallahan arranged for him to do a job with him. They would hold up the manager of the National Hotel on his way home, tie him up, steal the keys to the hotel safe and then go back to the hotel to empty the safe of the Saturday night takings.

Born in England, Vincent had been christened Alan Rogers and come to Australia at 15. The first entry on his criminal record was being fined a pound for not paying his rail fare at Richmond, Queensland, at a time when Hallahan may well have been the arresting officer. The crimes became progressively worse, resulting in a prison sentence. According to Rogers, he decided to try to start a new life and adopted a new name, Perry Alan Vincent. He even tried a new country, emigrating to New Zealand where he got married. But debts mounted and when he couldn't pay them he returned to Australia and robbed a Melbourne bank.

"Bail had been posted for me of $1000 by some pretty notorious underworld characters," he said. "My wife and children had been threatened and I absconded." He found sanctuary, a home for his wife and two children, and work at a dairy farm near Beaudesert south of Brisbane. That's where Hallahan found him.

The third man in the job was 31-year-old Don Maher. An only child, he was born in Sydney and when his father died suddenly was sent to be a boarder at the ultra-strict St Bernard's College run by the Roman Catholic De La Salle brothers at Katoomba in the Blue Mountains west of Sydney. One former pupil remembers being given the strap for not remembering the word for blackboard during French lessons. Maher left at the age of 15 to join the Air Force but a year later was in trouble for stealing a car and spent three months in Pentridge Jail. Between 1957 and 1965 he spent a total of six years in prison, mostly for car stealing. But he changed his life around in Brisbane and started a business, Maher Printing and Media Services at 19 Markwell St, Bowen Hills, a couple of kilometres outside the CBD, printing brochures and booklets. He married in 1967 but the marriage was dissolved three years later on grounds of cruelty. Nevertheless, life was looking up and he moved into an upmarket home in the university suburb of St Lucia.

Business had been going well for Maher but then Vincent and Hallahan intervened.

This is what happened on Saturday September 25 1971 according to Vincent's evidence in a magistrates court when police sought to extradite him to Victoria.

"I met Hallahan and Maher at the Acacia Ridge Caravan Park about 3 pm and we discussed the robbery and then left with the intention to return at about 10.30 pm. Hallahan and Maher picked me up in an old model light green Holden sedan and we travelled to Brisbane and we parked close to the National Hotel and Maher then left the car leaving Hallahan and myself seated. At about 2 o'clock in the morning he came back to the car and said he's coming now: you follow me. Maher drove past and tooted. We followed Maher for a few minutes. Then he stopped and we parked behind him. Then he left his car and told us to wait. He returned and said 'He's having a feed'."

Cooper had gone to the Lotus Room nightclub and restaurant in Elizabeth Street, in the CBD to have a meal with a friend, Ray Sue Tin, something he did on a regular basis after finishing work. Then he always dropped Sue Tin at his home in the suburb of The Grange, only five minutes from his own home at Stafford.

"We were - Hallahan and myself - still in the car and we stayed in the car until approximately 4 o'clock in the morning," said Vincent. "Maher returned and said 'He's coming now'."

Maher drove off by himself to put boxes across the road at a pre-determined spot where they intended to hold up Cooper at the point of a gun and relieve him of the keys of the safe of the National Hotel. Hallahan and Vincent followed Cooper's car as he dropped off his passenger and then followed him towards his home.

"We had in our possession an automatic rifle which had been cut and had a silencer fitted and around the cartridge magazine of the rifle was placed an amount of plastic or fibreglass to form a grip," said Vincent.

Cooper always drove to his home along Shand Street, which ran through park and woodland for hundreds of metres in the flood plain of Kedron Brook. On reaching an area of housing on the left of the road, he would take the third turning, Brennan Street, lined with single-storey homes on its left but with parkland on the right. At the top of the road, after a gentle rise, he would turn into the front yard of the house he rented and shared with his wife and three children.

At 4am the roads were virtually deserted. Maher reached Brennan Street ahead of the others and placed a line of six wooden fruit boxes across the road. When Cooper arrived he got out of his two-year-old Holden Premier, leaving his transistor radio playing on the passenger seat and the headlights on. He started moving the boxes out of the road.

Vincent said: "Hallahan and I jumped out of the car and I went to Cooper's car to turn off the headlights and at this time I heard the sound of muffled shots and saw Hallahan standing over Cooper's body in the road. Maher came running and said 'What have you done? What have you done? What did you do that for?'"

The big man was crumpled and lifeless in the middle of the road.

According to Vincent: "Hallahan said: 'It's done now, it's no good talking about it.' The body was searched and no keys were found and Maher said: 'Everything's gone haywire and the best thing we can do is clear off.' He was to stay and clear up the boxes that we left on the road."

That was Vincent's evidence on November 24. The story was not covered by the media and so did not appear in the public arena.

What should have been clear to everyone was that this wasn't a robbery gone wrong. It wasn't one or two bullets fired by accident, in a panic or as a result of Cooper going on the offensive. Sixteen bullets were fired at Cooper from the automatic rifle, an Armalite. Four hit him, one in the back killing him. This was a ruthless, cold-blooded execution. It looked like a warning to anyone thinking of talking to Whitrod's men.

How was Hallahan going to get out of this one? Could Whitrod's team nail him?

The story started unfolding in the media on September 29, three days after the murder, when reporters were informed that Detective Sergeant Hallahan of the Consorting Squad had been appointed to the group of detectives investigating the murder under the leadership of Fortitude Valley CIB chief Inspector Frank Gorman, acting Inspector Merton Hopgood and Detective Sergeant Brian Hayes of the homicide squad.

When police firearms experts discovered that the bullets that had killed Cooper had probably come from an Armalite they found a gunsmith named Gordon Kingston who had fitted a silencer to one recently and had tested it in his workshop. Two experts went through 12,000 discharged cartridge cases in a drum at the workshop and selected 100 which looked to be from Armalites and then narrowed them down to three which they believed came from the gun which killed Cooper. They then traced ownership of the gun to Maher.

Meanwhile, pressure on Hallahan was building to a point which would have reduced most other men to trembling insomnia.

On October 12 from the floor of Queensland Parliament Col Bennett sought advice from the Speaker about tabling copies of the letters Murphy had written to Shirley and copies of the police interviews with Shirley. He said the interviews alleged corruption against Murphy and Hallahan. The two detectives promptly fired a salvo back at Bennett, gaining headlines in The Courier-Mail: *'Detectives' denial of claims in parliament'*. That day Bennett told Parliament that Shirley had told how Murphy and Hallahan had coached her on her perjurious evidence at the National Hotel Commission and how they had both threatened her if she didn't follow their script.

Next day he got stuck into fellow parliamentarian Don Lane who, he said, had *"spent his time in this Chamber since winning the by-election in sabotaging all efforts to correct and clean up the Queensland Police Force"*. Lane had been closely aligned with the endeavours of Hallahan and Murphy, said Bennett. He made several references to Lane being a friend of Hallahan and Murphy which resulted in Lane leaping from his seat to say that he found the remarks offensive and asking for them to withdrawn. Bennett taunted him further: "I merely referred to his friendship with Hallahan and Murphy and I said nothing else about him. It is because I referred to him as a friend of Hallahan and Murphy that he accuses me of suggesting he is dishonest. What is the logical conclusion there?"

Bennett's attacks were becoming more of a problem to the corrupt police because people were starting to wake up to the fact that not all police were as squeaky clean as Dixon of Dock Green, Hawaii Five-O and Homicide. In addition to media reports of allegations of corrupt activity in the Queensland police force, Frank Serpico was hitting the international headlines with his testimony of the widespread and accepted corruption in the New York Police Department. And for the cinema-going public Popeye Doyle was taking the law into his own hands in The French Connection. A new era was dawning.

On November 2 Inspector Gorman and Detective Sergeant Kevin Ryan pulled over Maher in Ann St and told him he was being taken to Fortitude Valley Police Station. Detective Sergeant Hayes led the questioning. Maher was refused the use of a phone and refused access to a solicitor. He was grilled for hours by up to eight detectives shouting at him. In what Hayes later agreed was an unusual situation, Hayes left Maher alone with Hallahan for an hour at 9pm.

That night he was thrown into a cell with no bed and only a tarpaulin to cover him. He told them the gun had been stolen from him. He was only allowed to leave when he signed a document saying he had remained at the station voluntarily. But his freedom was short lived. He was picked up again on the 4th. He was beaten up, shaken, and knocked to the ground. Hallahan had been present at these beatings, he said. Maher was taken to an upstairs interview room. If he wasn't frightened enough already, he alleged he was now hung out of an upstairs window upside down as a demonstration that his life was now in the hands of corrupt police.

On Thursday November 4 Hodges announced that the graft and corruption inquiry headed by Assistant Commissioner Val Barlow, which had begun on September 9, had produced no evidence of graft, bribery or police protection of vice.

Maher appeared in Brisbane Magistrates Court on November 5 charged with murder. He appointed solicitor Cyril Murphy to act for him.

On Monday November 8 Vincent was arrested by Detective Sergeant P. Daly on a provisional warrant alleging he had failed to appear in the Victorian Supreme Court on May 5 on a charge that he committed a robbery while armed with a .22 rifle on March 22. He was placed in the remand section of Brisbane's Boggo Road Prison.

Maher's girlfriend, Susan MacKenzie, was at Maher's flat on November 9 when Hallahan came to search it. The flat had been searched by police, including Hallahan, three times before, on November 2, 3 and 5. Hallahan was there for a good part of the morning of the 9th and had searched everywhere very thoroughly, including the balconies, she noted.

How odd, then, that when Inspector Merton Hopgood turned up at the flat later that day he quickly found a spent shell on the balcony. Could it have been overlooked in all those previous searches or was it from the barrel of shells in the gun shop, carefully placed here for Hopgood to find? It would become a crucial exhibit in the court case, with the jury being told that a shell found at Maher's home had been fired by the same gun that had been used to kill Cooper.

What had led Maher to this position? At his trial Maher explained what had happened. In the second or third week of January 1971 his secretary told him a Peter Vincent had rung him. One evening a little later a showy American car pulled up outside his home in St Lucia and two men got out and walked up his drive. The bigger fellow came in first, aged about 35 to 38 and immaculately dressed. He said he was Peter Vincent. The smaller man was older than Vincent. Maher couldn't remember for sure but thought the smaller man was introduced as Jim, Gene or Jack Somerville. Vincent said he knew Maher from when they had both been locked up in Long Bay Prison several years earlier in New South Wales. He had a proposition that would be mutually beneficial and which they thought he would accept. If Maher did not co-operate Vincent said it might be a bit unpleasant if a few of Maher's customers discovered his criminal record. Maher told them he was not interested. Vincent had replied: "I'm going to have to show you that we mean business and I'm sure that you'll change your mind in the next 24 to 48 hours. Next day, while Maher was out running in the cool of the summer evening, he was almost run down by a car without lights and on the wrong side of the road. Next morning the phone rang. It was Vincent. "Did you enjoy your run last night?" he asked. A few days later Maher walked down to his car in the road outside his home to find it had been badly scratched. Other, unidentified, men started making the threatening calls. Maher told his close friends and business colleagues that if they needed to speak to him they should let the phone ring three times, put the phone down and ring again. He stayed away from his office and hoped that if he kept out of the way Vincent would lose interest and it would all blow over. But one day Maher made the mistake of picking up his phone to hear Vincent's threatening voice, this time asking for information on the floor layouts and security arrangements of companies which Maher dealt with. Once again Maher refused. Vincent warned him: "You probably don't realise the extent of our operation." He told Maher that certain detectives were his associates and that: "You really have had it good up to now. We're going to have to prove to you that we mean business." Maher was so worried that on July 12 he passed control of his affairs to a friend, John Selby-Brown.

Can we believe Maher's story about Vincent's persistent threats? When police seized Maher's diary for 1971 the name of Vincent was mentioned many times, starting in February. And the request for floor plans and security arrangements of businesses is identical to a modus operandi used by Hallahan on other occasions. The company's manager Ebbe Thomsen said Maher had refused an offer of $35,000 in mid-1971 to print pornographic work. The lucrative pornographic market could well have been what made Maher's printing business attractive to Vincent and his contacts. Maher's accountant Gerhard Bergmann said Maher was an extremely hard worker, working long hours and being quite proficient in salesmanship. The business had been successful and flourishing. But from January 1971 he noticed Maher's attitude to his work changing dramatically. "He lost interest in his work and it got worse and worse. He started to become absent from his business quite a deal and was difficult to contact. On some occasions I had to ring a certain code to get him. The business was no longer being run by him and that was when liquidity problems started."

Different stories told about the events that led up to the murder create many scenarios. However, there is no doubt that Maher owned an Armalite rifle. He said he used it for hunting. And there is no doubt that he was present when Cooper was assassinated. When it comes to the question of who pulled the trigger, we have Vincent's evidence that the gun was in the car with him and Hallahan rather than with Maher. And that it was only after all 16 shots had been fired that Maher came running to see what had happened.

Vincent was desperate to avoid being taken back to Victoria. He probably realised also that Hallahan had turned him in. So when he was taken to Brisbane Magistrates Court on November 24 to go through the formal process of the magistrate granting permission for him to be extradited to Victoria to face trial for the armed bank robbery he dropped his bombshell. He told the story of how he had been involved in the Cooper killing and that Hallahan had pulled the trigger. Faced with a man who admitted being involved in the murder of Cooper, the magistrate ordered that he be further remanded in Queensland to help police with their inquiries.

The usually imperturbable Hallahan must have been just a little worried. Vincent held to his story under intense questioning. However, Detective Sergeant Hayes went to see Vincent's wife and his employer. Hayes returned to tell Vincent that he had statements from both of them saying that Vincent couldn't possibly have been in Brisbane at the time of the murder and have returned to Beaudesert in time to perform his early morning duties. The police had gone out of their way to provide him with an alibi. Without further ado Vincent was put back in front of a magistrate on November 26 and shipped off to Victoria.

There was still a major worry for Hallahan. When Maher was brought to trial, the defence might well raise Vincent's claims. The jury would have to be presented with an explanation for Vincent's outburst.

On Sunday December 12 Maher's solicitor Cyril Murphy was sitting at home watching television when the phone rang. A male voice asked: "Is that you Cyril?" The voice then said "Don't you think that it's time you retired?" Murphy begged the caller's pardon. The caller repeated it. Murphy retorted angrily: "What sort of a mug am I talking to?" The voice said: "I'll spell it out for you – M-A-H-E-R." He repeated it before hanging up. Cyril Murphy received another unexpected call in the early hours of Thursday December 16. This time it was the police, telling him his office had been broken into. Murphy flung on some clothes and drove to his office where he discovered the place had been ransacked. Files had been pulled out, books were thrown down and drawers pulled out. But property which could have been stolen, such as tape recorders, had not been taken.

The first thing he did was to search for Maher's file. It had been removed from a secure area and dumped on a chair in the outer office near the counter.

But what would have caused serious concern in the minds of everyone associated with the case was the fact that a night watchman who surprised two intruders in the office had been so violently beaten up that his skull had been shattered. He had been found in a pool of blood outside the office and spent three days on the critically-ill list in hospital.

It appeared someone desperately wanted to know what Maher would be saying in court.

Hallahan needn't have worried. Cyril Murphy had arranged for Des Sturgess to act as defence counsel for Maher. Sturgess told me: "Donald Maher started telling me that Hallahan was the one who did the murder and all this business about Mr Big. I didn't believe a word of it. The result of it is that my solicitor Cyril Murphy was listening to this with ears flapping and he was carrying on about it. I said *'Cyril that's all bullshit'*. I said *'Look, I've been thinking about this. I am prepared to go so far with instructions that I don't have any confidence in but I am not prepared to go into court and accuse a person of murder. So if he wants to go ahead with that, tell him to get another counsel.'* Cyril told him that and he abandoned the allegation."

Chapter 24 - A Prostitute is the Next Victim

The shock waves from September's vice shake-up were still reaching distant shores. On December 1 1971 a good-looking blonde prostitute in her early 30s named Dorothy Edith Knight told Gulbransen's CIU she was so fed up with being stood over and having to pay Hallahan $20 a week protection money that she would give evidence against him. Gulbransen was the detective who Bennett had learned to trust when Shirley had started making her statements. Next day the CIU recorded a phone conversation between Knight and Glendon Patrick Hallahan in which Knight agreed to meet Hallahan on Monday December 6 in picturesque New Farm Park to hand over her protection money.

Gulbransen decided to bug the meeting but discovered that the force hadn't bothered to invest in any modern equipment. He quickly found an inventive officer who rigged up some do-it-yourself equipment. Then he found an old caravan and installed the bugging equipment. On December 6 the caravan was towed to the park where they tested the transmitter and receiver. They worked. The transmitter was then placed under Knight's blouse and the caravan parked about 30 yards from where she would be sitting under the avenue of jacaranda trees among the rose gardens close to the Brisbane River.

Gulbransen decided they would pounce when Knight was due to meet Hallahan on December 29. Gulbransen arrived at the CIU's surveillance caravan parked in Moray St, New Farm, close to the park, with Detective Greg Early, the shorthand writer. Already there, were Sergeant Basil Hicks and a radio operator. Gulbransen gave two marked $20 notes and two marked $10 notes to Hicks to pass on to Knight. Hicks left and at 8.20 he waited at a phone box as Knight phoned Hallahan. Gulbransen and Early towed the van into the park and stationed it on the circular park drive close to the river and about 55 metres from the seat where Knight had promised she would wait for Hallahan.

Gulbransen, Early and the sergeant from radio section kept their eyes glued on the seat as they sweltered in the intense heat inside the tiny van. There was relief as Knight turned up at 9 am. They all waited in nervous anticipation until at 9.10 there was the sound of a small car coming round the circuit. It stopped nearby. Hallahan, wearing a brown knitted open-neck sports shirt, beige shorts and shoes without socks got out and amazed Gulbransen by walking straight up to Knight and sitting down.

"I'll never forget this, he drove up, stopped, jumped out of the car and didn't look right or left - straight on in," Gulbransen told me. "If I'd have been doing something like that I'd have been looking under every leaf. Settled down. Not one word came through. How did I feel? Well she was a bit touchy too, this woman. We were desperate men. But we had the phone tapes."

After a few minutes Knight handed Hallahan something which he put in his left hand shirt pocket. Hallahan walked back to his car. Go! Gulbransen opened the caravan door to intercept him.

"I noticed you having a talk a few minutes ago with a girl who is a known prostitute," Gulbransen said. "Did you meet her for any particular purpose?"

Hallahan replied: "Well, I talked to her, that's all." He denied Knight had handed him anything. Then he admitted it and showed Gulbransen the notes. "I recognise the serial numbers on these notes," Gulbransen told him, adding those words which should have been only too familiar to Hallahan: "You are not obliged to say anything..."

Gulbransen shepherded Hallahan into his police car and told him it was not the first time he'd been seen meeting Knight and told him about the December 6 meeting. Hallahan countered by saying Knight had been an informant for two and a half years and owed him money. Gulbransen signalled Knight to come to the car and she braved Hallahan's stony stare to tell Gulbransen she had paid Hallahan for about four years so that she could work as a prostitute. "I deny emphatically that she was paying me money for protection," said Hallahan. After Knight had left, Gulbransen said: "I think it's only fair that you should know the whole story. She claims she met you in Townsville and later you met her in July 1967. She says you told her she had gone long enough without paying money for protection and that she was to pay you $20 a week."

Hallahan was driven off to the Police College at Chelmer and later that day, at 12.13 pm, Gulbransen played a tape to Hallahan of him talking to Knight on December 2 on the phone. At 4pm Gulbransen officially arrested him. Twenty five minutes later he was presented to the court ready for the initial appearance before a magistrate and, still in the clothes he had slung on that morning for his 'quick' meeting in the park, he stood in the dock. The charge was receiving corruptly $60 from Dorothy Edith Knight on December 29 1971 in consideration that he would omit to report and record that Knight was a prostitute and that he would provide her with protection in the event of her being charged with any offence arising from her activities as a prostitute. He listened intently as the prosecution alleged Knight had been paying him $20 a week for two and a half years. Merton Hopgood, who had worked with Hallahan on the Cooper murder investigation, now stood in court as his prosecutor, telling the magistrate that Knight was frightened of Hallahan. He asked for a special condition if bail was granted, that Hallahan should not attempt to contact Knight in any way. At 4.47 Hallahan was released on bail of $300 after promising not to contact Knight. He was suspended from the force with no pay. It had been an extraordinary day.

"Arrest a top criminal you have got a battle on your hands but if you arrest a detective you have got a war immediately," recalled Gulbransen several years later. "The night that I arrested Hallahan my wife got a phone call to say I wouldn't be home: there's no chance I'd make it through the week."

It simply reinforced Gulbransen's certainty that Hallahan would threaten, intimidate and even harm Knight if he had the chance. He had her guarded night and day by members of the traffic branch, which had not been infected by the corruption rampant among detectives. The traffic police even had to keep an eye on Dorothy as she plied her trade and looked after gentlemen's needs. Sometimes she was taken by police car to meet clients at motels. The police car would drop her off and wait around the corner for her to finish her appointment.

Hallahan was further remanded when the case appeared briefly in court again on January 6.

Shirley knew that Hallahan would be plotting to ensure he survived and she became more worried about her own future. Gulbransen had offered her protection but she didn't trust anyone to guard her. And the CIU believed that because Dorothy Knight's evidence was of a very recent incident and that because Shirley's testimony was eight years old, Knight was more at risk. At the beginning of January Shirley decided to move right away from the western suburbs where she feared she would once again be found. This time she chose one of three flats in a large, rambling wooden house not far from where Robin Corrie had lived in Clayfield, a well-to-do suburb to the north-east of the city centre. As soon as the upheaval was over she sat down and, in her flowery script, wrote to the Public Solicitor in Sydney saying that she was now living at Flat 3, 75 Bonney Avenue, Clayfield, phone 62-1833. She was frightened! And she knew where the danger lay. "Could you please keep this address away from all police as my life has been threatened a few times," she told the solicitor. "My husband is still in Wacol Prison and won't be out until some time in February."

"She became very erratic and quite fearful," said daughter Mary Anne. "She was frightened but, um, she was also very determined to go ahead with that and, um, I know that Tony Murphy did his best to talk my mother out of that….In the end it was stronger than persuasion because my mother grew really fretful."

Did Shirley reveal what Murphy was saying to her? "That she would die, that he would have her killed …she told my father that that's what he intended to do," Mary Anne told investigators. And Shirley told Col Bennett that Fred Krahe would come after her and that Hallahan had threatened her.

The pressure on Hallahan was also reaching stifling proportions. Gulbransen learned that Donald Ross Kelly had been arrested in Melbourne. He immediately arranged to fly there himself to interview him and have him extradited to Queensland. With him went Detective Sergeant Basil Hicks from the CIU. It took more than half a dozen meetings before Kelly was willing to talk, saying he was frightened of what Hallahan might do to him – a common reaction from criminals who knew him. Eventually, Kelly said he wanted to make a clean breast of things and furnished a 19-page statement in which he said that Hallahan had asked him to commit three robberies.

If word about Kelly's arrest had not already percolated to him, Hallahan would have realised on Saturday January 15 that he was in even bigger trouble. Kelly, represented by Col Bennett, appeared before magistrate Hickey, charged with the bank robbery and was remanded in custody to January 21.

Hallahan himself appeared before magistrate Fagg five days later on Thursday the 20th on the Knight offence.

While Gulbransen's battle against corruption was increasing in intensity, Don Lane was about to end the career of one of the Rat Pack's most active foes.

Don Lane had become a member of the Liberal Party Executive in 1969 while still a policeman. And while a ginger group in the party believed principle should come before political expediency, Lane was having nothing to do with that sort of attitude. He started work on behalf of the Government to redraw electorate boundaries as part of a plan to increase the number of electorates in the state from 78 to 82. He worked closely with Bjelke-Petersen, senior Liberals and Country Party president Sparkes on the Parliamentary Bill to amend the map of electoral boundaries. Lane must have chortled as he took revenge on Bennett with a manoeuvre which was clever and brilliantly executed. A large chunk of Bennett's South Brisbane electorate was carved off to become part of the Brisbane electorate. It included the area containing Bennett's power base, the West End branch of the ALP, of which Bennett was president and his wife secretary. It meant that in any party decisions, the West End branch's voice and votes would only count in the Brisbane electorate. On the other side of Bennett's constituency, the electorate of Norman was removed from the map, leaving the sitting Labor MP Fred Bromley without a seat. A new electorate was created but, in fact, most of it was the old seat of Norman with the remaining chunk of South Brisbane that had not been absorbed into the Brisbane electorate. But to avoid any allegation that Bennett had been singled out for destruction the new seat was called South Brisbane. The result was that Fred Bromley and Col Bennett were competing in the Labor Party for selection as the candidate for a seat which was called South

Brisbane but which was in reality largely Fred Bromley's old seat. It was Bromley's power base: Bennett had become the outsider.

On January 29 a State ALP convention selected Bromley as the new candidate for South Brisbane.

Bennett was understandably devastated. He had gone into Parliament more than a decade earlier with expectations of attaining senior status in the party, hopefully becoming the attorney-general of a Labor Government and, who knows, even Premier. He had fought long and hard against corruption but had received almost as much opposition from sections of his own side as he had from the Country Party. He had been belittled, threatened, and had watched his political career being demolished.

A couple of days later, on February 4, Detective Sergeant Anthony Murphy donned a smart dark suit for a 1pm appointment with Gulbransen, Inspector Dynes Becker, Detective Senior Sergeant Voigt and Detective Senior Constable Greg Early in the sober Queen St chambers of his solicitor John Elliott. For two and a quarter hours questions were fired at Murphy and he calmly and firmly answered each and every one of them.

Murphy told Becker: "I find myself charged because of the untrue, malicious statements of Shirley Brifman, a drug addict, a self-confessed perjurer, prostitute and police informer, who so obviously has fabricated certain statements about me, hoping somehow to evade the consequences of the law with respect to her in New South Wales introducing her 13-year-old daughter to the sordid life of a prostitute. She has retailed these stories to Mr Colin Bennett, barrister, who has carried a grudge against me and other police officers since his allegations in 1963 about the police force and the National Hotel the Royal Commission proved to be unfounded. These have been taken up by the Police Commissioner and the Police Minister because of my involvement as an executive member of the police union in the interests of my fellow unionists and the public of Queensland as opposed to the policy of the commissioner and the minister. I am not guilty of this charge."

Inspector Becker showed Murphy the undated, unsigned letter from Shirley. Murphy launched into an attack on Bennett, saying he had read extracts which Bennett had released. "Such extracts in fact it would appear were quoted out of context by Mr Bennett who has been carrying on a vendetta against me and other members of the police force for some considerable time," he said. He could not recall having sent the letter but in his opinion he probably had done so. He agreed he had sent the other letter.

Becker then read out loud part of the transcript of the National Hotel Inquiry dealing with Murphy's evidence where he had said he had no information where Shirley Brifman might have been in the preceding 12 months. Becker told Murphy: "Now, that is the evidence you gave on oath and it is clearly indicated by those letters that you knew where she was in Sydney. Do you wish to say anything about that?" Murphy launched into a long and detailed explanation in which he said he had written to Shirley care of a post office and when he had tried to trace her just before the Inquiry started he was told by Sydney police that she had shot through.

Becker formally arrested Murphy and they all then moved on to the City watchhouse where Becker told him he was charged with having committed perjury at the National Hotel Inquiry in that he had sworn he was unable to get any evidence that Shirley Brifman was a prostitute. Murphy replied: "I shall be giving further evidence in connection with this charge at a later date."

Then the circus moved off again, this time to the magistrates court where Murphy arrived at 4.08. His case was called by senior magistrate Kingston at 4.21. Murphy, described as a 44-year-old father of six, appeared to be righteously indignant at being hauled before a court when all his life he had been fighting crime. The major events of the day were recalled and then Becker asked that Murphy be remanded until February 18. Elliott told the court of Murphy: "He is probably one of the best known police officers in Queensland as a result of his police work. He believes the charge to be the result of a political vendetta."

In the last week of February 1972 the murder case against Maher was outlined to a magistrate, with Maher being remanded in custody to face trial in the Supreme Court.

Next week, on Thursday March 2, Lily Ryan, who could have told the Murphy court hearing so much about the National Hotel Inquiry, died in Mount Olivet Hospice, Brisbane. The cause of death was given as cancer. A friend said that Murphy was at her bedside when she died. What was Murphy doing there? Further light on Lily's death was shed in 1987 when Hallahan alleged in a statement to investigators "she made what virtually amounted to a dying declaration about a week before she died" saying Shirley had visited her in the hospice. Hallahan alleged: "She told Ryan that she intended to make up stories about certain detectives, including myself, to get even for not helping her get off the charge of procuring her daughter for prostitution. Ryan later gave a sworn statement regarding this conversation and it was witnessed by a Justice of the Peace."

It was certainly a fortuitous death for Murphy, for Val Weidinger had died some time before. Two of the three prostitutes who had worked together at the National Hotel and lied together at the inquiry were now unavailable to give evidence against Murphy. Only Shirley was left.

Shirley's daughter Mary Anne was 15 in 1972. Sixteen years later she told investigators her memory of what happened on the evening after Lily Ryan's death.

Mary Anne, her two sisters and brother, and father Sonny were watching television in their first floor flat in the wooden house on the corner of Milne Street and Bonney Avenue while Shirley was in her bedroom.

Mary Anne answered a knock on the door to find a woman wearing a big coat, a scarf around her hair and wearing glasses. There was someone who had driven her there, waiting in a car.

"And then my mother came out of the bedroom and she introduced us and she seemed quite happy and quite, um, delighted," Mary Anne said, explaining that the woman was someone very close to Tony Murphy.

"I think she felt that she was winning for the fact that (the woman) had come there…and she took (the woman) into the bedroom and spoke to her in there.

"When (this woman) and Shirley came out and (the woman) was about to leave… (the woman) kept trying to give my mother something…and my mother said no, that she definitely didn't want it and that she was definitely going to court…'Well', she said, 'Shirley, you know what we've spoken about and, um, I'm going to, I think I should leave this with you, cause you know what'll happen'.

"So I don't know if she was threatened about one of the children or if she was threatened with her life in the end, although she always said it was her life…that went on for a few minutes and my mother accepted the small thing… and we naturally assumed that it would probably be tablets."

Asked why it was assumed tablets were being given to Shirley, Mary Anne said: "Because, um, if my mother could have got hold of enough tablets – I mean she tried with all her, with so much effort towards the end not to overdose because, um, we used to, my sister and I used to guard her like anything, um, and my mother had so many overdoses that we would, we were just so perceptive…"

Question: "Overdoses which were attempts to take her own life?" Mary Anne: "Yes. Which were, um, we'd just grown accustomed to that, we had years of that…and, um, because it was small we assumed that it was just tablets.

"We were very in tune and perceptive towards those type of things, you know. I mean for six months one year she overdosed every weekend so we were very perceptive into looking after her like that….we said: 'Well then, show us what (she) did give to you then if it's not tablets mum'. And, um, she wouldn't show us. So we knew it was tablets."

A thorough search of the flat had failed to find any tablets and eventually everyone went to bed.

Sometime after 8.30 in the morning of Saturday, March 4, when noise was starting to fill the Brifman flat and Shirley hadn't made her usual shout for quiet, daughter Mary Anne and her brother went into her bedroom. This time it was too late for a dramatic dash to hospital. She was dead. She was, despite all that she had crammed into her life, just 36.

Was Shirley's death as simple as that?

According to David Hickie's 'The Prince and the Premier', "Several police attached to the (NSW) CIB at the time said there was much talk that Fred Krahe had gone to Brisbane and, with a Queensland policeman, forced the drugs down Brifman's throat with a tube."

And many years later a major drug smuggler named John Milligan told senior Narcotics Bureau officer John Shobbrook that he was terrified of Hallahan who was bankrolling one of his heroin importations. Shobbrook recalled: "Milligan claimed that if he talked then his life would be in danger. He later informed me that Hallahan had claimed that he had already murdered a prostitute named Shirley Brifman."

The Friday evening visitor would have been able to tell Shirley's former lovers that Shirley's bedroom had a large window immediately next to the front door. They would have been able to quietly climb the brick steps leading up to the front door and climb through the window.

Mary Anne remembered that when detectives arrived on the Saturday morning they noted how easy it would have been for someone to use the outside stairs and climb into Shirley's bedroom through windows which were very easy to open. Commissioner Whitrod certainly believed Shirley had been murdered but Inspector Dynes Becker, in charge of the investigation, was satisfied it was a case of suicide.

Shirley had told police: "I'm more frightened of Glen as far as violence goes. I don't mean physical violence with Tony but Glen would be the type...Tony wouldn't hurt me. Glen would."

Tony Murphy had a watertight alibi. He had flown to Sydney and was 1,000 kilometres south of Brisbane on the night of Shirley's death.

There was a final indignity. Mary Anne told investigators: "Szama still couldn't read or write English. He was quite desperate for money and my father said that, um, by having...my mother's body taken to Cairns to be buried, um, that there were, um, also a shipment of drugs went up with my mother...um, and he got the money from that...I was horrified at my father."

The funeral took Shirley all the way back to her childhood home at Atherton. She had once told a reporter: "You have to live this life to know it and I don't think anyone has lived it better than I have. And as I've said before, I've met some of the nicest people." She had also met some of the worst!

Chapter 25 - Hallahan and Murphy in the Dock

It was Hallahan's turn to appear before a magistrate on March 13 1972 when the case against him on the Dorothy Knight charge was due to be decided. But when the case was called Hallahan was missing. His barrister, Kev Townsley, told the magistrate that Hallahan had a backache and was confined to bed. He presented the magistrate with a medical certificate, saying the incapacity could last for a fortnight but there was a chance it could last longer. His request for an adjournment till March 27 was granted.

Hallahan would have been waiting every day for a knock on his door from the CIU wanting to talk to him about the Kedron bank robbery. It came on March 20 when he found a member of the CIU on his doorstep with a summons alleging that between August 1 and 7, 1970 he counselled Donald Ross Kelly to steal from the Bank of New South Wales at Gympie Road, Kedron, with actual violence, a sum of money which was the property of the bank "and Donald Ross Kelly thereupon did". His house was thoroughly searched. Not surprisingly nothing incriminating was discovered.

The pressure on Hallahan was reaching crushing proportions. He was facing the might of the CIU and two people ready to testify against him for two crimes for which he had been charged – and the risk that Maher would throw caution to the wind and tell a court that Hallahan had killed Jack 'Bingo' Cooper.

Two days later Murphy appeared at his committal proceedings in the magistrates court. Despite all Bennett's stirring to try to raise public awareness of the issues involved, there were more journalists in the court than members of the public. J L McNamara, a silver-haired prosecutor, was up against Des Sturgess, a man whose name was to become familiar in cases such as this where a detective was up against it. Tall, dark and eloquent, Sturgess was, at 42, recognised as being the best defence lawyer in town and was 'enormously influential'. He was an advisor to the police union during its quarrels with Whitrod. Standing straight, he was 188 centimetres tall but he tended to hunch and appear smaller. A dog lover, he was a bit of a loner. He would arrive in the city each day not in a Mercedes or Jaguar but by train in his short-sleeved shirt. In court he hectored and harried prosecution witnesses into corners. Like Whitrod, he had spent some years in New Guinea. Four years later he would take part in the Lucas Inquiry into police verballing.

Sturgess's opening remarks were: "The case for the defence is that this is a malicious prosecution. For a considerable time past people in high places have set themselves at prosecuting Detective Tony Murphy at a criminal level." Further, a malicious set had developed against him because of his interest in union affairs and his frequent public statements naming the police commissioner and police minister. So this was a purely malicious prosecution of a political nature, he underlined.

On day two of the committal, Inspector Becker was in the box being cross-examined by Sturgess. He agreed with Sturgess that the signed letter was such as a detective might write to an informant.

Becker said Murphy had told the National Hotel Inquiry he had been unable to find any evidence that Shirley had been a prostitute. But Becker had clear evidence that Murphy knew she was a prostitute. He had a document in Murphy's handwriting indicating that Shirley was an inmate of a brothel and he had a statutory declaration from her confirming that. The document had been found in a notebook issued to Murphy in 1959 and was a list of prostitutes. Becker admitted to Sturgess it was possible to forget a routine interview when giving evidence.

The cross-examination continued into day three when Becker said it was obvious from the unsigned letter that Murphy had known where Shirley was staying. It mentioned police turning up on her doorstep and Becker inferred from this that Murphy knew where that doorstep was. The letter had also included the passage: "I'm sure you will realise under all the circumstances that I will do all in my power to ensure that your name is not mentioned and that the source of any information you give me will not be disclosed." And later in the letter: "I'll close now, hoping the young 'Briffman(sic) Boy' is picking up fast and will soon be out of hospital." Then Detective Sergeant Syd Currey told the court what a wonderful detective Murphy was. "He's one of the best," said Currey. "I've always known him as a man of integrity."

The case was unfinished at the end of the three days set aside for it and it was adjourned until April 7.

One of the courts was needed to hear accusations against Glendon Patrick Hallahan. Previewing the case, the Sunday Sun (as Sunday Truth had become) reported: "Hallahan is widely known interstate as the outstanding detective who has solved some of the country's most baffling crimes, including internationally publicised homicides."

It did not say which cases.

On Monday, March 27, Hallahan fronted magistrate Peel for the committal proceedings on the corruption charges involving Dorothy Knight. But first he had to be remanded on the Kelly charge. Barrister Kev Townsley appeared for Hallahan and said the Kelly charge was one of the most serious on the calendar and overshadowed the corruption charges. They were all unfounded, he said. The counselling charge involved setting the word of a criminal and associate of notorious bank robber Darcy Dugan against that of Hallahan, an outstanding detective and a George

Medal winner. Members of the CIU had been involved in both investigations and the defence would claim that certain reprehensible methods had been used in both cases, said Townsley. Townsley told Peel the defence wanted the bank charge heard before the corruption charge but in any case it wanted both matters delayed until a murder trial had been completed.

Townsley said that Hallahan wanted to be represented by Des Sturgess. However, there was an ethical reason why Sturgess could not do so until after the trial of Don Maher had been concluded. "It is a unique situation," said Townsley. "The only reason Hallahan can't have that counsel is because of his own outstanding police work. In the case against Maher, Hallahan is a witness for the police force which is now trying to pull him down. I seek an adjournment of the hearing until Mr Sturgess becomes available." On the bank robbery charge the magistrate remanded Hallahan on bail of $400 until May 22 and said he would continue to deal with the Knight case.

Gulbransen took the witness box and told how the CIU had set traps for Hallahan. Knight had told him she had paid Hallahan, either personally or through Lily Ryan, since July 1967 apart from a period when she had moved south and when she had given birth in 1969. She had been afraid of Hallahan because of what he could do to her as a detective, Gulbransen told the court. When he reached evidence about phone tapping, Townsley jumped up and asked if the prosecution intended to show that Gulbransen had been a party to phone tapping. Crown prosecutor J H Hair said it was not a case of phone tapping - a recording had been made with the permission of the subscriber. Then Townsley objected strenuously to the recordings being played. But magistrate Peel said he would listen to all 12 tapes taken by the police.

On the second day, Knight, an attractive blonde in her 30s took the stand. One of life's losers, she had never been to high school and had hit rock bottom when her husband had walked out on her. Penniless, she had started dishing out dud cheques all over the country. And that had led to her first meeting with Hallahan who had accompanied her back to Townsville on a plane to face a court. She had been jailed and it had been there that she had learned about the easy money to be had from prostitution.

She had next seen Hallahan in 1967 when she was working as a prostitute at the National Hotel, Brisbane. Hallahan had called at her home and protection had been mentioned. She had paid him $20 that day and had continued paying him regularly at the National Hotel, the Belfast Hotel and the Port Office Hotel. Payments had continued until about January 1969 when she had ceased work because she was pregnant. She said she had rung Hallahan and asked if she could drop the payments to $10 because she was no longer working. He had agreed and she had paid him until she went into hospital in April.

In cross-examination Townsley tried to establish that Hallahan had used her as an informer. She indignantly replied she had only ever given him one lot of information about criminals. Townsley asked: "Didn't Hallahan put you into the Playboy Club to find out what you could about the man who did away with Gary Venamore, whose body was found floating in the Brisbane River?"

"No," she said.

Hallahan denied receiving protection money from Knight and said he had lent her money and she had got behind with repayments to him. She still owed him $40, he claimed.

After three days the committal was adjourned to May 5.

At the end of the week the Sunday Sun started its page-long story on Hallahan's committal on the charge of having taken graft from Dorothy Knight, not with a highlight of the evidence but with the sort of acclamation given to a star topping the bill at the theatre: "Detective Sergeant Glen Hallahan is a George Medal winner and a man who has solved some baffling crimes, including the famous Sundown murder." Only then did it get round to saying that he had been charged with being corrupt.

Next day, bank robber Donald Ross Kelly was in the magistrates court, conducting his own defence. He was still so frightened of Hallahan that he had an iron bar down a leg of his trousers. First witness was Detective Senior Constable Doug Murray from the CIU. He told how he had been on patrol in May 1970 in the Valley and had seen Kelly walking with his wife and had watched as both of them got into a 1963 Holden, registered number PHZ 433. After the bank robbery he had taken charge of 146 photos taken by an automatic camera.

When Kelly cross-examined him, Murray admitted that on the night of the hold-up he had suspected someone else completely. But next morning he had examined the photos in the presence of Detective Hallahan. Imagine Kelly's shock and panic when Murray revealed to the court that Hallahan had been the first to suggest that 'Donnie' Kelly might have been involved. One of the photos showed one of the men with the end of a finger missing. With Hallahan's suggestion in mind, he remembered Kelly did, indeed, have the tip of a finger missing. Murray said he had next interviewed a woman who had seen two men leave the getaway car and jump into a Holden, registered number PHZ 433.

Kelly would have felt as though he had been hit with a mallet in the midriff. Hallahan, the mastermind of the robbery, the man who was supposed to be his protector, had told him that it had been a junior detective who had noticed the deformed finger and come up with the name of Kelly as the robber. Now Kelly had learned in court that Hallahan had been the man to identify him. He realised with horror that he was doomed, that he wouldn't be going home to his wife and child, and that he was going to prison. He immediately changed his plea to guilty. Magistrate Martin committed him for sentence to the Supreme Court.

On April 7 Murphy was back in court. The main witness against him was not available. Neither were her two friends. Sturgess told the magistrate there was not the slightest evidence on any of the charges that would convince a jury that the detective was guilty. Magistrate Martin agreed with Sturgess, saying: "I don't believe any properly instructed jury would convict Murphy on the evidence." He discharged Murphy, who went off with jubilant colleagues to celebrate at the Belfast Hotel with a crowd of cheering colleagues.

Next day Murphy told the people of Queensland via The Courier-Mail: "There was no evidence against me in the first place. The charges were brought simply because of my union activities." Union president Ron Edington said the union had now paid out $20,000 in 12 months defending members. "We think this proves that charges are being brought against police that should never be brought," he said. The case had destroyed the men's confidence in the police administration and no policeman was now prepared to take the same professional risks Murphy took in mixing with prostitutes and criminals to gain information about crimes. "This is one reason why the clear-up rate of crimes has dropped so much since Mr Whitrod took over," he alleged.

The Sunday Sun carried a large, smiling photo of Murphy and reported that 'even the crims are wishing him well'. It recalled how all the police who had given evidence to the National Hotel Inquiry had been 'completely exonerated' by the Inquiry. "I never had any doubts about British justice but it's been hard on the kids," said Murphy. And: "I have been fingerprinted, photographed and placed on file. It stinks and I'm as dirty as hell. I have not been feeling well. I may have to take a holiday." He promptly took sick leave - until May 22.

On April 17 Donald Ross Kelly appeared before Justice Campbell for sentencing. He was not going to go quietly and told the court exactly how Hallahan had pushed him into the crimes and of Hallahan's role in each of the crimes. The account did not seem to help Kelly. He was sentenced to eight years' jail.

Chapter 26 - How to Confuse a Jury

and Get Away with Murder

We don't know what sort of persuasion and encouragement Vincent would have been subjected to regarding his account of how Hallahan had shot Jack Cooper. By the time he gave evidence at Maher's trial at the end of April 1972 he was serving six years at Pentridge Jail for armed robbery. Apart from the fact that an accident could be arranged in Pentridge, there was also the fate of his family to be considered. But it may have been as simple as telling him that if he changed his story he would not be prosecuted for his part in the murder of Cooper.

Whatever the methods used, Vincent had a brand new story to tell the trial which started in the Supreme Court on April 26, 1972 before Chief Justice Mostyn Hanger. It was tortuously convoluted and would certainly have baffled the jury about what part, if any, Hallahan had played while still accounting for what had been said at the extradition hearing.

The jury would have been further amazed when the Phantom Ferret Society wriggled into the case. Instead of cross-examining Maher about some of the more pertinent aspects of the case, Crown prosecutor Lloyd Martin seized on an entry from Maher's diary for April 12, 1971, in which boys were ferrets and girls were minks. The first aim of the society was The Liberation of Virgins.

Martin asked: "What do you mean by that?"

Maher: "Exactly what it reads."

Martin: "Just what it reads?"

"Ferreting."

Judge: "How do you liberate a virgin?"

Maher: (silence) (Suppressed hysterical laughter in court)

Judge: "I do not see it's funny."

Maher: "I'm sorry."

Martin: "You say it means just exactly what it says?"

"That's correct."

"How do you liberate a virgin?"

"Generally, sexually."

"By having sexual intercourse?"

"That's right."

"Is that an object of the society?"

"No, it's not at all."

"What heading is it under?"

"That is under aims."

"That is not an object?" (more laughter in court)

Judge: "That is not funny ladies and gentlemen. This is most serious."

Maher: "Ferreting of new burrows."

Martin: "What does that mean?"

"Generally in preparation for the liberating of virgins"

This absurd cross-examination in the middle of a trial to decide whether Maher had shot Jack Cooper in cold blood continued. The society included 'the order of the crutching crop' and there was a yearly order of a set of silver spurs. Maher had been a founder member. Those present at the second meeting had included Pubic, Passion, Lurch and Snatch. A head ferret had been appointed.

Hallahan was unable to be present for the whole of the defence case as Maher fretted in the dock watching witnesses giving evidence on his behalf. On Friday May 19 Hallahan himself was in the dock - of the magistrates court on the charge of corruptly receiving money from prostitute Dorothy Knight. Crown prosecutor J. H. Hair told the magistrate that police had discovered a Catch 22 problem. It seems Hallahan had been so successful in protecting Dorothy Knight that she had never been booked as a prostitute by any Queensland police officer. Therefore he could not be charged with protecting a prostitute. Hair sought to change the charge but counsel for Hallahan said he would want to spend a long time examining the new charge before making a decision on whether to accept the change. The case was adjourned once again.

Back at the Maher trial, Sturgess cross-examined Hayes about the number of times detectives searched Maher's New Farm penthouse including the balcony and suggested the shell on the balcony had been planted there. In his summing up he said there had been two attempts to frame his client - the shell and Vincent's story - "And an attempt has been made, we would submit, to ascertain what instructions he has been giving his solicitor."

Sturgess came close to putting a smoking gun into Hallahan's hand when he told the jury: "People who had been putting pressure on Maher since early last year probably were also those now trying to ensure his conviction. It is implicit in the account of the accused that the persons responsible for the pressure on him also were responsible for the death of the unfortunate Mr Cooper. Their safety from prosecution would be ensured by the conviction of that man in the dock. It was obviously those people who were responsible for placing a .22 cartridge case on the balcony of Maher's penthouse in Oxlade Drive." But then he seemed to distance himself from this argument by saying: "These people, if they existed, would have everything to gain by injuring Maher's defence…"

But Sturgess never cross-examined Hallahan about Vincent's naming of Hallahan as being present at the murder.

On May 24, as the closing speeches in the trial were being made, a police report to coroner Bill Laherty said there were no suspicious circumstances about Shirley Brifman's death. Laherty passed the report on to the Justice Department's under-secretary. The news disappeared under the media's radar but Hallahan, Murphy and Lewis would have had a drink or two that night. Gulbransen, the Poirot of Queensland detectives, had made up his mind: "I am satisfied she was murdered," was his verdict. He did not have the time or resources to investigate.

On Thursday May 25 Chief Justice Mostyn Hanger summed up the case against Maher and told the jury what they needed to consider. He made no reference at all to the story told by Vincent, with its references to Hallahan having literally been the man with the smoking gun. The judge used the timing of a radio announcer to finish his summing up in time to send the jury out to consider their verdict at precisely 12.59. They had their lunch and spent only slightly longer in digesting all the evidence before returning at 2.36 pm. Their unanimous verdict: Guilty.

Luckily, Queensland had abolished the death penalty for murder back in 1922, more than 30 years before any other Australian state. So there was no black cap for the judge this time. But it meant a life sentence for 32-year-old Maher.

In 1988 a friend of gunsmith Gordon Kingston said: "Over the years Mr Kingston had expressed his concern over the Maher conviction…Kingston's concern arose from conversations he had with an employee of his who had given information to the police that he had fitted a silencer to Maher's rifle. The police apparently were not looking for this particular firearm. The employee said that Maher's residence had been searched thoroughly by the police however nothing was found. The police returned to Kingston's gun shop where they obtained some cartridges for test firing and it was after this that another search of Maher's residence revealed a cartridge case. Evidence of the cartridge case was instrumental in Maher's conviction. Kingston's concern was that the cartridge case may have been planted on Maher and may have been one of the cartridge cases which they obtained from Kingston's gun shop after their initial search of Maher's residence."

The big question – if Hallahan did pull the trigger, why didn't he quietly kill Cooper in secret? Perhaps because if he was the only one, the police hunt could have uncovered him. It was a murder, after all. With others involved, he could arrange a frame-up. And, perhaps boldest of all, word was meant to get around to those thinking of blabbing to the corruption inquiry.

Hallahan was not in the Supreme Court to hear the Maher verdict because he was once again in the magistrates court as a defendant in the Dorothy Knight case. Stipendiary Magistrate Peel said the prosecution depended mainly on Knight's evidence and, therefore, "on the evidence put before me she could be held to be an accomplice of the defendant and, as such, her evidence would require corroboration. It seems that corroboration could be found in the tape recordings of the conversations between Knight and the defendant over the telephone and the conversation transmitted from New Farm Park of which there is also oral evidence."

Kev Townsley, Hallahan's lawyer, had argued that the tapes were not admissible but the magistrate said he had decided to admit the tapes in line with procedure approved by the Victorian Full Court as recently as June 1971. In other words, one of the highest courts in the land had accepted tape recordings such as the Hallahan tapes as legitimate evidence. Peel said: "I am of the opinion that the evidence is sufficient to put the defendant upon his trial for the offence charged. He committed Hallahan to the July 3 District Court sittings and allowed him bail of $300. Hallahan pleaded not guilty.

The action on Saturday May 27 1972 was not in the courts for a change but in polling stations. This was the day feisty Col Bennett, barrister, MP, corruption fighter and battler for the underdog was himself the underdog in the state election.

Across the State more than 54 per cent of the electorate voted for the two Labor parties but due to the internal strife in the party and the rigged boundaries that Don Lane had helped draw, instead of winning more than half of the 82 seats only 33 Labor members were elected. The number of rural Tories voting for the Country Party dropped but there was still one in five of the adult population prepared to vote for it and return 26 members. The Liberals, the city Tories who propped up the Country Party, lost a few votes but won two more seats to give them 21. Twenty per cent of the votes was enough to make the Country Party the dominant party in a coalition government with the Liberals.

Bjelke-Petersen ignored the fact that four out of five people hadn't voted for his party and boasted that he had once again been given a mandate to carry on with the recipe as before.

In South Brisbane Fred Bromley scored 4907 votes for the Labor Party, the Liberal 2576 and Bennett, with no Labor backing, 2101. So much for speaking out against corruption. Bennett's dream of becoming a senior minister in a Labor government was gone. His career as an MP was over. And, crucially, the platform from which he was able to expose corruption and gain headlines had been removed. Hallahan, Murphy and Lewis had cause to celebrate for the second time in two days.

They launched a counter-offensive against Police Commissioner Whitrod and Police Minister Hodges through Brian Bolton, who had taken on Ron Richards's role as police roundsman at the Sunday Sun. On June 4 the newspaper told how the reforming Hodges and Whitrod were under threat. A section of Hodges' own party did not like what he was doing and Whitrod was being attacked by the Police Union. In the provincial cities of Rockhampton, Townsville and Toowoomba members of the union had passed votes of no confidence in Hodges and Whitrod. Bundaberg and Mount Isa were expected to follow.

Two days later Justice Department under-secretary Skinner decided, having read the report forwarded to him by Coroner Laherty, that there was no need for an inquest into Shirley's death. It would be nearly five months before Sunday Sun became the first newspaper to discover this when it would tell readers – erroneously: "Her claims proved in court to be groundless," telling in another story how information on criminals had dried up because of merciless raids on vice and gambling clubs.

Hallahan was back in the magistrates court on June 26, this time before Mr Jacobs SM. This was on the summons that he had counselled Kelly to rob the bank.

Inspector Dynes Becker said Kelly's story could be summed up as that of a man trying to go straight but who had been pressured into committing crimes by Hallahan. He said a number of Kelly's allegations could only have come from Hallahan. But under cross-examination he agreed someone could have obtained Hallahan's silent phone number, address and the shifts he worked without being told personally.

Kelly told how he had paid $900 to Hallahan after the robbery. In 1969 he had brought stolen jewellery worth up to $28,000 with him for Hallahan's inspection after he had said he had a market for it. Kelly had handed it over to the detective at CIB headquarters and Hallahan had put it in a locker. When it was handed back a few days later, some of it was missing.

On June 29, the fourth day of the hearing, the magistrate said that if Hallahan was guilty then Kelly would be an accomplice and the Criminal Code stated that a man could not be convicted on the uncorroborated evidence of an accomplice. He said: "Kelly, who gave his occupation as 'thief', is a criminal who on his own evidence is capable of, at the very least, unlawful killing. To my mind he would be capable of committing perjury in court proceedings, especially against the defendant, whom he must have known - certainly his wife knew - was one of the first persons to name him as a suspect for the robbery." There were obvious discrepancies in Kelly's evidence, said the magistrate, and he would go as far as to say Kelly did not tell the truth, the whole truth, and nothing but the truth.

He finished: "To my mind there is not sufficient evidence to put the defendant on trial."

Sitting at home in Main St, Kangaroo Point that night, Hallahan crowed to a reporter: "I was always confident my name would be cleared. But there has been a terrible strain on my wife and family in the meantime."

The interview was constantly interrupted by congratulatory phone calls - as many as 15 in all.

Union president Edington told the media the CIU should either be scrapped or reformed. He was greatly concerned that since the CIU's inception two of the State's best known officers had been charged.

Chapter 27 - A Friend in a High Place

The Knight case was back in court on July 17 1972 but Hallahan's barrister, Kev Townsley, successfully had the matter adjourned when he asked Judge Seaman in the District Court to consider whether a re-worded charge was in order. The case was adjourned yet again.

At this point let me introduce you to Judge Eddie Broad.

Broad, appointed a judge by the state government four years earlier, had been dux of his private school, an outstanding athlete, a capped Wallaby and a champion bridge player. In the Second World War he enlisted with the RAAF and became a squadron leader, flying more than 30 missions as a Lancaster pilot with Bomber Command and being awarded the Distinguished Flying Cross. A dashing hero he may have been but that was no guarantee of a flawless character. Not only was he a friend of Terry Lewis but he was also a good friend of a well-known SP bookie. Ronnie Richards, the newspaperman, was always saying what a larrikin Broad was, recalls Ken Blanch, the reporter who knows more than most about the characters and events of this period.

Barrister Des Sturgess recalls: "Eddie Broad only appeared occasionally in this jurisdiction. He worked very slowly and most of his work was done in the licensing court."

However, his name appeared on the list of judges who would be sitting in the District Court in August.

Townsley approached Sturgess to argue Hallahan's defence against the Dorothy Edith Knight charge with him at the District Court.

"The case depended on the tape recordings," Des Sturgess told me. "When Kev Townsley came to see me I said 'What's the case Kev?'.

Townsley told Sturgess that he believed there was a loophole in the law dealing with tape recorded evidence. Sturgess believed Townsley was wrong and, along with the magistrate who had committed Hallahan and the ruling of the Victorian Full Court, believed that the prosecution case on tape recordings was unassailable.

"I'd been through a (similar) case. The Mayor of Cairns, Pembridge, who was charged with seeking to secure a bribe from a large real estate agent, and I thought I had a pretty good grasp of the law," Des Sturgess told me. "I heard Kev's arguments. I didn't agree with them. I said 'You have got more confidence in this than I have so you handle that side of the argument'."

Des Sturgess recalls that on the Friday before the case was due to start the following week: "Kev Townsley, the solicitor and Glen were in my chambers and talking about the trial. Glen was very interested in what judge would be hearing the case and our conference was interrupted several times by the solicitor going across to the registry to find out who we had been listed before. He finally came back with the information it had been listed before Eddie Broad.

"The relief on Hallahan's face was quite obvious. Within minutes he stood up and grinned, brought the conference to an end and said he was going to have a beer."

Was it an accident or careful engineering by Hallahan which resulted in the case being heard by Judge Eddie Broad?

There had been four successful requests to delay the case as it progressed towards a trial.

Norm Gulbransen, who knew nothing of the Friday meeting, was convinced the fix was on.

The case opened on August 10 1972 with Des Sturgess appearing for Hallahan who pleaded not guilty to a new charge that on a date unknown in 1968 Hallahan, a member of the police force, corruptly agreed to receive money from Dorothy Edith Knight in consideration for which he would, with a view to protecting Knight from detection and punishment, arrange that no action would be taken against her. The prosecution outlined its case. Dorothy Knight would tell the court she had met Hallahan at the National Hotel in 1967. She said: "He said he could never ever stop me from being arrested but he could offer me protection as far as if I was hot around the town or anything like that."

The prosecution alleged: "The agreement referred to was made orally between the accused and Mrs Dorothy Edith Knight at 89 Butterfield St, Herston, (her home). Mrs Knight believes the date was early in February 1968 and a diary of the accused reveals that he visited Mrs Knight at 89 Butterfield St, Herston, on February 2, 1968.

"The depositions disclose that Mrs Knight was an offender against the law arising from her activities as a prostitute during the years 1968-1971 and that the accused was aware of her activities."

After just over a day of legal argument without the jury, Judge Broad adjourned the court from 11.10 am until 12.55 pm to weigh up what had been said and then declared: "I have considered the whole of the evidence to be called by the prosecution. I am satisfied that at the conclusion of this evidence it would be my duty to direct the jury to return a verdict of not guilty."

The prosecutor, Mr Hair, was shocked. It was effectively the end of the trial. But he announced: "I intend to proceed with the trial, your honour."

Judge Broad: "Yes, you are entitled to call all the evidence. Is there anything further at this stage?" He adjourned for lunch until 2.30 pm.

The jury entered at 2.32 and were told they still were not wanted and they should return on the Monday at 10.00

Evidence to the magistrates court revealed that Knight had received three phone calls from Hallahan. Sturgess objected to this evidence being given to the jury. Hair said it was given apparently to indicate that the accused had contacted Mrs Knight after being warned not to and she had refused to speak to him.

His Honour: "At some stage the prosecution alleges Mrs Knight worked for Mrs Ryan. The further I read into this record the more I believe some of the names are familiar to me. I appeared for two ladies in the National Hotel Royal Commission. I rather fancy one of them was Lilian Ryan. Does anyone have any objection to my sitting up here in these circumstances?"

What a golden chance for the prosecution. This was an opportunity to have the case moved away from a judge who had already decided to clear Hallahan. Now, because Broad was duty bound to report that he had a link, however tenuous, with the main prosecution witness, there was a chance for the prosecution to ask for a new trial before a new judge.

The prosecution failed to object to Broad continuing!

Judge Broad said, despite the ruling of the Victorian Full Court: "It seems to me that if there has been an interception within the Act an offence has been committed. I think it probable that the evidence of the tape recordings is not admissible. If it is admissible I order that it not be given in the exercise of my discretion. I should point out that in my view even if evidence of the tape recordings was admitted it would still be my view that as a matter of law I should direct the jury to return a verdict of not guilty."

In other words, the judge was going to tell the jury to find Hallahan not guilty whether the tapes were admitted or not.

Hair was forced to ask for the return of the indictment and three minutes later Judge Broad told the jury: "Gentlemen, in your absence the Crown prosecutor outlined the nature and limits of the evidence that the crown proposed to call in relation to the charge against the accused. I then ruled that at the conclusion of such evidence it would be my duty to instruct you the jury to return a verdict of not guilty.

"The Crown has now announced that it will not proceed further on the indictment. The accused is therefore discharged."

Hallahan was a free man. He told the waiting media: "Naturally I'm pleased. I was always confident there would be a successful conclusion." He was about to leave for a holiday on the Gold Coast with his wife Heather and his daughter. "The main thing is I'd like to say thank you to the large number of friends who stuck with us through all this."

Sturgess recalls: "I thought there was a very real chance that the Crown might come again on the basis that a very serious error had been made by the judge.

"I said to Glen: 'Look, I don't think you've got a very bright future in the police force, do you?'. He said: 'No'. He was also worried about the contents of his locker which he'd lost access to when he was charged. I said: 'Would you like me to go to see Whitrod and offer a deal'? You'll get out of the police force if he'll let bygones be bygones'. He authorised me to do that. He was very relieved when that offer was accepted."

There were still 16 outstanding departmental charges against Hallahan. Most of them involved guns.

At 9 am on October 9 he walked into Police Headquarters and was re-instated after nine months without pay. He resigned from the force immediately. His solicitors released a statement which read: "Detective Sergeant Hallahan has today tendered his resignation from the Police Department. All matters of complaint against him have now been resolved and he was this morning reinstated. However, he feels his interests for his future and that of his family will be best served in other spheres." Whitrod issued a similar statement.

Norm Gulbransen remembered: "Later we discovered there was one room in the Criminal Investigation Branch for which he had a key and no one else did. Space was always a problem but he had this entire room under lock and key. It was off a normal passageway with rooms along it, just with numbers on the doors. It was one inspector who knew he had the room - Austin Kunst. There were large cartons of cigarettes piled up high. I don't know how many thousands. There was jewellery. 95 per cent of this was all stuff where people had been arrested for possession of property suspected of having been stolen but the necessary report hadn't been furnished: some on a desk, some in draws. And there were guns. I think it was five guns – pistols - in his locker."

The Sunday Sun ran an extensive tribute to Hallahan that weekend. Reporter Ken Blanch called him 'One of the most brilliant detectives Queensland has known'. And he added Hallahan had 'become a living legend since he leapt into public prominence' with the Sundown case. The 'brilliant' investigator was not saying what the future held for him now.

Six months later Ron Richards arranged for Glen Hallahan to become a special reporter for the Sunday Sun. The front page headline read: ACE COP ON OUR TEAM. The story said: "Mr Hallahan, regarded as one of the top CIB investigators by police throughout Australia, resigned from the force as a detective sergeant last October". It referred to his "brilliant career". There was no mention of any of the allegations which had been constantly made against him throughout that career.

After three sensational front-page crime stories which no other newspaper could follow-up because no names were mentioned, Hallahan disappeared from the Sunday Sun without any explanation to readers.

Hallahan bought a post office in the tiny township of Kin Kin, a tiny township of less than a dozen streets half way between chic Noosa on the coast and staid Gympie to the west. After a few months he sold the post office and bought a farm south of Kin Kin at Obi Obi which didn't even have a hamlet, let alone a township. Des Scanlan, a friend of Hallahan's from the National Hotel days, told reporter Ken Blanch that Hallahan grew marijuana between rows of sweet corn.

In April 1974 someone with inside knowledge of local Post Office procedures arranged the armed hold-up of a mail truck carrying half a million dollars as it travelled through the nearby Beerburrum State Forest. Hallahan was immediately suspected and Detective Basil Hicks put him under surveillance. Nothing could be found to implicate Hallahan but one of his former informers, Donnie Flanders, was arrested along with a criminal named Jack Wilson and charged with the robbery.

Barrister Des Sturgess told me: "Jack Wilson fled eventually to Sydney taking with him a girlfriend who was a prostitute and half the loot which was in the region of $400,000. He booked into a pub. The fellow from the hotel who lifted the port up to the room said it was so heavy it nearly broke his arm. It was full of money. It was wet. It had been hidden."

Wilson had only been in the pub a short time when a notorious bent Sydney copper burst in to the room, arrested Wilson and took the money.

Des Sturgess became Donnie Flanders' barrister. He was surprised when he entered the court on the first day of the trial to find Hallahan sitting at the back of the court. He believes that Hallahan was in league with the bent coppers from Sydney.

Perhaps he had tipped them off for an extra share of the loot.

"We asked for the money that had been recovered to be presented in court," said Des Sturgess. "It only filled up a corner of the port."

Sturgess says that both defendants told him Hallahan had not been involved. Flanders was saying nothing about who planned the robbery. He told police he was too frightened to talk.

Maybe he was frightened because Hallahan was sitting at the back of the court as a reminder not to talk.

Chapter 28 - Exit an Honest Commissioner

The Rat Pack might have lost Hallahan but the campaign to get rid of Whitrod continued. Votes of no confidence were passed by police union branches. Every reform, especially education, promotion on exam results and merit, were met with resistance, including media campaigns and political pressure. The media was fed a steady stream of allegations that crime rates were increasing under the Hodges-Whitrod regime.

But Hodges and Whitrod carried on with their program of modernisation, even though the personal cost was draining. Whitrod believed that Shirley Brifman had been murdered and was aware of the allegation that Hallahan had shot Cooper. The police commissioner feared for his life so much that he took to sleeping with a revolver under his pillow.

When Lewis qualified as an inspector at the age of 45 in September 1973 he was said to be the youngest inspector in Queensland and, possibly, Australia. Lewis reached his lowest point when he was moved out of Juvenile Aid and given a succession of low-key jobs, including the night shift in unfashionable Woolloongabba. He told bagman Jack Herbert he was going to resign and try his luck selling real estate. Queensland's future may well have been dramatically better had he done so. But he stuck it out and by the time he was sent to be the officer in charge of Charleville, he was a changed man. The town, Hallahan's birthplace, is 750 kilometres into the Outback, a town that had seen its best days decades earlier. Its population had reached more than 5,000 but now it was shrinking and peeling under the baking summer sun and freezing winter nights. Nevertheless, on the day he was transferred Lewis told a fellow officer: "I will go. But don't be surprised if I come back as commissioner." Something was afoot.

Whitrod sent Murphy to the farming capital of Toowoomba, perched on the crest of the Great Dividing Range which was then about two and a half hours' drive west of Brisbane, and then, in 1976 when Murphy qualified as an inspector, to Longreach, a town of about 4,000, 1,200 kilometres from Brisbane and more than 500 kilometres from Charleville. It was the first time in their careers that Lewis and Murphy had served outside the cushy confines of Brisbane.

But Don Lane, who would eventually become a Minister in the Bjelke-Petersen Government, was not only in Brisbane but he was also rubbing shoulders with the Premier in the wood-panelled, red-carpeted corridors of Parliament. Lewis regarded Lane as one of his very few 'special friends'.

It is inconceivable that as the self-proclaimed chairman of the 'get rid of Whitrod committee' and as a senior office holder of the Liberal Party

Lane did not take the opportunity to badmouth Whitrod to Bjelke-Petersen. In 1974 he had further reason to try to push Whitrod out of the job. Lane's name and home phone number were discovered by Whitrod's untouchables in the contacts book of prominent police bagman Jack Herbert who was collecting $1500 a week in protection money from illegal SP bookies. Lane would not have wanted inquiries to progress in his direction. The Rat Pack was further threatened in August 1975 when two major corruption inquiries were announced. Hodges and Whitrod asked Scotland Yard to investigate corruption in the force.

Bjelke-Petersen announced on August 11 there would be an open judicial inquiry into police corruption as soon as a major criminal court case involving allegations against police had finished. Detective Chief Superintendent Terence John O'Connell and Detective Superintendent Fothergill arrived later that month.

This could bring them all undone. Perhaps the Premier had suffered a brainstorm but Murphy had underlined the Rat Pack's strength and determination four years earlier when he told Shirley Brifman that they would not allow another government inquiry into corruption.

It wasn't long before O'Connell of the Yard discovered that the room they had been allocated for their interviews with potential whistleblowers was bugged. "I was warned within a week of arriving that I should not drive a car because it would be pulled in for some reason or other, so we didn't drive a car," he later recalled.

Was it Lane who first told the Premier that Whitrod was a Labor Party supporter? Bjelke-Petersen had a ridiculous hatred of the Labor Party and its supporters, labelling them socialists and communists: he thought the Labor Party was "the lowest form of human activity". He ordered his party's MPs not to eat, drink or fraternise with Labor MPs in the Parliamentary dining rooms. His attitude to Prime Minister Gough Whitlam infuriated the PM to the extent that he called Bjelke-Petersen a Bible-bashing bastard…"the man is a paranoic, a bigot and fanatical". If it was Lane who made the false assertion about Whitrod to Joh, it wouldn't be the first occasion on which Labor Party support would be a matter raised by Lane with the Premier. Several years later Justice James Douglas was in line to be appointed the Chief Justice of Queensland but Lane told the Premier he had seen a postal vote cast by the judge in his seat of Merthyr: it had been for Labor. The news was sufficient for the Premier to scupper the appointment of the learned and experienced judge to the top job. Such loathing for Labor supporters would have added to Joh's determination to get rid of Whitrod (who was, in fact, habitually a conservative voter). However, the Police Commissioner was anchored in his job by Police Minister Hodges. If Whitrod was to be forced out, Hodges would have to go first.

In January 1976 "government sources" (surely Don Lane) tipped off Ron Richards' Sunday Sun that Premier Bjelke-Petersen "was out to get" Hodges and Whitrod.

But who could be trusted to fill the role and do the right thing by the Premier and the National Party – as the Country Party had been renamed? Without prompting from someone like Lane it is unlikely that Bjelke-Petersen would have looked far enough down the ranks to find Lewis, for although by now he had become a junior inspector, he was still more than 100 places down the seniority list and had been banished by Whitrod to the Outback. It's a reasonable bet that Lane would have suggested to the Premier that Lewis would make an ideal police commissioner, being a loyal National Party supporter, having the support of the Police Union and being an opponent of Whitrod's policies. If he didn't, he wasn't half the conniving, Machiavellian, opportunist that had been evident in his grabbing the seat of Merthyr for himself and his redrawing of the electoral map to get rid of Bennett. Bjelke-Petersen visited Terry Lewis's patch from May 16 to May 18 1976 on an official visit to the tiny outback township of Cunnamulla. Lewis, always seeking to be urbane but coming over as unctuous, was invited to one of the dinners held by the Premier and seemed to be constantly close to the Premier. It was so blatant that Police Minister Hodges told a colleague: "Mark my words, Lewis will be back in Brisbane shortly."

Back in his office, Bjelke-Petersen created a file on the junior inspector. At the beginning of July the Premier asked for advice from his department on paying out Whitrod's contract. A month later the Premier took the next step in replacing Whitrod by sacking Hodges from the police portfolio and installing a totally compliant minister, Tom Newbery, who became derisively known to both sides of the battle as Uncle Tom for his subservient attitude to the Premier.

Immediately after his appointment as police minister he accepted an invitation to dinner at bagman Jack Herbert's home with Lewis and Murphy. Whitrod was now unprotected in Cabinet.

Bjelke-Petersen announced there were to be no further charges against police. Someone had got to the Premier and persuaded him against investigating allegations of corruption. The message was clear: carry on corrupting. But it went over the heads of Joh's Christian supporters, a group of whom formed a Fair Go for Joh campaign and paid for large newspaper advertisements which read: *'Deliberate and malicious attacks against our Premier are UNCHRISTIAN'.* Whitrod noted that Queensland did not have a government – just Joh Bjelke-Petersen and 17 yes men sitting round a table.

On 15 September, 1976, Gulbransen, now an assistant commissioner, turned 65 and was forced to retire. Whitrod lost his most senior trusted colleague within the Police Force. He was becoming isolated.

On Saturday November 6 Bjelke-Petersen returned to Lewis's patch with a Cabinet meeting in Charleville. With plenty of other regions to choose from in a state two and a half times the size of Texas, it seems likely that the reason for returning to an area he had visited only six months earlier was to hold further talks with Lewis to cement the plan for replacing Whitrod.

On the Tuesday Lewis phoned Tony Murphy in Longreach from Charleville to tell him that Don Lane had told him about the result of the Cabinet meeting. Premier Joh had asked how Lewis and Murphy were faring; Tony was to be promoted next to be in charge of the criminal investigation branch

On 15 November, Whitrod received a phone call from new police minister Tom Newbery to say Lewis was to be promoted to Assistant Commissioner. Whitrod was flabbergasted and told Newbery it was widely known in the force that Lewis had been one of Bischof's bagmen. Whitrod asked to address the Cabinet about Lewis but was refused. In Cabinet, Industrial Relations Minister Fred Campbell raised the persistent rumours about Lewis having been a bagman for Bischof.

He wasn't alone. Max Hodges recalled: "Murphy and Lewis were out in the country because we hoped by doing that, the corruption might die down a bit and I drew Cabinet's attention to all this and the reasons they were out there but I don't think anyone listened. I always referred to Lewis as one of Bischof's bagmen but the Premier refused to believe it…telling me to forget about it."

The premier's close confidante and media advisor Allen Callaghan also warned him. "Assistant Commissioner Bill Taylor came to me at the Premier's Office and tried to see the Premier. He came to warn me that Lewis was corrupt and part of a gang including Hallahan and Murphy. I passed this on to the Premier."

But Bible-reading Bjelke-Petersen was determined to appoint the corrupt Lewis.

A 'senior government source', presumably Don Lane, told the evening Telegraph: "The aim of the move is to force the resignation of Commissioner Whitrod. The whole deal has been organised by the Premier who has been trying for some time to get rid of Mr Whitrod."

Whitrod realised that he could not continue as commissioner when Lewis and Bjelke-Petersen would be working in tandem and leaving him as a lame duck. The dedicated reformer, Queenslander of the Year in 1973, Commander of the Royal Victorian Order for personal services to the Queen, tendered his resignation.

There was one crucial action that had to be taken. He entrusted the head of his criminal investigation unit, Basil Hicks, to methodically examine all files and destroy anything which could lead to informants and honest police who had ratted on the Rat Pack being hunted down by the new regime.

That same day Bjelke-Petersen announced that the "open judicial inquiry into police corruption" that he had announced in August 1975 would be specifically barred from examining claims of corruption. It would now only focus on police procedures. It seems obvious that someone from the dark side had got to the Premier. The Rat Pack and all their crooked colleagues were safe.

If anyone still had doubts about where Bjelke-Petersen stood in the battle between honesty and corruption, it is clear the Premier would almost certainly have been told in the days following the Cabinet meeting that Scotland Yard Detective Chief Superintendent Terence John O'Connell had discovered that corruption was rife in the Queensland force and that Lewis and Murphy were of particular concern. O'Connell and Fothergill had interviewed hundreds of Queensland police officers at the behest of Whitrod and Hodges. On the very day that Lewis was appointed an assistant commissioner, Queensland Cabinet Minister Bill Lickiss, who was visiting London, summoned O'Connell to Queensland House in the Strand to ask him about his findings. These made it clear that Lewis should not be appointed as Commissioner. Lickiss said he would pass on the information to Premier Joh. Knowing of the plans to promote Lewis, Lickiss, if he was an honest man, would have been remiss in not passing on the information about Lewis and Murphy as a matter of priority.

But a week later, on Monday November 22, Cabinet took only 10 minutes to decide not to advertise the position of Police Commissioner but to appoint Terence Murray Lewis as commissioner from the following Monday – November 29. The notes of this meeting are the only ones missing from the archives. Police Minister Newbery told Whitrod that Bjelke-Petersen had insisted on Lewis's appointment. Former Police Minister Max Hodges said that Lane claimed responsibility for getting Lewis appointed. And Sir Thomas Hiley said: "I recall a night shortly after Lewis was appointed Commissioner of Police. I was at a reception in Brisbane. I overheard a comment made by Mr Don Lane. He openly stated to the group in which we were standing: 'We got our man home'.

Ironically, neighbouring New South Wales was also in the process of selecting a corrupt officer, Mervyn Wood, as its next commissioner, ensuring that the force remained in corrupt hands.

Tony Murphy, once the target of the Criminal Intelligence Unit, would be appointed its new chief and would go on to head the state's CIB.

Lewis, having been part of a vicious, lengthy and well-organised attack on Whitrod with a focus by the union on maintaining a system of promotion based on seniority, had become commissioner by pole-vaulting over about 120 more senior officers.

This state of affairs is well documented. But there is another possibility worth considering.

According to a highly-intelligent and well-educated criminal partner of Hallahan, John Milligan (who we will meet soon) a triumvirate of Hallahan, Lewis and Murphy had compromised Bjelke-Petersen. Milligan, a long-time criminal associate of Hallahan, told an investigator in 1979 that this triumvirate had got rid of Whitrod and "…they compromised Joh Bjelke-Petersen, and by 'they' I mean the triumvirate, this particular three, with a great deal of assistance. Basically, they were dealing very closely with Jack(sic) Lickiss, the Minister for Justice. In fact, Jack was their man." Unfortunately, only this scrap of the interview is available publicly today. But it would fit in with the way the corrupt police operated. They had considerable experience of investigating people who stood in their way and of threatening, compromising or blackmailing them. There were David Young and John Komlosy at the National Hotel Inquiry, two people whose characters were ruthlessly destroyed. There were the homosexual businessmen who were blackmailed.

Every aspect of Whitrod's background had been examined in an attempt to reveal a dark secret which could lead to his downfall but nothing had been found. Could it be that corrupt police had carried out the same exercise on Bjelke-Petersen and had let him know what they had on him? A story told by Cabinet Minister Ron Camm to honest detective Basil Hicks supports this possibility. Camm told Hicks: "They've been following me, trying to get something on me, ah, trying to, ah, show that I had some affair with Vickie Kippin and they followed me to the airport when I gave her a lift to catch a plane home. There's nothing wrong with me just talking with Vickie Kippin, she's in the electorate next to me." Hicks said in a statement: "I could see that Mr Camm appeared to be very frightened."

It is also worth remembering that the police spy unit in which Don Lane had served, the special branch, was used to try to find dirt on members of parliament. The Fitzgerald Report on corruption found that after Lane had become an MP he: "…*seems to have been able to obtain access to its files himself. On one occasion, he was supplied with information which was used to disadvantage a member of the Australian Labor Party. He denied that he sought intelligence from Lewis on members of the Australian Labor Party. Lewis provided a similar service on occasions for each of Bjelke-Petersen and Hinze, for whom opponents or critics were investigated.*"

This could have been another option for corrupt officers searching for some dirt on Bjelke-Petersen to compromise him. If this was the case, had they then advised Lewis that they were confident of his elevation to commissioner? There is no evidence that this happened but it would go some way to explaining Lewis' confident comment about returning as commissioner even as he was being bundled out of Brisbane by Whitrod. It would also explain why Bjelke-Petersen had dropped his promise for an open inquiry into corruption.

In addition to this, Joh was a Lutheran sectarian bigot who loathed appointing Catholics to high office. Only one of the ministers was not a Protestant Freemason. Lewis and Murphy were both Catholics so their appointments were highly unusual, especially after the conservative government had appointed three Protestants in succession.

In October 1978 Premier Bjelke-Petersen revealed there was, indeed, a dirt file on him. He told the Sunday Sun he had discovered he was the subject of a police dossier. Who had compiled it is a mystery but news of the file surfaced in the middle of a power struggle for control of the licensing branch, headed at that time by an honest detective. Lewis had twice gone to Bjelke-Petersen seeking to have him transferred out of the potential gold mine. It is also worth noting that the journalist who broke the story was not a political reporter but police reporter Brian Bolton, so it is likely that the story was passed to Bolton by Lewis rather than Bjelke-Petersen, who told Bolton some 'Whitrod supporters' had compiled dossiers on leading citizens including him and Terry Lewis. Bolton wrote: "The Premier told me the dossiers contained scandalous and blatantly dishonest accusations which, if ever made public could ruin the standing and private lives of decent law-abiding citizens." Could that file on Bjelke-Petersen, in fact, have been compiled by corrupt police and used to lever Lewis into the commissionership? Was this revelation to the Sunday Sun Lewis's way of putting pressure on Bjelke-Petersen to move the honest man out of licensing by signalling to the Premier that he was letting the media and public know there was a dirt file on him and the next stage would be to release some of the contents?

One final point. There were occasions when Hallahan or Murphy would sit at the back of courtrooms when the accused was in a position to reveal something harmful about the Rat Pack. One suspects that Hallahan or Murphy would not have been there to take neat shorthand notes but as a warning to be very careful about what was said. Many years later when Bjelke-Petersen was on trial Murphy sat at the back of the court every day.

Lewis refused to talk to me when I called at his home so it's all conjecture. But then again, the appointment as police commissioner of a very junior inspector who the Premier knew to be the subject of corruption allegations goes against all the norms of government appointment procedures.

Chapter 29 – Hallahan Moves into Heroin

This is where we hear from one of Hallahan's long-time criminal contacts, John Milligan, who had the IQ of a genius but the commonsense of a fool and chose to use his intelligence to try to earn a quick buck on the wrong side of the law. He was a 33-year-old single, slim, dapper, slightly effeminate figure who came from a well-off family in northern New South Wales and needed to live constantly on edge.

Milligan had been a judge's associate in Brisbane's District Court in the mid 60s when he got to know Hallahan. He had mixed with judges and barristers during the day and ne'er-do-wells and violent criminals such as John Regan at night. Hallahan had used Milligan as an informer to keep tabs on what Regan and other crims were up to. While in Brisbane Milligan enjoyed the protection of Hallahan and only suffered two prosecutions – for traffic offences. And when he left Brisbane for the big-city crime that Sydney offered he built up a reputation as something of an untouchable. It may well be that Hallahan used his Krahe connections to protect Milligan in Sydney. A charge of selling heroin in September 1972 was dismissed when the prosecution announced it had no evidence to offer. Two months later, with Frenchman Jean Louis Guidoni and an Italian Giuseppe Saba, he was arrested and charged with armed robbery at Rose Bay. The charge related to the rip-off of a known heroin dealer. Milligan and Saba were committed for trial but the Attorney-General declined to file a bill. In other words, the State's top law officer decided not to go ahead with the prosecution. March 1973 saw Milligan up again for drug dealing. He was discharged when it was decided the case didn't stand up. And so it went on. By 1977 he was flying frequently to South East Asia, using a courier, Bryan Parker, to physically carry the heroin into the country.

The account of what happened over the next couple of years is basically Milligan's, as given to senior Narcotics Bureau officer John Shobbrook. Hallahan's denials can come later.

In 1977 Milligan came up with a scheme to import heroin through Australia's empty back yard. Cape York is the pointy bit on the top right of Australia which reaches out to the almost deserted jungle of Papua New Guinea, a country not renowned for strong border protection. Lying between the two land masses is the Torres Strait with its 40 shades of aquamarine and mix of islands, some of them picturesque low, forested hills, some beautiful palm-lined coral cays intricately fashioned by winds and currents and some of them just ugly alluvial mud dumped by the huge rivers of Papua New Guinea and infested by mosquitos. It doesn't bother the Islanders that some are owned by Australia and some by Papua New Guinea: they constantly cross between the islands with no passports. The big attraction to Milligan was not just the proximity of the two countries but also the fact that Cape York is almost empty. It's the same size as England but in 1977 was officially home to 3,838 people, if they were all at home. About 1,000 of them lived in the idyllic old goldrush port of Cooktown, on the site where Captain Cook had beached the Endeavour in 1770 after it had been badly holed on the Great Barrier Reef. The entire town is on the south bank of the picturesque Endeavour estuary. Stand at the top of the hill where Cook climbed to try to spot a way out through the Great Barrier Reef and if you look north you will see the same undeveloped coast that Cook saw in 1770. Outside Cooktown there is about one person for every 44 square kilometres of the Cape. Horizon after horizon of coastline contains no sign of civilisation: no buildings, no roads, not even a footprint on the beach. Areas the size of an English county are roadless. The first major population centre heading south from the tip is the city of Cairns on the east coast, about 950 kilometres south of the Cape, with 58,000 people at the 1976 census. It had grown rich on sugar cane. Set at the foot of the rain-forested Great Dividing Range and the mouth of Trinity Inlet, with the Great Barrier Reef just over the horizon, it had an airport serviced only by domestic airlines.

Milligan's idea was that a light plane flying from Papua New Guinea to Cairns could easily drop packages of heroin at an obvious landmark in deserted country and then land and clear Customs. Hallahan liked the idea and agreed to bankroll the purchase of the heroin from Thailand.

Milligan's pilot was a suave-looking businessman by the name of Ian Barron who he had met in a Sydney club. Barron was assistant national service manager for Sharp, the Japanese electronics group. He was nearly bald, what hair he had left was dark and he wore a black beard. Approaching middle-age, he wore business suits, striped shirts and ties and looked totally respectable. But he was naive and would do anything for a quid. And he was a pilot. When Milligan asked him if he fancied the chance of earning some easy money by flying across international borders, he jumped at it. They met Bryan Parker, the drug courier, at a hotel in Sydney and all agreed to work together.

To be closer to the action, Milligan moved into a unit in the Brisbane suburb of New Farm on July 1, 1977. He and Hallahan met at a room which Hallahan rented at the Travelodge, Kangaroo Point, whenever he wanted to conduct clandestine meetings. Hallahan gave him $1,000 for Barron to charter a plane to fly to New Guinea and back to acquaint himself with the route and Customs procedures. On the 13th he rang Hallahan at his Obi Obi home to tell him they were setting off the next day. Barron left Sydney by scheduled flight for Cairns where he then chartered the plane and flew on to Port Moresby, capital of Papua New Guinea, the next day. Milligan met him in Port Moresby to discover if he had experienced any trouble with Customs. Barron flew back to Cairns on the 17th looking for a suitable place to drop packages of heroin. He chose a massive plateau which rises from the surrounding lowlands. The plateau, called Jane Table Mountain, lies between the Normanby and Bizant Rivers to the south of the magnificent white sand dunes that line Princess Charlotte Bay. It was deserted but was reasonably close to the tiny town of Laura when it came to retrieving the drugs by four-wheel drive.

Barron told Milligan the plan was perfect and Milligan rang Hallahan at Obi Obi next day to pass on the news. They agreed to meet at the Travelodge where Hallahan handed over $3,000 for Parker to buy the heroin in Thailand.

Towards the end of July Milligan asked Barron to find another light plane and prepare for the actual drug run. Barron arranged a cheap and devious way of flying the heroin in from Daru, a mud island just off the Papua New Guinea coast which had an airstrip half the length of the island, a very low-grade hotel and not much else to recommend it. The owner of Cairns Aerial Services, Charles Du Toit, had advertised a twin Commanche light aircraft, VH-FAY, for sale in the Aircraft Owners and Pilots Association magazine. Barron met Du Toit at Cairns Airport and drove to his home to discuss the possibility of buying the plane. Barron told him he was a representative of Sharp Electronics and that he wanted to open an office in New Guinea. This meant Barron would be flying to New Guinea at least once a month. Could he test fly VH-FAY?

During last-minute preparations Milligan phoned Hallahan on August 12 and again on the 13th when he and another associate, Graham Bridge, an aesthetic-looking bloke with a whispy beard and moustache and a high forehead, left Sydney for Bangkok on an Alitalia flight while courier Bryan Parker travelled between the same cities on Singapore Airlines. Parker was to courier the heroin from Bangkok to New Guinea. Milligan and Bridge did not want an obvious association with Parker but wanted to be nearby in case of rip-offs. They bought a kilo of heroin which Parker then took to Port Moresby where it was left in a safe place. Parker and Bridge returned to Sydney on August 30, while Milligan treated himself to a foreign holiday.

A fortnight later, on September 14, Bryan Parker flew to Port Moresby from Brisbane on Qantas flight QF25 ready for the smuggling of the heroin into Australia. Next day Milligan returned to Brisbane from Bangkok and phoned Hallahan. A day later, Parker flew to Daru Island, taking with him the heroin and booking into the Daru Hotel. On the 17th Milligan, Barron, with his thick black beard, and Bridge, with his whispy version, arrived in Cairns in preparation for the heroin importation and retrieval. Milligan and Bridge booked a double room and Barron a single room at the Lyons Motel, Cairns. The two-star motel might not have been

The Ritz but it had a pool and air conditioning and was a whole lot better than being in Daru.

On the 18th the three of them walked in to the Budget Rent-a-Car office in Cairns and at 11.30am hired a Toyota four-wheel-drive wagon. They drove to the light aviation centre of the airport where the black-bearded Barron had arranged to test fly VH-FAY for no fee and which he flew to Daru.

Milligan and Bridge carried on driving towards the tiny hamlet of Laura, comprising only a dozen homes, a general store and the Quinkan Hotel, 300 kilometres to the north. They planned to stay the night here and set off in the morning for Jane Table Mountain.

Now, Barron performed his part of the scheme immaculately, meeting Parker in the Daru Hotel, picking up the heroin, dropping it in two packages on to Jane Table Mountain and landing at Cairns Airport where he had nothing to declare. Parker flew to Port Moresby and then on to Brisbane on a regular flight, his job over.

But Milligan and Bridge were about to have one of those gut-wrenching moments when you realise you've made a dreadful mistake. It was only now, as they talked to the locals in the Quinkan Hotel that they realised they would need a boat to get them across a river to the mountain. Jane Table Mountain is, in effect, a giant island. Bridge asked about the rivers flowing into the bay and how far up those rivers a boat could go. Milligan and Bridge tried for two days to find a way through but gave up and returned to Cairns on September 22, forking out $181.05 for the car before continuing their journey to Brisbane. Next day Milligan took a deep breath before phoning Hallahan to tell him his $3,000-worth of heroin was out of reach on a lonely plateau. They may have been business partners but Milligan knew of Hallahan's history and reputation and feared him. Hallahan was short and to the point: Go and get it.

On the 28th Milligan was back in North Queensland. This time he hired a vehicle from Townsville, a Ford F100 utility, registration OTO 819, from Budget. He told the staff he was taking a few friends fishing up north. And with a friend he borrowed a dinghy and outboard from a mate and headed back to Princess Charlotte Bay. It was a nine-hour, 650 kilometre drive before they reached the coast, launched the dinghy, crossed the bay and travelled up the Normanby River to the base of the mountain where they set up camp. Next day they climbed up the hill and spent hours with the tropical sun beating down on them, combing the long, brown grass that covered the plateau. It had all looked so easy from the air but on the ground a package might only have been a few metres away and remain hidden by the grass. The heroin could not be found. What on earth could they do next? Milligan travelled back down the river until he came to a fisherman's camp. Here he found Dave, an easy-going bloke who, besides fishing, loved nothing better than a cold beer on a hot day. It was pointless trying to invent a fanciful story about why they would be looking for a parcel on the plateau. Milligan asked Dave to help in the search, with a $5000 success fee if they found the parcels. They divided the plateau into sections and walked up and down in line for four hot days. The main plateau is only about a kilometre long by half a kilometre wide but they found nothing. Milligan and his friend made the nine-hour journey back to Townsville where the car was returned on October 3 at a cost of $352.24. This time it took Milligan two days to pluck up the courage to phone Hallahan.

They came up with plan B. Milligan telegrammed Dave at his base asking him to meet them at an isolated airstrip on Princess Charlotte Bay called Marina Plains on October 9. Milligan, Barron and Bridge flew in a chartered plane to Marina Plains. The plan was for Barron to do a repeat run and drop two brightly coloured dummy parcels on to the mountain in the same place as the first two parcels while the vaguely effeminate Milligan, the professorial-looking Bridge and the down-to-earth fisherman Dave watched from the top of the plateau. The trio took up their positions at different points of the plateau and listened for the engine. Barron's plane appeared over the northern horizon and they watched as the parcels dropped. Again, it seemed very easy. Again, they were very wrong. They searched for four days under the searing tropical sun. The score? Both dummy parcels but only one of the heroin parcels. Exhausted, they gave up once again. On the 13th Milligan and Bridge left the area on the tiny Cooktown Air Services mail plane with Milligan carrying the heroin hidden between frozen barramundi fillets which Dave had provided. Next day, back in his unit, Milligan made a phone call to Obi Obi 25.

Barron was paid $1,000. Hallahan received $26,000 as his share of the profits from Milligan. Dave received nothing for his trouble. Which might have been Milligan's biggest mistake. Because Dave went back to Jane Table Mountain and came back with the second parcel. If he had received his promised $5,000 he might have contacted Milligan. As it was, he tried to sell the heroin himself.

Chapter 30 – John Shobbrook Builds a Case

It was nearly a year later, on August 21, 1978, when John Shobbrook, the 30-year-old deputy head of the Queensland and Northern Territory region of the Australian Narcotics Bureau was given a report by a senior investigator regarding heroin obtained from Cairns at the start of the year.

Shobbrook had come a long way since leaving school at 14 and working on a farm. Life had not been easy for his parents. They had never owned a car and food was prepared on a wood stove. But that had not stopped them from adopting him as a baby and bringing him up with much love and affection. Dad had been a truck driver and he and his wife had shared a lot of very old fashioned views about life and its values. They were practising Christians. John had been brought up to believe you don't cheat and you don't lie. Honesty and straightforwardness were the important things in life.

A small, neat house on Kangaroo Point had been home, a home without books, for mum and dad never had any need for books and John would never need them because, of course, there was never any doubt that he would leave school and become a labourer. There was no motivation to do any better in life. So John had obtained mediocre levels in exams. But it was a happy home, filled with love. After working on farms he had developed an interest in photography. Despite the lack of motivation in his school days, he had never been happy unless there was a challenge to be overcome. And this desire to find and answer challenges brought him a job as a photographer on a passenger liner sailing to Europe and back. For a year he had a ball. And then his number came up in the ballot for Vietnam conscription. So be it. It was another challenge. He received a letter while in Southampton saying next time he was in Sydney would he go in for a medical. Then he could go back to Southampton and next time he was in Sydney after that, he would be called up. He passed the medical and after his next trip he resigned from his perfect job and waited to be called. He waited and waited and waited. And while dozens of other lads were doing everything they could to avoid conscription, John phoned the Army and said: "Hey, you've forgotten me."

His file had been lost and because more than three months had elapsed he would have to have another medical. This time he failed it because of an attack of acne on his back. Apparently this was a big 'no, no' in the steamy conditions of Vietnam. With his prize job gone what could he do? What did he know?

By chance he saw an advertisement in the paper for Customs prevention officers. He had always had a love for boats and planes. Normally this sort of job would have been out of his reach but fortunately in this case, school certificates and degrees were not necessary. He would have to complete an aptitude test. In November 1969, at the age of 21, he sailed through it and the next month obtained 100 per cent passes in every subject in the induction course examination.

In August 1970 he completed a four-week investigation course run by Victoria State Police Force's detective training centre. He passed all exams with an average mark of 84 per cent. Four months later he passed an investigator techniques course run by Customs with a final mark of 94 per cent. In April 1972 he was promoted to Investigator (narcotics agent) with the Federal Bureau of Narcotics and was transferred to Sydney. Two months later he attended an advanced training seminar on the techniques of dangerous drug investigations. On July 27, 1973, barrister and New South Wales Legislative Member Louis Solomons appearing for the defence in a drugs case, commended Shobbrook for the way in which he had conducted the investigation. Other commendations followed from impressed magistrates. In March 1974 he attended a specialised intelligence surveillance and undercover operations course run by the Australian Secret Intelligence Service and at the same time was promoted to senior investigator.

He became the first officer in the country to receive two certificates of recognition for outstanding performances in narcotics investigations. One of the citations mentioned his initiative, diligence and devotion to duty of a high order. The other said that over a period of months he had demonstrated personal qualities and professional skill of a high order. His supervising officer later wrote of his ability in solving problems: "This officer displays ability in this regard which is well above that which would normally be expected of an officer of his age and experience." He successfully completed a specialised detective training course at the Australian Capital Territory over three months. Despite missing eight days of lectures and study because of court commitments in Sydney, he scored 1422 marks out of a possible 1600 in criminal law, evidence, brief preparation, practice and procedure. And he scored 350 out of 400 for forensic general, crime scenes, fingerprints and search. The instructor wrote on his report: "The overall marks are an indication of his intelligence, personal drive and ability to absorb the complex areas of law and procedure relative to criminal investigation. His obvious personal application and effort reflects creditably upon him and his department." In May 1978, after his promotion to supervising investigator (inspector), he attended two months of courses in the USA organised by the Drug Enforcement Administration of the US Department of Justice.

Through it all he had been dedicated to the job and the bureau. He even spent his own off-duty time constructing special surveillance vans because the bureau was so under-funded. One big old van had been bought at an auction. Shobbrook painted it and fitted it out inside so that through the rear windows it looked as though it was full of carpets and goods. In fact, what was inside was a typist's swivel chair from the office and a roof-mounted video camera utilising sophisticated equipment such as bits of an old vacuum cleaner. To stop the van from rocking as the men moved around inside, four 'legs' could be lowered through the floor to press down on the axles to neutralise the springs.

The report that was handed to him by the senior investigator on August 21, 1978, appeared at first glance to be not much different from many other reports that landed on Shobbrook's desk at the Brisbane headquarters in an Eagle Street high rise, close to the Brisbane River. He was used to dealing with routine requests to destroy drugs when an inquiry could be taken no further. But this report concerned 380 grams (nearly a pound) of heroin - perhaps the largest amount seized in Queensland by the bureau. Yet as he read through the file he realised hardly any checks had been carried out. The report suggested the heroin be listed for destruction and contained a rebuke by the investigator complaining about the bureau's lack of ability and initiative in following up the investigation. Shobbrook picked up the file and carried it into the office of his chief, Max Rogers, to suggest something was wrong and that something should be done to rectify the situation.

The report had been made on April 24 - four months earlier. And nothing had happened since then.

Shobbrook was told: "Look, if you want to do something about it then you get in touch with Canberra and sort it out yourself." Shobbrook went back to the report's author and asked him for a summary of what had happened.

It had all started in January that year when a Cairns informant had taken a matchbox full of heroin to the Cairns Customs sub-collector Peter Gerry. Gerry had sent the box on down to Brisbane. This was eye-popping stuff. Normally, samples were only a couple of grains. Here was high grade heroin worth thousands and thousands of dollars. Officers had flown to Cairns to follow up the lead. The informant told them how a fisherman called Dave had been wandering around town trying to sell the heroin. They put Dave under surveillance but he was soon on to them and they had to confront him. Dave explained that the heroin was hidden at his camp way up on the Normanby River, a day's drive to the north. The officers travelled there by the local Customs launch. It was so informal that the first thing they did on arrival was to have a few cold beers courtesy of Dave because it was a hot day. They also said 'yes please' to some barramundi. Then Dave said: "You sit there and I'll go and get the stuff." And they did just that while Dave went into the bush and returned with 380 grams of heroin. Dave said it had been dropped by a plane on nearby Jane Table Mountain.

The owners had been unable to find the packages and had enlisted Dave's help in the search. Mixed up in the scheme somewhere had been the name of John Milligan, a man who had frequently been linked with major drug importations but who for some reason had only been busted once. Nothing further seemed to happen and on April 24 the senior officer had submitted a report requesting directions as to what action he should take next. There had been no reply. And that, thought Shobbrook, was where he had come in.

Now the report went to Chief Inspector David Schramm, the national enforcement officer in Canberra. Schramm directed that the investigation should be upgraded but it was the end of November before Shobbrook was told to start work on Milligan. Before this could happen, Shobbrook, at just 30 years of age, was upgraded to acting regional commander for Queensland and the Northern Territory when Rogers went off on leave. It meant he was too busy to look at Milligan.

It was January 4, 1979, before Shobbrook was able to start a mammoth task. But would he be able to complete the job? The Daily Mirror reported on that day that the Narcotics Bureau could soon be disbanded and become part of a new Australian police force. The newspaper had received a tip that the Williams Royal Commission into Drugs had already decided to disband the bureau as a result of severe criticism of it by senior Commonwealth police. One Commonwealth officer in Brisbane had told the Royal Commission in secret hearings that he considered the bureau totally inept and that narcotics officers were not capable of presenting matters in court. Narcotics officers had learned of the criticism, said the Daily Mirror, and had called for an inquiry.

Shobbrook was acquainted with Milligan, even though the two had never met. While he had been working as an investigator's aide in Brisbane at the beginning of the decade he had become aware of an importation of drugs addressed to a non-existent company called Asiatic Interiors in Ann St, Brisbane. Milligan had turned up at the airport to collect the parcel but had claimed to be only the messenger and that he knew nothing about the contents. It had become a talking point that no one could wrap a brief round him. Despite being widely known as a drug importer he had only been taken to court twice, and one of those charges had been so insignificant he hadn't even bothered turning up for the case.

In 1978 Milligan was named at the Royal Commission of Inquiry into Drug Trafficking in New South Wales run by Justice Woodward as a Sydney-based heroin importer who had police and political protection in Queensland. It was alleged two MPs paid for 2.5 kg of heroin brought into Australia by a diplomatic courier and arranged by Milligan. A large number of overseas flights had been booked by a tiny real estate company run by

Milligan. In a five-week period the company had chalked up $8188 in airline tickets.

Shobbrook was given the go-ahead to investigate Milligan. He asked to be allowed to concentrate solely on this importation and to be allowed to choose the officers he wanted to help him instead of just having officers assigned to him. The answer was 'Yes'. It was the first time it had happened in Shobbrook's long experience. He even had his own office and equipment! To help him he chose Senior Investigator Noel Lester Caswell, a Christmas Day baby who had grown to be a big, tough, solid formidable man, and Investigator John Eric Moller, a studious man with a needle-sharp mind.

Shobbrook had met Caswell while on a detective training course in the Australian Capital Territory in 1976. Caswell had then been a Northern Territory policeman. He was a good, tough cop, the sort who would play rugby league on bitumen car parks without fretting. Slightly younger than Shobbrook, he was a nice guy, with a good sense of humour but fearsome-looking and the sort of bloke who it was comforting to have beside you when walking down a dark alley. Moller, bespectacled and in his late 20s, later became a university lecturer. All three were married. A senior officer decided the inquiry should have a name and christened it Operation Jungle.

The team started work on the phone. Moller was especially good at finding the right people to speak to. Instead of using conventional methods, such as sending a report to a sub-collector somewhere and asking him to ask one of his officers to look into it, the team searched out the names of other keen, efficient investigators and rang them direct. They started with all the routine, background questions they could think of: light aircraft sightings, strange vehicles. Nothing!

On to another tack. Dave, the fisherman, had talked of a group of strangers searching Jane Table Mountain looking for packages. If this was true, perhaps they had hired a four-wheel drive for the purpose? Customs officers were sent to every car hire company in Cairns to photocopy every contract to hire vehicles for two months around what Dave had mentioned as being the time when the heroin had been dropped. The copies were sent down to Operation Jungle HQ. The team pored over the piles of contracts. Not one name or detail rang any bells. They did exactly the same with Townsville, 375 kilometres further south and the next big town with an airport. They would do the same all the way down the coast if necessary. It was while they were going through the Townsville sheets that they struck gold. Like a rich nugget after much digging, the name lay there on a contract for a four-wheel drive - John Edward Milligan. One of them grabbed the RACQ map of the area and worked out the mileage from Townsville to Jane Table Mountain and back and compared it with the mileage recorded for the vehicle. The distances were spot on. They were triumphant but amazed at how Milligan had so brazenly used his own name. It was something that would be repeated all through the operation with airline tickets and hotel rooms. Milligan and his men were so cocky that the team began to wonder if there was some sort of protection involved. Day after day they checked. They tracked down each hotel members of the gang had stayed in and visited them. It took a lot of footwork but every address was examined and anybody who might have seen the gang was questioned.

As they buckled down to their mammoth task their chief, Max Rogers, was replaced by John Robinson, a former member of the Queensland Police Force. Queensland Police Commissioner Terry Lewis would later deny having anything to do with engineering his appointment. What would he be like? Sunday Sun reporter Brian Bolton reported on March 11: "On Friday former Detective Sergeant John Robinson, 37, was appointed commander of the Federal Narcotics Bureau based in Brisbane. Commander Robinson, who joined the Queensland police force in 1958, served in Mt Isa and on key CIB units in Brisbane until he joined the Feds in 1974. He was nicknamed Black Robbie by retired Det Sgt Jack Linthwaite who founded the Queensland CIB drug squad in 1957 and recruited Commander Robinson and Insp Horrie Robertson to his new team."

Interestingly, according to an entry in Police Commissioner Terry Lewis' diary, Robinson was mentioned in a bizarre case in 1978 when, claimed Lewis, a drug importer had evaded all security checks at police headquarters and walked into his office with a gun and wads and wads of cash. Lewis had recorded on October 13 that the importer had 'called' and: "Produced pistol on entry to my office. Said he had about $150,000 which he wanted me or Premier to take. Had been given to him by associates of (censored), son of person arrested in Bangkok this week with about $2.5 million drugs. Feared Ned Smith or some unnamed police from NSW will murder him for the money. Mr (censored) obtained services of Mr Barbi, solicitor, interviewed in conference room." Three days later Lewis wrote that he had told the Premier about the strange visit. On November 9 Lewis wrote: "Messrs J. Rogers and J. Robinson served seizure notice re $145,000." The missing names were censored by the Fitzgerald Inquiry into corruption.

One of the first things Shobbrook did was to put a check on the calls made from Milligan's unit. There were a large number of calls to a number at Obi Obi. He checked the number with Telecom. The registered owner was a man called Glendon Patrick Hallahan. The name rang a bell with Shobbrook. It didn't take long to discover who Hallahan was.

Over the coming weeks Shobbrook and his team filled one wall of their office with a calendar of events in which Milligan and his team were linked. Complicated charts with dozens of names were compiled and then regularly scanned.

There were other importations, too, which they examined. And Shobbrook liaised with another team, down in Sydney, which was putting its own jigsaw together. A New South Wales State police drug squad member called Harrigan had used an undercover policewoman using the name Sue White to infiltrate a section of Milligan's syndicate. Shobbrook flew to Sydney several times to liaise with the police team. In June 1979 Harrigan created a calendar of events similar to Shobbrook's. Harrigan's list showed Milligan had a home in Sydney. A number of calls were recorded between his phone there and Obi Obi, which had now become part of the subscriber trunk dialling network with the new number 46-9125. The 1979 calls correlated with an importation of heroin Milligan made from Bangkok via Noumea. In July Milligan was planning to bring in heroin from Manila aided by Graham Bridge.

By now the Narcotics Bureau was under further pressure. The Federal Government announced that police would investigate claims that the Mr Asia drug ring paid a Sydney Narcotics Bureau officer for inside information.

At nine o'clock on July 20 undercover officer Sue White and an informant named McGovern met Milligan in a room at the Westend Hotel, Pitt St, Sydney, to discuss their intended heroin importation. White was to leave for Manila in a few days using a ticket supplied by Milligan. Milligan said he would phone a contact of his to make sure that all would go smoothly when the courier left the country. The contact would also be able to ascertain if she was on any police or Customs blacklist. McGovern watched the dial spinning as Milligan made the call and then left the room on the pretext of wanting to get some cigarettes. Outside the room he wrote down on a slip of paper what he thought the number was. It was 46-9126, within one digit of Hallahan's number. Milligan also said: "There's been a meeting at Canberra today but my informant 'His Excellency' wasn't included. I'll be making more inquiries to find out what the meeting was about and whether it's cool for me to leave Australia. It's probably something to do with the bullshit task force that's starting soon."

The bullshit task force referred to by Milligan was meant to be a top secret, top level, high-powered group of the nation's foremost drugbusters created by the Federal and New South Wales Royal Commissions which were both examining illegal drugs. The joint task force was searching for targets to justify its existence. Sue White contacted one of the joint task force investigators to tell him of Milligan's knowledge. By August 2 McGovern was in fear of his life because Milligan had been told by one of the joint task force officers that McGovern was informing on him.

Shobbrook was intrigued by the implication of the phone number dialled from the Westend Hotel, which suggested Hallahan had high-level informants in both the police and Customs, but alarmed in case the Sue White importation meant Milligan would be arrested in New South Wales on this much smaller matter. There was another thing worrying him. He had just about enough evidence to put Milligan and all but one of his accomplices away but now Milligan had moved on again. Where was he putting his shoes at night? Shobbrook asked for help from those NSW drug squad officers he felt he could trust.

There was one suspect less on August 11 when Bryan Parker, the courier, died in the Royal Prince Alfred Hospital, Sydney, the cause of death being put down as rheumatic heart condition.

At 3 pm on September 10 Shobbrook picked up the phone in his office in Eagle House. On the other end was a Sydney drug squad member who gave him the address of a unit in the upmarket suburb of Edgecliff where John Edward Milligan was living. Shobbrook shouted out the news, made a few hurried phone calls and rushed out to the airport with the beefy Caswell. At the bureau's office in Sydney, in Customs House, they picked up a car and drove out to the address. It turned out to be an imposing block of units. TV identity George Negus was a neighbour upstairs. Shobbrook knocked on the door not knowing quite what to expect. It was opened by a man Shobbrook had never met but who he knew so well. It was an incredible feeling. It was much like a fan meeting a pop star: the person was real: flesh and blood, reach out and touch him.

Shobbrook was amazed at how cool Milligan was after he had identified himself as a Narcotics Bureau officer. He was very confident, as if he knew a secret which Shobbrook did not. He oozed self-assurance, as if he was acting in a play. Shobbrook had arrested dozens of people and for the first time here was a man who wasn't at all nervous, not paranoid. Nothing. He wasn't screaming for a solicitor. Here was a man who had studied law and been a judge's associate and would therefore know the ropes. But he never asked for a solicitor. "What's all this about?" he asked calmly in a vaguely effeminate voice. They searched the unit but it was squeaky clean. There wasn't a skerrick of evidence or documentation in the place.

Shobbrook took Milligan back to the Narcotics Bureau and started to reveal just how much detail of Milligan's operations had been catalogued. For the first time Milligan began to heat up a little. Shobbrook made it clear he would be vigorously opposing bail. Milligan blurted out: "Why should I abscond? I knew about your silly little Operation Jungle." It was Shobbrook who was shocked. The team had kept a tight ship - or so they had thought. How, then, had the leak occurred?

Later that afternoon Hallahan was at home in Obi Obi when there was a firm knock on the door. Chief Investigator Ray Cooper of the Federal Narcotics Bureau told Hallahan he had a warrant to search his home. With him was a team of agents. To minimise the chance of a tip-off from a corrupt Queensland Police officer, Shobbrook had arranged for Cooper to be flown from Melbourne to Queensland specially for the raid.

Hallahan explained to Cooper that he had known Milligan for 15 years. He said the only contact he had had with Milligan after leaving the police force was in 1977 when Milligan wanted to buy a couple of acres of land from him at Obi Obi, and two phone calls from South-Africa. He said Milligan had paid him $26,000 for some land. And he said it had been Milligan's job to prepare all of the necessary documents for the sale.

The team spent hours combing Hallahan's home, outbuildings and land. There wasn't anything that seemed incriminating and a key that was found on the front seat of Hallahan's car didn't seem to be much of a prize. It came from a unit at Kangaroo Point Travelodge in Brisbane. Among the paperwork seized was a list of phone numbers.

In Sydney Shobbrook formally charged Milligan with one of the many offences he had been investigating - conspiracy to import heroin into Australia in the false bottom of a suitcase from Noumea between January and May 1977. Shobbrook told Milligan that Hallahan's premises were being searched at that very moment but Milligan didn't seem worried. He denied any involvement and declined to be interviewed. He wasn't going to talk but that was exactly what Shobbrook had expected. This was why he had spent so long on gathering the minutiae. He did not need a confession. Other cops might collect a bit of evidence and then forge a confession or persuade a couple of crims to give false evidence. But Shobbrook relied on facts. Milligan was still indignant about the lack of bail. Shobbrook told him: "Look, if you were to be granted bail, you would have to surrender your passport. Where is your passport?" "I lost it." "Fair enough," said Shobbrook, without necessarily believing him.

It was a short walk from the bureau to Phillip St Police Station where Shobbrook lodged Milligan for the night. Shobbrook bade Milligan 'good night' and told him he would pick him up at 9.30am ready for a Special Federal Court at 10am. But this was not the end of the day for Shobbrook. It still wasn't time for a celebratory drink. He drove over the Harbour Bridge to North Sydney and the address of a barrister who happened to be married to Milligan's sister. She opened the door. Shobbrook showed her his ID and said: "I'm sorry I have some bad news for you. Your brother, John Milligan, has been arrested for being knowingly concerned in the importation of a prohibited substance."

"Where is he?" she asked. And could she see him? Shobbrook told her he was at Phillip St Police Station and would be at the Special Federal Court next morning.

"Look, the question of bail will probably come up tomorrow," said Shobbrook, explaining how Milligan would have to report frequently to a police station and hand in his passport to the court.

"Oh well, I can give that to you now if that will save time," she said.

Shobbrook stifled a grin of amazement and calmly said: "Oh, well, I suppose it would save a lot of problems. Has he left anything else?"

But there was no other booty there. It meant there had to be another room somewhere: somewhere where Milligan had stashed all his paperwork and anything else that was incriminatory after he had been tipped off about Operation Jungle.

Back in Queensland Hallahan would have started talking to fellow conspirators and highly-placed contacts.

Next morning Shobbrook had Milligan before the Special Federal Court of Petty Sessions. Milligan asked for bail. Shobbrook stood up on behalf of the Crown and opposed it, telling the court how Milligan had said his passport had been lost and how an hour later his sister had provided it. Milligan was furious. Shobbrook thought that if looks could kill he would die there and then. There was no hesitation. Bail was refused.

It was all over. Shobbrook's knees had become alternately jelly and lead. The pressure of months and months of investigation was off. It had been a long night. They had come to Sydney with no spare clothes, no toiletries, nothing. It was time to go. Time to start putting the brief together. He turned to go.

Suddenly, he realised Milligan was calling out to him, wanting to know if he could talk to him privately. "You had your chance last night," said Shobbrook, who was already booked on a flight.

"Look, it's important. Can I talk to you?"

Chapter 31 – Milligan Tells All

Shobbrook reluctantly agreed. Milligan's solicitor agreed. So the two of them found a barrister's briefing room where Milligan asked why Shobbrook had opposed bail. Shobbrook said it was mostly to do with the chance of Milligan absconding. Milligan said he had known he was being investigated and that if he had wished to abscond he would have done so before. He repeated the bombshell of the previous night. He had known all along that Operation Jungle was in progress. This time he revealed the name of his informant – a senior officer who had just resigned. Shocked, Shobbrook said: "That's no reason to grant you bail." Milligan then became emotional and told Shobbrook: "You don't know how big this is. You're only a boy. You don't know what you've gotten into." He claimed he was not the mastermind, he was just a small fish and there were people of greater importance involved.

Shobbrook thought: "I mightn't have been around as long as some of the wallopers that you've had dealings with but I can pick a fairy tale when I hear one coming." Yet on this occasion Milligan's cocky bravado of the previous evening was giving way to an air of desperation. Shobbrook knew Milligan had either conned, blackmailed or bought his way out of sticky situations for more than a decade and a half. If nothing else, a front row seat at one of his performances would justify rebooking the flight back to Brisbane.

"Go on, you're doing the talking," said Shobbrook.

Milligan said: "Look, I'll tell you who's involved. The system as it has been explained to me: there is Terry – I don't know whether you know the triumvirate but Terry Lewis is the commissioner, Tony Murphy is his right-hand man and Glen is supposed to be the – what can you call him? – the civil organiser; the sort of planner; the ways and means man; the sort of inspector-general."

He also referred to the triumvirate as a 'board of directors' which had been created while Hallahan was still in the force and had continued to operate. Shobbrook knew there were those who spoke badly of Murphy. Hallahan he, of course, knew all about. But Queensland Police Commissioner Terence Lewis! Shobbrook had heard nothing against him at all. The implications were staggering.

"What's the phrase you used, the triumvirate?" asked Shobbrook.

"The triumvirate. These three have been together for many years as a group. Tony has been the other main partner in all the conspiracies, the corruption that has gone on in the Queensland police force. Glen was put out of the police force over all this. He had the opportunity of going back, incidentally, when Lewis became commissioner."

Milligan explained that because of Hallahan's role as organiser it had been decided it was important for him to have a low key image and remain out of the force.

"Glen is the civil arm and Tony is in charge of security. That's how the outfit operates up there. Tony does the dirty work. Terry is 'Our Friend'. That is in inverted commas, a nickname 'Our Friend'. In telephone conversations everybody has been referred to by some sort of pseudonym. Tony is 'Across the Road' – that is in quotes – usually. There are others, most certainly there are others. They got rid of Whitrod, they compromised Joh Bjelke-Petersen, and by they I mean the triumvirate, this particular three."

Shobbrook asked: "The Queensland three?"

"The Queensland three with a great deal of assistance. Basically, they were dealing very closely with Jack Lickiss, the Minister for Justice. In fact, Jack was their man."

Milligan said he had rung Murphy using a general police phone number to complain that his car had been stolen. Murphy had chastised him for not using a direct line to his desk.

Milligan said all this was heavy and his life was in danger if he talked. Shobbrook asked him if he trusted Harvey Bates, head of the bureau in Canberra. Yes, he said. Would Shobbrook ring him and tell Bates he was going to co-operate? Shobbrook felt Milligan was still after bail and would then toe it for safety. But he decided to test him out. "Look, I'm not going to ring Harvey Bates and tell him you've seen the light and you're a changed man just like that." He wanted proof of Milligan's bona fides before he went to Bates with such a story. What was the biggest thing Milligan had to offer?

"Where's the Markesteijn passport, John?"

Shobbrook knew Milligan possessed a false passport in the name of Markesteijn which he had used on the Noumea suitcase importation which was the subject of the first charge. It was in essence Milligan's ticket to freedom in some foreign country if things went wrong. But perhaps if he was prepared to give it up he might really be on the level.

"It's in a room at Paddington," said Milligan, without prevaricating.

Shobbrook was used to crims hedging for time, giving false information which led nowhere. But Milligan even drew a map in Shobbrook's official notebook showing an address on the corner of Sutherland St and Point Piper Lane, Paddington, Sydney.

Shobbrook believed that there and then Milligan had given up the ghost. He had named three accomplices, given up his ticket to freedom and even given up the room where his secrets were kept. Why he had chosen Shobbrook to confess his life of crime to he was never sure. Perhaps it was because he was so patently honest and this was the first time Milligan had ever come across a totally honest officer. There was another map showing how to get into the building and where the keys were. The external key was with Graham Bridge who would be returning from Grafton that afternoon. Milligan wrote down a message for Bridge in Shobbrook's notebook: "Graham (David) please just hand to this gentleman the key which you have to Paddo. Stay cool and come see me. John." Milligan said the room contained a lot of documentation which could incriminate him in a number of offences and pleaded with Shobbrook: "Look, anything else you find in there - you will not charge me with anything else, will you?"

"Well, if there's a dismembered body under the bed, John, we probably will take some action," Shobbrook joked as the two of them departed, Milligan making the lonely trip to Long Bay Jail.

Shobbrook phoned Brian Bates, brother of Harvey Bates and a senior officer in the Bureau, and told him of the conversations. Bates ordered him to go to Paddington and wait for Bridge. Inspector Phil Lawrence from Sydney narcotics bureau, a red-haired officer known affectionately as the Red Baron, and Caswell went with him. The front door of the rooming house was ajar. Inside were individually rented rooms. Milligan's key was where he said it would be - on a door ledge. Inside was the Markesteijn passport. And there were other passport applications in other names but all accompanied by Milligan's photo. There was also a document which said in part 'HOW GET MONEY - Hallahan to collect 2400 for M from ORTT of Bne - in trust a/c John Robertson Elliott and Co Sols 40 Queen St, Bne Re home unit in Bne H agreed to lend M 2000'. It was dated 22-3-78.

"What a goldmine," thought Shobbrook, rifling through the papers and finding two more documents which mentioned Hallahan. Then there was a cheque stub for $1000 from Milligan to Hallahan dated 12.8.77, the same day a phone call had been placed between Milligan's unit and Obi Obi. There were other payments from Milligan to Hallahan - between November 1977 and January 1978 after the Jane Table heroin would have gone on sale in Sydney - three payments totalling $3000. Other documents referred to Bridge, Parker and Barron. He put the documents in a suitcase and took them back to Customs House, Sydney.

The list of phone numbers from Hallahan's home would also prove to be interesting. It contained an entry "Tony M 221-7148" which turned out to be a direct line to Superintendent Tony Murphy, officer in charge of Queensland's Criminal Investigation Bureau, who would have been able to tip off Hallahan and Milligan about police knowledge of their smuggling operations.

Next day, Wednesday, Shobbrook obtained an order from the Department of Corrective Services, collected Milligan from Long Bay Jail and took him to Customs House, Circular Quay. Milligan was more subdued now, less cocksure. They crossed Customs House's echoing marble mosaic floor with its inlaid swastikas and caught the lift to the second floor where the bureau had its offices. Milligan found himself being led through a public reception area, through a waist high swing door behind the counter and round to his left into a private corridor where the pair walked through the first door on the left. They were in a small, windowless room about three metres by three metres with cream walls, no pictures to relieve the monotony and lino on the floor. In the middle of the room was an office table with two plain chairs, one on each side. There was no other furniture. Shobbrook motioned to the chair furthest from the door for obvious reasons and sat down himself. Milligan, slim and graceful, slipped into his chair. This was the way they would spend the rest of this day and every day for five days, locked in conversation, with a rapport and understanding growing all the time. They only stopped when Shobbrook escorted Milligan to the toilet and for hamburgers brought in from a take-away just down the road. Coffee would be brought in to keep them going. On the table was a small cassette recorder and a pile of Telex brand C120 cassettes. Here he was, he thought, about to record the most important allegations, involving a police commissioner and a CIB chief, and the bureau had, typically, gone shopping on the cheap.

Milligan opened the floodgates. Shobbrook felt he was holding nothing back. At times Milligan was in tears as he revealed what he knew. All the time Shobbrook was nursing him along, cajoling, agreeing, putting his hand on his shoulder, saying: "It'll be all right John, get it off your chest." He showed respect for him. All Milligan wanted now was to trade what he knew for bail. "Have you spoken to Harvey yet?" he would ask, referring to the bureau chief. Shobbrook slowly built a rapport and trust. As the recordings were made they were flown from Sydney to Canberra for the assistant commissioner and commissioner. There was only one small drawback: as Milligan reached a point in his story where he was dealing with someone who he feared or who he had a soft spot for, he would motion to the recorder and wait for it to be turned off. Then he would continue the story for Shobbrook's ears alone. Next day Shobbrook introduced Milligan to Daniel Scullion, the bureau's assistant director (intelligence). Shobbrook told Milligan: "Mr Scullion is the personal representative for Mr Harvey Bates and in view of the seriousness of your taped allegations, Mr Scullion will be present to monitor the tape." Milligan, with his love of the dramatic, was clearly impressed when Shobbrook mentioned that Scullion was there because he was the bureau's international expert.

What Milligan did not know was that in the interview room next door, amid all the junk that was kept in what had become a storeroom, was David Schramm, chief inspector, national enforcement, armed with a second tape recorder. A small hole had been drilled through the wall and a tiny microphone hidden behind a hole in the pegboard. Now whenever Milligan motioned for Shobbrook to stop the cassette recorder on the table, the master tape would continue recording, catching all of Milligan's off-the-record information about names, dates and places. On and on went Milligan's confessions and allegations, through coffee after coffee and hamburger after hamburger; through tears and tension. And every time Milligan motioned to the tape recorder and Shobbrook turned it off, all of Milligan's closest secrets wafted into the microphone stuck in the wall and were recorded on the master tape. Through Saturday and Sunday Milligan talked. He sang at length. And he cried as well. Sometimes the tears would flow as fast as the names. There were judges, politicians, immigration officers and other police whose names cropped up.

A rapport had built up between the two men, the hunter and the hunted. Shobbrook felt the room had become something of a confessional. It seemed to Shobbrook even then that there would obviously have to be a special task force set up to investigate all these allegations. On the evening of Sunday the 17th, exhausted, Shobbrook took Milligan back to Long Bay Jail. Then he flew back to his family in Brisbane, proud of the operation that had revealed so much.

Milligan said among other things that Hallahan was his direct principal for drug imports and had financed them. Hallahan had received up to $26,000 for the Jane Table importation. Hallahan had told him that should he ever be questioned he would say the money he had gained from Milligan was for the sale of some of Hallahan's land, even though there were no sale documents, receipts or contracts. Whenever Milligan was required to meet Hallahan to discuss imports, a unit at Kangaroo Point Travelodge would be used. Part of the Jane Table money had been transferred by Milligan to Hallahan's bank at King George Square, Brisbane.

Milligan also claimed that he had gone overseas that year under Hallahan's directions to conduct a feasibility study on another major heroin importation.

Back in Brisbane Shobbrook learned of Hallahan's story that he had only met with Milligan regarding a land transaction. Shobbrook wrote: "Following the discussions with Hallahan and Milligan the question arose as to why a former Detective Sergeant of police (and former consorting squad member who would be aware of both Milligan's criminal record and reputation) would sell to a convicted heroin trafficker and prostitutionist a portion of the land on which that former police officer had established his home and business, and where he resided with his wife and step-daughter? A check with the Land Titles Office has shown that no sales are registered with that office in connection with a sale of land from Hallahan to Milligan. Five blocks of land were found in the name of Hallahan. All five are still in that name. Why hadn't any documentation or receipt exchanged hands following this $26,000 cash payment, then or in the following two years?"

And Shobbrook wondered about some diary notes in Milligan's room mentioning GP in the same entry as the names of the drugs conspirators - hardly to do with buying a 'couple of acres of creek flats and rain forest', he decided.

On Tuesday the 19th Shobbrook received a phone call from a Supt Hanslow, at Long Bay Jail, telling him that Milligan had sought his assistance in contacting Shobbrook. Hanslow said he could have Milligan in his office at 3pm so that he could speak to Shobbrook. At 3pm Milligan said to Shobbrook on the phone he had given considerable thought to recent events and in spite of what other people might have led Shobbrook to believe, he would like Shobbrook to come to Sydney to interview him in relation to the Jane Table heroin drop - an admission in writing, despite his fears for his life!

So on September 24 Shobbrook found himself once again commuting to Sydney. He arranged for Milligan to be released under escort from Long Bay Jail and taken to Customs House. At 11.30 am Shobbrook started to interview him regarding the importation which became known as the Mallouhi suitcase conspiracy. It wasn't until 4.45 pm that he started the Jane Table interview. During this interview Milligan repeatedly mentioned "The Unnamed Man". Outside the interview Milligan said this was a reference to Hallahan but he was so frightened of him that he dare not even mention his name on tape.

Shobbrook recalled: "Milligan claimed that if he talked then his life would be in danger. He later informed me that Hallahan had claimed that he had already murdered a prostitute named Shirley Brifman."

At one stage Milligan rose from his chair and exclaimed "Evidence, evidence!" Shobbrook asked what he was talking about and he replied: "I know where you can find evidence to show Barron's involvement." Such was Milligan's co-operation.

While Milligan languished in jail and Shobbrook arranged the prosecution details, one of the 'triumvirate' named by Milligan was going up in the world. Terence Lewis, Queensland Commissioner of Police, was back amid the pomp and pageantry of Government House on September 28 to be awarded another medal from the Queen's representative, the Governor, to join his George Medal, this time an OBE for his services to the community. Some service! For instance, what the public did not know was that Lewis had put virtually no resources into the drug squad. Despite a massive increase in the number of heroin addicts the size of the drug squad remained pitifully small. Seized heroin would disappear from police custody. Those found in possession of heroin found that when charged, only a token amount would be mentioned, the rest having been sold by police.

On the last day of the month Shobbrook and Caswell were due to arrest Ian Barron, the pilot. Would he play hard to get? Would he insist on calling a solicitor? They arrived at the Sharp building and had a quiet word with the general manager to tell him his assistant national service manager was about to be interviewed about his part in a major heroin importation. The general manager's face fell. What would Japan think? Discretion was essential. The manager left to tell Barron that someone wanted to see him outside - and you'd better take your jacket!

Out came Barron. Shobbrook calmly introduced himself as if it was the most normal thing in the world for a Narcotics Bureau officer to turn up like this. Intriguingly, Barron treated the event the same way. "Let's just sit in the car," suggested Shobbrook. In jumped Barron. "Let's just go for a drive," said Shobbrook, churning out small talk like a mincing machine. And off they drove to Customs House, 90 minutes' drive away. But then again, Barron was that sort of guy. It was partly that sort of attitude that had led him into Milligan's clutches in the first place, thought Shobbrook.

He knew he was on the point of breaking what appeared to be a large conspiracy. He was a methodical man who was carefully dotting his 'i's and crossing his 't's. And he would wrap up the entire business given time. And now, as acting commander for the Northern Region of Australia, the lad from Kangaroo Point had come a long way. He had wrapped up a Mr Big and believed he had a strong case against Hallahan. And who knew where the Milligan tapes would lead?

On Monday, November 5 Graham Bridge was arrested in Grafton. Bridge would go on to plead guilty with Barron and Milligan. With Shobbrook's evidence against them, they did not have much choice. Next on the list was Hallahan. Shobbrook was enormously pleased that all the exhausting work had been so worthwhile.

It would have been unusual if Hallahan and his crooked mates were not aware of these developments. It seemed that finally Hallahan was about to be cornered. Shobbrook was not bribeable. If Hallahan was to escape there would need to be a major turnaround of miraculous proportions.

Chapter 32 – A Major Turnaround

of Miraculous Proportions

The first Tuesday in November in Australia is an immoveable feast. It is known as the day when all Australia stops for a horse race. Once-a-year-punters jam the tote agencies, women take as much care, time and money with their hair, frocks and hats as they would for a wedding and long lunches are taken by just about everyone. It's Melbourne Cup day. In parliaments it is a day for governments to slip through something controversial in the hope that opposition members will be more intent on finding a winner and in partying than in listening to what's being said in the chamber. The media might not notice through their amber-coloured glasses what's going on. And even if they do, there won't be much room in the news for anything that doesn't mention the Cup.

On Tuesday, November 6 1979 Shobbrook and Caswell were driving home from Grafton in northern New South Wales this Melbourne Cup day, deeply satisfied that another objective had been attained after having arrested Bridge the previous day. They had stayed overnight in Grafton and had seen Bridge safely through the court hearing that morning. The radio was on and tuned into the Parliamentary broadcast when deputy prime minister Doug Anthony made an announcement which devastated the two men.

Mr Anthony said: "In July 1979 following allegations of leakages of information from an unknown officer of the Sydney office of the Narcotics Bureau, the Government decided it was appropriate to consider general matters relating to the Narcotics Bureau." He told how the Government had asked Mr Justice Williams to examine the matter as part of his Royal Commission of Inquiry into Drugs. "The Government has given careful consideration to the chief recommendations contained in the interim report and has decided to adopt in principle, the recommendation that the Narcotics Bureau be disbanded and that responsibility for enforcing, at the Customs barrier, Commonwealth law against imported drugs remain vested in the Bureau of Customs and responsibility elsewhere be vested in the Australian Federal Police."

Shobbrook was stunned. What reasons could the Commission have for scrapping the whole organisation? Mr Anthony supplied the answer a few moments later: "The Royal Commission identified three main factors in support of its recommendations. In brief they are: 1. the Narcotics Bureau is founded on an insufficient legislative base; 2. persons who by any standards would be classified as criminals are deeply engaged in the illegal trade in drugs; 3. the total staff of the Narcotics Bureau is too small. The

Narcotics Bureau claims that the simple remedy for any deficiencies it may have is to increase its staff, powers and resources. The Commission rejects this cure which, in its opinion, would compound the problem not solve it. The solution is to attach the main functions of the Narcotics Bureau to the Australian Federal Police."

The attack continued: "The Narcotics Bureau was incompetent and failed dismally in every important respect to protect the interests of this community... For too long we have been fed this nonsense, this fiction, this deceptive fabrication that the Narcotics Bureau was fulfilling its job, that it was a very skilful organisation...Let us look at the essential features of this report of Mr Justice Williams. He condemns the Bureau of Narcotics for being amateurish, for being incompetent, for effectively being dishonest and for being obsessive about its own reputation instead of getting out and getting done the job it was charged to discharge. He suggested that perhaps it was corrupted on a significant scale. We know that it is the belief of State law enforcement agencies that it was infiltrated at the higher levels by organised crime."

Outraged, Shobbrook wondered about the phrase '*suggested* that *perhaps* it was corrupted' and waited for some sort of proof or explanation. Mr Anthony went on: "What about the disturbing allegations which have become public issues in recent days, that the Commonwealth Police passed on information to the Narcotics Bureau about suspects and potential drug hauls? Allegedly that information was not acted on. So offenders escaped and drug hauls were not seized. One draws the obvious conclusion that there was either incompetence, corruption or a combination of both."

It was not a member of the Opposition who came to the defence of the bureau but a fellow Minister. Despite the fact that he should have given wholehearted backing to a Cabinet decision, Wal Fife broke Cabinet solidarity to say: "The source of the criticisms levelled against the Narcotics Bureau was never made clear and has not yet been made clear. The Royal Commission does not suggest in its interim report that there is corruption in the Narcotics Bureau."

Opposition leader Bill Hayden said: "If the Bureau were anywhere near as successful and as faithful in its service to the community as the Minister would have had us believe, then let him explain why the Government quite peremptorily this afternoon moved in behind the findings of the Royal Commissioner and endorsed them by terminating the existence of the Bureau. There is evidence of corruption. The Queensland Police Force, among other law enforcement agencies, has said that. For the last two and a half years it has been a frequent complaint by law enforcement officers in State police forces that the Bureau has been heavily infected with corruption."

Was this what it was all about? wondered Shobbrook. Had the allegations come from the Queensland force, the head of which, Commissioner Terry Lewis, was now the subject of serious allegations, and which had supplied investigators for the Williams Commission?

Hayden added: "I stand by those allegations and I repeat that it is on public record that the Queensland Police Force has said as much." This was an odd comment from a former Queensland Police officer who had warned Whitrod in 1970 that the force was riddled with corruption.

Later that day Democrats leader Don Chipp said in the Senate of the bureau: "I still believe that it is one of the most efficient law enforcement agencies of its kind in the world. Its integrity is beyond question and it is composed of dedicated, hard-working men and women who virtually place their lives in their hands every day. I go this far: I say that there are two groups tonight who, when they hear the news, will be laughing all the way to the bank. I refer to the crime syndicates and the corrupt police throughout Australia...They have won a long battle, a battle that has been devastatingly planned and magnificently executed. Let me trace the history of this attack on the Federal Narcotics Bureau. I wish to ask some questions of the Government in good faith. Why was there such indecent haste to disband the Federal Narcotics Bureau? What was the urgency of it?

"The Government set up an inquiry. It did not have to do that, Mr President. Every dog in Australia has been barking for a year now that the Wilsons, who were murdered in Rye in Victoria, disclosed to the Queensland Police - I repeat, the Queensland Police - this information more than 12 months ago. The Queensland Police, the Press and the Commonwealth Police were informed. On that basis the Government was prepared to conduct an inquiry into the Federal Narcotics Bureau. Why? Did the allegations come from a respectable source? They came from the Wilsons, two notorious New Zealand heroin pushers who had been operating on a massive scale. That is where the allegations came from, via the Queensland police, against whom more allegations of brutality, bribery and corruption have been made than against any other police force in Australia, with the possible exception of the New South Wales Police Force. Therefore, on the basis of information supplied by two confessed, convicted felons, heroin pushers - information passed on, filtered down by the Queensland police - and exposed by the notorious enemies of the Narcotics Bureau, the Commonwealth Police Force, an inquiry was held. Today's announcement of the disbanding of the Federal Narcotics Bureau was made before the report on those allegations has been received.

"Why was the announcement made today? There is nothing on the notice paper. Why rush in with the announcement today? Was it because the Woodward Report was expected to be released today and that it was hoped that that would result in the announcement being buried in tomorrow's news? Or was it because another event in Melbourne this afternoon might be expected to take the front page of the newspapers tomorrow? Why were 17 or 18 Commonwealth Police officers seconded to assist the Royal Commissioner, Mr Justice Williams? They are members of a police force that has had since its inception, and continues to have, a manic hatred of the Federal Narcotics Bureau. Why was the offer of the bureau to second one of its officers to the Royal Commission rejected?"

Later he would say: "The disbandment of the Federal Narcotics Bureau was announced...at precisely the time the Melbourne Cup was run. I do not regard that as fortuitous. Something stinks about the reason why the Federal Narcotics Bureau was disbanded."

Why, indeed, was there a mad rush to start closing down the Narcotics Bureau? Federal Government cabinet records report that in May 1979 a high-level police team had been commissioned to investigate allegations that an unknown officer from the Sydney office of the Narcotics Bureau had leaked tape-recordings of police interviews with the Wilsons.

Then, on August 7, 1979, before that team had reported on its findings, the Federal Government had requested the Williams Commission to deliver an interim report on general matters relating to the Narcotics Bureau. (This was soon after information had been received that Milligan had appeared to be making contact with Hallahan to check on Customs and police knowledge of a heroin importation – and soon after feedback to Milligan that there was an informer in his camp.) In record time – less than five weeks - the Williams Commission had delivered that interim report, with its recommendation to close the Narcotics Bureau.

What nobody outside the Federal Cabinet and a few senior Government figures associated with the Cabinet process knew was that the Williams recommendation to axe the Narcotics Bureau had not reached Cabinet until that very morning. Someone in Cabinet convinced fellow ministers the Narcotics Bureau should be abolished and that this was so urgent that the decision should be announced that afternoon during the Melbourne Cup despite the fact that the Cabinet submission dealing with the recommendation had stated that the news of any decision should be announced later that month. There was also a requirement that the Governor-General, the Opposition in both Houses of Parliament and the leader of the Australian Democrats, Don Chipp, had to be briefed before the announcement was made. The six state premiers and the chief minister of the Northern Territory were also supposed to receive letters advising them of the proposed action before it was announced to the public. So it would have been far more sensible to attend to this process in a timely manner and make the announcement at a later date. Instead, this lengthy protocol was abandoned in the rush to announce the axing of the Narcotics Bureau in the next few hours.

Intriguingly, other major recommendations contained in the same report of the Williams Commission were left to a later date.

Cabinet Minister Wal Fife, who was responsible for the Narcotics Bureau, had been outraged by the findings. He presented a damning assessment of the Commission's actions to his fellow Ministers at the Cabinet meeting, saying that as the Commission had progressed it had become abundantly clear that the Narcotics Bureau:

> "was on trial on the basis of confidential evidence which it had no opportunity to test or refute except in respect of a series of generalities and sweeping assertions contained in correspondence from the Commission. The situation became so bad that the Department found it necessary to engage senior counsel to protect its interests in appearances of its officers before the Commission."

One of the criticisms by Williams of the Narcotics Bureau was that it had exercised central office control over the Milligan case without involving the police. Minister Fife advised his colleagues: "The reference to the Milligan case is interesting. As a result of Narcotics Bureau efforts, Milligan and six others have been arrested on charges relating to the importation of drugs. Subsequent interrogation of Milligan has justified the stand of the Bureau not to prejudice its operation."

In the car on that fateful Melbourne Cup day, Shobbrook and Caswell found it difficult to come to grips with what had happened. From being euphoric they had slumped to a feeling of despair. What did it mean to the Milligan case? What about their own future. Why had Mr Justice Williams, despite saying he had no feelings against the Narcotics Bureau, failed to include any of its officers on his team of investigators, choosing instead Federal Police and detectives from the Queensland force run by Lewis and Murphy.

On that same Melbourne Cup day in the New South Wales Parliament, the Woodward Report on drug trafficking was tabled in three heavy volumes running towards 2,000 pages. It had been completed the previous month but for some reason had not yet been tabled. Most of New South Wales was interested in the murder of anti-drugs campaigner Donald Mackay and what the report had to say about him and the involvement of corrupt police and officials.

But elsewhere in the report John Edward Milligan received plenty of mentions. In fact, Woodward identified him as one of the country's major heroin importers. An entire chapter was devoted to 'The Milligan Group'. Woodward said of Milligan: "He has been involved with well-known criminals since at least the late 1960s and the organised importation of, and trafficking in, drugs since 1971."

Woodward did not mix words in his appraisal of Milligan: "On the evidence before me I am satisfied that John Edward Milligan has been a professional criminal since the late 1960s and that since at least 1971 he has been actively trafficking in heroin, principally in NSW and Queensland but also in Victoria. Further, I am satisfied that since about 1974 he has been part of a number of groups of people who have imported substantial quantities of heroin into Australia by the use of couriers and light aircraft.

"I do not accept that Milligan played only a minor role in this activity; merely carrying out the instructions of others. Rather, I regard him as the instigator and principal of much of this activity. I do not believe that I have been able to uncover all of that in which he has been involved. But even the limited amount of activity dealt with by me discloses a pattern of continual and persistent drug importation and trafficking activity over the years."

A man called Terence Lance Hadaway said Milligan had brought in more than 2.2 kilos of heroin so pure he could turn it into nine kilos. The report said: "Hadaway said it was brought in by a diplomatic courier to John Milligan in Brisbane. He said that it was also paid for, to the best of his knowledge, by two Parliamentarians and 'we did three runs like this altogether and it went down pat each time'."

With one group Milligan was alleged to have been responsible for bringing in kilos of heroin which were dropped from cargo ships and left tied to buoys at the mouth of the Brisbane River in batches of up to 25 kilograms. With another group of criminals Milligan had helped to organise the importation of Chinese tables whose legs had been hollowed out in Bangkok. Woodward reported: "The shipments usually arrived in Brisbane where Milligan allegedly 'used to have a special deal going with a Customs Officer and they would bring it in in the furniture and the Customs Officer would just let it go through'.

"A witness suggested (perhaps with exaggeration) the group was responsible for 75 per cent of the heroin that hits Australia."

Woodward hit the nail on the head when he emphasised the way in which Milligan seemed able to avoid trouble with the law: "Milligan was the ideas man of the group...yet he was able to remain at liberty for over three years after he was arrested in possession of two ounces of heroin."

The whole tenor of the report confirmed what Shobbrook had himself discovered. But where just about every other officer of the law had failed, Shobbrook had succeeded. He had got Milligan locked up.

Back in Brisbane, Moller was already having thoughts of what he must do regarding the kiss of death from Drugs Inquiry Commissioner Williams. Moller had been off work with a back injury for a couple of months after a road accident. Next day, as acting regional commander Shobbrook set off for Canberra for discussions on the disbanding of the bureau, stand-in radio announcer Mike Higgins was taking phone calls on Radio 4IP's talk back show. At 10.27 a caller announced himself as Paul and said he was a Narcotics Bureau officer who wanted to talk about the way the bureau was being disbanded and to allege deep-seated corruption at senior police and Parliamentary levels in Queensland.

"Well Mr Higgins, I'll make it known at the outset that I am speaking on behalf of the Federal Bureau of Narcotics officers in this Brisbane office and I do have their support in what I am saying," he told listeners. "What we are most naturally upset about is that the Bureau has been axed through what is known to be a well-orchestrated conspiracy by persons with criminal and other vested interests in the abolition of the bureau."

And he alleged those conducting the conspiracy were: "(1) We've got the criminal element, (2) we have vested interests in the police forces and (3) we would have certain interests in the Royal Commission itself." He went on at length to talk about corruption, alleging politicians were involved as well as top level police officers. In fact, 'Paul' was Moller. These revelations were to have enormous repercussions.

The furore continued next day with a story in the State's only morning paper, The Courier-Mail, which said: "The agents feel they have been stabbed in the back by Federal and State police who, they claim, gave unfavourable reports about the bureau to the Federal Royal Commission on Drugs headed by Mr Justice E. S. Williams. "We do not have a lot of faith in them because as far as we are concerned they have too many rotten apples in their own barrels," the agent said. He also said a former policeman was connected with the Milligan syndicate and that several Queensland politicians were named in bureau files as having had connections with people in the drug smuggling world.

The ripples caused by Shobbrook's investigations were still spreading. When the Fitzgerald Inquiry released Terry Lewis's diaries several years later, the entry for November 9, 1979, had been censored. It read: "(censored); 'bugging' Murphy and Hallahan's phones; Hallahan still claiming friendship with Murphy and me and an anonymous call re me heading drug smuggling ring."

It seemed reporter Brian Bolton was on the ball with a report on November 11 headlined: Shock report on narcotics soon? Premier Bjelke-Petersen was reported as saying there would be no inquiry into 'Paul's' allegations of political involvement in drug smuggling. Senior National Party MP Bill Glasson swore in a statutory declaration a few years later: "The premier had often stated a view that an inquiry should never be started unless the result is known beforehand."

Despite all the fuss, Shobbrook was still working on his case and on November 12 he further charged Milligan with conspiracy to import the

Jane Table drugs. All next week the State Opposition in Queensland made it plain it was going to name big names in Parliament in connection with the furore which had been sparked by Paul's broadcast. It intended to do so on November 21 in the debate on matters of public interest. But the canny Bjelke-Petersen called a snap Cabinet meeting during the evening of the 20th and caught the Opposition half-cocked by bringing on a debate in Parliament at 10pm that day.

After four hours of debate Bjelke-Petersen announced the Opposition's claims would be investigated by a new session of the Williams Royal Commission. The Sunday Sun had reported earlier that year: "Sir Edward (Williams) is being tipped as the National Party nominee on the (racing) commission and has close links with the Premier, Mr Joh Bjelke-Petersen."

Shobbrook immediately tendered his massively-detailed and well-researched case to the Commission, including a 10-page closely-typed summary of the events from 1977 onwards together with 13 folders. The folders included: a copy of the original anonymous letter; copies of Monaghan's information; the report from the 1977 investigation; Shobbrook's 28-page report from February 6 that year; a detailed calendar of events from January 1977 to February 1978, including the links between Hallahan and Milligan; Cooper's report about Hallahan's key to the Travelodge; and Shobbrook's interviews with Milligan. Most of the documents were later sent back to him.

Opposition leader Ed Casey said he was confident the guilty would be exposed, especially as the Commission had the power to subpoena books, accounts and information in the course of its inquiries. Next day an event which appears to have no significance to the commission occurred. But for some reason it is included in a running sheet at the end of the completed report by Justice Williams. Notorious former New South Wales policeman, alleged murderer, standover man and partner in crime of Glen Patrick Hallahan, Frederick Krahe flew in to Brisbane Airport and was intercepted and detained by Federal First Class Constable B C Halliday. There is also a reference linking Krahe to Hallahan and Milligan. Why would the arrest of Krahe be linked officially with the inquiry? Perhaps Krahe had been in touch with people who might give evidence to the inquiry – or people associated with the inquiry itself – to talk about their health and life expectancy. Things were hotting up.

They certainly were for Police Commissioner Lewis. His diary for Sunday November 26 reads: "Insp L. Pointing called re interview with a Mr Milligan wherein he stated that ex-Detective Hallahan said that he would have me give any necessary assistance to Milligan. Phoned Mr Justice Williams re info we receive re drugs. Phoned Cedric Hampson QC re my giving evidence. Phoned Stan Wilcox re copy of Woodward Report."

Cedric Hampson QC, a former Rhodes Scholar, was President of the Queensland Bar Association, leader of the bar and the barrister who was counsel assisting the Williams Royal Commission. He was much respected by his fellow lawyers to whom he was always available for advice. It was his job to impartially assist Mr Justice Williams in discovering the truth. Stan Wilcox was a senior public servant in the Premier's Department.

Chapter 33 – But it's Shobbrook Under Attack

The grand-sounding Williams Royal Commission Special Investigation into Allegations Against Senior Police Officers and Parliamentarians held its first public sitting on January 3, 1980, in court number two on the first floor of Brisbane's Magistrates Court complex - a modern, medium-rise building overlooking the river in North Quay. It promised it would investigate any wrongdoing involving drugs by Parliamentarians and senior police. This would include not only actual involvement in drug trafficking but also any deliberate provision of assistance in any way whatsoever to persons involved in that traffic. Sixteen years after Hallahan, Murphy and Lewis had been at the centre of the National Hotel Inquiry they were now at the centre of another Royal Commission. Could they survive this inquiry as well? Shobbrook was not sure what the inquiry would mean to him but on this stinking hot morning he walked into the welcome coolness of the air-conditioned courtroom ready and waiting to offer any help necessary as Hampson rose to start proceedings.

Hampson, a large, severe, Teutonic-looking man, with closely cropped hair, said: "Allegations have been made and a lot of them have been examined. A lot have been passed over to enforcement bodies to investigate. And quite a lot of the material of course, as your honour knows, is quite ill-founded. It has been the experience that rumour is a currency much more favourable in this area or much more in use than are hard facts."

It was an opening which was to set the scene for much of what followed.

"What we propose to do today, your honour, although the allegations in the Queensland Legislative Assembly concern Parliamentarians and police, is to *not* deal with the allegations against police or the investigations of those allegations today, but to try to deal with what appears to us to be a completely discreet and separate matter - the allegations made against Parliamentarians."

In particular the commission would examine in some depth a mention Milligan had made in relation to Cabinet Minister Bill Lickiss, the man who had been in London in November 1976 when Lewis was being considered by Cabinet for the position of Commissioner.

Instead of summarising the grave and extensive allegations made by Milligan, and detailing them so that as the Commission unfolded, it would become clear whether they were being rebutted or reinforced, Hampson launched into an account of how Milligan, faced with an interview by an officer from Terry Lewis's own force had back-pedalled furiously from what he had told Shobbrook. It would not be until a month later, on

February 4, that a list of the actual allegations against Lewis, Murphy and Hallahan would be tabled. And it would not be until almost the very last - on March 20 - that large extracts of the taped allegations made by Milligan against Lewis, Murphy and Hallahan would be revealed.

Hampson said: "Our investigators went to interview (Milligan) and they interviewed him, I think, on 3, 4, 5, December. The account he gave them was that he did not know anything about any politicians at all of his direct knowledge having any involvement in drugs. This was all completely new to him.

"The first he had known really about these allegations was when he read them in the newspapers. (Milligan) really suggested that his situation was that he thought Mr Shobbrook would really like him to involve people in high places because Mr Shobbrook seemed keen to find some smut or scandal against other people."

Shobbrook jolted upright in his seat. What on earth was going on? For weeks Shobbrook had been in touch with inquiry staff and this was the first time anyone had said anything about Milligan claiming words had been put in his mouth. No one from the inquiry had come to him to ask him about this apparent change of heart by Milligan. And the Commission could choose to listen to the non-stop master tapes of the Milligan interviews to gauge the manner of his revelations.

One of the investigators who had discovered this change of heart in Milligan was Detective Sergeant Barrie Cornelius O'Brien, an officer from Lewis's Queensland force. With him had been Federal Police officer Ray Phillips, who was also on attachment to the commission.

I wrote to Mr O'Brien asking him for an interview about his part in the investigation but he failed to respond. It's worth examining what's on the public record about Mr O'Brien through the years.

In 1986 Det Sgt O'Brien was found by a court to have illegally taped a conversation between a suspect and his solicitor. A Supreme Court judge found that Det Sgt O'Brien had then fabricated evidence to justify his 'reprehensible' conduct.

A few years later, in a totally different matter, former Judge Bill Carter QC conducted an inquiry which resulted in him reporting "my total dissatisfaction with O'Brien's performance as a witness. He was, I am satisfied, intent on evasion and prevarication, and a significant body of his evidence was patently false". And, he said: "O'Brien's responses to the obvious questions were pitiful and inadequate. I reject his evidence as untrue." And on another point he said: "Once more O'Brien was untruthful…his denial of another important matter of fact…is disturbing." And on a further point: "I cannot accept this evidence." Det Sgt O'Brien was guilty of "a fraudulent pretence", said his honour, and he had made "false denials" on another point.

In this same inquiry, barrister Shane Herbert labelled Det Sgt O'Brien and a compatriot as "Keystone Kops" and "greedy, grubby people." Counsel assisting that inquiry, Russell Hanson, said: "Anything that O'Brien says that is not corroborated by independent evidence should not be accepted."

How close was Det Sgt O'Brien to Terry Lewis and Tony Murphy? Bagman Jack Herbert, who gathered corruption money from prostitution and illegal gambling for all the police who were on the take, told the Fitzgerald Inquiry into Queensland corruption that Det Sgt O'Brien was a member of a Lewis and Murphy clique of officers who regularly drank at the home of a publican.

Was there a history of Lewis placing officers he trusted in other jurisdictions? Jack Herbert told the Fitzgerald Inquiry that Commissioner Terry Lewis had told him: "We need someone in the BCI". What he had meant was that they needed to place someone in the Australian Bureau of Criminal Intelligence (created to combat organised crime across the country) to report back to Lewis. Two officers had been found to fulfil that role.

So, if sworn testimony at the Fitzgerald Inquiry is to be believed, it would mean that Lewis, one of the supposed targets of the Royal Commission's investigation, had an alleged friend of his on the team which was delegated to investigate him, a feat which would run a close second to Commissioner Bischof using Murphy to lead investigations in the National Hotel Inquiry.

Det Sgt O'Brien and Phillips had spent three days early in December with Milligan.

Hampson summed up the line of questioning from that interview: "A lot of this is speculation by Milligan, I suppose, but it was on the basis that the narcotics bureau had been disbanded and it would be good to throw stones at somebody else. To put it shortly, that is what Milligan sort of told Phillips."

What did Hampson mean? The decision to disband the bureau had not been made by the Federal Cabinet until November 6, well over a month after Milligan had sung his head off to Shobbrook! Hampson went on to place greater and greater store on the O'Brien/Phillips interviews, virtually ignoring the Shobbrook tapes and the uninterrupted master tapes.

He continued: "Anyway, the important thing about it is, that he (Milligan) did not support allegations whatever they might have been, made against Mr Lickiss and indeed - I do not want to go into the senior police officers today - the same thing was true to them. In fact, he said that in so far as anything like that was said on tape it was really at Shobbrook's instigation for whatever reason."

Shobbrook could hardly contain his anger over lunch at the way the inquiry was shaping. Soon after it reconvened at 2.14 he was sworn in.

The tapes he had made with Milligan on the recorder on the desk in that tiny room in Customs House, Sydney, became confidential exhibit 377. Their transcripts became confidential exhibit 378. The confidentiality meant that the media were not allowed to know what they contained. Public exhibit 699 became a portion of the tape in which Milligan referred to Lickiss while talking to Shobbrook. And 700 was the same topic with Scullion.

There are many ploys used by lawyers when it comes to cross-examination. Some cajole and caress. Some lay traps and guide the prey into the snare. Others hector and bully. And some, of course, use a mix of all these tactics and more. Hampson was direct and to the point.

Hampson drew Shobbrook's attention to what could have been a break in the tape. It was to be the beginning of a long-running battle with Hampson which was to end in the denigration of Shobbrook and his interview with Milligan.

Shobbrook: "It could have been because Milligan, during my conversations, frequently sort of pointed to the recorder and wanted me to stop it. So I could have perhaps momentarily touched the pause button or the stop button and kept going."

Commissioner Williams, the dapper, silver-haired judge known for his love of foreign travel and horse-racing, interrupted: "What did you want these stops for?"

"Mainly when he mentioned people that he had a degree of concern for, perhaps affection for."

"To talk off the record?"

"Yes."

"How much time was spent with that type of discussion, what percentage?"

"I'd say in my tapes perhaps about 10 per cent."

Hampson: "After that break he said basically they were dealing very closely with Jack Lickiss, the Minister for Transport and you said '*Yes, I heard that*'. Did you hear that?"

"No. This is the first time I've ever heard it."

"Why did you say '*Yes, I've heard it*'?"

"To be quite honest, I don't know. Perhaps the phrase '*I've heard that*' is another way of saying '*Yes, I heard that, go on*'."

"'Go on?'"

"'*Keep talking*' to Milligan to encourage him to keep on talking."

"What about the involvement of Mr Lickiss according to Milligan?"

"I don't recall."

"That would be pretty hot news, would it not?"

"There's a lot of hot news. There's a lot more hot news than Mr Lickiss's name by my standard."

"There is the Queensland triumvirate?"

"That was the hottest news that year. The allegation in relation to Mr Lickiss was a minor one compared to the allegation in relation to the triumvirate and the persons concerned in that triumvirate. The members of the triumvirate - we know who they allegedly are - were responsible or played a role in getting rid of Mr Whitrod of the Queensland police."

Hampson then questioned him about how word of some of the allegations on the Milligan tapes had apparently leaked. This was to be a major feature of the commission. It spent hours inquiring into how word of the Milligan case had leaked rather than into whether police and politicians were involved in illegal drugs.

Hampson asked: "What is Milligan like in your experience? Is he a big noter? A con man type? Very reliable, reserved sort of person?"

"All of that," said Shobbrook. "He is - I don't know. He is an incredible person. I could sit here for days talking about the type of person Milligan is. He is very intelligent, that he is. Very questioning. Very cunning. He is a big noter. He does have, or did have, a considerable reputation amongst police circles."

"As what?"

"As being a Mr Big although I think as we have looked at him now, perhaps not as big as the image but he did have the image of an untouchable. He could virtually get away with anything."

"Because he was supposed to have powerful friends?"

"Not only for that reason, perhaps. He was intelligent and the way he went about things. He used for the North Queensland job three light aircraft - one for a dummy run, one to bring in heroin and then another one to find the heroin when it went missing. And all for a kilo of heroin. He does things on a big, grand scale, because, I think, he likes the excitement. He is not in it, I think, for the money but for the glamour, for the excitement. He likes to manipulate people."

"Is he sort of a Walter Mitty?"

"Not so much a Walter Mitty because he does manipulate people. Walter Mitty dreams of it but does not achieve it. He does! I remind you that the people who he mainly manipulates are small, weak people and perhaps people higher up manipulate him."

"He may have manipulated a lot of police over the years?" suggested Hampson.

"I believe he has manipulated a number of police. I do not doubt that for a minute. Also he has been a great informant for the police, too. He is a very dangerous character," replied Shobbrook.

"Of your knowledge, were any of those that he mentioned as knowing them, false?"

"No. I tended to believe it was true. Graham David Bridge and Bryan Parker I knew of extremely well. And what he was saying about them was correct. Sir, one surprising thing about all of those tapes was that I couldn't catch him out, which surprised me. And perhaps in all the things he said, over all the days, I couldn't catch him out as lying with my knowledge of the people he knew."

"You could not get him back-tracking, as it were?"

"That is right. And you know, when you sit there with someone for about five days and they talk and you can't catch them out and they tell the same story days apart, and it is exact, you start thinking, perhaps there is truth in it."

"Or he has an exceptionally good memory?"

"Yes."

Hampson then put it to Shobbrook that when Milligan was interviewed by the Commission's men, Milligan said he had only told Shobbrook what he thought he wanted to hear.

Shobbrook said: "I quite admire him for saying that because if I had said what he had said on those tapes - and they are there to be heard - and I had regretted what I had said, I would think 'How can I backtrack?'"

He reminded the commission that the test of Milligan's confession lay in the master tapes, saying: "You have just got to listen to the tapes, the tone of voice. You have to listen to the off-the-record tapes, you know..."

Commissioner (interrupting): "The off the record tapes? We cannot listen to the..."

Shobbrook: "Yes you can, because Scullion..."

Hampson interrupted: "I see what you mean."

Shobbrook explained about the master tapes catching Milligan's secret asides. "You have just got to listen to the tapes," he said.

Despite Shobbrook's urging, his plea was not to be even remotely heeded in open session and there was no reference in the final report to the fact that the tapes contained crucial corroboration of what Milligan had confessed to.

Hampson continued: "The problem is that he has very seriously told you one story and he very seriously told the commission investigator a completely opposite story. It is the old question: how do we know he was telling the truth, or on either occasion, telling the truth?"

Shobbrook replied: "I don't know if what he told me was the truth because I haven't investigated it. I don't know. I believe that when he told it to me he believed it. Perhaps if our conversations had taken place for an hour or two he could have fooled me. But not over five days. Not with the tears. Not with the pleadings as we drove back to Long Bay jail. Not with the grabbing of my arm as the Long Bay warders were about to take him away and pleading with me to keep talking with him. No, I went through the whole scenario with him."

Shobbrook finished his evidence feeling quite punch drunk and unable to work out what had hit him or why. He sat there in a daze as the man himself was brought into the court.

The rather frail-looking figure of Milligan stood in the box and took the oath. He gave his occupation: "I am an inmate of the Metropolitan Remand Centre at the moment." Then with all the self-assurance of a former judge's clerk and with typical bravado he interrupted the well-ordered and forbiddingly formal proceedings.

"Excuse me. At this stage Mr Hampson, might I ask a question of his honour?"

"Sure."

"Your honour, I was informed that the hearing today was only in relation to the politicians."

"That's right," said Sir Edward.

"And I would ask of your honour if anything at all in relation to the evidence I might give, tends to go beyond evidence to the politicians, for your honour to advise me. I would like to make an application to your honour in that case, but in relation to politicians I have no application to your honour."

What he may have had in mind was an application to give any evidence involving Hallahan, Murphy or Lewis in camera.

Hampson then suggested to Milligan that in his interview with O'Brien and Phillips in early December he had in effect said he did not know anything against Lickiss, there were no allegations against Lickiss and that he didn't know him from Adam really?

In fact, the transcript of the tape makes it very clear that Milligan had told Shobbrook that Lickiss was closely involved with Hallahan, Lewis and Murphy. But Shobbrook had no one representing him who could jump up and object to leading questions.

"That's right, yes," said Milligan.

The counsel assisting a commissioner is there to assist in uncovering the truth. Leading questions are used from time to time where an issue is clear cut.

Hampson asserted: "You know nothing to his discredit, certainly nothing to do with drugs, and in fact, the only reason he comes to be mentioned is that Shobbrook in a sense put you up to it because Shobbrook let you understand, or you came to understand, that he liked to hear sensational allegations against highly-placed persons outside the Federal Bureau of Narcotics and in particular in the State areas because the Federal Bureau of Narcotics at that point of time was under siege of some kind?"

"Yes, that's so."

"That's what you told Phillips and O'Brien?"

"That's right. Yes."

"We have two opposite views. We have Shobbrook believing you are making sensational disclosures to him that are truthful about this triumvirate in Queensland - the unclear but nevertheless illegal activities of Mr Lickiss even if they don't involve drugs - and you told Phillips and O'Brien that that is not true at all, that you know nothing to the discredit of Mr Lickiss and, in effect, Shobbrook led you on, or you led him on - I don't know who led who on - but you knew what he wanted and you gave it to him even though you knew it wasn't true and you had no basis for saying it?"

This leading question was too much of a whitewash even for Milligan: "I don't know if I go that far in my questions to Mr Phillips and Mr O'Brien," he replied.

"How far are you prepared to go now?" Hampson asked Milligan. "I suppose that is the real question. What is the truth of it all?"

Commissioner Williams interrupted: "You are on oath now?"

"Yes."

"And the other times you weren't on oath."

"Yes."

"Let us have the truth."

This was where Milligan might have decided to start naming names. He said: "Could I make an application to your honour to be heard in camera?"

Hampson: "What for?"

"There are reasons I'd like to make in camera. I'd like to make the application in camera."

Seven years later there would be bodyguards and massive security for those who named names at the Fitzgerald Inquiry. Milligan was by himself and was greatly frightened by Hallahan. Several times the commission would go into private session. But not now.

Chapter 34 – Milligan Insists Shobbrook is Right

Hampson: "There is nothing very difficult before we get to that. There might be some information but you are really being asked that there are two different stories."

"Yes."

"You are really being asked to say at the moment which one is true, the one you gave Shobbrook and Scullion or the one you gave Phillips and O'Brien?"

"Well, when I made the tape with Mr O'Brien and Mr Phillips I wasn't aware of all the things that were on this tape that had been tape-recorded. I genuinely had forgotten most of them."

And then, despite his fear of Hallahan and the fact that he was on remand and at risk of a prison attack being arranged, he confessed: "What was said on tape with Mr Shobbrook was basically true, in that that is what I had been told," he said under oath.

"What does that mean - that what is there in front of you in exhibit 699 [the tape regarding Lickiss] is true is it?" Hampson asked. "Whatever is said in there is true, is that what you are saying?"

And again Milligan backed the Shobbrook tapes: "I'd have to go through it in detail but that's what - just from looking at it here - that is a true account of what I told Shobbrook and what I had been told," he repeated under oath.

"Can you say who told you?"

"I'd prefer to say it in camera."

Presumably, he was fearful of mentioning Hallahan's name in public.

"Let us look at page one, the first page, you have this triumvirate who has organised this coup which got rid of a commissioner of police of Queensland, right?"

"Yes."

Shobbrook felt that Milligan was being side-tracked away from his application to give evidence in camera.

"They were connected very closely with Jack Lickiss, the Minister for Justice?"

"Yes."

"Very closely, in fact, Jack was their man - all right?"

"Yes."

Milligan then alleged that Shobbrook had first mentioned the name Lickiss.

And Hampson then asked: "Who told you that Lickiss was connected with this triumvirate?"

"Hallahan told me that."

"Is he the only source for that piece of information?"

"For that piece, as far as I know, yes."

"I would be interested to know whether Shobbrook put you up to it in the sense of raising with you first, off the record, you know? Because the problem is you have read through that transcript this afternoon of what you told Phillips and O'Brien?"

"Yes."

It appeared from this answer that Milligan had been given a copy of his interview with O'Brien, the Queensland police officer, to remind him of what he had said. It would later appear he had not yet been given a copy of the all-important interview with Shobbrook.

The commission adjourned at 5.06pm, with Milligan being given a copy of a transcript - presumably the interview with Shobbrook - to take away with him to study to see if he could refresh his mind as to which tape was correct.

Shobbrook would later ask for access to that transcript - and be refused.

Milligan was not the only one with homework to do. With mind racing, Shobbrook walked right across the city in the extreme heat of the late afternoon to Eagle House in Eagle St where the bureau had its offices on the first floor. The department could confirm to the Commission that he had not acted in the way suggested by Hampson, thought Shobbrook. And he would ask for a barrister to protect his interests. At the office he told a senior officer: "I'm being crucified out there. I'm starting to get a bit worried. I've gone up there as an officer willing to assist the Royal Commission. But I think I ought to have a counsel helping me." A phone call to head office in Canberra resulted in the response: "You got yourself into this, you get yourself out of it." Shobbrook was rocked again. He was being abandoned, yet he had done nothing wrong.

Meanwhile, police chief Lewis recorded in his diary: "Phoned Cedric Hampson re evidence at Royal Commission."

Shobbrook had never been much of a union member but now he got straight on to the union and made an appointment to see if representation could be arranged for him. And he consoled himself with the thought that at least he had a firm brief of evidence against Hallahan.

Hampson asked Milligan in the morning: "You took with you a copy of that exhibit overnight. I would like to direct you back to what we were talking about when the commission adjourned yesterday afternoon and ask you what is correct, the account you gave to Mr Shobbrook or the account you gave to Mr Phillips and Mr O'Brien or is there some intermediate account?"

Milligan was emphatic: "No, I have already answered that. The account I gave to Mr Shobbrook is correct. Where there is variation in the account I gave to Mr Phillips and Mr O'Brien I think the Shobbrook account is correct."

That was three times Milligan had vouched that the Shobbrook tapes were correct.

Hampson continued to try to shake Milligan but he continued to bat for Shobbrook: "On oath I have to say I do recall having conversations, not of any great moment, but conversations with Hallahan about Lickiss."

The frustrated barrister questioned Milligan further about the O'Brien/Phillips interview.

"They ask you then *'Well, how did you start to talk about these things to Shobbrook?'* and you said *'Well, he said he wanted to and he spoke of Canberra wanting to know what I knew about corruption of the bureau because the bureau was under attack by such forces as the Queensland Police force and before they got to me, the bureau wanted to speak to me to see what I knew'* - is that right?"

"That is right."

Hampson then asked Milligan about Shobbrook having raised the name of Hallahan on the night of the arrest.

"Yes. He mentioned Hallahan at the very start of the interrogation on this night. He told me that at that very moment, that when I was in custody somebody called Ray Cooper had flown from Melbourne. Shobbrook had arranged for somebody called Cooper and another narcotics officer to fly to Brisbane to go to Obi Obi to raid Hallahan's house and Hallahan would think I had told the narcotics officers at Sydney that he was involved and would blame me for a raid on his house. And he also, I recall something to the effect that Ray Cooper from Melbourne, was brought in because they did not want Hallahan to get any tip off or wind of it or something like this in Queensland."

"And you named the persons and you said there were three persons (I do not want to name them now), there were three persons who organised illegal drug activities and you said *'If that was said, it was incorrect'*. O'Brien said *'Well, are you saying that you said that or that you didn't say it'*. You said *'I don't know I can't remember saying it specifically in those terms. I was saying a lot at the time to assist Shobbrook because Shobbrook had put me in a state of fear and he had put the proposition to me that if I could come up with a good story before Scullion arrived to tell Scullion that he would assist me in many ways which he named.'* Is that true? Is it true, first of all, that you told Phillips and O'Brien that?"

Milligan said it was not true that Shobbrook had put him in a state of fear.

"He made a suggestion?"

"Yes, a suggestion."

"That if you could come up with a good story before Scullion arrived?"

Milligan bridled at this suggestion: "It is unfair to Shobbrook to say anything that infers that we concocted a story or he was concocting a story. He believed that what he was doing was in the best interests of the bureau and was honest. So it is untrue to say that, that he wanted me to come up with a good story. But he wanted as much information as I could give him."

Hampson tried a different tack: "He thought you knew a lot more than you in fact did?" he asserted, putting words into Milligan's mouth and downplaying Milligan's importance at the same time, and then accelerating the process, despite evidence elsewhere to the contrary - evidence that was never touched upon in open evidence at this inquiry.

"Yes," said Milligan.

This attitude of Hampson's is difficult to understand bearing in mind that he and Williams had been told in a memo of August 2, 1979 by Mark Le Grand, the Royal Commission liaison officer on the joint task force created with the New South Wales drug commission, that the NSW commission had found Milligan was "a major figure in the importation of heroin into Australia".

Despite this, Hampson put it to Milligan that Shobbrook "thought you were a real big wheel?"

"Yes, exactly."

Another barrister might have asked: "And you were, weren't you?" But Hampson asked, despite all the NSW Commission evidence that Milligan was a pivotal wheel: "And you were not?"

"That is right. That is the whole story summarised."

"Exactly?"

"Exactly."

"He was sitting there open-mouthed waiting for this big man to tell him everything and you did not have much to tell him?"

"Well, no, I told him all I knew."

"So you had to put forward hearsay?"

"Yes."

"Rumour?"

"Rumour."

"Speculation?"

"Well, it wasn't speculation. I repeated what I had been told."

"Anything at all to try to give him, as it were, what he wanted to know?"

Again Milligan bridled at Hampson's negative line of questioning: "No, it wasn't anything at all. I gave him what I had been told from a number of sources, which he suggested to me, which he questioned me on. I did not invent things," Milligan emphasised.

Hampson, whose job it was to assist in an inquiry into whether or not senior police or politicians had been involved in drugs, switched to an adversorial role: "Knowing that he seemed to be a dedicated officer who had some information you thought he wanted to get confirmation from the big guy, Mr Milligan. You were quick, I suggest, to offer him anything at all, even though it would have been hearsay eight times removed to confirm or to assist him in obtaining any confirmation of the matters he put to you?"

"That is so. I told him anything that I, any information whatsoever I had in relation to anything he asked me about," said Milligan in an answer that came nearer to satisfying Hampson's line of questioning.

"But I did not invent things or fabricate things," came the counter punch to the jaw.

Commissioner: "Really, what Mr Hampson is putting to you I think is that you have put it in as strong a light as you possibly could?"

"Yes, I appreciate what your honour is saying. I told to Shobbrook a hearsay as who had told me and I told him that I believed that situation."

In his line of negative questioning, Hampson now touched on a similarly negative section of the O'Brien interview from December, saying: "I did not want to go through the lot but O'Brien finally said this after all the talking about Hallahan '*You are saying that you fabricated almost everything that you said to Shobbrook in relation to Hallahan's involvement in your drug dealings*' and you said '*No, I am saying that some of it was fabrication by me and the rest of it was supplied by Shobbrook and I said it*'. I know that touches Hallahan at the moment but is that correct?"

This was again too much for Milligan. "I said that but it was not correct," he said categorically.

"Is it a case of it being supplied by Shobbrook and you agreeing to it?"

"No. This is where I am saying that what I said to Phillips and O'Brien is in fact incorrect. I did supply most of the information about Hallahan on tape, yes," said Milligan, once more emphasising the Shobbrook tapes were the ones to be heeded rather than the commission's.

But the questioning continued in the same vein. And once again Milligan said that his answers to O'Brien were the ones to be disbelieved and the interview to concentrate on was the in-depth Shobbrook chat.

Hampson: "You did not ever say to him '*Look, Mr Shobbrook, you've got this all wrong I am only a pretty little guy really?*' You wanted to impress him really so you did not correct his mistake or his wrong assumptions so you went along with him?"

"No, I said '*No I am not Mr Big*' but I said, you know, '*I'll tell you about Hallahan, he is*'!"

Now we are getting down to it, thought Shobbrook. A line of questioning about the allegation of Hallahan being Mr Big in the heroin importation business was going to change the emphasis. The bureau had drawn up calendars showing how Milligan appeared to ring Hallahan only at crucial points when Milligan was involved with drug importations. So Shobbrook, sitting in the gallery, was amazed when Hampson phrased his next question: "But you are not saying that he has got anything to do with drugs, Hallahan?"

"I don't know now to what extent," said Milligan, giving a qualified yes.

But instead of asking Milligan what that extent had been, Hampson followed up with another negative question. Shobbrook was well aware as an interviewer himself that people being asked questions find it easier to agree with the question rather than disagree. He knew a negative question, such as: "You don't want to rock the boat, do you?" is likely to be met with the answer 'no'. Ask: "You would rock the boat, wouldn't you, if it was necessary?" and you might get a different answer.

Hampson asked: "You are not saying he ever had anything to do with drugs are you?" "Well, I don't wish to answer that question."

Shobbrook waited for Hampson to ask him why not.

"You apparently told Phillips and O'Brien you had nothing at all to connect Hallahan with drugs."

"Did I tell them that?"

And then, after these few negative questions, the learned barrister moved away from the topic of Mr Big and drugs. But the negativity continued.

"What about the board of directors, that was pretty ridiculous, was it not? The idea that the criminal activity had this corporate structure?"

"Well, it, the board of directors, was first used by someone called Ceruto in the evidence of the NSW Royal Commission."

"But it was ridiculous?"

"It is a ridiculous term, yes."

"Too ridiculous for words, right?"

"Yes."

"But here were you and Mr Shobbrook solemnly trading the word backwards and forwards as though it had a sensible meaning."

"Yes."

"You were too intelligent to believe that there was a board of directors constituted at the top of the pyramid of crime or something?"

"There is no such thing as that in those terms. It was a term that was used, as I said, by Ceruto first, and then by me in the NSW Royal Commission and then Shobbrook seized on the term and I used the term in relating information to Shobbrook because it was a handy term to use."

Milligan seemed to be admitting he had given evidence to the NSW Royal Commission into drugs and that he had told that commission about the board of directors in Queensland.

The world had long before learned of meetings of various boards in organised crime, especially in America. Shobbrook thought to himself: "He obviously hasn't heard of organised crime."

Hampson went on: "There would have to be directors' meetings and all this kind of stuff. It was all ridiculous?"

"That didn't go on as far as I know, meetings and so on."

"Of course, that didn't. It wouldn't have kept minutes anyway," said Hampson pedantically. "It wouldn't have complied with the Companies Act?"

"No."

Shobbrook was about to be shocked again. Part of Milligan's story had been that if he or Hallahan was ever caught, Hallahan would tell police that the money he had earned had come from the sale of land. No registration of such a sale had been found. Shobbrook expected at some stage that Milligan would be faced with probing questions designed to establish how, why and when he had paid money to Hallahan, seeking to establish links with Milligan's drug dealing. Instead, Hampson asked a question that assumed that indeed any money that had changed hands between Milligan and Hallahan had been for land.

"With your land transactions, was he reliable?"

"I don't know what has happened there."

"He might have ripped you off for the money you paid him?"

"Very well could have."

Shobbrook thought long and hard about the evidence, asking himself why Milligan was privately prepared to name names and reveal details of drug deals and criminals but in public would appear to be vague or unsure of his recollection. He decided the answer lay in the fact that Milligan had believed all his revelations were made only when the recorder had been switched off. He had not wanted anyone to know he was dobbing people in. It must have been a shock to him when an officer from the Queensland force had confronted him in his cell with details which he had thought were strictly confidential. Milligan had been forced to save face and pretend that he hadn't done the dobbing but had just agreed to what had been put to him. Now, in open court he was not going to name names. But in camera perhaps??? Shobbrook was convinced Milligan, The Cardinal, as he had been nicknamed, had been telling the truth.

William Daniel Lickiss, of 62 Greentrees Avenue, Kenmore Hills, occupation Minister for Justice and Attorney-General, stepped into the box and denied knowing Milligan and Hallahan.

Lickiss had been told by a senior Scotland Yard officer a couple of years earlier that corruption was rife in the Queensland force, had been warned about particular activities in the force, and been told of the Scotland Yard officer's concerns about the Rat Pack. Here he was giving evidence to a major investigation into the activities of the Rat Pack, yet he never volunteered a word about this knowledge.

He was not asked any questions about his finances.

Between now and the next session of the inquiry a month later, Shobbrook desperately tried to get something done about the Hallahan investigation. But wherever he turned he ran into a stone wall. He even wrote to Democrats leader Don Chipp in the Federal Parliament, asking him to meet him next time he was in Brisbane to discuss the case and the apparent refusal by senior officials to show any interest in following up Milligan's allegations.

Shobbrook also kept his appointment with the union in Adelaide Street. For the first time he received some constructive help. Yes, the union would provide someone to look after his interests. Solicitor John Robertson was appointed.

It was February 4 before the commission reconvened and Police Commissioner Terry Lewis, GM, OBE, made his long-awaited appearance.

The Inquiry report would later say: "As soon as evidence connected with alleged senior police involvement was ready, the Commission sat to hear it on 4 and 5 February 1980."

But unlike the evidence from January 3 and 4 involving the fluffy, filmy scraps of suspicion against Lickiss when Milligan had been marched in to give evidence, he was not called on when it came to the far more substantive case involving Murphy, Lewis and Hallahan.

For some reason the commission abandoned its previous modus operandi and did not call Milligan to give evidence against Lewis, Murphy and Hallahan before they were questioned.

Instead, a summary of allegations was read into the transcript:

"John Edward Milligan was interviewed by Shobbrook. His main source of information about Queensland people was Glen Patrick Hallahan, formerly a member of the Queensland police force. Milligan said that prior to Hallahan leaving the Queensland police force there had been established in Queensland a board of directors. This was an informal group consisting to Milligan's knowledge of three persons. Those persons were Terry Lewis, now commissioner of the Queensland police, Tony Murphy, assistant commissioner for crime, Queensland police, and Glen Patrick Hallahan. Some excerpts from the tape are attached so that the accusations made against Mr Lewis can be better appreciated. It appears however, that the allegations are as follows:

"1. Mr Lewis was a member of the board of directors which Milligan also refers to as a triumvirate.

"2. Mr Lewis's codename as such member was 'our friend', Hallahan was GP, Murphy was 'over the river'.

"3. The board of directors or triumvirate was concerned with protecting their interests of an illicit kind and in particular:

"a. Conducted a conspiracy which Milligan referred to as a coup to cause the dismissal from office of Mr Ray Whitrod, commissioner of police;

"b. Endeavoured in combination with one Jack Rookland(sic) to have poker machines made legal in Queensland. In their efforts to achieve this and also to achieve their object referred to in a. above they were assisted by the Minister for Justice, Mr Lickiss;

"c. Endeavoured to retain in office Max Rogers, regional commander of the narcotics bureau based in Brisbane, and when this was found to be not possible, to have appointed in his place one John Robinson, formerly a member of the Queensland police force;

"d. Showed considerable interest in the narcotics trade in Queensland by endeavouring to be possessed of whatever information could be obtained regarding this traffic."

Chapter 35 – Sorry to Have Bothered You Mr Lewis

Lewis then read a statement into the transcript. It included:

"The position of commissioner of police was not advertised and as far as I know applications were not involved," he said. "About two weeks prior to my appointment as the commissioner, Cabinet did appoint me as assistant commissioner to take effect from early 1977. I was first made aware that I was being considered for commissioner by media people phoning me at Charleville in the week or so before the appointment to ask did I think I might be appointed and I assumed they knew more than I did. The appointment was very unexpected. I had not received any notice beforehand that I might be appointed assistant commissioner which was to replace one of the assistant commissioners who was due to retire."

His statement continued: "When I went to the juvenile aid bureau (Hallahan and I) never worked together and I would have only seen Hallahan in the same way as I probably would have seen most other detectives. He resigned from our force, I understand, in 1972 and I have not seen him, or spoken to him or communicated with him in any way since 1972. At the time Hallahan resigned I was a detective senior sergeant in the juvenile aid bureau.

"Mr A. Murphy and I went to the CIB at about the same time and he and I also worked on individual jobs from time to time and I don't know that we were ever really paired together. If we were it would have been at the time when we had a very involved abortion case many years ago which quite a large number of police officers worked together on for many months and I could have been paired with him at that time but I did, as I said, work with him on numerous jobs over many years. We were much the same rank. He was about a year senior to me. While I was in the juvenile aid bureau I would have seen Mr Murphy from time to time. I maintained social contacts with him but from a work point of view we wouldn't have worked on any jobs together. He may have referred jobs to our then section but I can't think of any jobs which we would have done together. While I was in the juvenile aid bureau Mr Murphy was in the CI branch in Brisbane but I don't recall on what sort of work. Then he went to Toowoomba, either as a detective sergeant first class or detective senior sergeant. I think he went direct from Toowoomba to Longreach as inspector. I suppose it would be around 1975."

Terry Lewis was conning the Royal Commission. The man he was referring to as "Mr A. Murphy" was his close mate Tony – as he swore on oath a few years later.

"To the best of my knowledge I have never met John Edward Milligan or ever had anything to do with him. I can't even place the chap. I am told he was Judge Seaman's clerk but to the best of my knowledge I have never had occasion to talk to Judge Seaman. I had never heard of Milligan until his name seemed to have been bandied around in relatively recent times. He has never given me information and his name has never been mentioned to me as an informer to other police officers.

"I have been told that it has been alleged that there was in existence a coup or conspiracy to remove Mr Whitrod and replace him with me as commissioner of police and the suggestion that I was in some way part of that coup. I know there were numerous persons who were not happy with Mr Whitrod's administration. At the time of Mr Whitrod's departure or resignation there was some publicity that there were people who weren't happy with him. To my way of thinking the main group of people that seemed to be saying the most at that time was in fact our union and political leaders. I certainly did not join with any group to unseat Mr Whitrod if there was such a group. The late Sergeant Walker used to run around talking about the rat pack and that sort of thing. I am afraid that in life, particularly in our job you are going to upset people and if you get reasonably rapid promotion you are going to upset a number of police officers, some who, of course, are not frightfully happy about such promotion. The term rat pack was a term, apparently, the late Sergeant Walker got into his mind and when he talked about people he didn't like he would refer to them as the rat pack. But nobody could ever find out who the members allegedly were. The term was used prior to Mr Whitrod's leaving. That seemed to be the main thrust of the derogatory term."

In fact, Lewis would later state in a writ that Murphy was a close personal friend and that each had been identified as a member of the "Rat Pack" since the 1960s.

Lewis's statement continued: "I have been told that a suggestion has been made that meetings would take place between Milligan and Hallahan after which Hallahan would speak to me about the matters raised in that meeting before again speaking to Milligan. If that type of statement has been made it is absolutely inaccurate. I have had no communication with Hallahan whatsoever since 1972. I haven't even seen him, spoken to him or communicated with him in any way or he with me on any matter at all.

"I am quite happy to attend the commission and answer any queries put to me. I do not require representation.

"I have been informed that a suggestion has been made that I, as part of what is called a triumvirate, consisting of me, Mr Murphy and Mr Hallahan, with the assistance of Mr Lickiss, has been attempting to introduce poker machines into Queensland. I don't think I have ever even played a poker machine. If I did it must have been some years ago when I was inter-state. They are one area I know little or nothing about."

Lewis said: "I have heard the name Jack Rooklyn who I am told has been said to be the person behind the introduction of poker machines. I think he has been named for many, many years. I think I can remember that from a poker machine inquiry in New South Wales. I have never had anything to do with him in any way."

According to Lewis's own diaries, this was not true. For he had actually noted Rooklyn's address and phone number in an appointment book for January 3, 1978. He had received Rooklyn in his own office at police HQ. And he had been seen meeting with Rooklyn in a private room at the Crest Hotel.

Lewis, presumably in answer to a line of questioning prompted by Milligan, talked about his drinking days at the National Hotel and his relationship with former crooked commissioner Frank Bischof.

"I had a lot of dealings with Mr Bischof, a former commissioner of police, both before he was commissioner and while he was a commissioner. He was the chief of the CI branch for years while I was there so I would have had numerous dealings with him. I never visited his home or anything of that nature. My dealings with him were as a junior officer of his staff. In the same way I had dealings with Mr N. Bauer, another commissioner of police. He was a detective senior sergeant at the CI branch when I went there as a police constable. I had dealings or contact with Mr Bauer from then on and off."

How very odd. He had never visited Bischof's home – yet, while the Commission had been sitting Lewis had made a special visit on January 5 to Bischof's home. He recorded in his diary: "At 7.30am to The Gap and the home of the late Frank Bischof. Collected medals and uniform from Mrs Bischof." What else might he have collected? Perhaps some evidence which showed their true relationship and which Lewis would then have destroyed?

Apart from a very brief cross-examination by Lickiss's counsel, Derrington, that was it.

Appallingly, there was absolutely no cross-examination on questions posed by the Milligan tapes!

No cross-examination about his relationship with Hallahan.

There were no questions about his finances nor any attempt to examine them, despite the commission having the power to do so.

Nothing more at all.

An examination of his income would have proved interesting, especially as Police Commissioner Lewis was raking in so much corrupt money that he had started making diary entries of massive winnings on horse races, exhibiting a strange sense of humour by deciding that his first winner would be Ima Cheeta (which he returned to, tongue firmly in cheek, five more times) and that his 13th entry would be his first loser. This attempt to explain his sudden wealth would not have stood up to scrutiny because he was claiming an 88 per cent success rate for his betting. It would have been fascinating if Lewis had been asked to supply the Inquiry with his bets in advance of each race meeting for a month or so.

It would have been fitting if someone had thanked him for finding the time to pop in to the Inquiry. Or maybe even apologise for having bothered him.

The Inquiry then heard from one of its own investigators who told how: "On 15 January, 1980, I interviewed Mr Colin Maxwell Brumby, a business executive at his place of business at 39 York St, Sydney. Mr Brumby confirmed that he had first met Milligan in jail about October 1977 and became closely associated with him. Milligan began to confide in him and told him of a number of alleged activities, many of which have been repeated by Milligan in his interviews with investigators.

"Brumby is obviously convinced of the truth of Milligan's statements. He bases this on his acceptance of Mr Milligan and information supplied by other prisoners.

"Mr Brumby has never met Hallahan or any Queensland police officer or politician mentioned by Milligan. He states that he did ring a number which he believed belonged to Hallahan, namely 071-46-9125 on two occasions on behalf of Milligan. On those occasions he had been told by Milligan to ask for a Mr Williams. He was to ring at either 8am, 12 noon or 7 pm. Mr Brumby stated that he had made these calls from his home at Darling Point while on leave from the prison attending an education course about March 1978. The first occasion related to the fact that Milligan was in jail and the second was in respect to Milligan being about to give evidence before the New South Wales Royal Commission into Drug Trafficking headed by Justice Woodward and he was asked to convey a message that Milligan would not be mentioning Hallahan and his associates!

"Mr Brumby stated that Milligan had told him on one occasion that an amount of $27,000 had been raised in a hurry to pay a Member of Parliament."

Hampson: "The reason I am not seeking the (names of the) members of Parliament at this time ... may be obvious. We would like to hear it from Mr Milligan."

But there would be no harm in it whatsoever and there was a risk that Milligan would not answer or would now deny it. In fact, Milligan would never be faced with the question in open inquiry. So a crucial name was omitted. Was there another Cabinet Minister against whom allegations had been made? Or was this another allegation against either Lickiss or Martin Tenni whose name had cropped up in the tapes? Had the financial records of these two politicians been examined?

The officer said: "On January 17, 1980, I interviewed a medical officer in relation to a patient named John Edward Milligan. This doctor declined to discuss matters relating to his patient in respect to treatment. However, it was established that Milligan was a person of very high IQ with an outstanding memory.

"At 1 pm on Friday January 18, 1980, in company with Investigator Stoll I visited the premises at 19 Bayswater Road, Kings Cross, Sydney, which are the business premises of the late Royden Joseph Pettiford, a solicitor who acted on a number of occasions for John Edward Milligan. I there spoke to the bookkeeper, Miss Phylis Bessy Little. She stated that she had kept the books of the firm since 1961. She recollects that Mr Milligan informed her and Mr Pettiford on a number of occasions that he could expect help from a Member of Parliament if he needed it. He had given Mr Pettiford a present approximately three years ago which was a gold 18 carat calculator as a present. At the time of giving the gift to Pettiford Milligan stated that he had given a similar present to a Member of Parliament."

No evidence was given as to whether inquiries had been made about whether or not a member of Parliament had been seen three years ago using a gold calculator.

"At 2.45 pm on January 23, 1980, I interviewed a Richard Mallouhi, at the Sydney Customs House. During the interview Mallouhi stated he had been accompanied by Milligan to a branch of the bank of New South Wales at Homebush on a date approximately two to three years ago and a sum of money had been withdrawn which had then been placed into a bank cheque in the name of Hallahan, which had then been handed to Milligan."

Hampson: "The proceeds of Mallouhi's account were used to get the bank cheque?" - "That is correct."

That had been April 5, 1977. Mallouhi was another drug dealer.

"In pursuing operational records of the former Federal Bureau of Narcotics in relation to matters alleged to involve John Edward Milligan I found that a number of telephone calls had been made from unit 6, 19 Cooper St, Paddington, to the telephone connection held by Glen Patrick Hallahan. The premises were rented to a man named Julal Raad. Raad is at present under remand in respect to a number of charges including drugs!

"However, he has failed to appear on two particular charges and bench warrants have been issued. I produce a list indicating the dates which show connections between the number at 19 Cooper St and the premises of Glen Patrick Hallahan."

Raad had been arrested in Sydney by Shobbrook on July 28, 1979, on a charge of importing heroin for Milligan.

Despite the links between Milligan and Hallahan, the officer finished his evidence by saying: "Throughout all my inquiries I have not detected any information which relates to any corruption or illegal activities of any member of the Queensland Police Force or former member of the Queensland Police Force or any politician."

Exhibit 716 set out how many times Hallahan had booked into the Travelodge where Hallahan had a key to room 25. No details were revealed in evidence.

Tony Murphy said in his statement: "I know of John Edward Milligan. I know he has a criminal history. I have to the best of my knowledge only spoken with him once in my life and that was on the telephone in about 1977. He phoned me at the crime intelligence section where I was at that time attached. He introduced himself in a mysterious type of manner and then told a story of a black man stealing his car. I was highly suspicious of his bona fides and after discussing the nature of his call with my counterpart in the Sydney crime intelligence department of the New South Wales State Police I directed Detective Glancy who attended to Milligan's complaint to prepare a statement about the matter. A copy of that statement was forwarded immediately to the Sydney crime intelligence section.

"I have never been a member of any board of directors or triumvirate as claimed by Milligan. I know of no such board of directors and regard such suggestion as a fiction. I have never to my knowledge been called or known as 'Over the river' or 'Over the road'. I have never known Mr T. M. Lewis to be called or known as 'Our friend'. I know that ex-Detective Sergeant Hallahan was at times called GP, which, as far as I am aware, was an abbreviation of his two Christian names, Glendon Patrick.

"I have never been a party to any conspiracy or coup in order to (sic) the dismissal from office of ex-Commissioner Raymond Wells Whitrod. I know of a person called Jack Rooklyn. I have never met or spoken to this person. I have never endeavoured alone or with others to have poker machines made legal in Queensland. Nor have I ever consulted or spoken with the honourable the Attorney-General Mr Lickiss about poker machines. I know Mr Lickiss by sight only. I have never met him or spoken to him. Any allegation or statement to the effect that I have been involved with Jack Rooklyn and Mr Lickiss in any matter concerning poker machines is a fiction.

"Any and all interest shown by me in the narcotics trade in Brisbane has been directly and solely related to my position as detective superintendent in charge of the CIB. The State police drug squad comes under my superintendency. Any allegation or statement to a contrary effect is a fiction.

"I have never caused Milligan to be supplied with a telephone number in order that he could ring or contact me if he ever found himself in trouble. Likewise, I have never reprimanded Milligan. Any allegation or statement to the contrary effect is a fiction. I know narcotics officer

Shobbrook. I met him personally on October 17, 1979, when he came to my office in consequence of a phone call by me to the narcotics bureau. The contact between us was official in nature and I have placed the original of my file in connection with same before this honourable commission."

There was no cross-examination on questions posed by the tapes; no questions on the mysterious phone call from Milligan. What was it that made him suspicious about Milligan? Why did he file a report with the New South Wales police - a report which was to become so handy in backing his story to the commission? Why was this report not admitted as an exhibit? If Glancy carried out the investigation, why was Murphy's phone number in Milligan's possession? How did Milligan gain that number? How difficult was it to obtain? Why, of all the detectives in the force, had Milligan chosen to ring Murphy?

What was Murphy's relationship with Hallahan? If there was a relationship, why was an assistant commissioner still in touch with an officer who had left the force under a severe, black cloud?

Immediately after this evidence the inquiry went into secret session and took confidential evidence which filled 12 pages of transcript between pages 24722 to 24733. From whom was not made public.

Chapter 36 - Hallahan Takes the Stand

Immediately after lunch Glen Hallahan appeared in the witness box. A tall, imposing, dominating figure with piercing, intense blue eyes, he appeared relaxed but in charge.

Hallahan said he had joined the force in 1952 and had resigned at the end of 1971. Then he had worked as a collection officer part time on the Sunshine Coast for a friend of his, Mr Scanlan, who had finance dealings with AGC. Apart from that he had been farming.

In fact, Scanlan was another of the people who had given evidence at the National Hotel Inquiry whitewash and who had recently been recorded in Lewis's Diary as being in contact with Lewis.

Hallahan had first met Milligan in 1962 when Milligan had been associate to Judge Seaman of the District Court. Milligan had some personal problems and had come to Hallahan for help, having come into contact with him at the court.

Hallahan said he had lived at Red Hill before he got married in 1966 or 1967 and then he had moved to Kangaroo Point and stayed there until he left the police force.

Of Milligan he said: "There was just something in his nature that he appeared to enjoy being in the company of what we call criminals and knockabouts and that type of people. He did get into the company indeed, on occasions, at our instigation, with some fairly, I suppose you could say, notorious people."

"Confidence tricksters or people who exhibited violence?" asked Hampson.

"Killers, one particular one. One particular incident concerned the movement of quite a notorious killer who is now dead - a chap named Regan, Stuart John Regan. He had moved into Queensland and was dealing in real estate but setting up other deals and Milligan ingratiated himself with him and we were able to keep a fairly extensive tab on Regan's comings and goings and his dealings in this state. Those matters are recorded."

"How did he support himself after he left his position with Judge Seaman?"

"I was always given to understand - this is from him mind you - that his grandmother was a titled lady. He has mentioned her name quite a few times to me. Whether it is his grandmother or not I don't know. She was a person of independent means and she supported him. His people actually come from northern New South Wales."

"Was he still living in New South Wales when you left the police force?"

"He was. I had a small farewell, a number of them. He actually attended one shortly after I resigned. At one stage he suggested I go into some sort of business that he could finance through money from this grandmother of his. That was discussed and I decided against it. He then decided that he was going to let his law studies go and go to Sydney and he actually left with me a lot of his law books. I left Brisbane. I went to a place called Kin Kin where I bought a Post Office and I carted his books around with me. We stayed at that place for about four months probably until I bought the property I am on now."

"What business did he suggest that you should go into with the assistance of the finance from his grandmother?"

"He was talking about a restaurant which had no appeal to me at all. And then he mentioned the lease of a pub, a hotel probably."

"Did you see any indication that he had the ability to finance you into a restaurant?"

"Yes. Put it this way, just before I left I had some problems as you are aware and I was not earning any money before I left the police force and he did in fact loan me a couple of thousand dollars in cash which he got. I think he got some from his father. He told me a thousand, and I think the other thousand supposedly came from his grandmother."

The questions and answers continued: "Did you repay him that money?"

"Yes."

Hallahan said Milligan had gone into real estate and claimed he had sold land to Milligan for $26,000.

"Have you got separate title to the land yet?"

"No."

"Is there any reason why you did not get that title?"

"Well, what happened was that as he got through on the payments for it he did not want the piece of land, he wanted his money back."

"Have you repaid him the money?"

"No, I haven't."

"Did Milligan press you for the money?"

"No. When it could not be sold I spoke with Milligan again and I told him there was no way in the world we could sell it quickly because we had already waited for that time. I mentioned to him a proposition whereby I felt I could make the money viable if I had the use of the money for some time further. I told him how I proposed to do it with the money and what money I thought I could make from the property and if I succeeded with that venture he would have an excellent chance of getting his money back."

"Was this conversation about maybe developing the land and growing sweet corn?"

"Yes."

"Did he want interest?"

"No."

"Where did you meet him to talk about that?"

"At the Travelodge on many occasions."

"How many occasions in all did you meet him?"

"I guess it would be half a dozen. I used to live close to there and always since I left Brisbane in 1971 or 1972 I have stayed there any time I have come to Brisbane on business."

"The only money you got from Milligan was the $31,000?"

"Yes."

Despite Milligan's criminal record and Hallahan's appalling record in the police force, the story of the alleged sale of land with no receipts, no deeds, no pressure to return money was accepted without a murmur! There was no question about proof. No question of: "Why should we believe you?"

Hallahan said that in the early part of 1979 he had read Milligan's name in The Courier-Mail and the Bulletin in connection with the royal commission into drugs. He had been concerned and asked Milligan about it and Milligan had said he was employed by the narcotics bureau.

It is worth noting that when Milligan was recalled he was not asked about this claim.

"Did you know at that time whether he had any convictions?"

"No, I did not know that he had any convictions," said Hallahan despite the evidence he had given earlier about Milligan being associated with one of the most vicious, cold-blooded criminals ever to set foot in Queensland.

Then Hallahan was asked about the list of phone numbers found in his home.

"What happened was as I told you. When I left the police force I was friendly with Mr Murphy, Mr Lewis and many other police. The circumstances of my leaving, you probably know there was some dissension between elements of the police force."

Hallahan was telling less than the whole truth here. He had, in fact, left under a giant black cloud with departmental charges left untested.

Hallahan continued: "I decided on my own initiative that I would have no contact with any of my former friends because I just felt that it could prejudice their career to be associated with me. There was nothing at their instigation. So I purposely contacted no one. Not only does that apply to police but to many other people with whom I was associated. As Mr Lewis said the other day: I haven't been in contact with him since leaving the police force.

"With regard to Mr Murphy, I think I saw him about five or six years ago. I have spoken with him about twice in that time. He rang me one New Year's Eve three or four years ago just to wish me all the best for the following year. Some time about six months ago he rang me at home and he was looking for information about a murder investigation they were doing. The person who was suspected for the murder was somebody who was known to me...

"He said if there is anything further would you ring me back on this number. He gave me his number at the CIB. I wrote his number there and then in the teledex. I had it under T. That is the only telephone number that was found at my place and those are the circumstances of it being there. It might be TM, I am not sure."

What about the board of directors?

"My comment is that it is absurd. Absolutely absurd."

"Why would Milligan have made these stories up if they are completely ridiculous?"

"That question has troubled me but to my mind it would appear to me that the narcotics bureau - they have been anxious to prove some sort of corruption in the Queensland Police Force for some reason or other, I don't know what it is. I can see why Milligan would say something like that."

"What do you mean, he was on a promise?"

"Yes, exactly."

Shobbrook was appalled. Why not ask Hallahan what he meant by saying he could see why Milligan would say something like that rather than put words into Hallahan's mouth? But worse was to come.

"On a promise of more lenient treatment if the narcotics bureau agent who arrested him would tell the judge he co-operated with their investigation?"

"Exactly! Something like that."

Shobbrook listened to the next question and answer with mounting horror.

"And therefore Milligan would say things on the tape that he believed the narcotics interrogator wanted to hear?"

"Yes. Somebody has put two and two together and found five. They found my number. They knew I used to be associated with certain police. Somebody has told them something and they have heard I was involved. And I think they thought in this context that Milligan is too silly to do anything off his own bat. And to use the term of Mr Milligan, it was me. This is the proposition they put up to Milligan and of course he has accepted it under the circumstances you suggest."

...under the circumstances you suggest! Hallahan was acknowledging that Hampson was inviting conjecture. Yet there had been no attempt by the Commissioner to prevent it.

But questions that had not been posed - at least not in open session - included queries about the phone calls from Milligan; his relationship with Brumby; his knowledge of Mr Althaus/Harvey; his relationship with Julal Raad; and payments from Milligan. Nor had he been questioned about Milligan's statement about the unnamed man. And what about the two phone calls from Brumby to Hallahan's number when Milligan was in jail? Who had answered Hallahan's phone? And who was saying Milligan was "too silly to do anything off his own bat"?

But that was the end of Hallahan's questioning.

On February 6 Lewis noted in his diary: "Ex Asst Comm Duncan phoned re his dealings with Milligan. Supt A. Murphy called re aspects of connection by Milligan and Peter Monaghan in Royal Commission." And Don Lane MLA phoned. Presumably, the Rat Pack was making sure any loose ends were tied up.

Five days later Lewis noted in his diary: "Hon Camm phoned re Milligan's history." Mr Camm was the Queensland Police Minister.

After a break, the Inquiry sat again on February 19 and while it was going about its business, Lewis was out and about in the Sunshine Coast area on an official inspection of police stations. For some reason he specifically mentioned in his diary that he had been to a place that only exists on maps, a place name that does not actually have an existence, miles off the beaten track in the vast hinterland behind the Sunshine Coast. He did not mention why he had singled out this one spot for special mention. He merely noted: "Drove through Obi Obi."

Back at the inquiry, David Geoffrey Schramm, now a chief investigator with the Australian Federal Police in Canberra, answered a question about a reference to Milligan as an untouchable in a telex he had sent.

Question: "It expressed not what was in the telex but your view that Mr Milligan was a Mr Big?"

"A personal observation only."

"Why untouchable? Why did you have the opinion that he had been regarded as untouchable?"

"There had been over the years - I cannot specify how many years, but over a number of years - there had been information, generally rumour, nothing substantiated, that Milligan was a major heroin dealer in New South Wales."

"And that he had friends in high places?"

"And that he was regarded as having friends in high places, yes."

"And is it fair comment, then...that things which are said on the Shobbrook tapes at face value often sound quite convincing because - I'm overstating it, of course - but they sound a lot better because when you come to compare similar things on the Scullion tapes, the bubble is pricked a bit because there is an absence of any corroboration or supporting detail and there is obviously some mistake made in connection with what Milligan has alleged?" asked Hampson.

"Yes. There were many areas that were not programmed. But in fairness to the officer, that was not what he was instructed to do. He was instructed to find out what Milligan wanted to talk about because Milligan, as we knew, had a reputation for wanting to talk his way out of a tight situation."

"So, therefore, it would be fair to say that Shobbrook's instructions were really to give Milligan his head?"

"Yes."

After digesting Milligan's lengthy confessions Harvey Bates had recommended that a small investigation team be set up with the agreement of Federal police chief Sir Colin Woods to pursue checkable facts.

"In fact, that did not happen, is that right? The recommendation was made but Sir Colin Woods did not join in the idea that there should be an investigation?"

"To my knowledge there was no investigation!"

So here was an officially-identified Mr Big of the drugs world alleging that Terry Lewis and Tony Murphy were involved in organised crime and it appeared that the Federal Police commissioner had decided against any investigation.

On February 20 Lewis told his diary: "Phoned Hon Lickiss re representation at Royal Commission."

That night Shobbrook was working late in his office when two former colleagues walked in. The senior of the two had been a good friend to him in the early days. Shobbrook had been to dinner at his home. The officer's two young children had kissed him good night. Shobbrook had been at the Australian National University on a foreign languages course and a long way from home. Shobbrook had been impressed that a man holding a very senior rank would invite one of the troops home to dinner and pass on words of advice that might assist his future career. It had been a warm and memorable evening.

Now, almost five years later to the day, the officer was passing on more advice about Shobbrook's career. Shobbrook recorded in his diary the officer told him: "Move interstate or be buried. The Australian Federal Police don't need crusading investigators."

The two officers told him that if the AFP supported Shobbrook and his case against Hallahan, it would lose the support of the Queensland force. On the other hand, if the Jungle file was closed, the Queensland force would remain on side. The AFP needed the Queensland force if it was to function in the state because of its fingerprint and document examination facilities, access to modus operandi records and co-operation at local stations during arrests.

He was given some options: if he voluntarily terminated Operation Jungle perhaps a drug liaison trip to Fiji could be arranged for Shobbrook and his wife. If he did not and wished to stay in Queensland, he would be switched to a clerical area and no longer be involved in investigations; if he wanted to remain as an investigator with the AFP he should apply for a transfer to another state; if he did not wish to go interstate but wanted to be an investigator, he should get out of the AFP and go to Customs.

"I've done nothing wrong - charge me with a departmental offence," challenged a very angry Shobbrook. "That'll bring the matter out into the open. I'm not running away from anything."

On February 22 Lewis wrote in his diary: "Phoned Mr Justice Williams re copies of his report and absence at Commissioners' conference."

John William Robinson, the man who Lewis was alleged to have wanted to take the place of Max Rogers - and who, in fact, had been appointed to that position - was now a special member of the Australian Federal Police and the officer in charge of the narcotics operations, AFP northern region.

He had used a man named Monaghan as an informer, he said. "At no time have I discussed with Monaghan the allegation that Commissioner T Lewis of the Queensland Police Department, Detective Superintendent A Murphy, CIB, Queensland Police Department, and former Detective Sergeant G P Hallahan were involved as a syndicate in the distribution of narcotics. I have no evidence to support the allegation. The suggestion that I discussed this matter with Peter Monaghan can only be described as a figment of his imagination."

Where that suggestion came from was not clear. Later it would be alleged Robinson had met Monaghan in a pub favoured by members of the Rat Pack - the Belfast Tavern. He was not recalled to answer questions about that meeting.

Robinson continued: "Monaghan has mentioned to me that Supt Murphy is closely associated with Hallahan."

The attacks on Shobbrook continued. A Queensland police officer came up to him at the end of one of the sessions and spat out: "You are ratshit with the Queensland force." It was an ironic choice of mammal to include in the putdown.

Shobbrook was recalled on March 6 and he was asked by Hampson about his relationship with Monaghan.

"He is not the type of person that I would reveal operational facts to and that has been born out in an independent report I submitted on Peter Monaghan. My attitude to Monaghan was clear," he said.

This was not Milligan or Hallahan in the box but the much-commended Shobbrook. Hampson exploded: "I am not asking you for your attitude. Please be responsive. You cannot pull yourself up by your bootstraps by attacking Peter Monaghan. I am asking you a simple question."

Mr Robertson (representing Shobbrook) was quickly on his feet: "I object to Mr Hampson interrupting the witness. I submit the answer is responsive and it is relevant that the man is not prepared to relate operational facts to Monaghan."

Shobbrook then tendered a 23-page calendar of events linking Milligan to Hallahan and it was admitted as confidential exhibit 427.

A few days later Milligan appeared in Sydney's District Court for sentencing. Shobbrook had flown down for the brief appearance and presented the facts and antecedents. He told Judge Thorley of the part played in the importation by Bridge, Barron and Hallahan. Judge Thorley asked why Hallahan had not been arrested with the other three. Shobbrook replied that the prosecution brief of evidence was not quite ready. Milligan then stood and said he was prepared to give evidence against others. Barrister M. Finnane asked if he was prepared to give evidence against Hallahan.

"I'll delay sentencing for a week to give you time to think about it," said the judge. In that period in his cell Milligan completed five pages of hand-written notes revealing that Hallahan had been instrumental in smuggling heroin to Australia. Shobbrook had nothing to do with this statement. It was taken by an officer completely divorced from him.

His five-page written statement said Hallahan had talked to him in 1977 about bringing drugs into Australia; Hallahan had agreed to finance a trip by Milligan's courier, Parker; Hallahan had given him $1000 for Barron to charter a plane for the initial trip to New Guinea; Hallahan had paid $800 towards the cost of Parker flying to New Guinea; he had met Hallahan at a service station at Nambour. Hallahan had given him $3,000 or just over in cash at the Nambour service station to pay towards Parker buying drugs in Thailand; it was all in $50 notes; Milligan had met Hallahan at Mapleton, near Hallahan's Obi Obi home, where Hallahan had told Milligan to keep looking for the lost Jane Table heroin; and money from the sale of that heroin had been transferred to G P Hallahan's account at the Commonwealth Bank, King George Square, Brisbane.

Chapter 37 - Milligan Fingers Hallahan Again

Milligan's voluntary statement did not prevent Judge Thorley from sentencing him, on March 19, to 18 years' imprisonment with hard labour, with a non-parole period of nine years – one of the longest and toughest sentences ever given to a drug importer – a man painted by the Williams Royal Commission as a bumbling, petty criminal.

If Milligan was big enough to deserve an 18-year sentence how should his paymaster and puppeteer Hallahan be viewed and what length of sentence might be sensible? Judge Thorley said he would like the case against Hallahan to come before him when it was ready.

Shobbrook was stuck in Sydney when the commission sat again on March 20. Milligan now had nothing to hope for – he had been sentenced. He had nothing to trade. He did have a lot to fear, being open to attack at any time in the confines of prison. Any answers he gave in public session at the inquiry would be designed to protect himself from retribution by Hallahan.

But Hampson now had Milligan's detailed, hand-written, five-page statement damning Hallahan plus the master tapes, in which Milligan revealed how Hallahan had conspired with him to import heroin.

Hampson started by asking Milligan about the hearsay evidence he had received from Hallahan about Lewis and Murphy to which Milligan could only respond by saying it was all secondhand.

"I want to ask you now, what do you know about Commissioner Lewis in an adverse sense?"

"I don't know anything. I have never met the man," said Milligan.

"Well, if you know nothing adverse to Lewis, for instance, how is it that the tape records your voice as identifying him as one of this trio overseeing illegal activities of different kinds in Queensland?"

"Those tapes, as I have explained before, were tapes of part of a long conversation, five days of conversation in a dramatic and ridiculous atmosphere with Shobbrook running around wanting to arrest the commissioner of police for Queensland. I have explained that before, the last time," said Milligan.

"One of the things you are recorded as saying is: '*The system as it has been explained to me: there is Terry - I don't know whether you know the triumvirate but Terry Lewis is the commissioner, Tony Murphy is his right hand man and Glen is supposed to be the - what can you call him - the civil organiser; the sort of planner; the ways and means man; the sort of inspector general.*' And Shobbrook is recorded as answering: '*What's the phrase you used, the triumvirate, is it?*' And you are recorded as saying: '*The triumvirate. Years ago the days of the stories of the Rat Pack, you see these three have been together for many years as a group.*' All right?"

"Yes, I read that part, yes."

For the first time, the extent of the allegations on the tapes was being made clear. It was not made clear at this stage why Milligan had not been questioned about them before, back at the beginning of February.

Hampson: "I am going to the next page and I am going to read some extracts: '*Tony has been the other main partner in all the conspiracies, the corruption that has gone on in the Queensland police force*'. Now, it's another story with another tape at another time. A story of the political overthrow of Whitrod (who had been) installed as Commissioner of Police. '*These groups were persecuted. Glen was put out of the police force over all this. He had the opportunity of going back, incidentally, when Lewis became commissioner, because his role now in the civil arm, as inspector general, and so on, is more important - vital he keeps a low-key image. So they have always stuck together. And as I say, it was a fairly sophisticated political plot that overthrew Whitrod. He literally had to run out of the State.*' And then it goes on. Do you accept that you said that?"

"Yes, I accept that."

"And again you refer to the trio in relation to an affair where you had made a complaint that went to Tony, took it up with Tony.'*Glen is the civil arm and Tony is in charge of security. That's how the outfit operates up there. Tony does the dirty work!*'

"You went on: '*Terry is 'Our Friend'.*' That is in inverted commas, a nickname '*Our friend*'. '*In telephone conversations everybody for years in telephone conversations, everybody has been referred to by some sort of pseudonym such as 'Our friend' which refers to Terry. Tony is 'Across the road',*' - that is in quotes - '*'Across the road' usually.*' Do you accept that you are recorded as saying that?"

"Yes."

"And then a little later on you are asked: '*In total now, who are the members of each organisation in Queensland? You have just got the three: Glen Patrick Hallahan, Tony Murphy and Terry Lewis, or are there other members of the organisation?*' You are recorded as answering: '*There are others, most certainly there are others.*' Do you accept that you are recorded as saying that on the tape?"

"Yes."

"Now I go over quite a way and there is a reference to: '*I was doing a particular job under instructions. What Jack Rookland said was accepted as a directive by Terry Lewis, by Tony and by Glen in Queensland and this was in relation - and I know also what Jack says is in turn decided at the moment – and then too - by San Francisco and I even know names but I can't remember them at the moment. But that is getting sort of waffly and vague. In those days - I am being specific here because I can be - because in those days after the Whitrod coup they got rid of Whitrod, they compromised Joh Bjelke-Petersen, and by 'they' I mean the triumvirate, this particular three.*' '*The Queensland three?*' You are reported as answering: '*The Queensland three with a great deal of assistance.*''*How did they compromise him, just very quickly? If you can tell us we can corroborate your story.*''*Basically, they were dealing very closely with Jack Lickiss, the Minister for Justice.*' Interviewer: '*Yes I heard that?*' That is a question.

You went on:'*Yes, very closely. In fact, Jack was their man.*' And then there was a part which you looked at last time which had been edited but it went on to deal with poker machines and so forth. Do you remember that?"

"Yes."

"I do not want to go through all the rest of it. There is a lot obviously on the tape," said Hampson.

There were many other allegations on the tapes. But just what they were and what the answers to them could possibly be would never be revealed to the public.

Hampson continued: "Why did you say there was this triumvirate of the three persons, Lewis, Murphy and the former policeman Hallahan?"

"Well, that is what Shobbrook had already told me, that he thought was going on in the State of Queensland. I think I told you last time that when he arrested me he told me that he thought that Hallahan was Mr Big, involved in the drug trade, and he was going to arrest him that night, he thought, and then over the next five days of tapes it was what I would call, well, the first two days were mainly, not mainly, but a very large portion of them I suppose, was swapping of facts - swapping of information. Shobbrook spent most of the two days telling me what he thought the situation was in Queensland, and that is when I am going on tape and repeating it. I have noticed from just reading those transcripts this morning that most of the facts that are outlined in green in the first part of the transcript are what Shobbrook had, in fact, said to me and then I go on tape saying it. At the last there are some things, obviously the tapes were made in the last few days, where I am giving him facts. For example, the mention of the Solomon Islands and things like that. Now most of those facts that you have read out this morning were things that Shobbrook told me he thought were going on and I confirmed it by going on tape and saying what I thought he wanted me to say."

"Shobbrook has given evidence and he denies that he said any such thing to you?"

"Well, you know, he did. He said lots of things and while I was reading the tapes something else occurred to me which, you know, I think should be said in closed court. For example, just on those facts that you read out there I knew nothing about the Rat Pack. I had never heard of that term until Shobbrook mentioned it to me."

The questions and answers continued: "Was this the first time you had ever heard that Murphy and Lewis and Hallahan had some sort of combination?"

"I knew. I didn't know. I thought they knew each other. I just don't know how but I felt they knew each other."

Having elicited so many negative answers from Milligan, Hampson now moved on to deal specifically with drugs. In front of him, with the ink barely dry, was Milligan's detailed description of how Hallahan had laid out thousands of dollars to import illegal drugs into Australia.

It would have made sense to go through this statement sentence by damning sentence, and to present Milligan with the hard evidence of Hallahan's bank statements and the records of phone calls.

"Do you know anything to Hallahan's discredit in relation to drugs?"

"Not really, not directly in relation to drugs."

Another barrister might next have asked 'What do you mean by 'not really'?' Or 'What do you mean by 'not directly'?'

Instead, Hampson asked: "Do you know anything so far as Lewis is concerned to his discredit in relation to drugs?"

"I know nothing whatsoever."

"What about Murphy?"

"And the same there."

"You are recorded on the tape as having reported to Murphy that a black man stole your car and that Murphy chastised you because you had rung him at the wrong number. You were supposed to ring him on a special telephone number?"

"I don't know about that."

"Is it true or not? First of all, it is recorded on the tape, so you said it. Are you saying it is not true?"

"I just can't remember it now."

Here was a crucial point. There had undoubtedly been an unusual contact between a drug importer and a top police officer. Just how and why had Milligan chosen to ring Murphy rather than anyone else, and how had he obtained the phone number? But the questioning switched.

"Did Hallahan ever tell you anything adverse about Lewis?"

"No."

"Or about Murphy?"

"Not that I can remember."

"You had some financial transactions with Hallahan that we discussed – the last time you say in relation to the purchase of some land from him?"

"Some land, yes."

"Did you ever have any other financial transactions with him?"

Even now, Milligan couldn't resist pointing out the error: "There were transfers of money to Hallahan which were *supposed* to have been for the purchase of land," he said, inviting a question of what the payments had *actually* been for.

But for the most part it appeared that Milligan had become extremely concerned with his future health. The man with the big IQ and photographic memory had suddenly developed a severe case of amnesia.

"Did you ever have any arrangements with Hallahan in relation to drugs?"

"Drugs were discussed but, you know, I really can't remember here."

"You probably could remember this - did Hallahan have anything to do with you in your operations relating to drugs?"

"Not that I can recall at the moment."

Hampson asked: "It does seem, forgetting again what you might have said to other people, it does seem a little odd to me that you can't clearly say whether or not Hallahan was to his knowledge associated with you in your drug smuggling ventures?"

"Well, I can't because I really can't recall what happened."

"So really, what you are saying is that you can't recall whether he ever gave you a couple of thousand dollars or something for a share in one of the undertakings to import drugs?"

"No. I am saying I can't recall this now. My head is so confused over what has happened."

"You said you discussed drugs with him. What were the terms of the conversations in which you discussed drugs with him?"

"I can't remember now. I really can't."

"Did you tell him, for example, that you were involved in importing drugs?"

"I don't know," said the man with the photographic memory to the barrister in possession of his two-day old five-page admission.

"I have no further questions," said Hampson. "But there is a short in-confidence matter that Mr Milligan did raise. He would like to mention something in camera."

In open session, Milligan was not asked for his explanation of how he had come to know Hallahan and how their relationship had developed. What was said in camera Shobbrook would never know.

And then Milligan was led away to start his long, long sentence.

Shobbrook picked up his morning paper next day and groaned. His reputation, already severely damaged, he believed, had taken another broadside. The headline read: "Never heard of 'drug rat pack' says witness" The story said Milligan had told the inquiry: "He did not know anything which could discredit CIB chief Supt Tony Murphy or former policeman Glen Patrick Hallahan with respect to drugs." And: "He had never heard of the three men referred to by the expression 'triumvirate' or 'rat pack' until he was interviewed by a former Federal Bureau of Narcotics agent, Douglas John Shobbrook. Shobbrook had mentioned these things about Lewis, Murphy and Hallahan, he said. He had confessed this in a tape recorded interview with Shobbrook because he believed it was what Shobbrook wanted him to say." And so it went on. If only his representative had been present! Still he was determined not to give up. He tendered documents on Hallahan from his interview with Milligan. It became confidential exhibit 452.

A little later a barrister assisting the commission said: "The next open exhibit is two statements in the form of records of interview by Reginald Ernest Kennedy, who is the deputy commissioner of the AFP, of Superintendent Gillespie and Bardin Charles Halliday. And they relate to the arrest of a Mr Krahe."

That became exhibit 754. Kennedy had interviewed Constable Halliday, who was based at Brisbane Airport, regarding the detention and charging of Freddy Krahe, the former crooked NSW police officer and alleged murderer. The second statement concerned an interview with Superintendent Gillespie concerning Krahe, Hallahan and Milligan!

At last - and perhaps most important of all - the barrister assisting said: "Finally, when John Edward Milligan was giving evidence yesterday your honour will recall he had some handwritten notes, or some handwritten notes were referred to. I now tender as a confidential exhibit those notes or copies of those notes."

The transcript records: "Admitted and marked 'confidential exhibit 471 - copies of handwritten notes supplied by John Edward Milligan on March 20, 1980."

On March 24 Lewis wrote in his diary: "Det Sgt B. O'Brien called re Milligan and Royal Commission; phone tapping; narcotics squad; help from Det Sgt J. Seedsman, NSW; phoned K. Gluck re...Milligan's background."

Seedsman was a long-time member of the Drugs Commission investigating staff, seconded from the NSW force.

I managed to trace former police officer Halliday and asked him why it was that Krahe had been arrested. Unfortunately, Halliday was suffering from dementia and could not help me.

I sent a long list of questions to Cedric Hampson. He said he had not kept any aide memoir and had burned all documents from the inquiry soon after the end of the inquiry. He referred to a question about why he hadn't cross-examined on a certain line and said he had a very hazy memory that "they" had thought Milligan's story was an invention.

"It's quite impossible. I can't remember anything about it to be honest," he summed up.

Chapter 38 – The Winner and the Loser

On March 26 Shobbrook submitted a report: "Attached is a report completed on March 10, 1980, which deals with those items giving rise to the belief that Glen Patrick Hallahan and John Edward Milligan are jointly involved in illegal narcotic activities. Further to the details contained in the report, on March 18, 1980, Milligan supplied a hand-written statement outlining Hallahan's involvement in, and knowledge of, the Jane Table importation. A copy of that report has been forwarded to Mr D. J. Schramm. The attached report has been read by Mr Thomas QC...and Mr G. Spender, barrister...Both have commented that...they feel that the department already has a basis of a sound prosecution case against Glen Hallahan. The question has also been discussed with Mr M. Finnane, barrister briefed by the Crown in the prosecutions of Milligan, Bridge and Parker. He has stated the continued investigation should receive immediate attention."

He asked for the assistance of an ACT fraud squad member to help with the investigation of Hallahan's financial situation.

On April 3 Lewis wrote in his diary: "Saw Asst Comm Duffy re having Det Sgt O'Brien on Williams Report Committee." This was probably a reference to making sure that O'Brien, who had played such a big part in the December interviews of Milligan, would now play a part in shaping the commission's report.

Shobbrook was still hanging on. The threats now were that he would be given a job in stores counting paper clips if he did not give up on Operation Jungle.

He was then told that he was being taken off Operation Jungle because he was too personally involved.

He realised it was all over.

With all his years of experience he was still only 31 years old.

On April 16 Lewis confided in his diary about a lunch he had enjoyed at the Cricketers Club with a small circle of friends including fellow 'target' Murphy, and commission investigator Barrie Cornelius O'Brien. The commission report was due to be released the following day.

The report contains 155 pages.

It contained no suggestion that the finances of Lewis and Murphy or anybody else had been examined in any way to see if they were living beyond their means or owned property which they could not explain.

The first 83 pages deal only with the weak and flimsy allegations involving Lickiss, allegations so insubstantial that Shobbrook had taken virtually no notice of them. Amazingly, the thrust of the report is not on an investigation into Lickiss's activities, but on how the allegations came to be made and who knew about them. This is also illustrated by the number of pages in the transcript used to record evidence: politician Ed Casey, who had been examined on how he had discovered that the name of Lickiss had been mentioned in a Bureau investigation - 64 pages; his secretary Malcolm McMillan 33 pages; his press secretary Jack Stanaway 48 pages; Lickiss himself, a mere seven pages.

In the report, the weak evidence against Lickiss is used to discredit Milligan and Shobbrook. Milligan is painted as a petty criminal with a vivid imagination rather than as an incredibly intelligent man with a photographic memory. Or, as Justice Woodward found: "a professional criminal" who had been "the ideas man" and "the instigator and principal" of "groups of people who have imported substantial quantities of heroin into Australia" for several years. And Shobbrook is painted as a bumbling investigator who fed Milligan lies which Milligan repeated for the benefit of the tapes.

"The commission has no reason to disagree with the good reputation that Mr Lickiss should bear as Minister for Justice and which he swore to the Commission he had," said the report at the end of page 83. And that was that.

From page 84 to page 91 of the report, allegations against a senator are dealt with in similar fashion.

David Thomson, Federal member for Leichhardt, occupies pages 92 to 96 and Martin Tenni, State member for Barron River is given a clean bill of health in a little over five pages.

Only 21 of the 155 pages – from 103 to 124 – deal with the alleged involvement of Queensland's top police officer, the head of Brisbane's criminal investigation bureau and their old Rat-Pack mate Glen Hallahan. That's less than 13 per cent of the report.

Immediately, there is a major error. The report says that Hallahan had been identified as the person who did the dirty work. It seems Hallahan was to be the one man to whom a little dirt would cling. In fact, the transcript says that it was Murphy, the senior police officer, who was alleged to be the one who did the dirty work.

Lewis is on record as denying a close relationship with Hallahan. There is no word in the report of whether or not former Police Commissioner Ray Whitrod had been invited to give evidence.

The report says about Hallahan: "A short summary of his evidence will be sufficient." It does not explain why a short summary of the evidence of an alleged key player in an alleged conspiracy to import drugs would be sufficient.

It does say later that a public discussion of the evidence would very likely impede any police investigation and almost certainly be inimical to a fair trial if Hallahan was ever charged.

Shobbrook, after all the advice he had received from barristers about a possible case against Hallahan, was stunned when he read the

Commission's verdict on Hallahan. "The Commission merely records that evidence presently available to it falls *far* short of establishing as *even* a *reasonable possibility* that Hallahan has *ever* been involved in wrongdoing in connection with illegal drugs." The italics are the author's.

The report then carries conclusions from page 125 to 135 and then a summary of conclusions on page 136.

The first sentence of the conclusions reads: "The Commission has already expressed the view that the allegations relating to politicians and senior police which culminated in the naming of four politicians in the Queensland Legislative Assembly on 20 November, 1979 are *completely baseless.*"

On page 126 the report brutally labels Shobbrook a liar. It recalls how Shobbrook had sworn he had not told colleagues of Milligan's disclosures. "The Commission does not accept this," says the report. "It is inconceivable in the Commission's opinion, that Shobbrook, as Acting Commander of the Narcotics Bureau officers in Queensland, would not have alerted his subordinate officers to the danger of trusting the Queensland Police force in any way."

The report shows that not only had two Queensland police officers been requested to work for the commission, the Commission had also required a senior Queensland Crown Law officer to be attached to its staff. This was arranged with none other than the Minister for Justice and Attorney-General Bill Lickiss, one of the targets of the inquiry against whom allegations had been made. He had not even stood down nor been asked to stand down.

Narcotics Officer B M O'Connor had said he believed that certain members of Milligan's syndicate had been helped by senior police to get off charges. The report says: "This matter was returned to at page 25079 of the transcript where Mr O'Connor requested that his evidence on the matter be heard in camera. The Commission heard this evidence in camera and can record that what Mr O'Connor discussed had, as its ultimate source, Milligan."

But the report does not say what investigations, if any, had taken place as a result of O'Connor's allegations.

At another point the report says: "It must be remembered that Shobbrook *initially* believed that Milligan had given him important and true information." Shobbrook not only believed it initially. He had never stopped believing it.

On page 120, dealing with the police, the report says: "Milligan's sworn evidence to the Commission is that he has never met Lewis or Murphy and knows nothing, even by way of rumour, to the discredit of either of them. Milligan told the Commission that although Shobbrook undoubtedly believed that he, Milligan, was confirming matters that

Shobbrook mentioned to him, in reality Milligan generally knew nothing about these matters. He was afraid of a long sentence of imprisonment and he was anxious to obtain Shobbrook's favour by appearing to confirm to Shobbrook whatever he thought Shobbrook wanted confirmed."

It could just as easily have referred to the conundrum of Milligan repeatedly telling the Commission that what he had told Shobbrook was the truth.

Considering the Commission had been investigating two top officers of the Queensland police force and that if evidence had been found against them it might have expected the rot to have spread to other officers, the Commission might have been thought to have been naive in reporting: "The Commission records that it has liaised closely with the Queensland Police Force from the time that it was set up."

On the final page of its report, the Commission said: "The Commission is firmly of the view that any person, whether a Member of Parliament, of the press or of the public, who has any material suggesting that criminal offences have been committed should make that material available to the Queensland Police or to the Australian Federal Police Force and should reject the temptation to publish the material."

And that was it.

It has to be remembered that there would have been no raid on Hallahan's home without firm evidence of links between Hallahan and Milligan. Milligan had paid Hallahan a large sum of money but there was no transfer of land. Hallahan was not even questioned about why kept a key to a motel unit. Did he have a room permanently booked? Under his own name? Had motel staff seen Murphy and Lewis entering the unit?

One odd point: Williams was chairman of the 1982 Brisbane Commonwealth Games Foundation. Despite the Commonwealth Games Foundation warning that clothing or equipment used officially at the Commonwealth Games shall not be marked conspicuously for advertising purposes unless otherwise approved by the Executive Board, the foundation allowed a commercial organisation to parade its members before sell-out crowds with prominent advertising on their clothing. The company was run by a man who was later alleged at the Fitzgerald Inquiry to have been running an extortion racket and other illegal activities. A senior police officer told the Fitzgerald Inquiry the man was a thug.

On April 18 the evening Telegraph carried a story saying that Hallahan was bitterly disappointed the commission had not completely cleared his name. "I had no doubt in my mind the commission would come out unilaterally, publicly and absolutely absolving me," he said. "Why wouldn't I? I was not involved. The suggestion I am still under investigation is wrong. If there was any evidence connecting me with any wrongdoing of any sort, someone would have done something about it by now."

Shobbrook thought to himself: "Someone did try but he's been stopped. But who had told Hallahan that he was no longer being investigated?"

Within five weeks of Judge Thorley saying that he would like to hear the case against Hallahan when it was ready, it had been dropped. The Federal Cabinet decision of November 6 the previous year to axe the Narcotics Bureau had resulted in Hallahan escaping justice yet again.

The Telegraph story continued with Hallahan saying: "Milligan has sworn in court the allegations he made about me were false. The Commission is satisfied he had told exaggerated, false stories of his involvement with police and politicians...big-noting himself." He said he was deeply disappointed the same total exoneration had not been extended to him as it was to the others falsely named.

On April 19, according to The Courier-Mail, Murphy took out writs against newspapers for defamation for $350,000.

Shobbrook's anger and frustration continued. On June 24 he was found psychologically and physically fit to join the Federal Police and was formally sworn in. Yet on July 22 a letter was sent to him by W L Antill, the Federal Police acting assistant commissioner, saying: "As a consequence of you undergoing medical examinations, I have been advised that you are unfit to discharge the duties of your position as a member of the police force or any other position in the police force. As a delegate of the Minister it is my responsibility under Section 38(2) of the Australian Federal Police Act to determine whether you should be retired from the Police Force. Before doing so, I have decided you should be given the opportunity to put forward in writing any matters which you wish me to consider in taking my decision."

Shobbrook replied on July 29: "On the 20th of February, 1980, I was discreetly informed by a senior member of the Australian Federal Police that I should consider leaving the Australian Federal Police Force as the Force did not require 'Crusading investigators'. I was told that should I choose to remain in the Force I would be denied promotion and restricted in my future duties. I chose to remain in the Force believing that Force to stand for high principles and knowing that I had committed no offence apart from conducting my investigations without fear or favour. A couple of weeks after making the decision to stay with the Australian Federal Police, the threats of that senior officer were put into effect. I was denied promotion to an acting position which I had satisfactorily filled on two previous occasions and I was instructed to cease my investigations on a major drug trafficking syndicate which I had been investigating continuously for the previous 13 months with considerable success. I now find myself unable to come down to the standards of the Australian Federal Police and am surprised that prior to this general letter, no senior member of the Australian Federal Police has wished to discuss this situation with me. I wish the new Force well in its endeavours to combat the growing Australian drug problem."

Despite the seriousness of these allegations, coming as they did from a senior officer, he never received a reply, either written or oral.

Shobbrook wondered why no one had ever suggested that a period of convalescence might restore the health of this valuable and experienced officer. The 'illness' which he was 'suffering' from was officially described as an 'acute situational crisis' - in layman's terms he was extremely upset about a situation. True! On September 23 he was told by the police: "Your retirement from the Australian Federal Police on the grounds of physical infirmity will take place on and from 29 October, 1980."

Having been classed as permanently and totally incapacitated for further Commonwealth employment, he applied to the Commonwealth Rehabilitation Department for an annual grant of $300 to help cover the cost of transport and text books to complete an arts/law degree. With a degree he would no longer have required the compensation payouts. He could have started work as a solicitor and been free to start a new and challenging career. But while money was found for John Edward Milligan to buy books and study to become a Master of Arts while a guest of Her Majesty, Shobbrook's request was turned down.

Two years later Senator Chipp told the Senate: "The disbandment of the Federal Narcotics Bureau was announced in this Parliament...at precisely the time the Melbourne Cup was run. I do not regard that as fortuitous. Something stinks about the reason why the Federal Narcotics Bureau was disbanded. The thing that stinks is the stench that comes from the Queensland Police Force, the Wilsons and the way in which information was leaked. The Queensland Police Force...would be one of the most corrupt, rotten and contemptible groups of people engaged in law enforcement in the world at this time.

"There is something that stinks and I hope that this task force can get to it. I hope that its report will be better than the comparatively useless reports of the Williams Commission and the Woodward Commission. If ever there was a joke, a total waste of public money, a waste of at least hundreds of thousands of dollars - I think it got to millions of dollars - it was the compilation of the Woodward and Williams reports. The dogs in Sydney and Brisbane are barking yet a judge, sitting as a commissioner, cannot find it."

In 1983 Senator Chipp told the Senate that in May 1982 he had hand delivered to yet another Royal Commissioner looking at drugs - Mr Justice Stewart - 376 pages of detailed notes and original documents regarding drug importations. Chipp later told me that the notes and documents were those handed to him by Shobbrook and that they had made him fear for his life.

"For my own protection - I do not want to sound melodramatic on this - I asked the then Prime Minister of Australia whether he would take carbon copies of the documents so that there would be some protection of me," he told the Senate. "He graciously agreed to do so. The information I provided to Mr Justice Stewart named names. It provided tangible evidence which suggested corruption on the part of very senior officers of the Queensland Police Force and others. By the very nature of the subject matter of my submission to the royal commissioner its undertaking was fraught with grave risks to the personal safety not only of me but also of all persons who could be traced as informants in those 376 pages of documents.

"Ten months later the Royal Commissioner, Mr Justice Stewart, wrote to me. The standing orders ensure that I say only this: I am deeply disappointed by his response. I wish the standing orders could allow me to say a lot more about Mr Justice Stewart. Mr Justice Stewart's letter fell into two sections. He told me, in general terms, how wonderful the commission was and how many exhibits, statements and witnesses the Royal Commission had considered. He then said how baseless and untrue were the inferences arising from the submissions I made. The most remarkable paragraph in the letter was perhaps the following:

"Only police forces have the basic resources to investigate criminal activities. Amateurs without access to criminal intelligence may cause sensations but they will rarely assist in catching the drug trafficker. The commission is firmly of the view that any person, whether a member of parliament, of the press or of the public, who has any material suggesting that criminal offences have been committed should make that material available to the Queensland Police or the Australian Federal Police and should reject the temptation to publish the material."

"In other words, a person who has evidence against a policeman should not publish it. He should go to the police so that they can investigate the matter. A royal commissioner told me this. I suggest, with respect, that that statement is one of the most ludicrous that can be imagined, when the Queensland police, including very senior police officials, together with other officials are under suspicion.

"When the officials themselves stand accused, with good reason, of major wrong-doing, they can hardly be expected to handle accusatory evidence against them and their colleagues in a fair and impartial way. Is it not Caesar being asked to inquire into Caesar? Only the very amateurs which the commissioner has derided can pierce the veil of official secrecy and corruption.

"In any event, Mr Justice Stewart knew that all of the 376 pages that I gave him were submitted to me by a fully trained former police investigator of the Federal Narcotics Bureau. That was known by Mr Justice Stewart, yet he said to me: 'Don't give me evidence submitted by amateurs'. I am sad to say on the basis of what I have seen of the work of the Stewart Royal Commission, that it has joined the ranks of the Woodward Royal Commission and the Williams Royal Commission in making little contribution to investigatory progress. It is a sad day when those persons who are courageous enough to bring the evidence to the one branch of officialdom where it might do some good - the royal commission - are made to feel that they have acted foolishly or precipitately.

"I ask the Attorney-General at least to allow (the commission) to put its fingers into the smoky corridors of corruption that exist in Sydney and Brisbane. If I go alone on this matter so be it. But I will not let it rest."

In the very month that Chipp delivered the documents to the commission, Police Commissioner Terry Lewis wrote in his diary that he had seen Detective Sergeant Barrie Cornelius O'Brien "re willingness to remain with Stewart Royal Commission." O'Brien, whose interview with Milligan had been a crucial part of the Williams proceedings, was also one of the nine detectives assigned to the Stewart Commission. It is not unlikely that he would have advised the commission of this evidence, leading to Stewart's response to Senator Chipp.

Although Commissioner Terry Lewis had sworn to the Williams Royal Commission that he and Hallahan were not friends and that he had had not had anything to do with Hallahan since 1972, Lewis went out of his way in 1985 to phone an executive at the Queensland Government-owned Suncorp insurance company to assure him of Hallahan's good character, saying he "always felt Hallahan OK". With one of the worst CVs possible for a position involving honesty and probity, Hallahan became chief claims investigator for Suncorp on January 13, 1986. The position had not been advertised.

After moving out from his farm he declared bankruptcy owing $180,118.

Chapter 39 - Bailey Tells His Story

We left Raymond John Bailey at the end of chapter 5 having only heard Hallahan's version of his involvement in the Sundown murders. Having followed Hallahan's career from hero to cheat, liar, perjurer, and alleged heroin importer and murderer, we should return to the case of the Sundown murders and listen to Bailey's story.

He was born into a poor, hard-working religious family in the small conservative farming town of Gilgandra in the middle of rural New South Wales. He was also a child of the Great Depression, his father David trying his hand at share farming and truck driving to make ends meet before settling into life as a builder and contractor. David and wife Mary worshipped at St Ambrose Church of England where, nearly a year after he was born on December 3, 1932, Raymond was baptised. The family then moved to Dubbo, 65 kilometres south on the Newell Highway with a population 10 times bigger than Gilgandra. It had all the shops and activities that the local community wanted so many of them never felt the need to venture to the state capital of Sydney, 400 kilometres away. Apart from three or four years when the family lived in Parkes, another farming community set in a basically featureless landscape, Dubbo was the community which shaped Ray.

He wasn't destined to be a rocket scientist. He left school at 14, which is what a lot of youngsters did in Dubbo unless you came from a well-to-do family or you were top of your class and your teacher believed you should continue your education.

Keeping up appearances and earning the respect of your neighbours and the community were essential pursuits in 1950s small-town Australia. Ray was proud to be able to say: "My parents are well known and respected in Dubbo. My wife's parents are also well known and respected in Dubbo, and have lived there for a long time."

But Ray wasn't exactly worldly wise at 14 and brought shame on the family when he went for a ride in a car with a 19-year-old friend. He gained a criminal record for aiding and abetting the illegal use of a car. Luckily, it didn't affect his career prospects because on leaving school he became an apprenticed carpenter with his father.

He fell madly in love with a delicate girl called Patricia. Mind you, he was hardly a Tarzan. At just 60 kilos he was slightly built, a thin-lipped, quiet, polite, phlegmatic, ordinary bloke. He was 20 when he married his sweetheart on May 18, 1953, two weeks before Queen Elizabeth the Second's Coronation.

"After our marriage we lived at Dubbo with my parents for a time, then in a rented house," Ray recalled. Nearly a year after they married, they had a son, Michael on April 29, 1954.

Ray remembered that midway through 1957: "My wife was not in good health. She was run down and nervy and I decided to go away on a working trip and see if it would do her any good. We took our little boy with us."

His wife told police he had been a loving husband and doted on their son.

"Before leaving Dubbo I had been working for Walkom Bros builders and contractors," said Ray. "I had saved a certain amount of money and I obtained an International utility on hire-purchase from Skirman Motors, Macquarie Street, Dubbo. I got that about one month before leaving Dubbo. The cost was 350 pounds. I paid 130 pounds down on the utility and the rest was on hire-purchase."

The International was fine when it came to pulling the caravan on the flat roads around Dubbo. But when Ray reached the first hills on his route he found the car hadn't got the necessary grunt. At Renmark, a town of 7,000 built next to the mighty River Murray which irrigates the town's orchards and market gardens, he took the car into Renmark Motors, a major service station, on August 27, to have it examined.

"The garage chap there told me it would cost more to fix it up than it was worth so I traded it in for the DeSoto," said Ray. "The cost of the DeSoto was 200 pounds. I was allowed 220 pounds on the International. The DeSoto was therefore fully paid and I got a cash refund of about 20 pounds. I was well known to the people of Dubbo from whom I got the International and the caravan and I thought it would be all right to trade in the International so long as I kept up the hire purchase instalments, which I intended to do."

They stopped in Wirrulla, a tiny hamlet of half a dozen streets with a population of about 60, a general store and a pub in a vast, flat empty landscape.

"After arriving in Wirrulla I worked at various jobs including wheat stacking. When the wheat stacking finished I did 8½ days' work at 10 pounds per day roof painting and fixing up a house – re-roofing a house. While I was in Wirrulla I got a Huntsman single shot .22 rifle from a chap named Dave. I used to go out shooting sometimes while I was at Wirrulla and when I left I bought the rifle from him for 8 pounds. The hotel keeper there owed me 10 pounds for work I had done and I told Dave to collect the 10 pounds from him."

When there was no more work in Wirrulla he drove on.

"I was making for Mt Isa. I had heard from some foreigners at Whyalla that there was plenty of work at Mt Isa. I had heard they were putting up a new hospital there and that there would be work for me as a carpenter. We travelled via Port Augusta, Kingoonya and then up the main road to Coober Pedy."

It was a journey of 2,500 kilometres north into the heart of the baking interior where you might not see another human for three or four hours. Just past the tiny hamlet of Kingoonya, set among the horizon-wide panorama of brown plains and grey and white salt lakes and pans, Bailey stopped at the million-acre Wirraminna Station to use the station's workshop equipment to repair the caravan. It was now about the end of November and he was about 150 miles north of Port Augusta with about 450 miles to go on the drive north to Kulgera on the South Australia-Northern Territory border and then on to Alice Springs. On this section of the desolate dirt track the family celebrated Ray's 25th birthday on December 3.

"I sold the Huntsman rifle at the next windmill north of Coober Pedy to a dark skinned fellow for some opals," he said.

In Mount Isa he did, indeed, find work as a carpenter on the construction of the new hospital.

He recalled: "The hospital was near the police station and I used to drive the DeSoto to work and leave it in the main street all day. I made no attempt to hide it or alter the number. The caravan was parked out by the caravan park and we all slept in it at night.

"While we were on this trip was the happiest time of my life."

On January 21, more than a month after arriving in Mt Isa and starting his job as a carpenter at the hospital, Ray returned to his car which he had left just around the corner from the building site. As he was about to get into his car he was suddenly shouted at by two men. He stopped and turned round. There were two men looking threatening and waving something in their hands. It took a moment for him to realise they were saying they were police officers. The sheer suddenness and unexpectedness of the drama completely unnerved him. Many an innocent motorist has suffered a racing heart when being stopped by the police. Ray's heart would have started thumping as Hallahan introduced himself and his colleague Reg Pfingst and the nightmare started unfolding.

After initial questioning, Hallahan jumped in to the DeSoto and told Bailey to drive to the caravan while Pfingst followed in the police car. Red dust from the dirt road flew up in a thick, blinding, choking cloud behind the first car as they drove for about two miles to the spot beneath a large tree where the caravan was parked.

At the caravan Ray told Patricia the men with him were police but he had no idea what they wanted. The police then searched the car and caravan. When Bailey asked what they were looking for, Hallahan said "You'll find out".

They were then both put in the police car and driven to Mt Isa Police Station.

"I was taken to the end room on the first floor," remembered Bailey. "My wife was in the next room and I could hear them questioning her from soon after they brought her to the Police Station until after midnight. I could hear some words which were said but I couldn't make out the conversation. I heard my wife crying."

The South Australian police had done their homework well. Hallahan had a warrant which had been issued in Adelaide in August for Bailey's arrest on a false pretences charge for trading-in the International while it was under a hire-purchase agreement for the DeSoto. Bailey protested that he was continuing to pay for the International. They also accused him of possessing an unlicensed pistol. But that night he was only charged with possessing the pistol. And then the relentless interrogation continued: where were you at the beginning of December and what did you do? Can you prove it?

"I was taken away and locked up in a padded cell some time after midnight. I could hear my wife still being questioned in the next room when they took me away. During the night I was woken about every half hour by a torch being flashed in the trap and if I didn't move, they came in and woke me."

In the morning he was charged with false pretences and then Hallahan, Reg Pfingst, Inspector Norwin Bauer and another officer took him into the interview room and got stuck into him, telling him that the DeSoto was a minor problem for Bailey. We know you killed three people at Sundown Station. Tell us how you did it. Tell us why you did it.

"They didn't tell me that I needn't answer their questions or that what I said might be used in evidence. I thought I had to answer," said Bailey.

Hallahan told him he would be taken into court that morning for a mere formality. There would be no chance for him to plead his innocence. The charges would be read out and Bailey would be asked if he had any questions. He should answer 'No" and that would be the end of it. He would have his chance to put his side of the story in court on another day.

At 10am Bailey was marched to the courtroom. It was a shock after being held incommunicado since about 7 pm the night before. As he stepped through the door he found himself in a crowded room with every single face turned towards him and every eye staring at him, weighing him up. They saw a slim, dark-haired and sunburnt man with a dirty open-neck shirt, dirty shorts and sandals. The number of sweating bodies made the 40 degree heat even more unbearable. All the seats were taken and men were standing around the edge of the room. Among them were 10 police officers. The local court reporter from Mt Isa's newspaper was sitting near the front. Bailey scanned the faces anxiously. Where was Patricia? Where was Michael? They were not there. He was as friendless, bewildered, alone and helpless as a sacrificial offering. He was stunned but to the crowd he appeared to be self-possessed. He spoke only two words when Inspector Bauer asked if he wanted to question the arresting police officers: "No questions".

He was remanded in custody for eight days and taken straight back to the interview room

"During the morning I could hear my wife crying downstairs," he recalled. "I told them where I had been and what I had been doing but they just kept on questioning me and didn't seem to believe me. By midday I was in such a state I didn't know what I was saying. From then on I think I just answered the questions in the way I thought they wanted me to.

"I was questioned from soon after breakfast until about half past one. Several times Hallahan went out and came back and said he had been speaking to my wife and went on asking questions. All four of them asked me questions but mostly the questions were asked by Hallahan or by the inspector. The police had morning tea about 10am but they didn't offer me any. They brought me some food at dinner time but I couldn't eat it."

That afternoon two more big, imposing, authoritative men arrived in the interview room to bully and cajole Bailey.

"Detectives Hopkins and Moran questioned me until about 8 o'clock that night," he said. "Hallahan was present most of the time while they were questioning me. Towards the end of their questioning they said to me: *'They are still questioning your wife and you won't be allowed to see her until you sign a confession and they won't stop questioning her until you do'.* They also said: *'Do you love your wife?'* I said: *'I do'* and they said: *'Well then, sign it and we will leave her alone'.* By this time all I wanted was for them to stop questioning my wife and leave her alone. Moran typed out a statement and asked me to sign it and I signed it. They asked me to write the word "Yes" after some questions at the end of it. I do not remember writing anything in my own handwriting at the end of it but I could have done so. I was in such a state at that time that I would have done anything they told me to do.

"The reason why I signed the confession was so that they would stop questioning my wife and leave us both alone. They had her at the Police Station all day. I could hear her crying. I asked to see her but was told that I could not. I wanted to send a telegram to my father the night I was arrested and I asked could my wife send it to let him know what was going on. Hallahan said she was not allowed to leave the police station. I also asked to see a lawyer but Hallahan said I was not allowed to speak to anybody and even refused to let me speak to my wife."

On Thursday morning, the 23rd, he faced more questions from Moran and Hopkins until Hallahan arrived just before midday and told Bailey: "I have in my possession a provisional warrant for the arrest of a man named Raymond John Bailey charging him with the murder of a woman named Thyra Bowman at Sundown Station in South Australia on or about 5 December 1957." Bailey agreed he was the person mentioned in the warrant and was told he would be arrested and charged with the murder of Mrs Bowman. The indictment was on the information of Detective Inspector Gilbert Leonard Gully. The warrant, issued on January 22, 1958 before a justice of the peace, was that Raymond John Bailey of no fixed place of abode, carpenter, on or about December 5, 1957 at Sundown Station did murder Thyra Bowman.

Patricia, only 22 years old, pregnant, distraught, with a three-year-old son to nurture and a husband who had been spirited away by the police to be charged with murder, had herself been questioned by the police late into the night. Now she was left to make do in the caravan parked tantalisingly close to the police station and court. During the day she sat on the tree-shaded police court veranda, one of the few cool spots in Mt Isa where the shade temperature once again reached 40 degrees centigrade. Now that Hallahan had engineered a confession from her husband, police told her she was completely free to go her own way and could see her husband for a short time twice a day in the watch house. She told police she would go with her husband to South Australia and vowed to stick with him as closely as possible. A slim, almost frail woman, she continued to cook, sleep and look after her son in the caravan.

On Friday 24th more than 100 members of the public crowded on to the veranda and courthouse grounds when Bailey was due to appear in court. He was brought from the watch house at the rear of the police station at 10am, dressed in a clean check shirt, fawn trousers, socks and sandals, dwarfed by Detective Pfingst and the even bigger and bulkier Hallahan. When Magistrate Mr Sutherst explained the proceedings to him, Bailey responded: "Yes, Your Honour." They were the only words he spoke during the 20-minute hearing. He stood with both hands gripping the rail of the dock while the charge of murder was read to him by Mr Sutherst.

Among the crowd, sitting quietly on the balcony, was Patricia. The cold words of the dreadful charge were too much for her. She collapsed. Police carried her into the police station recreation room and called for a doctor. She lay there for half an hour receiving treatment. It was probably the first time she had realised the enormity of what police were alleging her husband had done.

Granting the application, Mr Sutherst said it would be necessary for Bailey to be remanded until January 31 to enable the original warrant to arrive. Bailey, who showed no sign of emotion apart from repeatedly licking his lips during the proceedings, replied: "Yes, Your Honour."

Bailey was remanded until January 31. As soon as he got back to his cell he asked for a Church of England minister. What he said is unknown.

He recalled afterwards: "I was locked in the same padded cell at Mt Isa every night I was there. For the first three nights I was awakened about every half hour. If I didn't turn over they came in and woke me. The only time I was allowed out of the cell was when someone wanted to question me. I was not allowed to have a bath and only had one shave and that was on the day I went to court to be extradited to South Australia."

Patricia was still in a terrible state later in the day and collapsed again. A doctor was called and she was injected with a sedative. She was still suffering next day. The shock and treatment she had suffered was too much for her to bear. Six weeks pregnant, she suffered a miscarriage. On the Saturday evening Patricia's parents arrived from Dubbo after a 2,000 kilometre drive of worrying, fretting, baking, sweating, aching, cramping, sorrowing and wondering what on earth had happened to their daughter. They found her in the caravan by the police station with son Michael and gave them both a big hug. Her parents had a couple of hours sleep but at 1.45am couldn't wait any longer to get her out of Mt Isa and set off on the 2,000 kilometre journey back to Dubbo.

Patricia never saw her husband again. He had lost his wife, son and unborn baby and was now alone in facing his ordeal.

Monday 27th brought another court hearing, with 12 police standing in the courtroom and at least 20 members of the public peering in the windows from the veranda. Dressed in a clean white shirt, blue trousers, socks and sandals, Bailey, for the first time, was brought from the watch house to the dock handcuffed to a police officer, burly Sgt Alan Cleland. The handcuffs were removed while the hearing was under way. He remained composed, despite having lost the physical support of his wife, and appeared to listen intently as the charges of murder and false pretences were read to him. The prosecutor, Senior Sergeant J E Linane, told Mr Sutherst the original warrant had arrived from Adelaide and called Detective Edwin Charles Hopkins to give evidence. Hopkins said he had in his possession two warrants issued in Adelaide for the arrest of Bailey, one charging him with the murder of Mrs Bowman and another on a charge of having obtained the DeSoto valued at 300 pounds in Renmark in August 1957 by falsely pretending he owned an International utility.

Hopkins said he had executed the murder warrant on Bailey earlier in the day and asked the court to order that the prisoner be delivered to his custody to be returned to Adelaide. Asked if he had any questions to ask the detective, Bailey replied: "No sir." Mr Sutherst then directed that the man be delivered to Hopkins' custody for return to South Australia. Sergeant Linane said that on another charge of possessing an unlicensed pistol, no evidence would be given as it might interfere with proceedings against Bailey in South Australia. Sutherst then discharged Bailey on the pistol charge. Bailey, asked if he had anything to say, made the longest statement of his three court appearances: "No, Your Honour, no."

The media was still being told that Bailey would be taken to the stretch of road where it was believed the murder weapon had been ditched. Police had hoped to be able to fly to Kulgera, only 48 kilometres from the murder scene but were told the freighter would be unable to land there. Instead, it was decided to fly to Alice Springs, travel to the murder scene by road on Thursday to look for the gun, and fly to Adelaide on Thursday night.

However, after spending Wednesday night at Alice Springs police station Bailey was driven straight back to the airstrip and the plane took off for Adelaide just after 10am on Thursday the 30th. There was no search for the murder weapon.

Chapter 40 - An Innocent in Jail

We're in the City of Churches in the only one of the Australian states that was created as a destination for free settlers and did not receive convicts under the transportation system.

Some cynical people suggested this gave South Australians a sort of snootiness, or moral righteousness and wowserism, a state of mind defined by Australian writer C J Dennis as an ineffably pious person who mistakes this world for a penitentiary and himself for a warder. There was still no television service in the state, no state lottery and no late night shopping in the city. And when we're talking about churches, in Bailey's case it was the creed of an eye for an eye rather than turning the other cheek. The people of South Australia wanted vengeance and retribution for the atrocities at Sundown Station.

Bailey landed at Adelaide's Edinburgh Airfield on the afternoon of January 30 1958 and was taken to the city watch house.

Next day he was taken to the splendidly imposing Adelaide Police Court, a beautiful two-storey golden sandstone building dominated by a Doric portico with its four fluted columns occupying about half of its frontage in King William Street, the city's main north-south artery. At least there was more room in this court room and it was blessedly cooler. He was remanded until February 14.

Bailey was then loaded on to a truck with barred windows and driven from the centre of the city all the way up King William Street to the northern edge of the city centre and then west along North Terrace, past the imposing Parliament House and the city's main train terminus, out to the north-west corner of the gridded city centre, out past the railway marshalling yards and down the narrow, bush-lined Gaol Road to the fortress-like Adelaide Gaol with its towers and turrets and to a world which hadn't changed much since it was built in 1841. This was to be his new home. And his last home.

Men were still whipped here. Men were still hanged here. There was no plumbing in the cells. Prisoners had a bucket for a toilet which they then had to carry out and clean each morning. Each cell came with its share of rats, cockroaches, bedbugs, lice and ticks. In winter the stone cells with their barred windows often meant the prisoners would have been more comfortable in a refrigerated storeroom: it would have had no drafts.

The gaol is built in a semi-circle, with the only entrance at the centre of the diameter. The wide main gates are set in a beautifully-proportioned building set in the massive outside wall. Inside the gates Bailey was taken through a cavernous hall to the far side of the entrance building. Here, the only way forward was to enter the sally port, a cage with two locked gates big enough to contain a large truck. Entry could not be gained through one of its gates unless the other one was locked. Once inside the sally port, the first gate was locked and only then was the second unlocked.

Now Bailey was in the hub of the jail, an open area surrounded by a second wall, as tall and intimidating as the first. From this operational centre, six doors placed at regular intervals in yet another, and much smaller, semi-circular wall lead into six large enclosed exercise yards fanning out from the core, with each yard containing cells and other prison buildings.

Bailey found himself governed by the gaol bell which was rung to signify meal times and parades. Breakfast was delivered to the cells at 7am. Prisoners ate their meals in the cells by themselves before inspections to make sure that cells were clean and tidy. Toilet buckets were then taken into the yards for emptying. Prisoners were returned to their cells at 11am. After lunch in the cells, prisoners were released back into the yards and recreation rooms until tea was served at 4pm. On average prisoners spent 18 hours a day in their cells. At the beginning and end of every 'session' prisoners were counted and a roll call taken.

The only break from this Spartan, miserable existence was when solicitor John Mangan came to see him to prepare his case for the committal proceedings at the Police Court. Mangan explained to Bailey that to avoid the possibility of prosecutions arriving at the Supreme Court with little or no chance of success, the prosecution first had to persuade a magistrate that there was a case to put before a jury and that there was a reasonable chance that the jury would find the defendant guilty. The magistrate would then decide whether to send the defendant for trial at the Supreme Court.

Bailey also talked to A L Pickering, an experienced barrister who Mangan would be instructing and who would do all the talking and questioning in court. They told Bailey that when Hallahan had started asking him questions about the murders the detective should have cautioned him that he need not say anything and that if he did say anything it could be used against him. Because of this failure they would seek to have all of Hallahan's evidence rejected. This in turn would rule out the evidence from Moran and Hopkins because they had depended on a 20-minute speech from Hallahan for the statement that they drew up for Bailey to sign. Without this incriminating evidence the prosecution did not have a case.

There was a second part to the defence plan.

Pickering was faced with a major problem. He had a client who appeared to have talked long and loud to the police and given them a highly-detailed account of how he had killed three people. The possibility that Hallahan could have heavied Bailey and invented the confession was beyond his comprehension. But wait – this case had striking similarities with the Bodkin Adams case in England in which a self-incriminating doctor had been tried for murder less than 12 months earlier. The case had made headlines all over the world and was still fresh in people's minds. Perhaps he could adopt a similar strategy to the one which had resulted in the surprise acquittal of Adams?

The Bodkin Adams case had been labelled the murder case of the century and no less than the British Attorney-General, Sir Reginald Manningham Buller, had appeared in person to lead the prosecution of the killer. And it was true: Bodkin Adams had confessed to killing patients: he called it 'easing their passing'. Nowadays the term is mercy killing. The problem was that large numbers of the patients whose passing was being eased by Bodkin Adams were leaving him large bequests in their wills. A further problem was that some of the patients did not appear to be particularly ill and it seemed the doctor was merely easing his way to a fortune as he eased them out of this world.

The son of a Northern Irish Plymouth Brethren watchmaker, he had settled in Eastbourne, an English seaside town laid out in 1859 by the Duke of Devonshire on his land to be a resort built for gentlemen by gentlemen. It had attracted well-to-do families and, in the 20th century, those who aspired to gentility and a peaceful retirement by the sea. The result was a town with lots of wealthy widows who had outlived their husbands.

The 18-room mansion in which he lived and practised had been bought with the help of a large loan from a patient in 1929. As early as 1935 he received the equivalent of a six-figure sum in the will of an elderly patient, Matilda Whitton. Rumours began to circulate behind the net curtains about the number of bequests the doctor was receiving from patients who had died suddenly and quickly.

Bodkin Adams' multi-will-winning bedside manner was not immediately apparent. He bore no resemblance at all to the matinee idols whom the widows worshipped. It didn't matter which way he was measured, the answer was about 165 centimetres. He weighed about 115 kilos, wore little round glasses and was almost certainly homosexual. Perhaps the large doses of morphine and heroin he administered made him seem more attractive.

When police started investigations in 1956 the Home Office pathologist looked at about 400 wills from Adams's patients and found that he had been a beneficiary in 132 of them. It was said he was the richest general practitioner in the country. When he eventually died he was worth 400,000 pounds – several million dollars in today's money.

Towards the end of 1956 the future for Adams started to look as bleak as it did for some of his patients: police found him particularly garrulous about his affairs. In October 1956 Dr Adams was asked by police about the death of a Mrs Morrell. Adams replied that she had been suffering terrible pain and wanted to die. He argued that it wasn't a crime to ease the suffering of someone who was terminally ill.

When asked why he had always stated on cremation forms that he had not benefited from the patient's will he told the Scotland Yard detective superintendent: "Oh, that wasn't done wickedly, God knows it wasn't. We always want cremations to go off smoothly for the dear relatives. If I said I knew I was getting money under the will they might get suspicious and I like cremations and burials to go smoothly. There was nothing suspicious really. It was not deceitful." Also to the superintendent: "Easing the passing of a dying person isn't all that wicked. She wanted to die. That can't be murder. It is impossible to accuse a doctor."

Police eventually focussed on two deaths. Edith Morrell had been partially paralysed after a stroke. He had prescribed her a cocktail of morphine and heroin. She had left him a vintage Rolls Royce Silver Ghost. Gertrude Hullett left him a Rolls Royce Silver Dawn. Her husband had died and she was suicidal. He prescribed large amounts of sodium barbitone and also sodium phenobarbitone. Perhaps he was over excited about this bequest when he rang the local coroner to arrange an autopsy. She was as yet only unconscious and not dead at all. She did die, on July 23, 1956, aged only 50 with twice the fatal dose of sodium barbitone in her body. And Adams did receive his Roller.

The trial began on March 19, 1957. The media had been talking of up to 400 suspicious deaths and there was a widespread belief that Adams would be found guilty of murder.

But the defence counsel, Geoffrey Lawrence QC, taking part in his first murder trial, created large holes in the prosecution case with some astute cross-examinations and a surprise exhibit which undermined the case further. These setbacks were judged as no more than a couple of early punches from the underdog before the knock-out blow was delivered when Adams took the stand.

He had proved to have very loose lips. It hadn't needed any strong questioning from the police before the case for Adams to dig a large hole for himself. The newspaper-reading public waited with eager anticipation for Adams to start answering difficult questions, especially as prosecuting counsel Sir Reginald Manningham Buller was feared in courts, with good reason, as Sir Reginald Bullying Manner.

Reporters packed the court in anticipation. Sir Reginald announced that he had come to the end of the prosecution case. Now the forensic dissection of Bodkin Adams would start. Lawrence QC rose from his seat and took Sir Reginald and Fleet Street completely by surprise by announcing that he was not going to call the doctor to defend himself. The legal world struggled to find precedents for people charged with murder not giving evidence in their defence.

The trial judge, Patrick Devlin, said after the case: "To imagine such a voluntary action is an exercise to bring the word 'boggle' briefly into its own."

Lawrence used his closing speech to argue, essentially, that a mercy killing was not murder. It took the jury only 45 minutes to find Adams not guilty.

No wonder this approach looked so attractive to Bailey's defence team. It seems reasonable to believe that Pickering decided that Bailey was liable to be bullied under cross-examination into saying things he didn't mean to say and that because of that it would be best for him not to take the stand to give evidence if he was committed for trial to the Supreme Court. What we have to remember is that we have travelled back to 1958 to a world with different values and behaviours. Today credit cards are thrust at us. Banks beg us to spend more than we earn. Back then if you wanted an overdraft you put on your best suit and tie (there was no point in a woman even contemplating asking), made an appointment with the bank manager and walked into his office, cap in hand ready to genuflect. These were the days when bank managers, doctors, politicians and lawyers were ranked only just below the level of gods. And when they spoke, their words were treated as sacrosanct. Watch the old newsreel footage as even rude and belligerent reporters approach cabinet ministers with great deference, doff their hats and politely ask: '*Excuse me Minister but would you care to say a word?*' Thus it was that Bailey would have accepted the decision of his barrister without a murmur. His word would have been final. Just as Pickering could not envisage the police inventing Bailey's confession, Bailey, the boy from the Bush who had left school at 14, would not have contemplated questioning Pickering's decision that he should not give evidence. "I have every confidence in Mr Pickering QC for he is a very brainy and clever man and knows what he is doing," Bailey wrote in a letter.

On February 25 Bailey was taken from the gaol back to the Police Court for the start of the committal proceedings. Probably for the first time since he had married more than four years earlier he was wearing a suit, white shirt and tie. They had been supplied for him by his solicitor. It was important for him to look respectable in court. And, anyway, he was bigger news than the Queen Mum. Queen Elizabeth the Queen Mother was making her first visit to Australia since she had visited as a duchess in 1927. But the media was far more interested in Bailey. The court case stole the front pages. Queuing started at 8am and when the doors opened at 9.30am there were about 150 people, mostly women, waiting to enter the court. Many were turned away. Even so, about 130 people were crammed into Court One.

At 10am the court usher announced: "All stand". A magistrate with letters before and after his name but, seemingly no Christian name, walked into the court and sat on high. Mr L E Clarke SM, the SM standing for stipendiary, or paid, magistrate, was in his 50s, a severe-looking man with his dark hair slicked down to his skull and wearing heavy-rimmed round spectacles.

The charge was read out. Raymond John Bailey, you are charged with murdering Mrs Thyra Bowman of Glen Helen Station in the Northern Territory, at Sundown Station, South Australia, on or about December 5, 1957.

When the court adjourned at 1pm for lunch the court was emptied. The huge audience had made the court very hot and uncomfortable but most of the crowd immediately started queuing again. They were determined not to miss a moment of this ghoulish free drama.

On Tuesday the 26th queuing started about 7.30am and by 9.30 there were about 200 people in an orderly queue winding round into Victoria Square. Most of them were middle-aged women, some of them carrying Thermos flasks and sandwiches. But with an even hotter day forecast, only 82 were admitted.

Thursday was to be the big day. There was increased animation and chatter in the court in the morning as the crowd filed in. Hallahan would be giving evidence.

Chapter 41 - Bailey's Longest Speech So Far

Hallahan took the stand, a big man with an air of great confidence about his abilities. As soon as he gave his name Pickering applied for the court to be cleared while Hallahan read his statement. This was the first big test of the defence strategy.

Defence counsel Pickering, with a long, lean face, a receding hairline and spectacles, was the older of the two barristers in court. He said he was seeking to prevent any prejudice being formed in the minds of the jurymen should Bailey be committed for trial. He was making the application because newspapers had given wide coverage of the case and it could be presumed that every potential juryman who might be required if the case was to be committed to the Supreme Court was likely to read Hallahan's evidence.

Magistrate Clarke: "Yes, that's what happened in the Dr Adams case. But Dr Adams, of course, was later acquitted."

He was pointing out to Pickering that despite incriminating evidence being given at a committal, that harm could be undone at the trial.

Clarke asked Pickering if he had seen the prosecution evidence by Hallahan. "No", he answered.

Clarke: 'Is there any reason why you should not be shown the evidence?'

Prosecuting counsel E B Scarfe, a chubby man with round, metal-rimmed glasses and a round, chubby face, intervened: "Certainly not. I would be only too glad to show it to your honour and Mr Pickering".

There was a fascinating link between the two barristers. When Scarfe had been a law student at Adelaide University Pickering had been one of his lecturers. In court the student would certainly want to demonstrate to the lecturer how much he had learned.

Clarke agreed to adjourn the hearing at 12.50pm so that he and Pickering could read the 12 foolscap pages of evidence to be given by Hallahan.

On resumption Pickering said he had no objection to the witness starting his evidence in chief but at an appropriate time he would apply to question the witness on a voir dire. A voir dire is a mini case within the main case when a section of evidence is tested by cross-examination for the magistrate or judge to decide if it should become part of the main case.

On this basis Hallahan started giving his evidence. He had only reached the point where he claimed that Bailey had said he had no objection to searching the caravan when there was a sudden commotion. Bailey was up and out of his seat in the dock, turning and running out of the little low wooden enclosure, yelling. No one will ever know exactly what he had been expecting Hallahan to say. But it was now clear to him that right from the beginning Hallahan was going to lie to the court.

"Can I leave the court?" he asked as he turned determinedly towards the door leading to the cells. A court orderly grabbed him.

"He's telling lies', he told the magistrate, breaking into loud sobs.

He turned to Hallahan and shouted: "Tell the truth. That's all I want."

Clarke said firmly: "Calm yourself and sit down. This evidence has to go on."

Bailey returned to his seat and sat crying with his head pillowed on his arms on the edge of the dock for the next 10 minutes as Hallahan continued his evidence as if nothing had happened. Later, Bailey turned his back to the court and sat staring at Hallahan, as though willing him to tell the truth.

When Pickering called for the voir dire examination Clarke ordered the court to be cleared except for counsel and police. It took nearly 10 minutes to clear the public. At 4pm the hearing was adjourned until Monday March 3 at 10am.

It appeared that other people, outside the court system, had also been preparing for Hallahan to give his evidence. The Golden Fleece chain of service stations had been running a series of display ads in newspapers extolling the virtues of the Australian way of life. It would seem that one of the detectives, probably Hallahan, Moran or Hopkins, had talked to the Police Association of South Australia and that the Association had chatted to an executive of Golden Fleece. The report of Pickering's challenge to the evidence of Hallahan appeared on page 4 of that day's The News. Occupying more than half of that page was a display advertisement featuring a boy of about seven talking to three other children.

The headline ran: "My dad's a policeman…". The blurb ran:

"I remember the ring of pride in my voice as I said it…the phrase that made me the last authority on the important things of my small life…stopped many an argument in its tracks…saved many a roughing from local bullies…a respect for the police comes early to young Australians…Additional to their job of crime detection, our police forces have established Boys' Clubs throughout this land…keeping young hands and minds busy…leading youngsters away from those things that lead to the tag 'Juvenile Delinquent'…I followed my dad into the Force…no other jobs had such attraction for me. I love this land of mine and it gives me an immense satisfaction to be one of its 14,000 guardians of the law, for I am proud to be Australian."

This sentiment of support for the patriotic police was followed by some words from the proud sponsors:

"Because we are an Australian organisation and have faith in this Nation and its people, we have dedicated ourselves to the inspiring task of building a greater spirit of national pride in the boundless heritage that is Australia. Let us all speak of Australia

with pride. Let us join in a concerted effort to be rid forever of the apologetic note that underlies each hour of attainment. A greater Australia for us, and for generations of Australians still to come, will be our reward."

It was brilliant timing and placement.

Monday morning brought the continuation of Hallahan's evidence. There was a massive shock for Bailey.

"At 7.10pm on Saturday, 25th of January, 1957, I had a conversation with a man named Mr Hudson at the Mount Isa CIB Office. At 7.30pm on the same date I saw the accused at the Mount Isa Watch house. I said to him: *'Your father in law Mr Hudson has arrived from Dubbo and he wants to have a talk with you.'* I then brought Mr Hudson into the Mount Isa Watch house and he shook hands with the accused and said *'How are you Ray?'* The accused replied *'OK thanks.'* Mr Hudson then said: *'Did you kill those people back there?'* The accused replied: *'Yes I killed them alright.'* At that stage Mr Hudson collapsed and after some 10 minutes he was revived and he said to the accused *'Why did you do it Ray? Why did you kill those three people?'* The accused replied: *'I don't know why I did it. I don't know why I killed them. It must be my nerves.'* Mr Hudson and the accused conversed on other matters for about 10 minutes and Mr Hudson then left the watch house. I returned the accused to the lock-up portion of the watch house and he said to me *'It's going to be hard on him now.'"*

It was the first time Bailey had heard this allegation from Hallahan. It was completely untrue, he later told the court.

Cross examined by Pickering, Hallahan said he had made no notes at the time of the conversation he was alleging.

At the end of Hallahan's cross-examination the magistrate ordered: "The court is now open. I certify that the foregoing depositions of Glen Patrick Hallahan were read over to the witness and signed by the witness and by me at Adelaide this third day of March 1958. In my opinion the evidence is sufficient to put the defendant upon his trial for the offence charged."

Bailey said: "I am not guilty and I reserve my defence." He was committed to next sittings of the Supreme Court. Scarfe then dropped the charge involving false pretences.

When Bailey saw his solicitor he demanded that his father-in-law Hudson be called to refute Hallahan's damning allegation that Bailey had confessed to Hudson.

A day confined and humiliated in the 19th century atmosphere and culture of Adelaide Gaol – even the spelling is antiquated – was an assault on the senses. The identical, repetitious days blurred. All Bailey had to cling to were the memories of Patricia and son Michael, who, on one otherwise indistinguishable day, became a four-year-old without his daddy to help blow out the candles.

Chapter 42 - The Supreme Court Trial

Dial M for Murder, starring Ray Milland and Grace Kelly, was doing reasonable business at an Adelaide drive-in but the biggest murder drama in town starred a very unwilling, frightened Ray Bailey at the grand sandstone-columned Supreme Court building on the south side of Adelaide's major city centre square. The grey autumnal morning of Monday, May 12 1958 with patches of rain did not deter about 100 people from queuing outside the sandstone building where five broad steps led up to three tall, wide, arches, each guarded by wrought iron gates. Above this imposing entrance, four massive columns stood in front of a wide balcony on the first floor. Only 29 women and 24 men were admitted to the public gallery in Court Number Two when the doors were opened at 9.30. They included Thomas Whelan's mother who sat pale-faced in the front row with relatives. Bailey did not enter through the splendid front entrance. The barred prison truck deposited him at a back door and he was spirited up through narrow corridors to a holding cell with a door leading up to the dock of the court.

It was not just the architecture which was designed to create a cathedral-like building to put people in awe of the institution and the establishment and in which justice and her servants should be revered. At 10am sharp an usher demanded "All rise" and the Judge, Sir Geoffrey Sandford Reed QC, a 66-year-old Methodist, resplendent in his traditional medieval scarlet robes and white horsehair wig, took his place at the bench on high.

Below him, in the front row of the bar table, sat more bewigged figures. The state government's top barrister, Crown Solicitor Roderic St Clair Chamberlain QC, had decided he ought to lead the prosecution team to show how important the government considered this case. With him was Scarfe who had conducted the prosecution case at the committal hearing.

Chamberlain was very haughty and a great defender of the police. (Long after the police evidence in the ensuing Max Stuart murder case had been totally discredited, he said he would have pulled the lever to hang the defendant.)

They were all upstaged by Bailey, dark-eyed and wearing a blue suit, fawn shirt and maroon tie, as he entered the wooden dock to became the focus of attention. The ancient traditions of the court continued with a man known as the Clerk of Arraigns now taking centre stage. "Raymond John Bailey – you are charged with the murder of Mrs Thyra Bowman of Glen Helen Station, in the Northern Territory, at Sundown Station on December 5, 1957. How do you plead?" Bailey managed a quiet, subdued "Not Guilty".

The Clerk of Arraignment turned to Bailey and told him: "The jurors whose names you will now hear called are those that are to pass judgement between our Sovereign Lady the Queen and you upon your life or death. If, therefore, you would challenge them, you shall do so as their names are called and sworn." Fifty had been called in case of multiple objections by the defence but Pickering only challenged two as their names were read out. Bailey said nothing. The jury comprised an electroplater, a clerk, a painter, two drivers, a salesman, a merchant, an accountant, a cellarman, a farmer, a decorator and a mechanic. They were, of course, all men.

Immediately after the jury had been sworn in it was directed by Justice Reed to retire, which would have puzzled them greatly. It was so that they would not be influenced by the legal argument which Pickering now advanced

Pickering argued that the concepts involved in the Judges' Rules meant that the alleged confession to Hallahan and the South Australian police should not be mentioned by the prosecution in its opening summary of the evidence to the jury because it had not been voluntary. He then tried to put pressure on the judge by saying that if the alleged confession was allowed to be mentioned and it was later ruled to be not admissible as evidence he would have no option but to ask for a new trial on the ground that no direction by the judge for the jury to ignore what had been said earlier could remove its effect on the jury.

The judge interrupted: "You say the statement is not voluntary."

Pickering alleged Hallahan had used softening-up tactics on Bailey before questioning him.

Chamberlain: "That is quite unfair."

Pickering: "That is the way we put it. Bailey is arrested and taken into custody. He is questioned about other matters, charged with possession of an unlicensed pistol and locked up for the night. He is brought before the court next morning and remanded and after all that he is questioned on this matter. Hallahan questioned a man in custody at considerable length without giving him any caution and gave no caution until the accused had made a damning admission. That involves inadmissibility of that admission and all that followed on the ground that it was not voluntary. There is no ground to suggest that there was any threat or promise. That does not decide the question that the Crown has not shown this statement to be voluntary.

"The English Judges' Rules are a definition of the standard of propriety of what a police officer should do. If you read the evidence, he was taken into custody at 6.20pm, kept in custody at Mt Isa overnight, charged next morning over a pistol and questioned still in custody. The first confession was made about 12.10. He had been under interrogation from shortly after 10. In England that would inevitably have resulted in rejection of the confession. The High Court here has established the English position, that while the Judges' Rules have not the force of law, any flagrant breach results in rejection of a confession."

The Judge replied: "The onus is on the Crown to show the statement is voluntary. The High Court has said the onus is on the defence to show it is unfair."

Mr Chamberlain said that up to his first confession Bailey might have been merely a witness in the case because the police had no idea of his relation to the case.

Pickering said that if the judge decided it was unfair to admit the evidence of Hallahan, it would rule out what was said to Moran and Hopkins. They had gone straight on with the interrogation at 4.30pm and there was nothing to remove the effect of what Hallahan had done. Hallahan's recitation to Moran and Hopkins and their interrogation of Bailey based on what they had been told by Hallahan should be excluded. He submitted that Bailey had been questioned for two hours while in custody. It was contrary to fair play that he should have been questioned without caution.

The Judge was unmoved: "We have no Judges' Rules in South Australia," he responded.

Chamberlain said that at so many important points the confession was confirmed that one could have no uneasiness about it. When questioned, Bailey had denied owning a rifle. The police went away and spoke to his wife and he then admitted having one. Statements relating to the shooting and to concealment of the bodies had been confirmed by evidence otherwise obtained. The objection could only be taken if the Crown had failed to show that the statement was voluntary. There could be no suggestion that it was not voluntary as it had been given in the exercise of free will. Bailey had been in possession of a pistol in breach of Queensland law and had been told he need not answer any questions. Next day, with that disposed of, but not knowing anything except that he might be able to give them information…

"…who might have been able to keep his mouth shut if he were cautioned," interjected Pickering angrily but suggesting that Bailey had, indeed, made admissions!

Pickering and Chamberlain argued all morning. Finally, at 10 minutes to one, Pickering had exhausted his ammunition and Chamberlain had fired his last response. The judge adjourned for lunch until 2.15pm when he would announce his decision. Basically, Bailey's survival rested on the decision. Without the police evidence of the interviews the circumstantial evidence was likely to be inconclusive. Acceptance of the alleged confession was likely to convince the jury Bailey was guilty.

With each word of the judge's verdict, Bailey's stomach must have twisted tighter, his nerves jangled more uncontrollably, his terror soared. "It is my opinion that there are no disputed questions of fact calling for my decision at this stage. Upon the material before me I must assume that the interrogations of Hallahan and Moran were not accompanied by, or the result of, any overbearing of the defendant's will, or of duress, intimidation, persistent importunity or undue insistence or pressure. I see no ground whatsoever for even suspecting that any inducement by a threat or promise was made. So the impression I have formed on the statement is that the questions asked were answered by the defendant voluntarily."

Chamberlain, having won the argument about the admissibility of Hallahan's evidence, sat down. The job was done: the ace of trumps could be played. He played no further part in the trial.

At 2.55pm Scarfe opened the case for the prosecution by saying: "The case has captured the attention, it seems, of everyone in the land. The jury will have no doubt that Mrs Bowman was savagely murdered, her skull smashed in and had a bullet in her body. And the same applies to Wendy and Whelan. Three innocent people met their deaths in a hideous and ghastly way. Whoever it was who killed the three people had succeeded in destroying the unwritten code of the Outback – the code of hospitality to the wayfarer. The Crown case, that Mrs Bowman was murdered by Bailey, is composed of two branches, circumstantial and a confession by Bailey that he killed all three."

Circumstantial evidence of Bailey's movements, tracks, cartridge cases and other matters made a clear case against Bailey, he said. Evidence would show that empty cartridge cases found at Wirrulla and near where the three people were killed, and one in Bailey's car and one in his caravan all bore the same firing pin mark, showing they were fired by a Huntsman rifle which Bailey took with him when he left Wirrulla a short time before December 5. Circumstantial evidence, far from being dangerous, was often the most reliable, for facts could not lie, Mr Scarfe said.

The second branch was what Bailey said to Detective Hallahan of the Queensland Police, and to Detectives Moran and Hopkins of South Australia, and to his own father-in-law. At first denying, he had shifted his story until at last he told the police he had killed the three. The killing of Whelan was accidental but he killed the women because they were witnesses, Bailey had told the police. Even now Bailey had not told the whole truth. Members of the jury, you may think as the case goes on that the killing of Whelan was deliberate, with a motive of robbery because his wallet had been taken. Bailey had told police he had taken 20 pounds from the wallet and thrown the wallet away.

Scarfe outlined the story that the prosecution had put together about the progress of the Bowmans and Whelan after they had set off from

Glen Helen. He said that: "On December 6, a Kulgera storekeeper, Wilkinson, had a vague recollection of a car resembling Bailey's passing through."

Pathologist Dwyer would say that the fractures to the three skulls were consistent with having been caused by the Bowmans' broken Remington rifle. "Each of the three shots, he thought, through the heads, was fired while deceased were lying on the ground in the position they were found under the canvas."

"Other objects were found at the scene, items which were later confirmed by Bailey's confession to the police," said Mr Scarfe.

Scarfe finished his summing up of the circumstantial evidence and said he would deal with the confession next day. The court adjourned at 4.20. Bailey had hardly moved all day, sitting with his right arm resting on the brass rail of the dock.

Another dull day dawned on Tuesday 13th but by 8.45am there were about a dozen people queuing outside the court. The weather, like Bailey's future, grew steadily worse, with an inch of rain falling in the afternoon and drizzle continuing into the night. When Scarfe resumed his opening address the gallery was filled, mostly by men.

Scarfe then went through the whole of Hallahan's interview from the moment he confronted Bailey as he was about to get into his car right through to the confession as though it was the truth, the whole truth and nothing but the truth. And then he went through the continuation of the story as told by Hopkins and Moran, leading to the point where: "The statement was typed by Moran at Bailey's dictation and was Bailey's own narrative assisted only by questions such as: 'What happened next?' and: 'Was that on the east side of the road?' or questions to clear up times."

The signed confessional statement was then read out. Scarfe remarked on the way the statement contained three different stories and told the jury: "It will be for you to say whether that third story, even now, is the whole truth. Medical evidence was that the victims must have lived for some time after their skulls had been broken as the bullet wounds would have been immediately fatal. There had been much bleeding which would have stopped at death. We'll never know just what happened at the camp fire or how Bailey went about it. You might well doubt if it were really an accident when Whelan was shot. His confession is a full admission of his guilt. Whether or not what is in it is wholly the truth is another matter entirely."

Pickering grilled Bowman at length, his questions leading to a suggestion that he had killed his wife, which he denied. It emerged that since the enquiry started Bowman and Marion had been house guests of Inspector Gully.

Frank Wilkinson said he ran a store at Kulgera Station homestead which was owned by his father-in-law Noel Coulthard. He could remember many details of the Bowmans' car and its occupants passing through at about 4pm on December 5. Wilkinson swore that on the next morning the first car was a Morris going south, followed by a grey Zephyr and trailer going north, a Land Rover and trailer, a government vehicle and a black car and caravan.

He did not know who was in the black car. He told Pickering it had passed his store on December 5. He agreed that at the Police Court he had been unable to say this so positively, nor had he been able to speak positively on dates. His evidence in this court was the truth. He had been able to think things over since then. His answers at the Police Court were true at the time. No, his memory had not been stimulated by anyone since then.

But he did admit that his memory had been stimulated for the first time when police showed him Bailey's car and caravan in the police yard in February. And the wind was taken out of Scarfe's sails when, looking directly at Bailey in the dock, he said: "I have never seen this man before this court case."

Pickering cross-examined him: "Do you pledge your oath that the vehicle shown in this photograph passed your store on December 5?"

"Yes, I do."

"Do you agree that you were unable to be so positive at the police court hearing?"

"Yes."

"Do you agree that you were unable to be so positive about dates?"

"Yes."

"What happened to stimulate your memory?"

"Police showed me Bailey's car and caravan in the police yard in February."

Wilkinson then confessed he had not said anything about the black car and caravan until shown the DeSoto and its caravan in the police yard by the police.

The next witness, Hassell Gordon-Brown, who said he had seen Bailey driving north on December 4, admitted he, too, had been shown the DeSoto and caravan in the police station yard in February. Bailey had told him that a native had wanted to swap opals for his rifle at Coober Pedy but Bailey had wanted six pounds and so the deal had not gone through.

Pickering: "When were you first asked to recall this conversation?"

On January 14 when a Sergeant Buchanan had spoken of a black car and caravan.

Pickering: "Did you at any time see the defendant in possession of a .22 rifle?"

"No."

May 14 brought more cold rain, the complete opposite of the dust and heat that the jury was being asked to picture during evidence.

Pickering asked Brian Bowman: "Did you form the opinion from what you saw that the Vanguard car had been driven to the spot where it was abandoned by a woman?"

"Yes."

"Did you form the opinion that she had summoned a man to assist her in washing that car?"

"She could have done. I formed the opinion that a man had travelled to the spot in the Vanguard car by reason of the fact that his tracks went from the road to the car and back again."

"From that did you deduce that she had enlisted his aid in some way to wash the car?"

"Yes, that's what I thought substantially at the time. I see no reason to change my opinion now."

The gloomy weather continued on Thursday May 15th with more wind and rain.

Sydney Garneau Stanes, the 37-year-old pastoralist, said: "The woman's tracks went away from the Vanguard. They were 3½ to 4 size. I didn't see any sign of a woman's tracks leading from the road into the Vanguard. The man's shoe would have been 7 or 8."

And, demonstrating that people had already judged Bailey guilty of the murders he said: "There is a pretty strong feeling among outback people against Mr Bailey."

Noel Coulthard, the 22-year-old stockman who had been an early arrival at the scene of the murder, was shown a photo of the car and said that nearby footmarks had not been there when he first arrived.

Under cross-examination by Pickering, the police photographer and fingerprint expert Constable O'Neill had to confess that none of the tracks he had seen were worthy of a plaster cast being taken. None of them had a sharp enough impression to show any characteristics. He had only measured the size of the footprints in comparison with his own shoes. There were no wheel or footprints worth photographing. He was unable to obtain fingerprints from the car, rifle or spaghetti can.

Constable Grope and David Iles of Wirrulla told how they had gone out on January 22 and immediately found spent cartridges from the Huntsman gun from when Iles and Bailey had fired pot shots in the bush three months earlier.

Iles, Bailey's fellow wheat lumper said: "It was suggested I go out looking for cartridges in about January. Constable Grope suggested it."

Constable Grope: "On January 22 I went out with Iles in this way because I was instructed to do so by Inspector Gully. He is the officer in charge of CIB Adelaide. I just took the three spent cartridge shells identified to me by Iles."

January 22 had been the day Bailey was questioned for the first time about the murders.

The sun came out briefly on Friday May 16th but not for Bailey.

Hopkins: "I was present when the bodies of the three dead people were uncovered. Between the bodies of Wendy and Whelan I saw the broken Remington Sportmaster rifle. I saw an empty .22 calibre cartridge case." Cross-examined by Pickering, he said an intensive search had been made for spent cartridges and any other cartridges at the scene would probably have been found.

Halfway through Friday, Hallahan took the stand.

Hallahan started giving his evidence just before the court adjourned for lunch from 12.45 to 2.15. Pickering asked leave to question Hallahan on a voir dire and also asked that Detective Hopkins should retire. The judge agreed.

Pickering: "On Tues 21st of January the police at Mt Isa had received a phone message from the Tennant Creek police, which originated in Adelaide. Did you understand it to be an Australia-wide alert for a dark–coloured sedan car thought to be a Dodge, drawing a light-coloured caravan?"

Scarfe objected to the question and was overruled but Hallahan claimed privilege and refused to answer.

Pickering: "At the time when you first saw the accused's DeSoto in Mt Isa did you have in your possession the registration number SA 379-622?"

"No."

"It was acting on information received, was it, that you went and waited by the accused's car on 21 January?"

"Yes."

"When you took the accused to the police station at Mt Isa, you knew, didn't you, that he was wanted for questioning in respect of the Sundown Murders?"

"No, I didn't know that at all."

Bailey listened to the lie, a small, forlorn man, practically hidden by the size of the dock, frowning from time to time, with heavy circles under his eyes.

"Did you ascertain that before starting to question him on the following morning?"

"The only thing I had ascertained was that on the day preceding the murder, a similar type car and caravan was seen about 200 miles south of the murder site. I had no other information."

"Do you know whether lengthy phone calls passed between the police in Adelaide and the police in Mt Isa on the night of 21 January?"

"Not Mt Isa Police I don't think."

"Did the Mt Isa police on the night of 21/22 Jan obtain further information with relation to this dark coloured car and caravan?"

Scarfe objected but the question was allowed.

"I received information concerning the car and information relating to another charge on another subject. That related to a charge of obtaining a car by false pretences in Renwick."

"During any of the times you were questioning Mrs Bailey on 22nd was she in tears?"

"No."

Hallahan went on to deny all of Bailey's allegations of ill treatment apart from the fact he had been kept in the padded cell after confessing.

Pickering tried again to prevent Hallahan's evidence being admitted. The judge refused his submission. Hallahan then gave his evidence in chief and was cross examined by Pickering:

Pickering: "You told me earlier that you had no detailed information about the Sundown murders at the time of questioning Bailey."

"I had none connecting Bailey with them. I did have some details of the Sundown murders. I had a summary of what had happened. Including the fact that a rifle had been used."

"At one stage you put to Bailey 'Did you have one' - i.e. a rifle – 'when you left Whyalla?'"

"Yes, that was not as a result of my information."

"Wasn't that question as a result of information you had that a rifle had been used in the murders?"

"Yes, but I didn't have information that he had one."

"I am suggesting that from the very outset of you interrogation with Bailey, you were intending to question him to see whether he was connected with the Sundown murders."

Scarfe objected but was overruled.

"Yes. With a view to seeing whether he was the culprit or alternatively to see if he had any information connected with it."

Pickering: "Were you playing Mrs Bailey off against her husband?"

"On that day I would say I was not playing Mrs Bailey off against her husband."

"Mrs Bailey has never been charged in connection with these murders, has she?"

Mr Scarfe objected, saying it was impossible for a spouse to be charged in such circumstances. The question was allowed.

"I don't know."

Pickering then objected to further evidence being admitted from Hallahan and Moran on the same basis that he had argued on the opening day of the trial. The judge immediately ruled that it was admissible.

Hallahan then told his stories all over again, including the one about Bailey confessing to his father-in-law that he had killed the three people.

The hearing was adjourned at 4.30pm until 10am on May 19.

By the end of the day 26 witnesses had finished testifying and the 27th was midway through.

On Monday Hallahan's cross-examination continued. Pickering asked: "Would it be correct to say that Mrs Bailey on the night of Jan 21 was detained at the Mt Isa Police Station?"

"That is incorrect."

"Is it correct that she was still being questioned at midnight?"

"No, that is not correct. She was not questioned at night at all."

He had left the police station at about 9.40pm when Mrs Bailey was there talking to her husband. On the night of his arrest Bailey had been placed in an ordinary cell but on the second night, after his confession, he had been placed in a padded cell. But cross-examination revealed that Hallahan had no first-hand knowledge of whether Bailey had been in the padded cell on the first night. Hallahan insisted Mrs Bailey had always been free to go. He denied that Bailey had asked to see a lawyer and asked to telegraph his father. Bailey had been allowed to see his wife on January 22.

Pickering asked: "Is it correct that lengthy phone conversations took place between police at Mt Isa and Adelaide on the night of 21st January?"

"There was one conversation between them but that was in connection with false pretences. Nothing was said about the Sundown murder to my knowledge. I didn't answer the phone on that occasion."

Moran took the oath next. Moran started his evidence by reading out the 20-minute incriminating statement Hallahan had made to him in front of Bailey. Moran continued: "Hallahan read the warrant to him and said 'Are you the person mentioned in this warrant?' and he said 'Yes'. Hallahan said 'You will be arrested and charged with the murder of Thyra Bowman'. At this, the court was adjourned for lunch from 12.45 to 2.15.

Resuming his evidence, Moran said he asked Bailey if he would care to make a statement, telling him he did not have to and that what he said would be taken down and might be used in evidence. Then came an extraordinary Freudian slip. "The statement was taken down at his dictation, most of it voluntarily – from his own story." Pickering jumped on the phrase immediately and asked for the words to be read back to the court by the shorthand reporter. Moran said he wished to clarify that it was all made voluntarily.

Pickering objected to much of Moran's evidence on the basis that Bailey had been intimidated.

The judge said he saw nothing, on what was before him, to show that Bailey was overborne. He told the jury: "When you have heard what Bailey or someone else might have to say it is up to you to say what value is to be given to the evidence."

Under cross-examination by Pickering, Moran said that he knew everything about the case when he arrived in Mt Isa apart from who did it.

Pickering: "Is it correct that the police had a change of theory about this murder on about the 20th January from the fact that it was an oyster grey Zephyr drawing a trailer to that of a dark coloured Dodge or DeSoto sedan drawing a light-coloured caravan?"

"Yes but we did not know that the person in the car and caravan had committed the murders, but we did want to interview him."

"You had a very strong suspicion?"

"Yes."

"Was an Australia-wide alert put into operation on or about 20th January for a dark-coloured DeSoto sedan drawing a light-coloured caravan?"

"I believe so. But it would be a few days before the 20th January."

"May we take it that Hallahan's recitation of those facts [the confession] in Bailey's presence was of strengthening up the evidence?"

"I wouldn't say that."

"Was it for the purpose of getting corroboration of Hallahan's testimony?"

"No."

"For what purpose do you suggest (Hallahan having previously told you these facts) that Hallahan recited them in the presence of Bailey?"

"So that we could interview the defendant as we were more well-versed with the facts of the murder than what Hallahan was."

"But he had already told you those facts before you started questioning Bailey."

"Yes."

"Could there be any other purpose in reciting those facts in Bailey's presence than to get corroboration of Hallahan's testimony?"

"Only as I said before to question him more fully...I couldn't actually say why Hallahan recited those facts but it could have been what he thought the right thing to do and as I thought the right thing to do."

"And, incidentally, to get support for Hallahan's testimony as a sort of by product?"

"That is not the thought I had in mind."

"For the third and last time, was there any purpose for getting Hallahan to recite a summary of his questioning, other than for the purpose of strengthening up the case against Bailey?"

Scarfe objected and Pickering was forced to withdraw the question.

"Whose idea was it that Hallahan should make this recitation?"

"I believe it would be Hallahan's. He came up with us. He did recite it to me first without Bailey being present."

"Who first told you the name Iles?"

Scarfe objected and the judge agreed that the question should not be put.

"Was the person from whom you first heard the name Iles a policeman or a civilian?"

Scarfe objected. Again the objection was upheld.

"Do you feel yourself that any harm would be done to the public interest by revealing who first mentioned the name Iles to you?"

Scarfe objected. Objection upheld.

"At 4.30pm when you commenced your interrogation of the defendant, did you know the name David Iles?"

"Yes."

"How long had you known that name?"

"I would say approximately half an hour."

"Were you told that name by Detective Hallahan?"

"No."

He was questioned about the search of the car and caravan. "The DeSoto and caravan had already been searched by Detective Hallahan prior to my arriving and I also made a search in relation to the gloves we were looking for but I didn't make a minute search," he said. "There was quite a lot of junk. We took it out into the open and then returned it to the car."

Moran was asked by Pickering if two of the black trackers who had been at the murder scene were at Alice Springs when Bailey had stopped there on his way south from Mt Isa to Adelaide. One was called Larry but he did not know the other's name. Was it true that they had examined Bailey's feet and declared that he was not the man who had been at Sundown?

"Not to my knowledge," said Moran.

"Were two of the black trackers who had been at Sundown at Alice at the time Bailey was brought there?"

"Yes. They are Northern Territory police trackers."

"Did it suggest itself to you to ask these trackers to examine Bailey's tracks when he was at Alice for the purpose of comparing them with the tracks they had seen at Sundown?"

"No."

"It would have been quite an easy thing to get the police trackers to examine his footprints, wouldn't it?"

"Yes."

"As officer in charge of Sundown investigation did it occur to you of having a plaster cast taken of these footprints?"

"Yes. I didn't think that anything could be gained by it."

"It didn't occur to you to have a single photo taken of a single footprint?"

"It occurred to me. No, I didn't have it done."

He admitted he had taken possession of Bailey's shoes. "I had those with me on the plane at Alice. I didn't ask either of the trackers whether those shoes made any of the tracks that they had seen."

"Bailey was never taken anywhere to assist us in finding the Huntsman rifle?"

"No."

Intriguingly, the cross-examination then touched on an incident which had not been reported. A Mr and Mrs Robert McKenzie had been taken by police to Port Augusta Police Station at some time.

Moran agreed that a Detective Palmer from Port Augusta had been with him at Sundown.

"I couldn't say if it was he who arrested a Mr and Mrs McKenzie and took them to Port Augusta," he said.

Pickering: "And attempted to get them to sign a confession for the Sundown murders?"

"I wouldn't know about that."

Chapter 43 - The Biggest Frame-up in Australian History

The prosecution case was at an end. Pickering stood up and everyone in the court expected him to call Bailey so that he could explain how he was not guilty of the crime. Pickering shocked everyone by announcing: "I will not be calling anyone to give evidence."

Instead, Bailey made an unsworn statement from the dock. Reading in the dull, flat, hesitating voice of someone who has difficulty in reading, he said he had nothing to do with the three murders. Whelan's mother in the gallery screamed "Liar! Filthy murderer!" Police were trying to remove her when she shouted: "If they don't hang you I'll kill you myself." As police manoeuvred her through the door she screamed: "Your wife murdered my son – I know she did." It prompted a second, older, woman to rise from the gallery and shout "Hang him! He killed Tommy." Several officials around the court ordered silence. The woman's husband ushered her from the court as she turned and shouted once more: "Hang him. Hang him. He killed Tommy." Bailey moistened his lips and quietly asked the judge: "Will I go on?"

Judge: "Yes."

Bailey lost his self-control and continued haltingly in an unsteady voice. His voice began to break and when he reached the passage about the police treatment of his wife he broke down and cried. Several times he tried to start reading again with a wavering voice but broke down each time, wiping his eyes.

"My wife was about six weeks pregnant at the time and she had a miscarriage while she was at Mt Isa. She is still not well and I understand she is being treated by the doctor in Dubbo."

"I did not say to my wife in the presence of Detective Hallahan that I had killed these people.

"My father-in-law Mr Hudson came to see me on the following Saturday at Mt Isa. The evidence given by Detective Hallahan about Mr Hudson's conversation with me is not true. I did not tell Mr Hudson that I had killed these people or anything like that. I instructed my solicitor to arrange for Mr Hudson to come here from Dubbo to give evidence but I am told he has the mumps and is not well enough to come."

He eventually managed to finish his 2,500 word statement which lasted from 3.54 to 4.18. The court was then adjourned for the day.

Tuesday 20 dawned cloudy with a shower or two.

All the police who had been associated with the interrogation were recalled to refute everything Bailey had alleged against them apart from admitting Mrs Bailey did cry once - when told by her husband that he had killed the three people.

Now it was Scarfe's turn to sum up: "The clearest possible proof is that Bailey was on the spot at the time," he said. And: "There is only Bailey's word as to his wife's inability to drive a car."

Importantly, he told the jury that counsel's right was no more than to submit argument on what was proved in evidence. But then he went on to conject: "The whole situation points clearly at an attempt at robbery which went wrong. When Bailey held up the three travellers for money at gunpoint, Whelan tried to get the Remington rifle but Bailey shot him in the back. Bailey grabbed that rifle from Whelan clubbed the two women as they came to Whelan's assistance, broke the rifle, put in perhaps three more cartridges and tried to shoot them but the rifle jammed."

"It is too silly to suggest that Bailey would have confessed to three murders which he did not commit to stop his wife crying. If you think the police have made up the biggest frame-up in Australian history you should find him not guilty."

Pickering summed up by saying: "Circumstantial evidence can lie and can lead to a false conclusion. The duty of the prosecution is to close every gap. If there is any reasonable hypothesis consistent with the accused's innocence, then, however hard the rest of the evidence bears on him, he is entitled to the benefit of the doubt. There is no proof, after analysing the evidence, that Bailey had a rifle after leaving Coober Pedy. The Dubbo calendar was thrown away or lost by chance but there was nothing in the calendar to prove more than that the caravan was in the vicinity...You have as poor evidence as you could possibly get in a murder case as to the footprints. You are left with no satisfactory evidence connecting Bailey with the tracks at the murder scene."

The lunch adjournment interrupted Pickering, who continued in the afternoon: "I submit the cartridge cases do not point to Bailey. It seems from the expert evidence that the cases do not connect Bailey with the murders unless he had the rifle in his possession at the time of the murders. He had said he had traded it at Coober Pedy. The cartridges with the bodies prove nothing unless it can be shown he had the Huntsman rifle. Why wasn't there a search for the Huntsman? They've left the thing up in the air, like the tracks. Let's look at the situation with the bullet taken from Whelan's body. Constable Patterson could not, from the bullet alone, give a firm opinion about the sort of rifle firing it. It was only by matching the bullet from Whelan's body with a cartridge case that the ballistics expert could form the opinion that it had been fired from a Huntsman. It is a pretty slender thread on which to base a conclusion. You cannot match a bullet with a cartridge case. You must consider the absence of tracks from the caravan to the camp site. ...He was small. Is it a reasonable hypothesis that he could overcome and batter into insensibility three strong healthy people? Mr Scarfe's theory of an armed hold-up is pure speculation. In this case, with a man's life at stake, you cannot speculate. ...The murder weapon has not been found and no proper search for it has been made. There is not a single fingerprint of Bailey's. If Bailey were the murderer, working hastily in the dark, don't you think there would be some fingerprints of him lurking about? Until Mr Scarfe advanced the theory of robbery there appeared to be no motive for the crime. A motiveless crime is always harder to prove. Mr Scarfe's theory is a far-fetched one. There doesn't appear to be any motive, any satisfactory reason at all. His honour has told you he sees no legal reason to exclude the confessions but it is for you to consider their value. It does happen, though rarely, that people confess to crimes they did not commit.

"He should have been told he did not have to answer questions. Only after about two hours of being pressed did he make an admission. Once he's made a deadly admission, he can't go back. The questioning went on and on. A written document was produced and Bailey was invited to sign. There are more ways of breaking a man's will than by pummelling his body. They can put him in a padded cell, wake him every half hour. It is not suggested that Bailey was battered. He was told his wife would be questioned until he confessed. They produce the oral confessions, they produce the written confession. It is for you to say. Four versions did not satisfy the police, and on they went. You should suspect a confession supposed to be the offspring of remorse and penitence but repudiated by the prisoner in the court. All those of us defending him can say now is to take the Crown's proof and say 'There's a hole, there's a hole, it doesn't add up'. I submit that the case rests on the alleged confessions but there are so many loose ends. You cannot be satisfied that the Crown has covered the omissions by saying he confessed. It is unsafe to say anything but that it has not been proved that Bailey committed this crime."

The judge started his summing up at 3.30.

"You may well agree that an offence of this nature is bound to cause alarm and consternation amongst the people who live in the sparsely settled areas of the remote parts of this state and to shake the confidence that they have been accustomed to feel in the integrity and friendliness of those who may travel through their holdings.

"You can well understand the feelings of horror and revulsion which are engendered in the residents of those parts by such a terrible occurrence as this and their determination to bring to justice the person responsible for it if he can be found. It is quite natural that if suspicion falls upon the defendant he may be regarded as the culprit. I mention these considerations, gentlemen, merely for the sake of emphasising what I already said, that your duty requires you to act impartially. I put it to you that you are to hold the scales of justice with equal poise and find the defendant guilty only if you are satisfied beyond any reasonable doubt of his guilt."

"Now, gentlemen, Mr Scarfe, in the course of his address, propounded to you a theory as to the manner in which the killings occurred which involved the view that the three killings occurred at about the same time and during the night of the 5/6th of December. That may be a possible view and I do not think I will assist you by going all over the theory which Mr Scarfe placed before you. It does however of course raise the question of motive to which Mr Pickering referred towards the close of his address and you may well ask yourself gentlemen why anyone apparently sane should engage in an activity of this kind and commit such a fiendish crime. Why should anyone do it? The Crown's theory is that it originated in an attempt at the offence of robbery under arms and that as a result of perhaps as a warning by the dogs the three people at the camp were awakened or alarmed and it then proceeded as these things sometimes do from one stage to another rapidly and with increasing feelings because once a course of violence is embarked upon it is very difficult to say where it will stop and resort to weapons may become easier as feeling increases. But if it is not that motive, well, gentlemen, I suppose it is hard to say what other motive there is. Of course, the defence pointed out that it is not for the defence to suggest any motive and indeed no motive need be shown at all but it is an aspect. Motive is an aspect which you will, no doubt, give some thought to because you will have to consider who it might have been who could have done such a deed as this."

"You will take it that Mr Pickering said to you that these confessions are very often suspect. I will return to that in a moment. A possible view, of course, is that the defendant proceeded to make this confession because he had been subjected to very unfair treatment by the police of the nature which has been described. That is a possible view, I suppose. On the other hand, it is possible that the defendant was quite willing to make these statements and that what I may call the progressive admissions which he made were part of a willingness on his part perhaps to rid his conscience of guilt by confession producing a statement by him about which you can have no doubt."

"The Huntsman rifle is a very interesting point. Apart from what Bailey said, the only evidence he was in possession of it was that of Iles that Bailey acquired it at Wirrulla, the evidence of Gordon-Browne, which was open to doubt as to the accuracy of the witness's impression; and of Norris, who was not very interested.

"Now, you have the evidence of Mr Gordon-Browne, which as Mr Pickering has said, does not prove at all that the defendant had this rifle in his car when they had the conversation because you remember he says Mr

Gordon-Browne's recollection had to be jogged or assisted…and any impression that Mr Gordon-Browne may have formed that the defendant still had the rifle was clearly open to a good deal of doubt as to its accuracy."

"Next there was the question whether some search might not have been made for this rifle and that partakes of a line of criticism which the defence has offered to the Crown case. I do not think I am doing any injustice to Mr Pickering's contention when I put this to you: the police could have done a lot of other things. For instance, they could have had a black tracker look at the defendant's tracks at Alice Springs and they could have taken him down from there and said 'You show us the spot on the road where you threw the rifle away' or said 'Did you bury it or throw it on the earth or hide it?' In other words, they would have made an attempt to find this rifle although it may be thought that those who were responsible for this investigation thought: Well we have got a confession from the defendant, it does not matter very much about going and looking for this rifle or checking his footprints with the black trackers at Alice and so on."

"I think the evidence is that they made some search. Why make an intensive search which might take a long time and cover some hundreds of miles? That you will take into consideration."

The judge touched on the fact that the male shoe was a size 8 and the defendant took a shoe very much smaller – 5½ to 6.

"I am not quite sure but as far as I remember there is no evidence as to the size of the shoes put in as an exhibit. Those shoes were examined by you but I do not think anybody has proved what size they are but you can look at them yourselves and get what assistance you can," he said.

The jury retired at 5.38pm. Juries sometimes deliberate for several days when dealing with a charge as serious as murder. With a guilty verdict bringing an automatic sentence of hanging it might have been expected that the jury would examine every nuance of the evidence. After just 96 minutes the 12 men returned at 7.14pm. There was speculation they could have been back earlier but that they had waited sufficiently long to earn themselves a free dinner.

The jury had actually knocked on the door of its room to signify it had reached a decision at 7.06pm. It had taken another few minutes to bring the judge and barristers back into court. Bailey was brought from his cell to the dock. He stood for a moment and then sat down. He was pale. A small twitch flickered at the corner of his mouth. A court official ordered that the ventilator fans be shut off. Their faint humming stopped. Then the Judge entered the completely silent court and ordered the jury be returned.

The Clerk of Arraigns asked: "Gentlemen of the jury are you all agreed on a verdict?" "Yes we are."

"Do you find Raymond John Bailey guilty or not guilty?"

"Guilty."

"That is the verdict of you all?"

"Yes, it is."

It meant that the judge had to don his black cap before reading his dreadful script: "Raymond John Bailey, the jury has found you guilty of the charge of murder and the law prescribes the sentence which I must impose. The sentence of the court is that you be taken to the place from whence you came and then to the place of execution and that there you be hanged by the neck until you be dead. And may God have mercy upon your soul."

Bailey listened to his death sentence with the same calm acceptance that had marked his demeanour for most of the trial. He was asked if he had anything to say. He shook his head and said: "No." A crowd on the footpath clapped and cheered when a constable announced the verdict.

The hanging was scheduled for June 17.

Chapter 44 - Love Letters from a Doomed Man

Pickering said immediately afterwards that an appeal would be lodged - based largely on objection to the admission of certain evidence as to a confession.

Later that year a newspaper said that it had obtained copies of letters written by Raymond Bailey to his wife and family while in prison.

"May 5 – To my beloved father and mother. I'm writing this a week before I go on trial. I'm writing it now, for later on I might not have the chance. I think of you all the time and wish I could be with you. I know I don't have to tell you how much I love and miss you, for you are a mother and father to be proud of. I'm sorry if I've caused you any heartache or worry in the past. I thank you for giving me the chance of proving my innocence but the way lies are being told about me I don't have much chance. I'm going into the witness box under oath to tell that at Mt Isa I was forced to sign those papers. I did not know what they said. Even if I did, it wouldn't have made any difference. I loved my wife that much that if they said to kill myself I would have done it. That was the only way I could make them leave beloved Trish alone. The love I have for Patricia and Mike comes from my heart and soul. It is something I can't explain. I was happy in a wonderful way having her for my wife. And her returning my love and more if that was possible. To give me a son whom I love as I love her and companionship and love. They made her sign papers which they are going to use against me at my trial. But the jury will not know that, so if I'm found guilty do not stop loving her or my son for I shall always love her with all my heart and soul. Always remember that she is the woman I chose and married to share my love and my life. My last wish is that you always love my wife and son for in them you have me. This you must promise me, for if I die for something I did not do, I can die happy. My book of New Testament is for Patricia and tell her to keep it always."

"May 7 (5.30pm) – To my beloved wife. I call you my beloved wife because I love you with all my heart and know that you used to love me. But now I don't know if you do or not, for you have not written to me in the last three and a half lonely months I have been here. Remember the last time I saw you at Mt Isa? You said that you loved me and would write me every day. If you had done that I would have had 104 letters from you, but have none to read over and over knowing that you cared for me. You used to say that you loved me more than I loved you. I want you to write me a letter before I am hanged for even now I know I will die. I would like to hear from you that you still love me. Then I can die happy, knowing that I will die for something and not alone and unloved. Do please, my darling, write to me even if you have changed and don't love me any more."

"May 8 – My beloved Patricia: Here in my cell with nothing to do but think, my mind and heart wanders back over the happy times we have had together. The love and happiness inspired by you and our son is something I have always and will always hold dear. For you are the only woman I have ever loved. So my darling,if I must die, do not grieve for long but cast your mind back over the happiness we have shared. I signed that confession not knowing what I was signing, darling. I heard them asking if I knew them people, and you say no, but they would not believe me. I heard you crying, too, and that broke my heart and when they said we were not allowed to see one another again my heart went dry and numb. Seeing and hearing you being put through hell, darling, drove me out of my mind. I knew that if they kept it up with you expecting a child, it would kill either you or the child, or drive you insane. If justice is done, and I am released my love, we can try to make up for our loss, my darling, and still have those four children we planned to have. I hope Mike is being a good boy for you. Tell him I miss him and that there will be no games for a while. As you know I go to trial on May 12, seven days before our fifth wedding anniversary on May 18. So if things go right we can have our anniversary together. Do no worry yourself sick over me, darling."

"May 10 (written on the back of one of his mother's letters which reported *Poor Pat is very sick. She said she can't write, for as soon as she starts writing she gets ill and cries but she sends her love and she thinks of you all the time.*) – My beloved Patricia and Michael, I hope you get well soon. Don't worry yourself sick over me darling, for it makes me unhappy to hear you cry over me. It fills my heart with joy that you still love me and think I'm worth crying for. But, Love, don't be unhappy for if you are, so am I. How is my beloved son? Does he miss me very much? Tell him I love him and miss him. In one of the other letters I might sound cranky the way it reads. But it's not meant to be. What it shows is how much I love you and miss you and how much I'd love to hear from you. I'm going crazy worrying over you and Mike. How does everybody treat you at Dubbo? I don't know what to say to show you how much I love you and that you were the only woman in my life. How could I want anyone else when I had a woman that loves me the way you love me. Your loving husband, Ray."

"May 14: My beloved father and mother and beloved Trish and Mike…the blunders made by the police in not making plaster casts of car or man tracks was the biggest blunder of all for they could have given the size of the shoes worn at the crime if nothing else."

"May 15 7.30pm – My beloved mother and father: Tell Pat I miss her and love her and not to worry or be unhappy when the death sentence is passed upon me for everything will turn out OK in the end. Tell her I pray to God that He be with you all to watch over, to comfort and to protect you all. For I'm not going to defend myself in court so, therefore, I shall be found guilty. I am going to appeal to the High Court of Australia, for I'm not getting a fair trial. I'm not going to defend myself in this court for if I did, the Crown Prosecutor would know my plan of defence for my next trial. Don't worry for I have every confidence in Mr Pickering QC for he is a very brainy and clever man and knows what he is doing."

Chapter 45 - The Case Falls Apart Under Scrutiny

The prosecution case depended almost entirely on Bailey's alleged confession. The crime with which Bailey was charged was the murder of Thyra Bowman. This was the very crux of the case but the description of the murder of Thyra Bowman in the alleged confession is completely and utterly untrue.

The post mortems revealed that the two women had been bashed unconscious before they were shot. They were definitely not shot as they ran at Bailey in an upright position, as the signed statement says. They had been shot at close range while lying down, Mrs Bowman in the back of the neck and Wendy through the head with the right side of the head downwards.

The main thrust of the main piece of prosecution evidence is a lie. Unfortunately, Pickering did not cross-examine the pathologist to demonstrate that none of the bullet wounds was consistent with the signed statement.

Hours of the committal and the trial were spent following the trails of various footprints seen by different amateur trackers who descended on the murder scene and left their own tracks as they hunted for clues. Not one of the several experienced, specialist black trackers was ever called to give evidence. One reason given was that their command of English was poor. But interpreters could have been used. Maps were drawn of where various tracks led to and from. Witnesses travelled hundreds of miles to tell of the footprints they had seen. But no-one actually measured the footprints. No one photographed a footprint. No one took a plaster cast of a footprint. The woman's footprints were described as size 3, 3½ and 4. The man's footprints were described as 7, 7½, 8 and 10. But no one thought to ask Bailey at the trial what size shoes he and his wife wore. It was left to Bailey in his unsworn statement to reveal right at the end of the trial: "I take size 5½ shoe or if I can't get that size I wear a size 6." Patricia? We don't know.

Detective Hopkins was impressed by the tracking skills of Sydney Garneau Stanes who estimated the shoe size of the killer to have been 7 or 8. The judge pointed out to the jury that the size of the shoes worn by the killer was 8 while the "defendant took a shoe very much smaller – 5½ to 6".

On this evidence alone, Bailey could not have been the killer.

Bailey's fault was to be in the wrong place at the wrong time and find himself in the clutches of Hallahan.

The first thing to remember in examining his contact with the Bowman party is that in those days, with only a couple of dozen cars wending their way over dirt roads for hundreds of miles in heat that could kill within hours, it was usual to stop and chat to other drivers in passing to make sure that everyone was OK and to enquire about conditions on the road ahead. It was part of the Outback code of caring for one another in this inhospitable land. It was why Brisbane tourist Hassell Gordon-Brown had stopped to talk to the Baileys and why Bailey had no hesitation in telling Hallahan that he had, indeed, stopped to talk to the Bowmans.

Without the alleged confession obtained in the first instance by Hallahan, the case would probably not have succeeded. It could be argued very strongly that in today's judicial climate the case would be thrown out.

Was Hallahan prepared to lie to a court at this early stage of his career? The answer is, very demonstrably, yes.

South Australian police had linked Bailey to the murders at least two weeks before Hallahan arrested him. By January 19 even the newspapers had been given a description which fitted him like a bespoke suit. The Adelaide News carried this story on January 20: "From investigations there was no doubt the occupants of the car and caravan could help the police, Inspector Gully said. The car is an old black American sedan, possibly a 1938 Dodge. It was towing a dilapidated light to cream-coloured small caravan believed to have a blue or grey door. The tow bar may have been oxy-welded. There was a stove in the caravan. Descriptions of the people in the caravan were: Man – between 28 and 30 years old, clean appearance, about 170 centimetres tall, medium built, weighing about 70 kilos. He had a long thin clean-shaven face with a medium to sallow complexion. It is thought he was wearing a maroon windcheater, open-neck shirt and no hat. Woman – attractive looking 25 to 30, slim to average built, about 163 centimetres tall, fair to light brown hair recently permed. She was seen twice wearing red shorts and a white shirt. She wore a dress on other occasions. Boy – aged 2 to 5, hair inclined to be snowy, fair complexion, very active and talkative. The man had repaired the caravan at Wirraminna Station at the end of November. The man and woman said they were out of work. They had looked for jobs at Adelaide and Port Augusta. They were heading for Mount Isa or Darwin. Insp Gully appealed to anyone knowing of the car, caravan or the occupants to immediately communicate with the CIB or nearest police station."

On the 21st even the newspapers had been given the registration plate of the car driven by the wanted man – 379-622.

What wasn't known then but was revealed in 2010 by former Detective Hopkins was that the police even knew the name of the suspect – or "the offender", as Hopkins referred to him – in the lead up to his arrest.

Hallahan found Bailey late in the afternoon of January 21 and took him back to the police station for questioning. Someone, almost certainly Hallahan, then tipped off the newspapers that same evening that Bailey had been held in connection with the Sundown murders. As a result, Queensland's Courier-Mail reported in its next edition – "Sundown

Murders detectives fly to Mt Isa after three held – black car spotted – Two South Australian detectives investigating the Sundown triple murders will fly by specially chartered plane to Mt Isa this morning to question a man, woman and child. They believe the three may be able to help them in their investigations…Police early this morning were still questioning a 22-year-old woman." The South Australian Advertiser reported: "Man, car held. Two SA homicide detectives investigating the triple Sundown murders will fly by specially chartered plane from Alice Springs to Mount Isa today to question a man, woman and child…At midnight police were still questioning a 22-year-old woman, believed to be the man's wife."

Tellingly, the Advertiser also reported: "Lights in the Adelaide CIB building burned late last night as [police commissioner] Mr McKinna and Det Insp Gully conferred on the new Mount Isa developments. They made lengthy telephone calls to Mount Isa and to Alice Springs."

It is plain from these stories that on the evening Bailey was found, Hallahan knew that Bailey was wanted in connection with the murders and that Inspector Gully had made it clear there was no doubt the occupants of the car and caravan could be of assistance in solving the Sundown Murders case.

There were even long phone calls between Hallahan, as officer in charge of Mt Isa, with South Australia's police commissioner and head of the CIB – hardly an event which Hallahan could overlook. It is also obvious that Bailey's wife was questioned right through the evening and past midnight.

In court Hallahan lied.

Pickering: "When you took the accused to the police station at Mt Isa, you knew, didn't you, that he was wanted for questioning in respect of the Sundown Murders?"

Hallahan: "No, I didn't know that at all."

"Do you know whether lengthy phone calls passed between the police in Adelaide and the police in Mt Isa on the night of 21 January?"

"Not Mt Isa Police I don't think."

"Was his wife questioned that night?"

"She was not."

"Was she taken to the CIB building at any time?"

"Not that night."

"Do you swear she was not?"

"I swear she was not questioned that night."

"You told me earlier that you had no detailed information about the Sundown murders at the time of questioning Bailey."

"I had none connecting Bailey with them."

And on the question of the car registration: "At the time when you first saw the accused's DeSoto in Mt Isa did you have in your possession the registration number SA 379-622?"

"No."

Lie after lie after lie.

Detective Hopkins gave the game away in his memoirs in 2010, recalling: "On 21st January we returned to Kulgera Station and were advised by radio to return to Alice Springs immediately, because the offender had been arrested at Mt Isa."

The 21st was the day when Hallahan arrested Bailey. Yet Hallahan swore on oath in court that he had no information on that day connecting Bailey with the Sundown Murders.

Further, Hopkins, in his memoirs, reveals that the police at Mt Isa, which must have included Hallahan, were told on the 21st that the suspect's name was Bailey and he had been heading to Mt Isa to work on the hospital construction.

Hallahan's fabrications were then taken up by the prosecution to become an essential part of the case against Bailey, as evidenced by the pompous Roderic St Clair Chamblerlain telling the jury: "Up to his first confession Bailey might have been merely a witness in the case because the police had no idea of his relation to the case."

If we accept that Hallahan created the confession, he only had a few ingredients with which to construct a scenario which would stand up to scrutiny by a barrister and examination by a jury and result in the conviction of Bailey. As he was forced to admit in cross-examination: "I did have some details of the Sundown murders. I had a summary of what had happened, including the fact that a rifle had been used."

Some of the facts that had been made public and of which he would certainly have been aware included:

The three people had been bashed and shot;

At some stage they had been moved from their camp site to a second site where their bodies were placed under a tarpaulin and the car had then been driven to a third site;

A rifle with its stock broken from the remainder of the gun featured in the murders;

A newspaper report had said a theory had been advanced that the murder may have taken place after a large savage black and white kangaroo dog owned by Mrs Bowman and her daughter Wendy bit a stranger when he approached the spot where they were camping;

The car had been washed and a four-gallon drum was found empty nearby;

Someone had defecated twice near where a car and trailer had left tracks;

The murderer wore makeshift hessian gloves and used tools hurriedly made after the murder to avoid leaving fingerprints or shoe tracks;

A woman had left tracks at the murder scene.

This could explain how Bailey's admission he had talked to the Bowmans was developed by Hallahan to the point where he was able to recite a 20-minute 'confession' to the South Australian detectives when they arrived to interview Bailey.

This 'confession' wove together facts published in newspapers into a coherent story. There was even the fact that someone had defecated twice near the side of the road. But there were two glaring omissions from this story. It could be expected that a confession would contain an explanation of why the killings had taken place. Newspapers had referred to the lack of a motive so how could Hallahan overcome this problem? The "confession" should also have contained a blow-by-blow account of how the killings took place. But the exact details of the post mortem had not been released and therefore the injuries and how they were inflicted on each person were not available.

The "confession" contains the rather limp explanation that in reaction to a dog barking Bailey had swung round and fired a shot which had accidentally hit Whelan. There was nothing to explain why the frenzied and bloody beatings and the cold-blooded coups-de-grace had taken place.

On this thesis, the mysterious blackout cleverly explained the lack of motive and the lack of how each of the victims was killed.

However, in dealing with this major problem he had created another one. Despite the frantic phone calls between Adelaide and Mt Isa the previous evening when Hallahan would probably have been briefed about some aspects of the murder, he may have misunderstood the relevance of the rifle that had been found bloodied and broken in half by the ferocity of the assaults and left with the bodies. It seems Hallahan had assumed it had been the murder weapon and it had therefore belonged to Bailey. In fact, it had been the Bowmans' Remington that had been broken in half and bloodied during the attack. So Hallahan had woven into Bailey's 'confession' the fabrication that it had been Bailey's Huntsman that had been bloodied and broken in half. The words attributed to Bailey by Hallahan were: "I saw my rifle on the front seat. The wooden part of it was broken and it was covered in blood." There is no mention anywhere in the "confession" of the Bowman's rifle which was almost certainly the weapon used to bludgeon the victims.

There does not appear to be any other explanation for this part of Bailey's 'confession'.

If this scenario is correct, Hallahan now had another problem to overcome. When Moran and Hopkins took over the interrogation – as they had to do as the investigating police from the state where the murders had been committed – Bailey would protest his innocence and Hallahan would lose his starring role in the case. What he did was highly unusual and would attract comment and cross-examination during the court case but it worked. When Moran cautioned Bailey at 4.30pm on January 22, Hallahan told Bailey: These men are detectives from Adelaide. They are making inquiries about the murder at Sundown Station which is 20 miles south of the Northern Territory border where three persons were found murdered. This morning when I spoke to you, you told me that you had been working at Whyalla in a motorbike shop and you left there about the end of November…" and Hallahan spent 20 minutes – an eternity when it comes to reading aloud - recounting what he alleged Bailey had told him in the morning. Another effect of the recitation was that it forced Moran to carry on with this basic scenario in which Hallahan was the star. Interestingly, when it came to the actual court case Moran started his evidence by reading out the entire script Hallahan had delivered in front of Bailey.

It is also significant that in the finalised confession it had been considered necessary to insert the seemingly unimportant fact that the Bailey family had tea while they were parked by the side of the road with Bailey allegedly saying "I think it was spaghetti". What Moran and Constable Evans knew but Hallahan didn't was that Evans claimed to have found an empty spaghetti tin by the side of the road near the murder scene. It meant that when the court case took place, Constable Evans would reveal to the jury he had found an empty tin of spaghetti at the side of the road. And when Bailey mentioned in his confession that he thought he had eaten spaghetti for tea on the fateful day, the jury would see that all the evidence fitted together and pointed to Bailey being guilty.

It was the same with the pieces of wheat bag and wire which had been found with the bodies. In the enhanced confession Bailey says: "Before leaving my caravan that morning I took a wheat bag from out of my car, this was before my wife was out of bed, and cut two squares from the bag and wrapped them around my feet and went to the camp where I killed the dogs and then went to the car, and drove to the bodies. I did this so I would not leave any tracks. When I drove back to the bodies I put these pieces of bag off my feet under the canvas with the bodies. I had wire through the bags on my feet. I knew that I had left a bag under the car and caravan but I did not worry about it." The story is a nonsense because the murderer would have left dozens of footprints the previous evening when he went blundering around the bush in the dark. An earlier police theory, that the wheat bag had been cut up and used as gloves by the killer, is far more likely. While there were dozens of footprints, there was not one fingerprint anywhere.

Another fact that Adelaide police knew but Hallahan probably did not was that Tom Whelan was thought to have had a wallet which had not been found. So in the final version of the confession these lines were added: "I took a wallet out of the hip pocket of the dead man while he was under the canvas. It was a light brown leather wallet and I took a number of fivers and single pound notes from it and later threw the wallet away between Tennant Creek and Mount Isa but I cannot say when. I got about 20 to 25 pounds from him."

This finally provided a motive. But what the jury was never told was that, according to former Detective Hopkins in 2010 a purse containing 30 pounds was found at the site where the car had been abandoned. This is where Bailey was alleged to have spent a considerable time in daylight washing the car. If he had been short of money and robbery had been the motive, he would surely have taken the 30 pounds.

A police officer's need for exactitude resulted in more words being put into Bailey's mouth. The "young girl" by the side of the road from the original 'confession' had become "a girl aged about 14" in the final version, which, of course, was Wendy's exact age and which Bailey is highly unlikely to have known.

There was also the need to correct the mistake which had Bailey breaking his own rifle in the assaults. The signed statement has Bailey saying that his rifle was broken during the murders. Intriguingly, Moran swore in evidence that Mrs Bailey had told him that on the morning of December 6 her husband had his rifle in his hands and the stock was broken and there were blood spots on it. But Bailey's signed statement says that on this morning he went out and shot the dogs. At the end of the statement there is a further puzzle. Almost as an afterthought, the statement says that the gun was thrown away on the road to Alice Springs and: "The stock was cracked but it is not in two pieces." A further afterthought has him dismantling his rifle and throwing it away just before Alice Springs on the western side of the road.

This was not a confession. It was pure invention. As such it should have rung very loud and persistent alarm bells throughout the court. Pickering tendered a statement by Bailey in which Bailey clearly and unequivocally said: "I did not kill any of these people and I am not guilty of this charge."

Chapter 46 - Clues from the Max Stuart Case

We will never know what conversations took place between Pickering and his client but having examined Hallahan's record of inventing confessions it is likely that Bailey was able to tell Pickering with his hand on his heart that he was, indeed, innocent. It is clear that either Bailey's statement of innocence or Hallahan's evidence of a confession was a lie. It is also obvious that Hallahan's version of the shootings in the invented confession cannot be true because it does not tally with crucial facts. However, Pickering was unable to bring himself to argue in court that the confession was an invention.

He should have accused Hallahan with fabricating the confession and cross-examined him on that basis. He should also have challenged the prosecution to provide more substantive evidence, such as producing the Huntsman.

Why didn't he?

It was unthinkable in the ultra-conservative Adelaide Establishment of 1958 that the police would do, could do, anything wrong. To even suggest it was akin to treason. They were the front line troops in the battle for law and order, decency and protecting the fine upstanding, church-going people of South Australia and their hard-earned property from debauched low-life scum who needed to be taught a lesson and locked up for a long time without any namby-pamby parole and fed only bread and water. There is no better illustration than another case on which the Judge in the Bailey case, Sir Geoffrey Reed, sat in 1958 and which dragged on into 1959.

Aboriginal Max Stuart had signed a confession obtained by six police officers that he had raped and murdered a young girl. The "confession" was full of words and grammar that the illiterate and unschooled Stuart could not have used, especially as English was his second language. He could not read or write, apart from having been taught by his sister to print his name in capitals. At his trial his defending solicitor decided not to expose him to the cross-examination of a skilled and artful barrister but to have a statement by Stuart read to the court. Stuart could not read it so it was proposed that someone else should read it for him. Reed refused point blank. Stuart was found guilty as a result of his signed confession and sentenced to be hanged. But he was luckier than Bailey. Public pressure forced a Commission of Inquiry to investigate the case. In a blatant case of Caesar judging Caesar, Reed was one of the commissioners. When one of the police officers cracked and gave three different accounts of an interview, he was asked by J W Shand QC, appearing for Stuart, which one was correct. Mr Shand was told by one of the commissioners: "He is not obliged to explain anything Mr Shand." Reed put his name to the Commission's finding that any suggestion that the police had intimidated Stuart into confessing was "quite unacceptable". The behaviour of the police was "unblemished". The only criticism of the police was for not gaining independent evidence of Stuart's guilt. (Stuart's sentence was commuted to life imprisonment. He was released in 1973.)

Police jargon also litters the words Bailey is supposed to have uttered. An example is a totally unimportant but very telling exchange between Hallahan and Bailey in the street at Mount Isa when Hallahan says he asked Bailey what colour his caravan was. If the question had actually been asked Bailey would probably have said blue or even bluish and certainly nominated a colour. But the police had been looking for a "light-coloured" caravan. So Hallahan recorded Bailey's answer as: "light coloured".

It is important to remember Reed's support for the view that any suggestion that the police had intimidated Stuart into confessing was "quite unacceptable". This was the strongly-held view of the judiciary and likely to have been the strongly-held view of many barristers and a large proportion of the public. It seems certain to have been the view of Bailey's defence counsel. Pickering's membership of The Establishment detracted from the way he conducted Bailey's defence and may have cost Bailey dearly.

Bailey was alleging the police were guilty of bullying, blackmailing and fabrication. He was saying that one of the pillars that supported everything that was decent in South Australian society was rotten. This could not be.

But Bailey was insistent that he had been put in a padded cell, woken regularly and that "towards the end of their questioning they said to me "They are still questioning your wife and you won't be allowed to see her until you sign a confession and they won't stop questioning her until you do." They also said "Do you love your wife?" I said "I do" and they said "Well then, sign it and we will leave her alone".

"By this time all I wanted was for them to stop questioning my wife and leave her alone."

Which was exactly the same pressure Hallahan would apply to Tony Cavanagh after the non-existent theft of money from Lennons Hotel in Brisbane in 1961 when he told the man who would eventually receive a Royal Pardon: "You can either plead guilty, go before the court today and be home with your wife this afternoon or we'll throw you in jail until you come clean and your wife will be worried sick at home." And Cavanagh buckled, even though he was innocent of a crime that had never been committed: "I know I pleaded guilty but I challenge anyone else placed in similar circumstances to do anything different. I'd been taken away by the police and faced with a weekend in the watchhouse if I pleaded not guilty.

Let's put it bluntly, I was scared, scared for my wife and child, and with me they come first."

Bailey recalled: "Moran typed out a statement and asked me to sign it and I signed it. They asked me to write the word "Yes" after some questions at the end of it. I do not remember writing anything in my own handwriting at the end of it but I could have done so. I was in such a state at that time that I would have done anything they told me to do.

"The reason why I signed the confession was so that they would stop questioning my wife and leave us both alone. They had her at the Police Station all day. I could hear her crying. I asked to see her but was told that I could not. I wanted to send a telegram to my father the night I was arrested and I asked could my wife send it to let him know what was going on. Hallahan said she was not allowed to leave the police station. I also asked to see a lawyer but Hallahan said I was not allowed to speak to anybody and even refused to let me speak to my wife.

"My wife was about six weeks pregnant at the time and she had a miscarriage while she was at Mt Isa. She is still not well and I understand she is being treated by the doctor in Dubbo."

Confirmation of Bailey's story about his wife being questioned comes from the Advertiser in Adelaide which reported on the morning of January 22: "*At midnight police were still questioning a 22-year-old woman, believed to be the man's wife.*" And The Courier-Mail in Brisbane, Queensland, said: "*Police early this morning were still questioning a 22-year-old woman.*" Someone from Mt Isa Police Station had obviously given the facts to the newspapers. Hallahan was the officer in charge and he was hungry for publicity. In court he simply lied, saying: "*His wife was not questioned that night. She was not taken inside the CIB not at any stage that night. I swear that she was not questioned at all on the night of the 21st.*"

Bailey says he was kept in a padded cell and woken every half hour. He may have underestimated the disruptions to his sleep. The Adelaide News reported on Saturday January 25 that police were keeping a special watch on Bailey and inspecting his cell every 15 minutes.

Sleep deprivation and isolation have long been known as interrogation techniques. John Bradshaw, director of the Washington office of the Nobel Prize-winning Physicians for Human Rights, an American not-for-profit organisation, has said of the use of sleep deprivation, sensory deprivation and isolation: "Particularly when used in combination, these techniques amount to psychological torture."

A 2007 edition of Amnesty International USA's Amnesty Magazine features an investigation of how and why innocent people confess to murders they did not commit. It's headlined: When police interrogators manipulate suspects into confessing to crimes they didn't commit, innocent people end up on death row.

The article says: "Certain people — the uneducated, the poor, the emotionally insecure, the mentally impaired, the young — are especially susceptible to manipulation in the interrogation room. In cases involving the death penalty, such vulnerability is especially dangerous."

The magazine reported that the Innocence Project of New York's Benjamin N. Cardozo School of Law has recorded that 110 convicted people have had their innocence established by post-conviction DNA testing since 1989. The project also found that false confessions had played a central role in about a fifth of those reversals. In other words, in the past few years more than two dozen demonstrably innocent people admitted guilt for the most heinous of acts.

Social psychologist Richard Ofshe of the University of California, Berkeley, and Richard Leo, a University of California, Irvine, criminologist, have analysed the Reid Technique as outlined in the textbook Criminal Interrogation and Confessions by Fred Inbau and John Reid. The book claims the technique is taught to officers in many police forces in America, Europe and Asia.

The initial step is always the same: misrepresenting the nature of questioning. In Bailey's case he was held for questioning regarding Hallahan's claim of finding a pistol in the DeSoto.

Ofshe and Leo found that investigators commonly fabricate evidence, a technique designed to destroy a suspect's confidence. "They can lie about statements from a witness or accomplice, or about the presence of blood or other evidence," says the magazine.

In Bailey's case Hallahan admitted in his evidence that he had twice left the interview room, had a conversation with Patricia and returned to the room to tell Bailey his wife had completely contradicted him.

It is a Judges' Rule in the UK that: "It is a fundamental condition of the admissibility in evidence against any person, equally of any oral answer given by that person to a question put by a police officer and of any statement made by that person, that it shall have been voluntary, in the sense that it has not been obtained from him by fear of prejudice or hope of advantage, exercised or held out by a person in authority, or by oppression." The Oxford Journal of Legal Studies reports that it has generally been accepted, probably since 1964, that confessions obtained by oppression are inadmissible in English law and that it is not simply a matter of judicial discretion; they must be excluded as a matter of law. An English Appeal Court ruling held that the term oppression should be as defined in the Oxford English Dictionary: *The exercise of authority or power in a burdensome, harsh or wrongful manner; unjust or cruel treatment of subjects, inferiors, etc; the imposition or unreasonable or unjust burdens.*

That definition would certainly cover being locked in a padded cell, woken every half hour, hearing his wife crying and being told the police wouldn't stop questioning her until he signed a confession.

The full set of Judges' Rules was first introduced in England in 1912 to ensure that there were set procedures for questioning suspects and gaining statements and confessions which would be acceptable in courts. They had been introduced in many Commonwealth countries and in some Australian states but not in South Australia. However, this did not stop lawyers referring to them in South Australian courts and using them as a guide to what was considered acceptable behaviour and practice in other jurisdictions.

Having failed to ask questions about the possible fabrication of the confession, Pickering also failed to challenge Hallahan about the treatment Bailey suffered during the interrogation.

To be fair to Adelaide and South Australia it is worth pointing out the feeling that existed in London even in the swinging 60s. While civil libertarians continued to complain about police methods it was a commonly-held belief that the major effect of Judges' Rules was to help the criminal and hinder honest Mr Plod in his determined attempt to catch him. Traditionally it's been the Tories who lead the hue and cry for flogging and hanging but public sentiment was so much on the side of the police that even leading British socialist Dr Edith Summerskill was moved to ask the Government in the House of Commons in the 60s: "Will my honourable and learned friend bear in mind that the operation of the present Judges' Rules encourages crime by tying the hands of police officers, by protecting the guilty, and by discouraging innocent people from giving information to the police investigating a crime?" And the Minister's response reflected the mood of the people: "It may well be the case that at the moment the law of evidence is too heavily weighted in favour of the criminal, but I think that that is a matter which must be very carefully considered."

Be that as it may, the Judges' Rules state that every person at any stage of an investigation should be able to communicate and to consult privately with a solicitor. This is so even if he is in custody provided that in such a case no unreasonable delay or hindrance is caused to the processes of investigation or the administration of justice by his doing so. Bailey made it clear in his statement: "I also asked to see a lawyer but Hallahan said I was not allowed to speak to anybody and even refused to let me speak to my wife."

This was a flagrant breach of Bailey's rights yet again Pickering failed to launch an attack on Hallahan.

The only aspect of the interrogation that Pickering challenged under the procedures laid down by the Judges' Rules was the administration of a caution to Bailey by Hallahan before he was questioned about the murders. There would have been very little sympathy anywhere in Adelaide with what would have been seen as an attempt to rule the confession out of order on a technicality.

Pickering argued: "Hallahan questioned a man in custody at considerable length without giving any caution and gave no caution until the accused had made a damning admission. That involves admissibility of that admission and all that followed on the ground that it was not voluntary...If you read the evidence, he was taken into custody at 6.20pm, kept in custody at Mt Isa overnight, charged next morning over a pistol and questioned still in custody. The first confession was made about 12.10pm. He had been under interrogation from shortly after 10. In England that would inevitably have resulted in rejection of the confession. The High Court here has established the English position, that while the Judges' Rules have not the force of law, any flagrant breach results in rejection of a confession."

But judge Sir Geoffrey Reed was having none of that. As he pointed out so succinctly as part of his response to Pickering: "We have no Judges' Rules in South Australia."

The appalling sub-text of Pickering's submission is that in complaining about Hallahan's delayed delivering of the caution he states as a fact that "the accused had made a damning admission". That admission was that he had shot Tom Whelan. It seems Pickering did not believe Bailey's protestations of innocence. He must have believed that Bailey had, indeed, admitted shooting Whelan. His argument to the court was not that Bailey was innocent but that the admission should not be allowed by the court because Hallahan had not cautioned him appropriately. Further evidence of this attitude occurred in a heated exchange between Pickering and prosecuting counsel Chamberlain while the jury was out of the court. Pickering said it would be a very sorry day if what is held to be improper in other Australian states were not held to be improper here. Chamberlain said that at so many important points the confession was confirmed that one could have no uneasiness about what had been said by Bailey. Pickering interjected: "...who might have been able to keep his mouth shut if he were cautioned."

And then, despite Bailey's horror story of the interrogation, Pickering submitted: "There is no ground to suggest that there was any threat or promise."

Ironically, Pickering was tigerish when complaining that the lack of a caution meant that Hallahan's evidence should not be accepted at the committal proceedings in February nor at the trial in May. He continued the fight by going to the Court of Appeal on the same basis.

Judge Reed decided: "Upon the material before me I must assume that the interrogations of Hallahan and Moran were not accompanied by, or the result of, any overbearing of the defendant's will, or of duress, intimidation, persistent importunity or undue insistence or pressure. I see no ground whatsoever for even suspecting that any inducement by a threat or promise was made. So the impression I have formed on the statement is that the questions asked were answered by the defendant voluntarily."

Chapter 47 - Without Hallahan

There is No Case to Answer

Without Hallahan's evidence, what evidence was there that Bailey was involved in the murders?

Bailey puts himself in the Sundown area at about the same time as the Bowman party. So were many others. And with bad luck any one of them could have found themselves in the inventive clutches of Hallahan. There was the driver of the mysterious oyster-coloured Ford Zephyr towing a trailer which was never found despite the South Australian police putting so much emphasis on the driver being the prime suspect for the murders.

Wilkinson's evidence about the DeSoto was ambiguous and helps to show the sort of pressure and suggestion that the police exercised on witnesses. At the committal prosecuting counsel Scarfe was so sure of things that in his opening address he said categorically: "Next morning at about 10am Mr Wilkinson the storekeeper at Kulgera, saw a dark-coloured car and caravan which pulled up for petrol." By the trial Scarfe was reduced to saying: "On December 6, a Kulgera storekeeper, Wilkinson, had a vague recollection of a car resembling Bailey's passing through." The wind was taken out of Scarfe's sails when, looking directly at Bailey in the dock, Wilkinson said: "I have never seen this man before this court case." And under cross-examination he crumbled to say that he had not said a word about the black car and caravan until shown them in the Adelaide police yard in February.

The police were especially "lucky" in finding cartridge cases fired by the Huntsman. Cross examined by Pickering in May, Detective Hopkins said an intensive search had been made for spent cartridges at the scene of the murders. Three had been found and any other cartridges at the scene would probably have been found, he said. The assertion that all cartridges at the scene would probably have been found sounds very logical. So if they were so easy to find, why would the murderer pick up two and leave three behind? The police alleged they found one in Bailey's car and one in his caravan. Why on earth would a murderer, having picked up two incriminating cartridges, have put one in his caravan and the other in his car? If he had misplaced them, surely he would have searched his car and caravan until he found them.

Let's remember that many years later Hallahan was involved in the investigation of the murder of National Hotel manager Cooper. Fall-guy Maher's home had been searched three times, including once by Hallahan. Then Hallahan went to the unit for a fourth time and spent a long time on a balcony. Later that day police again went to the balcony and found a cartridge case which tied Maher in with the murder because it proved to be from the same gun that had killed the murdered man. The defence counsel alleged the cartridge case had been planted.

In the Sundown case, searches had been made of the DeSoto and the caravan in January by various police. Bailey's car and caravan were searched on the night of his arrest. Hallahan swore on oath that the car and caravan had both been carefully searched. There's even a photograph on the front page of the Adelaide News for Saturday Jan 25 of Detective Pfingst searching the DeSoto. Detective Moran searched the car when he arrived. We are certainly entitled to believe that in such an important and much-publicised murder investigation there would have been a thorough search of the car and caravan. Yet it was not until February that cartridge cases which were linked to a Huntsman rifle were found in obvious positions in the car and caravan.

Miraculously, ballistics expert Patterson was able to report that: "On Tuesday February 4 this year…I searched the DeSoto sedan car, registration number 379-622…and I found under the floor mat on the right-hand side of the front compartment…a .22 calibre ICI high velocity long or long-rifle cartridge case." It had been fired from the gun that no-one apart from David Iles had ever identified. It seems odd that neither Bailey when he was driving the car nor any of the other police who had searched the car had noticed the lump under the mat.

There was another miracle to come. The caravan had been searched by the police since January 21, yet on February 14 the incredibly lucky Patterson was able to find another cartridge case in a cupboard of the caravan – and identify it as having been fired by the Huntsman that no-one else apart from David Iles had ever identified.

The biggest question remaining is why, if the signed statement was true, was Bailey not taken to the spot where, according to the signed statement, he had thrown the rifle away?

On January 23, 24, 25, 28, 29 and 30, while Bailey was in Mount Isa, newspapers quoted police as saying it was their intention to take Bailey back to the road south of Alice Springs to search for the Huntsman rifle. Police even told newspapers that black trackers had been assembled ready for the search. They maintained this story that Bailey would be taken to the murder scene on the way from Mt Isa to Adelaide to search for the gun, even up to the time the plane took off. The Mt Isa Mail of January 30, obviously acting on what the police had told the reporter, had a headline across four columns which said unequivocally: "Bailey at scene of murder today". And the story read: "Homicide detectives escorting 25-year-old Dubbo carpenter Raymond John Bailey to South Australia to face a murder charge arising from the Sundown Station triple slaying, flew from Mount

Isa to Alice Springs yesterday, and today will take the prisoner 220 miles by road to the murder scene."

They never did. So there wasn't even a smoking gun at the trial.

There is a fascinating scenario which might explain why this was so. It is possible that police were looking for a Huntsman gun from December 19, just after the post mortems and more than a month before Bailey was arrested. Ballistics expert Patterson said it was not until he was given a cartridge case that he could give an opinion on what sort of gun had fired a bullet from the murder scene. This occurred on December 19. Patterson's verdict was that the bullet was from a Huntsman, a popular Australian sporting gun at the time.

Continuing with this scenario, we move forward to a series of articles in South Australia Police Association's magazine Hue and Cry at the end of 2009 and start of 2010 by former detective Charles Hopkins.

Hopkins recalled that when he had eventually returned to Alice Springs looking for clues he had interviewed a Mrs Oldfield who had been a passenger in a car driven past the Bowmans' campsite in December. Close by she had seen a car and caravan, together with a man, woman and young boy.

"Mrs Oldfield was an essential witness, because she said that the car was a large black one, and this persuaded us that it could not have been a Ford Zephyr," said Hopkins. "The new information was immediately despatched to Adelaide. Previous information conveyed to the public via the media was cancelled, and the new information was published."

What followed next in Adelaide is told in an article on page 124 of the Adelaide Sunday Mail of March 30, 1980, which extols the abilities of Inspector Gil Gully in the hunt for the Sundown murderer.

The story recounts the interview with Mrs Oldfield. The 1980 article continues: "Then the photographic mind of Gil Gully recalled that months before in a Police Gazette a man travelling in a similar car towing a caravan with...portholes was wanted in Renmark for false pretences having traded illegally an NSW registered car under hire purchase for a DeSoto." Police at Renmark came up with the name Raymond John Bailey, said the 1980 article.

Gully was quoted in a newspaper report on January 23, 1958, saying triumphantly: "South Australian police had tracked a black DeSoto sedan through the outback since January 9." It seems likely that the police would have also filled in Bailey's route from Renmark onwards. They certainly became aware of a Whyalla bike shop owner who said Bailey had taken a nickel-plated revolver from his shop. So it is possible they also found David Iles who would have told them about Bailey deciding to buy his Huntsman rifle. The police must have been cock-a-hoop. They had a suspect driving a caravan, apparently with a Huntsman gun. When they found him in Mt Isa all they had to do was seize the Huntsman rifle and pin him down to having been in the Sundown area at the time of the murders.

But Bailey maintained to the end that he had sold the Huntsman long before reaching Sundown Station. In his unsworn statement he says: "I sold the Huntsman rifle at the next windmill north of Coober Pedy to a dark skinned fellow for some opals. I have not seen it since I handed it over to him. I remember meeting Mr Norris but he could not have seen the Huntsman rifle in my car as I had disposed of that near Coober Pedy."

This has the ring of truth to it because it would have been easier to say that he sold the rifle after meeting Norris and Gordon-Brown.

If what Bailey says is true, it would be understandable for the police, faced with daily questions from the media while Bailey was in custody in Mt Isa about whether they would search the road near Kulgera for the gun, to have replied that they would conduct such a search – even though they realised it would be pointless.

Unfortunately, no-one asked Bailey if he still had the opals or, if not, what he had done with them.

There were other inconsistencies and things that did not add up. The 1956 calendar from Dubbo could have been dumped at the roadside almost two years earlier. Why would Bailey have been carrying an out-of-date calendar? And why would a murderer have chosen to throw it away to incriminate himself at the murder scene?

And the end of the prosecution case became farcical when Scarfe in his summing up to the jury was reduced to inventing a story: "When Bailey held up the three travellers for money at gunpoint, Whelan tried to get the Remington rifle but Bailey shot him in the back. Bailey grabbed that rifle from Whelan clubbed the two women as they came to Whelan's assistance, broke the rifle, put in perhaps three more cartridges and tried to shoot them but the rifle jammed." This was utter rubbish. There had been no evidence to support such a story. And if Whelan had been trying to get the Remington and had been shot in the back while doing so, he would not have had the gun in his possession for Bailey to grab. If, as Scarfe suggested, it was Bailey who put the cartridges in the Remington, why weren't his fingerprints on the cartridges which were jammed in the mechanism?

Like so much of the prosecution case it didn't stack up.

There is one more major fault in the prosecution case: motive. Why would Bailey, a man without any record of violence, decide to bludgeon and shoot three strangers? It was a problem with which, it seems, Hallahan had wrestled and given up, using the device of a blackout to avoid the necessity of explaining the reason for the crime. It was a problem which prosecutor Scarfe knew he had to deal with as part of his job of convincing the jury of Bailey's guilt. He invented a story in his summing-up (when he was only supposed to be covering evidence which had been tested): he suggested Bailey needed petrol money and that "the motive of robbery is not beyond the realm of reason". Police thought Whelan may have had 20 pounds in a wallet and that Bailey may have taken it.

Robbery as a motive does not bear much examination. Police actually found 30 pounds in cash left near the car with a diamond ring. The murderer would surely have seen it and, if robbery was the motive, would have taken the cash. This fact was not drawn to the attention of the jury.

No gun. No footprints. No motive.

Chapter 48 - What Patricia Bailey

and Detective Hopkins Say Now

One final point. Hallahan alleged that Bailey had said in his confession that when he was washing the bloodstained car at Sundown Station his wife had come over and *"asked me what I was doing and I told her that I had heard some shots during the night and went down and found the people were dead and I didn't want anyone to think that I did it."*

In 2010 I managed to trace Patricia Bailey to a neat 1920s brick bungalow. I sent her a letter explaining my quest but received no reply. So I knocked on her door. The small, frail woman with white hair combed ultra-tidily and close to her skull told me: "I've been under the doctor since I received your letter."

She told me twice that when it came to the crime: "I knew nothing about it then and I don't want to talk about it now."

I apologised to her and told her I wouldn't bother her again. But it could be argued that her emphasis that she had known nothing about the murders contradicts Hallahan's version of her husband's confession that he had told her about the murders and that he was washing the car to get rid of evidence.

On March 16, 2010, I sent 10 questions to former South Australian detective Charles Hopkins who had recently compiled a highly-detailed 7,700 word memoir of the Sundown murders, the police investigation and the court case. With his permission I have included several excerpts from his memoir in this book.

In my letter I pointed out:

Problem 1: Bailey's signed statement is not true. The post mortems revealed that the two women had been bashed unconscious before they were shot. They were definitely not shot as they approached Bailey in an upright position, as the signed statement says. They had been shot at close range while lying down, Mrs Bowman in the back of the neck and Wendy through the head when she was lying on the ground with the right side of the head downwards. The prosecution case depended almost entirely on Bailey's signed statement. And the crime with which Bailey was charged was the murder of Thyra Bowman. Yet the description of the murder of Thyra Bowman in the statement is completely and utterly untrue.

Question: Was Bailey quizzed on the fact that his statement about the three deaths bore no resemblance to what actually happened and, if so, what did he say?

Problem 2: You were impressed by the tracking skills of Sydney Garneau Stanes. From the tracks at Sundown he estimated the shoe size of the killer to have been 7 or 8. The judge pointed out to the jury that the size of the shoes worn by the killer was 8 while the "defendant took a shoe very much smaller – 5½ to 6".

Question: How could Bailey be guilty when his shoe size was smaller than the killer's?

Problem 3: Stanes was also convinced by the tracks that a woman drove the Vanguard to its final resting place and that she then walked out of the bush. Evidence was given at the trial that Mrs Bailey could not drive.

Question: Surely this is further evidence that Bailey was not the murderer?

Problem 4: If Bailey was involved, Stanes' evidence points to the fact that he had an accomplice.

Question: Was Bailey questioned about this and, if so, what was his explanation?

Problem 5: The woman's tracks were so clear that Stanes could say that she was wearing size 3½ or 4 shoes.

Question: Was Patricia Bailey's shoe size ascertained and, if so, what was it?

Problem 6: If the statement about the murders is untrue and Bailey's shoes could not have left the footprints at the scene of the murders, the murder weapon becomes all important. In Hallahan's account of what Bailey told him happened in the attack, there was only one gun mentioned throughout the story – his own. "I saw my rifle on the front seat," he said. "The wooden part of it was broken and it was covered in blood." But it had been the Remington owned by the Bowmans that had been broken in half by the ferocity of the assaults.

Question: Was he questioned about this and, if so, what was his explanation?

Problem 7: Bailey said he sold his rifle, which he thought was a single-shot Huntsman, at Coober Pedy. Hallahan said that Patricia Bailey told him that Bailey had not sold it at Coober Pedy and had kept it until he threw it away between Kulgera and Alice Springs. According to Hallahan, Patricia Bailey said her husband had "walked away from the car towards a hill" and had returned without it. In the signed statement there is even more detail: he was on the western side of the road and went in four or five paces before throwing the rifle. The judge said: "The Huntsman rifle is a very interesting point. Apart from what Bailey said, the only evidence he was in possession of it was that of Iles that Bailey acquired it at Wirrulla, the evidence of Gordon-Browne, which was open to doubt as to the accuracy of the witness's impression; and of Norris, who was not very interested." What puzzles me is that on January 23, 24, 25, 28, 29 and 30 newspapers quoted police as saying it was their intention to take Bailey back to the road south of Alice Springs to search for the Huntsman rifle. Police even told newspapers that black trackers had been assembled ready for the search.

Question: Why wasn't Bailey taken to the road between Kulgera and Alice Springs to find the rifle when, if Bailey's statement was true, it would have been just off the road and would have been a compelling piece of evidence in the trial?

Problem 8: Bailey said in the statement that his rifle was broken during the murders. Intriguingly, Moran said in evidence that Mrs Bailey had said that on the morning of December 6 her husband had his rifle in his hands and the stock was broken and there were blood spots on it. Bailey's signed statement says that next morning he shot the dogs.

Question: How could he have shot the dogs if his rifle was broken?

Problem 9: This was a glaring inconsistency.

Question: Was he asked about this in the interview and, if so, what was his reply?

Problem 10: Many years later Hallahan was involved in a murder investigation. The home of the suspect had been searched three times, including once by Hallahan. Hallahan went to the house for a fourth time and spent a long time on a balcony. Later that day a cartridge case was found on the balcony. The cartridge case proved to be from the same gun that had killed the murdered man. The defence counsel alleged the case had been planted. In the Sundown case, various searches had been made of the DeSoto and the caravan in January. It was not until February that cartridge cases which were linked to a Huntsman rifle were found in the car and caravan.

Question: Could the cartridge cases in the car and caravan have been planted by Hallahan?

On April 13 Mr Hopkins sent a reply to my 10 questions saying: "Due to my age, health and the fact that I have had problems with my memory in recent years, and the fact that more than 50 years have elapsed, I do not want to be involved (in) any matters associated with the Sundown Murder investigation."

After sifting through the evidence, you might agree with the damning summary advanced by prosecuting counsel Scarfe: "Bailey had claimed that the police forced him to confess to the murders by cruelly ill-treating his wife. If this was true, the police were guilty of 'the biggest frame-up in Australian history'."

Chapter 49 - Bailey is Hanged

Since his arrest Bailey had aged 10 years. His hair had receded. A tic had developed in his left eye. His face was lined and sallow.

After the death sentence had been pronounced Bailey was taken back to Adelaide Gaol, to a temporary home in the condemned cell. In through the big main gate, through the sally port and into Yard Four which fanned out towards an interior semi-circular wall as high and formidable as its twin exterior wall. The two semi-circular walls contained within them a part-paved, part-grassed area about seven metres wide which guards could observe from strategically-placed watchtowers. The condemned cell, number 21, was about two and a half metres by three metres. With six neighbouring cells, it was isolated from other blocks and sited close to the interior wall. In front of them was a covered walkway for the warders. Eight brick arches enabled prisoners to look out into the grim expanse of the yard. From the yard the cells looked rather like the cloistered corner of a monastery.

Each morning Bailey was taken from his cell while all the other prisoners were still banged up for the night. He was led on a lonely, unseen walk through the door in the big interior wall into the secure operational centre.

Here there were three solitary confinement cells even smaller than his condemned cell. And here, with the only light coming from a barred slit of a window, he spent each day until after the other prisoners were safely banged up again at the 4.30pm lock-up. Bailey was then walked back each evening as dusk arrived to spend the long, lonely hours of darkness in his condemned cell. The process meant he was never seen by other prisoners, minimising the risk of any sort of demonstration.

He was guarded 24 hours a day so he could not commit suicide and cheat the law which said he had to be killed in a special way.

Bailey signed his appeal documents on May 22. The grounds were that the trial judge had wrongly admitted evidence: evidence by Hallahan relating to admissions made to him by Bailey; evidence by Hallahan relating to prior caution of Bailey in relation to a charge of false pretence; evidence of Detective Moran of admissions made to him by Bailey; Bailey's written confession and the plan drawn by him; a plan drawn by the Lands Department; evidence by Dr Dwyer regarding the post mortems of Wendy Bowman and Thomas Whelan; and evidence by Constable Patterson and Mr J Warne relating to a bullet taken from Whelan's body.

The appeal was heard by the Court of Criminal Appeals on June 3 and 4. Less than a week later, on June 9, the appeal judges dismissed it. The appeal court held that the Crown had proved beyond reasonable doubt that Bailey's confessions were not obtained under such circumstances as to render them non-voluntary and so inadmissible as a matter of law. State's Solicitor-General Roderic Chamberlain QC spoke out in favour of Hallahan's questioning and said it would be calamitous if police were prevented from such questioning. "If they have to do what Mr Pickering is suggesting is proper, they would have had to release Bailey." The murder would have been left unsolved but a suspicion would have been left against members of the Bowman family, he said.

Warders N G Wood, A M Wildy and A D Ireland were assigned to him in prison. They played cards and draughts with him during the day. At night he was alone in his cell.

The realisation that his life was about to be extinguished led him to make one ridiculous, desperate attempt to fashion an escape opportunity by claiming that he had seen someone else commit the murders. He probably wasn't surprised when it failed.

Bailey received his one and only visitor on Monday, June 16 – from his brother Noel, giving him an opportunity to pass on his letters to the family.

The morning of June 17 was the coldest of the year, with widespread frosts. He was taken, shivering, out of the condemned cell at 5.50am by two guards and led on the last part of a journey which had started when Glen Patrick Hallahan found him in Mt Isa. It was about 40 paces from his cell at the end of the line of condemned cells out into the shock of a starlit, frosty morning and into the remand section; another 40 paces through the interior of the two-story block of 19 cells on the ground floor and a similar number which could be made out through the iron grates in the ceiling; then out into the valley of death – the strip of grass and concrete hemmed in between the dwarfing twin walls of the gaol and about 67 paces to the hanging tower set in the outside wall. It was still dark as massive bolts were drawn back and the door into the tower was opened. Imagine the shock when he was immediately confronted with the hangman's noose in the centre of an octagonal stone-walled cell some six metres from wall to wall. A ridiculously over-size concrete post stood towards the centre of the cell, supporting a beam which, at its other end emerged from the wall and from which the rope hung ready to break his neck and take his life just two hours from now. To reach his holding cell on the far side of the octagonal cell, he had to brush past the rope and actually tread over the wooden trap door which, next time he stood on it, would snap open and drop him into eternity. The rope which dominated the cell had been stretched to exactly the right length by having Bailey's bodyweight tied to it for 24 hours. Leaving nothing to chance, a spare rope had also been stretched.

For nearly two hours Bailey was confined in the claustrophobic irregularly-shaped holding cell only just a metre wide at one end and about four metres long. Worse, it had no windows. He never even saw dawn break before he died.

Just as the law had not wanted him to take his own life, reserving that barbaric task for itself, it also wanted him to die with a full stomach. The last breakfast was served.

What made this last isolated confinement even worse was the fact that one wall of his cell, the one on the left as he stood facing the door, was also the outside wall of the prison. Almost within touching distance of that outside wall is a railway track on a tight bend round the prison. Every three or four minutes the sound of a train filled the cell. Just two metres away from Bailey commuters from suburbs on the Grange and Outer Harbour lines were being carried forward to another new day, free to go wherever they chose and make plans for the future. Bailey was as close to the trains as if he'd been on a station platform.

James MacDonald, the prison chaplain, was the last person to hold a conversation with Bailey, talking about the condemned man's last journey.

At 7.55 the door of his holding cell opened and his hands were tied behind his back. He only had to move a metre from the cell door to reach the trap door over which hung the waiting noose. Another two steps comprised the last he would ever take as he reached the centre of the trapdoor. He said nothing as he glanced at the ring of official witnesses and officials. His ankles were tied together. The governor read the warrant. A white calico hood was slipped over his head. And the noose was placed over that, with its knot behind his left ear.

Bailey had walked from his cloistered cell in Yard Four. Now, in this awful tower, some seven metres up, in five of the eight walls, arched windows gave the tower a church-like appearance. On the outside, each window carries the illusion further, boasting two gargoyles where the arching begins. But there was no merciful God within these walls.

In a tiny room next to these grisly proceedings the hangman waited. Here was another link to that railway world outside. As trains rattled by outside, the hangman stood next to a long lever projecting up from the floor, looking no more sinister than a lever in an old-fashioned signal box. He could see nothing of what was happening next door. But in the tightly shut door leading to the hanging cell was a small opening. At exactly 8am one of the guards put his hand through the hole. It was the sign that Bailey's life was to be taken.

Perhaps the penultimate thing that Bailey ever heard was the sound of a train accelerating away from the prison.

A device like a handbrake on top of the lever was freed. The lever was pulled and the last thing Bailey heard was the trapdoor springing open. The verballed carpenter plunged into the pit until the rope jerked to break his neck.

The prison bell tolled slowly and monotonously above the empty cloister-like condemned cell with its gargoyles and Bailey's lifeless body which was left swinging until eventually all movement stopped and it came to a rest. The body was left for 45 minutes after the dreadful moment and then a doctor descended 13 stone steps into the pit to officially record that Bailey had, indeed, died.

A note dated June 24 was sent to the Government Printer: Will you please arrange for the publication of the enclosed notice in the Government Gazette: I, George Colin Henderson Nicols, being the Medical Officer in attendance on the execution of Raymond John Bailey, at the prison at Adelaide, do hereby certify and declare that the said Raymond John Bailey was, in pursuance of the sentence of the court, hanged by the neck until his body was dead." Witnesses J H Allen, Sherriff; E A Barbier, gaoler; J L Holland, turnkey; A C Horsnell, constable; J G McKinna, Commissioner of Police; James Younger MacDonald, chaplain; and five warders.

Bailey's body was placed in a wooden box containing lime and taken out into the bitterly cold morning another 75 paces along the valley of death from the hanging tower to the final resting place in the grassy area sandwiched between the massive walls where no grieving would ever take place. Lime was placed under and over the coffin. There was an anxiety that the body should decompose and disappear as quickly as possible.

Today, if you examine the massive expanse of the inside gaol wall you will eventually find a tiny marker which says only 'RJB 24-6-58'.

Many years later Hallahan's long-time confidante, mistress and prostitute Shirley Brifman told police: "Glen hit the pot over the Sundown murder. I used to cop it night after night. He said the real killer was free. It did really play on his mind and I thought he was going to go off his head over it. At that stage I would say he was not crooked but after that he went bad. I never saw anything eat a man inside like that did. I have seen him at his flat and at other places. I used to sit on the phone with Glen for hours even to early in the morning. All he used to talk about was this murder. He said: *'The man walks free. We know who he is.'* He said: *'I will never be able to live with myself again. He should never have been hung for it.'* That, I can really say, played on Glen's mind."

Chapter 50 - Conclusions

The analysis of evidence from the trial of Raymond John Bailey proves he could not have committed the Sundown murders. It is clear that Hallahan engineered a massive miscarriage of justice at his trial and that Bailey's conviction should be reversed and a posthumous pardon granted.

I believe the information provided in this book provides sufficient grounds for the murder of Jack Cooper in 1971 to be reinvestigated. Perry Vincent and Donald John Maher both alleged, on different occasions, that Jack Cooper had been shot by Glen Patrick Hallahan. Barrister Des Sturgess refused to defend Maher if he stuck to his story that Hallahan had pulled the trigger. Hallahan's consistent record of committing perjury in seeking to gain convictions must render his evidence at Maher's trial unreliable to say the least. The discovery of an incriminating spent shell on Maher's balcony soon after Hallahan had visited and despite three previous fruitless police searches is comparable to the incriminating shells found in Bailey's car and caravan during the Sundown murders inquiry. Without Hallahan's evidence and the incriminating shell, the prosecution case is very thin. Perry Vincent voluntarily put himself at the murder scene when he testified at his extradition hearing that Hallahan had murdered Cooper. How could he, and why would he, have done so if he was not, indeed, there? Remember, too, Maher's allegation he was left alone with Hallahan for an hour at the Valley police station (described by a detective sergeant as an "unusual situation") and that he was dangled by his legs out of a window. There was also the violent attack and break-in at Maher's solicitor's office.

The decision not to treat the death of Shirley Brifman as suspicious was a blot on the reign of Commissioner Ray Whitrod. Current Queensland law requires a coroner to investigate any unnatural death or a death which occurs in suspicious circumstances. But at the time of Shirley's death the law was looser, stating a coroner should inquire into a death if in the coroner's opinion there was reasonable cause to suspect the death was unnatural or had died in suspicious circumstances. Of course Shirley's death was unnatural and an inquest should have been held. Could she have committed suicide or might she have suffered an accidental overdose? These causes can't be ruled out but her actions after returning to Queensland point to a determination to gain her revenge on Murphy and Hallahan. Not only was her death by drug overdose sudden and suspicious, it followed a murder attempt only six months earlier by drug overdose – details of which had been made available to police in a statement by Shirley. In that attempt, the alleged assailant had been convicted thug and suspected murderer Johnny Regan, a man who stood to gain nothing directly from Shirley's death but who worked closely with Hallahan. CIU chief

Gulbransen believed it was murder but the man in charge of the case, Dynes Becker, believed it was suicide. Her death came only days before she was due to testify against Tony Murphy but the crimes and corruption of Hallahan and Fred Krahe featured far more prominently in Shirley's police statements than Murphy's. It seems logical to believe they would have been next in line for prosecution. With Murphy's prosecution imminent, he would have been an obvious suspect if Shirley was to be bumped off. On the night of her death he had an ironclad alibi. He was in Sydney. Johnny 'Shotgun' Regan had failed in his murder attempt. The question to ask is: who, apart from Murphy, had the most to gain from Shirley's death? The answer appears to be Glen Patrick Hallahan and Frederick Claude Krahe.

Harry Gibbs, later knighted as chief justice of Australia, wielded a large whitewash brush in his report of the National Hotel Commission of Inquiry so that he was able to clear corrupt police, including Hallahan. He has been excused by some of having failed to detect prostitution condoned by the police at the National Hotel, largely on the basis of the terms of reference being too restrictive. I argue that there was sufficient evidence for Gibbs to have delivered a much harsher report than he did. Even the Fitzgerald Inquiry report has been overkind to Gibbs, saying: "Nothing in the terms of reference or structures of the Royal Commission, including the range of parties represented before it, the assistance and facilities available to it, and the evidence which it received, or in the social and political environment of the time, would have alerted it to the possibility that it confronted an orchestrated "cover-up" based on, and supported by, institutionalized police attitudes and practices." This is plainly nonsensical. For instance, it would have been very plain to Gibbs that Tony Murphy was one of the officers mentioned as having drunk at the hotel after hours, that he was a friend of the licensee and that he should not have been placed in charge of gathering evidence for the inquiry. I argue that Gibbs tailored his report in a manner which enabled him to clear Bischof and his henchmen when there was sufficient evidence to have at least damaged and possibly ended the career of Bischof.

Sir Edward Williams receives a double 'F' for failure, for his Royal Commission's handling of the interim report to the Federal Government which led to the axing of the Narcotics Bureau, and for its failure to expose Hallahan, Lewis and Murphy when it had the resources and powers to do so.

It was tenuous in the extreme for the interim report to be only able to "*suggest*" that "*perhaps*" the bureau was corrupt. Williams wasn't even prepared to "report" or "find" that perhaps the bureau was corrupted. The sentence contains perhaps the strongest criticism of the bureau yet it is twice removed from being a substantive finding. Williams damned the bureau with faint criticism. There wasn't even a forecast in the interim report that the closure of the bureau would lead to an improvement in the detection of illegal drug dealing or importation.

I can't do better than to repeat some of the criticisms of the Williams Interim Report made in a secret report to the Federal cabinet by the minister responsible for the bureau, Wal Fife, and his department. It said the 'report was selective, subjective and open to challenge on almost every point'.

Fife and the department found: "As the commission progressed it became abundantly clear that…the Narcotics Bureau …was on trial on the basis of confidential evidence which it had no opportunity to test or refute except in respect of a series of generalities and sweeping assertions contained in correspondence to the commission. The situation became so bad that the department found it necessary to engage senior counsel to protect its interests in appearances of senior officers before the commission."

The commission alleged: "The existence of the Bureau as an "elite" force within the Bureau of Customs has…contributed to morale problems in other areas." The department countered: "This is not true." And explained why.

The commission alleged: "The Narcotics Bureau has depleted other arms of the Bureau of Customs of resources." The department countered: "This just isn't true." And explained why.

The commission alleged: "Too much centralised control impairs the bureau's operational efficiency." The department countered: "This is not substantiated."

The department's repudiation of the interim report's findings covers 17 A4 pages.

As minister Fife said of the report: "The source of the criticisms levelled against the Narcotics Bureau was never made clear and has not yet been made clear. The Royal Commission does not suggest in its interim report that there is corruption in the Narcotics Bureau." Yet the commission's recommendation to axe the bureau was rushed through as a matter of urgency.

It is astonishing that Williams managed to declare in April 1980 that the evidence against Hallahan fell *far* short of establishing as *even* a *reasonable possibility* that he had *ever* been involved in wrongdoing in connection with illegal drugs despite:

Several hours of tape recordings in which John Milligan provided detailed evidence of

Hallahan's key role in financing the heroin importation from Bangkok;

The five pages of damning evidence against Hallahan written by Milligan to be used in an intended prosecution of Hallahan;

The evidence of John Shobbrook, an officer with an impeccable record of success and honesty;

The frequent protestations of John Milligan in sworn evidence that Shobbrook's account of how Milligan had implicated Hallahan was correct;

$26,000 (the equivalent of more than $110,000 today) being paid by Milligan to Hallahan without Milligan receiving any apparent benefit for the money but at a time which fitted the explanation that this was Hallahan's profit from the Milligan heroin importation.

And despite having the mandate and power to examine the finances of Lewis and Murphy, and to cross-examine them, Williams failed to examine them in any way. Murphy was a very canny man and it may have been impossible for the inquiry to pin anything on him but it would have taken very little to detect Lewis's corruption. The failure to examine Lewis's income condemned Queensland to another seven years of corruption.

The linking of Hallahan's exploits during two decades, together with the activities of the rest of the Rat Pack and Don Lane, helps to demonstrate that the Queensland Government was in thrall to the corrupt leadership of the police force stretching from 1958 to the beginning of 1970 and from late 1976 until 1987 – under the premierships of "Honest" Frank Nicklin and "Christian" Joh Bjelke-Petersen. Between them these premiers and their governments:

Appointed Frank Bischof, known to be corrupt, as commissioner in 1958;

Acknowledged that Hallahan had committed perjury and had invented a confession from Tony Cavanagh when it granted Cavanagh a royal pardon in 1961 but, despite the fact that this was a crime with a sentence of up to 14 years' jail, and that action should have been initiated to deal with an offence that undermines the very basis of the justice system, signalled that the government was protecting Hallahan, then only a junior officer but already a Bischof henchman, by telling Cavanagh in a letter from the Justice Minister:

> *"As regards to your statements against police, they do not give sufficient details that are required";*

Saved Hallahan's career in 1964 by refusing to charge him for having given a court inaccurate, dishonest and misleading information when he verballed Gary Campbell and instead appointing a QC to hold a secret inquiry which resulted in him overturning the decision of three Supreme Court judges by declaring that the charges were "not proven" – a verdict not available to magistrates or juries in Queensland;

Refused to print the report of the National Hotel Inquiry, even though it was largely a whitewash;

Failed to sack Commissioner Bischof when it discovered he was heading a state-wide illegal betting system;

Forced honest police commissioner Ray Whitrod into resigning;

Installed a man it knew to be corrupt, Terry Lewis, as police commissioner and promoted fellow Rat Pack member Tony Murphy at the same time, despite a Scotland Yard report identifying them as corrupt;

Cancelled an inquiry into police corruption;

Hid the Lucas Report of 1976 which recommended ways in which to combat police verballing;

Attacked two honest police officers who appeared on an ABC television current affairs program in 1982 to present evidence that Lewis and Murphy were corrupt and, far from demanding answers from Lewis or holding some sort of inquiry, immediately joined Lewis in circling the wagons, refusing to listen to legal advice to hold a commission of inquiry;

Shielded Terry Lewis from scrutiny by the National Crime Authority in 1985 when the chairman of the Federal Joint Parliamentary Committee overseeing the authority, Alan Griffiths, told Federal Parliament: "The Committee has been gratified by the ready co-operation it has received from all States and the Northern Territory, with one exception, that exception…being the Premier of Queensland, who, for whatever obscure reason, refused to make the Queensland Police Commissioner available to discuss with the Committee the question of organised crime in his State and the broader issue of co-operation between States and the National Crime Authority. Having regard to the serious level of organised crime in this country and especially to the threat posed to young people by trafficking in narcotics, the Committee finds it inexplicable that any person in high office would refuse to co-operate in the fight against organised crime";

In November 1985 failed to act on the 'Sturgess Report on Sexual Offences Involving Children and Related Matters' which identified the Mr Bigs of prostitution, which criticised the licensing branch of the police for failing to perform the simple jobs of closing the illegal businesses, and which said its head was probably corrupt – thus condemning many under-age girls to another year and a half of exploitation.

The results of this corruption were far-reaching.

At one level innocent people were framed, demonstrators bashed by police, political opponents spied on, honest police bullied and vilified, and efficient companies failed to gain government contracts despite submitting the best tenders.

More extremely, lives were ruined or extinguished. There was a lack of action in tackling the growing illegal drug trade, with some victims becoming criminals to support their habits and others dying from overdoses. Families fell apart when gamblers at the illegal casinos lost vast amounts, even their homes. Young girls were allowed to become enslaved as prostitutes. Every year produced suspicious deaths and unsolved murders – prostitutes who perhaps threatened to make revelations and were found dead from overdoses, drug dealers who became a problem, and men involved with illegal gambling.

All empires eventually fall and I can report to readers unfamiliar with the modern 'Smart State' of Queensland that organised corruption is very much a thing of the past. The Crime and Misconduct Commission, a government-funded body which is answerable not to the government but to a parliamentary committee, has the powers of a standing royal commission and is vigilant in watching over the police and government.

I've been lucky enough to travel the world and have chosen to live in Brisbane, a world-class city which now has a low crime rate. I come home from my travels to a climate in which windows are always open, warm, sunny winters give way to springs of blue jacarandas and red poincianas and summers of fragrant frangipanis; a low cost of living but a high standard of living; modern infrastructure (which includes a growing, efficient, purpose-built express busway system and a modern international airport); clean air; Australia's best modern art gallery; the world-famous Gabba; one of the best football stadiums in the world; restaurants serving cuisines of the world using wonderful locally-sourced fresh ingredients such as Moreton Bay Bugs, mud crabs and mangos; the calm-water paradise of Moreton Bay to the east and the tall, graceful eucalyptus trees of Brisbane Forest Park to the west. I could go on – and on, for it's important to realise that Brisbane and Queensland have changed dramatically from the Rat-Pack-Bjelke-Petersen days, thanks in part to the brave, resolute people who opposed the Rat Pack and their political mates.

End Notes – What Happened To………?

GLEN PATRICK HALLAHAN: Seven years after his escape from the Williams Royal Commission, Hallahan had one more major inquiry to contend with. And this one seemed to pose the biggest threat of all.

In February 1986 Nationals MP Bill Gunn, a 66-year-old past assistant grand master of the Freemasons, farmer and grazier, became Queensland Police Minister. Bjelke-Petersen had sacked the last two police ministers when Terry Lewis complained to him they had been disloyal to his regime.

Perhaps Bjelke-Petersen thought Gunn, a National Party MP for 15 years, could be trusted not to interfere in the status quo which involved Lewis dealing directly with the Premier whenever he wanted to.

But Gunn was an honest man. He had been told more than 50 years earlier by his father that police in North Queensland were paid protection money in relation to Chinese gambling dens. The subject had cropped up when a police officer was moved to the area from the north. Death duties meant that his estate was publicised. There was general amazement at the huge fortune he had amassed. And as Gunn grew older he realised corruption had been endemic in Queensland more or less since it was founded.

On his first day as police minister he received a serious allegation of corruption in the force. He made notes and put them in his safe. Many anonymous phone calls and letters alleging corruption followed and he filed them all in his safe. But what could he do about it? He was well aware of the fate that had befallen his predecessors. Bjelke-Petersen backed police commissioner Terry Lewis to the hilt and refused to listen to Gunn's advice about corruption.

Gunn told me: "I had to await an opportunity. I was playing more or less a lone hand here. I didn't get a great deal of sympathy when I took on the ministry. There was a certain hatred towards me from some of them. I was absolutely determined that I had to do something about it. The situation was worsening. I had to have the numbers. I had good guys who wouldn't speak up. And if I didn't have the numbers it would have been the end of me."

His safe was as full as a bookie's satchel after the last race, when, on May 11, 1987, there was a miraculous conjunction of exploding political ego and determined investigative journalism which gave Gunn the opportunity to act. ABC TV broadcast a detailed expose of Queensland police corruption by reporter Chris Masters. Premier Bjelke-Petersen, who, in 19 years of iron-fist rule in Queensland had never managed to garner more than 39.6% of the vote for his National Party, had handed power to Gunn while campaigning on the federal stage, suffering from the delusion he had the ability to become Prime Minister of Australia.

Political decisions can take months or years to be fashioned. Gunn acted in record time, knowing that if he did not act immediately while he had the power and the opportunity, Bjelke-Petersen would return and slam the door on exposing corruption just as he had in 1976. Without consulting any of his colleagues Gunn announced next day that there would be an open inquiry into police corruption.

But this was still not enough to guarantee the inquiry would be able to do its job. The corrupt forces could still undermine the process if they believed they were in danger. One way to make sure the inquiry was not stillborn or aborted was to pretend it was not going to be any sort of threat. A press statement released by Gunn and fellow Minister Paul Clauson on May 26 says it was 'anticipated the inquiry would open about mid-June and run for up to six weeks'. There was little danger in an inquiry of that length and Lewis's chief bagman, Jack Herbert, cheerfully popped over to the Hamilton Island resort in the Whitsunday Islands for what he thought would be a six-week holiday prior to carrying on with The Joke.

With Cabinet facing a fait-accompli that nevertheless looked to be manageable, ministers had to decide who would chair the commission. Don Lane lobbied for Judge Eric Pratt, Terry Lewis's friend since 1957, but this was thwarted. A relatively unknown former judge, Tony Fitzgerald, was appointed. Now the momentum started to slip away from the corrupt. Unlike Justice Gibbs in 1963, Fitzgerald was not content to accept the initial terms of reference announced on May 26, which would have restricted him to matters occurring in the previous five years and obtained wider powers, eventually being able to investigate just about anything he deemed to be pertinent.

The wider powers meant Fitzgerald would be able to examine any wrongdoing involving Hallahan, Lewis and Murphy from the 1950s onward. It also meant he could examine the involvement of police in the lucrative illegal drugs trade.One of the most far-reaching social problems resulting from the Bjelke-Petersen-Terry Lewis regime had been the growth in the illegal drug trade in which corrupt police were involved in many ways, a situation aided and abetted by Bjelke-Petersen who talked tough but took virtually no action.

"Drugs are taken in raids but in court the quantities are halved," reported former director of Teen Challenge, the Reverend Charles Ringma. The rest would be sold by the police. Seized drugs disappeared from police stations. A corrupt detective already notorious from a case involving corruption was entrusted with transporting seized heroin worth hundreds of thousands of dollars from north Queensland, where it had been an exhibit in a court case, to Brisbane where it was to be officially destroyed. In Brisbane it was given a final test – and found to be chalk. Police launched a massive hunt to try to discover who had leaked the information to the media, said an honest officer, but there had been no real effort to discover who had performed the switch. On several occasions after police had kept surveillance on marijuana plantations, the resulting raids would result in the capture of minor players and the mysterious escape of the organisers. Bjelke-Petersen introduced legislation introducing mandatory life sentences for drug dealers. The hang 'em and flog 'em supporters of the Premier were reassured that he was being tough on law and order. But the police still continued to catch only the addicts who depended on selling minute quantities of drugs to support their own habits and who were then sentenced to life imprisonment. Money promised by Bjelke-Petersen to aid the fight against the drug trade had not been delivered five years later.

After his experience with the Williams Royal Commission, John Shobbrook, the former Narcotics Bureau officer, did not rush to hand his evidence about Hallahan to the Fitzgerald Inquiry.

But in September Assistant Commissioner Graeme Parker confessed to the inquiry that he was corrupt. He revealed Lewis was also corrupt, forcing the commissioner out of office.

"I was convinced that this inquiry was making an honest attempt to root out corruption, at least within the Queensland Police Force," Shobbrook said.

On September 24 he contacted the officers of the inquiry and supplied them with a 42-page statement about how Hallahan, now installed as a doyen of respectability and honesty at Suncorp Insurance, had funded a major heroin importation.

He was encouraged by their response and says he was later told that, with his help, the inquiry had gathered enough evidence to eventually place Hallahan before the courts regarding the heroin importation.

Shobbrook volunteered to give evidence to the inquiry about Hallahan's role. He says he was asked by investigators not to discuss this information with anyone until after he had been called as a witness at the inquiry. He was never called.

The Fitzgerald Inquiry sat for 238 days over 18 months, examined 339 witnesses and received 2,304 exhibits. It resulted in: the collapse, after 32 years, of the corrupt National Party-led government; the creation of a fair electoral system; the cleaning up of the police force; the formation of a permanent corruption watchdog designed to ensure that systematic corruption could never re-emerge; the prosecution of corrupt police and politicians; and the creation of a refreshed, vibrant culture and society.

But somehow, despite all the evidence and the promises of its investigators to Shobbrook, Hallahan escaped again. He was not even called to give evidence.

The report says: "No finding or recommendation adverse to Hallahan is made in this report. It is a matter for the Special Prosecutor whether Hallahan is charged with any offence."

And on the question of the illegal druge trade and the involvement of corrupt police the report says: "This report cannot adequately deal with the issue of drugs, and does not pretend to do so."

Former Queensland Premier Mike Ahern revealed that in 1989 Fitzgerald had asked him as Premier to provide $1 million to enable him to create a secret special drugs task force which would continue to try to nail the major drug importers and dealers. Ahern had taken Deputy Premier Bill Gunn with him to Government House with a secret order enabling the money to be paid with only Ahern, Gunn and the Governor knowing of the payment.

No doubt Glendon Patrick Hallahan put on an indignant and hurt air in the aftermath of the last of a long series of inquiries:

"I have been exonerated," he would have said.

Hallahan spent his final years in a very ordinary two-storey brick home on a busy main road to the south of Brisbane.

He died of cancer on June 17, 1991.

GUNTHER BAHNEMANN:Gunther Bahnemann was still hoping to have his conviction for attempting to murder Hallahan overturned in 1987 when the Fitzgerald Inquiry into Queensland corruption started its massive clean up. He wrote to the Inquiry saying he had been verballed by Lewis and Hallahan when he was convicted in 1959. His solcitors said he would be seeking a royal pardon. The case was not mentioned in the hearings or the report.

NORWIN WILLIAM BAUER:Norwin Bauer was Grand Master of Queensland's Freemasons from 1971 to 1974. In 1961 he had created a new lodge, Vigilance, where the majority of members were police. The Courier-Mail reported in 2002, 13 years after the clean-up of the police service, that Vigilance Lodge was attracting a mix of current and former officers, including two who had been named adversely at the Fitzgerald Inquiry into corruption. Bauer died in 1982 aged 76

COLIN JAMES BENNETT :Colin Bennett, born on 10 May 1919 in Townsville, died in 2002. In one of his first speeches in parliament, Col said: "It is rather amazing that at the CI Branch very few, if any, voluntary confessions are obtained from people who are allegedly invited to enter the CI Branch while in the company of friends ... But not long after they are separated from their companions, out pops a confession, freely and voluntarily admitting every element of the offence in such a fashion that one might believe that the accused was a lawyer who understood how to make admissions acknowledging the truth of every aspect of the charge." He and his wife Eileen founded the St Veronica Welfare Centre, an association for underprivileged children. He was also a member of the Brisbane and Sunshine Coast Hospital Boards, the Australian Workers Union, Lions and Johnsonian Clubs, patron and life member of the South Brisbane Returned & Services League, and patron, member and honorary legal adviser for many sporting and charitable organisations.

FRANCIS ERICH BISCHOF: In July 1974 Bischof was charged with shoplifting cigarettes and other goods worth $6.12 from a local supermarket. Des Sturgess appeared for him at the committal proceedings where it was argued he was suffering from a severe form of psychotic depression that had first manifested itself in 1967 when he suffered from unreasonable worries that he had done the wrong thing about 'quite trifling matters' and had been referred to a psychiatrist. The Crown later dropped the case. Bischof died on August 28, 1979 aged 74.

SIR JOHANNES BJELKE-PETERSEN KCMG:Sir Joh Bjelke-Petersen was found by a jury to have bribed construction company supremo Sir Leslie Thiess on a large scale and on many occasions. In turn, Thiess had bribed Bjelke-Petersen in order to win multi-million dollar windfalls. To facilitate secret discussions between them Israeli-manufactured scrambler phones had been installed in the Premier's office and at Sir Leslie's home. Another of these special phones enabled the Premier and the police commissioner to talk without fear of phone tapping by any Federal authority.

He was also found to have accepted $210,000 in cash from three separate donors, two of them allegedly anonymous. The money was placed in a slush fund run by the Premier and two business friends which eventually contained nearly $1 million.

The Australian Broadcasting Tribunal found that Bjelke-Petersen had commercially blackmailed $400,000 from Alan Bond in order for Bond to run Channel 9 in Queensland.

In 1986 drug trafficker Phillip Chan, who was convicted of conspiring to import heroin worth more than $2 million from Hong Kong, was found with a letter of introduction signed by Bjelke-Petersen under the official government seal. It said Bjelke-Petersen would greatly appreciate any facilities or courtesies which may be accorded to Chan by Australian and British consuls.

Bjelke-Petersen's successor as Premier, Mike Ahern, revealed that National Crime Authority chairman Donald Stewart had told him that Joh had refused to grant him the power to serve warrants on Queensland's Gold Coast to close a drug ring. Stewart said he had been subjected to a 40-minute diatribe by Joh. He had explained that this involved serious drug crime and the diatribe had only got worse. The result was that the crime authority had been forced to work with Terry Lewis who had assigned a detective sergeant to the case. When they arrived on the Gold Coast every one of the targets was missing from home and could not be contacted. Never mind, said the sergeant, come home for a cup of tea. He lived in a mansion. A large boat in the yard was named Corruption.

The Fitzgerald Report into corruption says: "During the period of over a decade in which Frank Erich Bischof (and briefly Norwin William Bauer) had been Commissioner, the Government had passively allowed, rather than actively encouraged, police misconduct." Under Bjelke-Petersen and Lewis: "...the deterioration accelerated."

In 1991 10 people on a jury found Bjelke-Petersen guilty of perjury in relation to evidence he had given on a gift of $100,000 in cash paid to him by a developer. Supporters at the court prayed for Joh, held hands while singing hymns and conducted faith-healing sessions. But any intervention came not from God but via the activities of the defence team which had helped arrange jury selection with the result that an avid Bjelke-Petersen supporter was on the jury. The supporter managed to persuade one other member not to find the former premier guilty. A key member of the defence team was Barrie Cornelius O'Brien. MP Henry Palaszczuk told the Queensland Parliament on November 12 1991: "With dozens of private investigators to choose from, the defence chose Barrie Cornelius O'Brien, a former associate of the Rat Pack which was so favoured by Bjelke-Petersen. O'Brien was adversely named at the Fitzgerald Inquiry."

Phillip Adams, who holds two Orders of Australia, tells a story of how Bjelke-Petersen was blatant in asking for a backhander. In the mid-1980s while Adams was Chairman of the Australian Film Commission a respected film producer told him that when he had asked Bjelke-Petersen for help in facilitating the production of a major film which would bring many benefits to Queensland, Bjelke-Petersen had twice asked: "What's in it for me?"

Having subverted democratic principles and presided over corruption for 15 years, he had himself nominated for a knighthood in 1983 with a citation straight out of the Idi Amin book of idolatrous self-praise. He was "not only an inspiration and a guiding light, but also a living embodiment of the spirit of self-sacrifice and service". And he had pursued his chosen path "with ability, with integrity, with dignity and, perhaps, above all, with humility, the true mark of greatness." Despite the fact that less than 4 out of 10 adults ever voted for him in an election, the citation continued "his leadership and his gentle care and attention to the needs of all who seek his assistance have endeared him to the people of Queensland". And despite the fact that he had rorted the voting system, refused to establish a public accounts committee or any other checks on his government's decisions and could not tell an interviewer what was meant by the separation of powers he was "a strong believer in the historic tradition of parliamentary democracy".

In 1995, when Terry Lewis was stripped of his $1.4 million superannuation, Bjelke-Petersen said: "I feel very sorry that a man who worked so effectively and efficiently and was decorated with bravery medals has been dealt with so badly."

Bjelke-Petersen died on April 23, 2005, aged 94. There are still many Queenslanders who believe he was a wonderful, God-fearing Premier who did no wrong.

BRIAN BOWMAN: Brian Bowman, the owner of Glen Helen Station at the time of the Sundown murders, wrote a detailed history of life on his property but despite losing his sister in law and niece, he does not even hint at the tragedy in his book.

EDMUND GEORGE BROAD DFC: Edmund Broad, a Lancaster bomber pilot and squadron leader in World War Two, became a judge of Queensland's District Court, Licensing Court and Mental Health Review Tribunal. He was also a member of the Courts Martial Appeal Tribunal. Broad was chairman of Brisbane Amateur Turf Club and of Brisbane Visitors and Convention Bureau. He was a flyhalf with the Wallabies who toured Europe and north America in 1947-48. He died in 1993.

SIR HARRY TALBOT GIBBS GCMG, AC, KBE, QC: The debacle of the National Hotel Inquiry did not prevent Sir Harry Gibbs from ascending to the top of the judicial ladder. After serving as a judge on the Supreme Court of Queensland from 8 June 1961 until 24 June 1967 he was appointed to the Federal Court of Bankruptcy and the ACT Supreme Court in 1967. In 1970, he was appointed to the High Court of Australia. Three deaths and a retirement meant Gibbs rapidly became second in seniority. In 1981, Gibbs was appointed Australia's Chief Justice, a position he held until retirement in 1987. He died in 2005. His name is perpetuated at the Harry Gibbs Commonwealth Law Courts Building in Brisbane.

NORMAN GULBRANSEN: Never one to do things by half, Gulbransen took up long-distance running at the age of 65, completing many marathons, winning veterans' titles and establishing age records. He died on August 16, 2006, aged 89.

CEDRIC EDWARD KEID HAMPSON AO, RFD, QC: Cedric Hampson QC was president of the Queensland Bar Association from 1978 to 1981, and again in 1995-96. He was counsel assisting at both the Williams and Stewart Royal Commissions investigating illegal drugs and several other commissions of inquiry. He represented Sir Terry Lewis and other senior police at the Fitzgerald Commission of Inquiry into corruption in Queensland. He retired from practice in 2006 after 35 years as a Silk and 49 years at the bar. He has since become an author of fiction and non-fiction books.

DONALD ROSS KELLY: Donald Ross Kelly, Hallahan's bank robber, was beaten and stabbed to death in a room at a service station in New South Wales in July 1988, half way through the Fitzgerald Royal Commission of Inquiry into corruption in Queensland.

DONALD FREDERICK LANE: For a while it seemed Don Lane, who was at least an associate rat in the Hallahan-Murphy-Lewis pack, might avoid jail. The Fitzgerald Inquiry into corruption discovered he had garnered more than $100,000 dollars in unexplained income over 10 years. Conniving to the end, Lane believed he would not be jailed if he denied that the money had come from corrupt police but claimed instead that it was the result of cheating on his ministerial expenses. He told reporters he didn't expect to go to jail for having misused public money. "I have done nothing that bears that penalty," he said. This time the joke was on Lane. He was jailed for a year. His "confession" triggered an investigation of all ministers' expenses and resulted in another three ministers being jailed. He died in 1995.

TERENCE MURRAY LEWIS: Terry Lewis received more than $600,000 in corrupt payments, bagman Jack Herbert told the Fitzgerald Inquiry into Queensland corruption.

Bjelke-Petersen nominated Lewis for a knighthood in 1982 but Buckingham Palace had the good sense to reject the recommendation. For some reason the knighthood was awarded in the 1986 birthday honours list. All honours have since been withdrawn.

He was charged with 15 counts of corruption, found guilty on each one and sentenced to the maximum 14 years' imprisonment on each. He was paroled in 2002 and, like Hallahan, continued to protest his innocence.

JOHN EDWARD MILLIGAN: Milligan was released on licence from prison on January 24, 1986, after serving only six years. The licence was revoked two months later on March 30 when it was alleged he had broken one of the conditions of that licence.

ANTHONY MURPHY: Detective Chief Superintendent Terence John O'Connell of Scotland Yard said of Tony Murphy: "He was obviously one they feared…and highly intelligent…They spoke of him in awe. You get this sense of fear. They were frightened of him."

Tony Murphy came under adverse notice in Operation Buckshot, a highly sensitive Australian Bureau of Criminal Intelligence probe into the importation and distribution of heroin in Australia, with the involvement of organised crime figures and the links between those figures and other criminals engaged in motor vehicle theft, gaming, prostitution, money laundering, and violent crime, including murder.

When the Fitzgerald Inquiry into corruption in Queensland reached the point where Lewis was about to be unmasked, Murphy went to Police Headquarters to access the "Brifman Suicide File".

The Fitzgerald Report noted: "There was undisputed evidence before this Inquiry from a former SP bookmaker that Murphy was paid bribes."

When Tony Robinson, shonky nightclub owner and self-confessed briber of police officers, died in 1989 Tony Murphy read the eulogy. Senior corrupt government minister and close friend Russ Hinze sent his apologies.

Now retired, Murphy kept a careful eye on the corruption trials of Terry Lewis and Joh Bjelke-Petersen, attending court every day.

In March 1979 Tony Murphy invited Sunday Sun reporter Brian Bolton to his office and told him the police had secret tape recordings made by leaders of the Mr Asia drug syndicate headed by Terrence Clark. Murphy had a transcript of the tapes with him. Bolton's story alerted Clark to the fact that Douglas and Isabel Wilson had spilled the beans about the syndicate. According to Clark's former girlfriend, Clark paid $250,000 for a copy of the tapes and then had the Wilsons killed. The Stewart Royal Commission: "…considers that it was most unwise for Superintendent Murphy of the Queensland Police Force to supply the material for Brian Bolton's newspaper article." It confirmed 'to a suspicious and vengeful Clark that the Wilsons had definitely informed on him'.

Sunday Sun reported on January 30, 1983: "Big farewell being planned for February 14 to mark the retirement of assistant police commissioner Tony Murphy, leaving the force after 38 years. Mr Murphy has been acknowledged throughout the Commonwealth as one of

Australia's most outstanding criminal investigators." The previous year two police officers and MP Kev Hooper had told the media and Parliament that Murphy and Lewis were crooked. Premier Bjelke-Petersen had refused to hold any inquiry into the allegations and now he signalled his allegiance to Murphy and Lewis by attending the farewell party at the Police Union Club.

Murphy died on December 21, 2010, aged 83 after a long illness. Unusually for a former assistant commissioner, there was no official representation at his funeral. Terry Lewis did not attend. Reporters were not admitted to the service. The state's only daily newspaper, The Courier-Mail, started its report of the death of this much-feared man: "Friends of alleged "Rat Pack" boss Tony Murphy have described him as a gifted crime solver who never had a corruption claim against him proven." The report referred to former colleagues saying he had left behind a legacy of excellence. "He had a brilliant mind. He was one of the most famous detectives Queensland ever had," a former detective was quoted as saying. "He was regarded as a legend in the police force. I could only speak well of the man."

JOHN STUART REGANL John Stuart Regan, the gangster who had tried to kill Shirley Brifman and was said to have murdered at least seven people, was exterminated in a Sydney street in August 1974 with three bullets to the head and four more in his back.

RONALD RICHARDS: Ron Richards became editor of the Sunday Sun (Truth) at the end of 1973. Lewis and Richards maintained their friendship to the end. Richards's name is mentioned 55 times in Lewis's diaries. Lewis told Bjelke-Petersen on more than one occasion that Richards should be knighted. But he couldn't recall any special qualifications Richards had which would have supported the awarding of a knighthood. After Lewis had spent several days giving evasive answers to the Fitzgerald Inquiry he recorded in his diary that Richards had congratulated him.

Professor Paul Wilson, a criminologist, became friendly with Terry Lewis. He tells in his book *A Life of Crime* how any police friendly with the Rat Pack were invited to police parties at Barry Maxwell's Belfast Hotel which were held two or three times a year. He was invited along with other friends from outside the force such as Ron Richards and Des Sturgess.

In February 1986 I wrote an article for the Sunday Sun naming and exposing the pimps who ran Brisbane's prostitution rackets in the guise of massage parlours. I used as a basis for the story a State Government report by Des Sturgess who had hidden the pimps' identities. The newspaper, headed by managing-director Ron Richards, refused to expose the men. It was another year before The Courier-Mail got round to printing a similar story which led ultimately to the establishment of the Fitzgerald Inquiry into corruption.

Richards, managing editor of The Courier-Mail's parent company from March 6, 1987, paid the corrupt and discredited Lewis a large amount of cash for an interview in February 1989. There was no denial to a report that Lewis had received $30,000 instead of the industry norm of a few hundred dollars. The fact that the story was worthless was demonstrated when no other newspaper in the Murdoch stable printed the ultra-expensive "exclusive", despite the vast cost.

Richards died in 2000 aged 71.

DOUGLAS JOHN SHOBBROOK: Shobbrook was accepted by the Royal Australian Air Force Active Reserve as an officer. He underwent a series of intellectual, physical and psychological tests at the Defence Force Recruiting Centre, Brisbane. He passed with flying colours.

He has a kind of fond affection for Milligan and contempt for those who failed to follow up the Milligan tapes.

Shobbrook was told during the cleansing Fitzgerald Inquiry into Queensland corruption that the inquiry had enough evidence to lock up Hallahan. He was told he would not be needed to give evidence.

DESMOND GORDON STURGESS QC: Des Sturgess made a name for himself as Queensland's pre-eminent defence counsel before surprising the legal world by acting as counsel assisting the coroner in the second inquest into the death of Azaria Chamberlain in 1982, joining the prosecution team for the successful prosecution of Lindy Chamberlain and becoming Queensland's first director of prosecutions in 1984. (Lindy Chamberlain was subsequently freed and exonerated.) Sturgess produced a report on the sexual abuse of children and ancillary matters in November 1985 after a year-long inquiry for the state government. It identified the people who ran Brisbane's prostitution empires and linked their activities to Lewis's licensing branch. It led eventually to the creation of the Fitzgerald Inquiry into corruption which exposed the extent of corruption in the government and police force. Sturgess is now retired.

SIR EDWARD STRATTEN WILLIAMS KCMG KBE QC: Appointed QC in 1965, Ned Williams was appointed a judge of Queensland Supreme Court in 1971 having been President of the Queensland Bar Association and an executive member of the Law Council of Australia.

He became chair of the *Australian Royal Commission of Inquiry into Drugs*, 1977 and from 1982 to 1987 was a member of the *International Narcotics Control Board*, headquartered in Vienna. In 1983 he became head of the National Crimes Commission.

In January 1977, Sir Edward became the chairman of the *XII Commonwealth Games Committee*, which organised the 1982 Brisbane Commonwealth Games. In 1984, Sir Edward was appointed Commissioner General for *Expo 88*.

He was created a KBE in 1981 and a KCMG in 1983, named Queenslander and Australian of the Year and was named Queensland Father of the Year.

He joined Queensland Turf Club in 1953 and was elected to the Committee in 1966. He served as Chairman of the Committee for 11 years, from 1980 to 1991, and was also a trustee of the Eagle Farm Racecourse for over 23 years. As a barrister, Sir Edward Williams acquired a reputation for defending disqualified or suspended racing people.

From 1971 to 1994, Sir Edward was President of *The Playground and Recreation Association of Queensland*. Sir Edward was also an active member of the *Queensland Cancer Fund*'s Anti-Cancer Council from 1983 to 1995, serving as Trustee of the Fund for 8 years. He was a founding member and trustee of the *Queensland Overseas Foundation* from 1976 to 1996.

He died in 1999.

RAYMOND WELLS WHITROD: The honest police commissioner driven out of Queensland by the Rat Pack and Premier Bjelke-Petersen lived to see the exposure and humiliation of Bjelke-Petersen and Terry Lewis in the hearings of the Fitzgerald Inquiry into corruption in Queensland. Whitrod had to give evidence to the inquiry without the aid of supporting documentation from his time in office: all his furniture, including filing cabinets containing all his documents, had been destroyed in early 1977 while in the hands of a removal company.

Whitrod taught criminology at the Australian National University and went on to establish in South Australia with his wife what was probably the world's first Victims of Crime Service. As Australian spokesman for the World Society of Victimology he even spent the holiday money he and his wife had saved to attend its annual meetings in Europe. He played a major role in engineering the passing of the United Nations Declaration of the Rights of Crime Victims.

He was the first national president of the Prison After-Care Council, a member of the South Australian Government's Commission for the Aging and became a Companion of the Order of Australia, the country's highest civil honour. He died on July 11, 2003.

Bibliography and Sources

Books and similar publications

Before I Sleep, by Ray Whitrod, University of Queensland Press, St Lucia, Queensland, 2001.

The Brotherhood, The Secret World of the Freemasons, by Stephen Knight, Granada, London, 1984.

Can of Worms, by Evan Whitton, Fairfax Library, Broadway, New South Wales, 1986.

Can of Worms II, by Evan Whitton, Fairfax Library, Broadway, New South Wales, 1987.

Corruption and Reform: The Fitzgerald Vision, edited by Scott Prasser, Ray Wear and John Nethercote, University of Queensland Press, St Lucia, 1990.

Don't You Worry About That, by Sir Joh Bjelke-Petersen, Collins/Angus and Robertson, North Ryde, 1990.

Easing the Passing: The Trial of Doctor John Bodkin Adams, by Patrick Devlin, The Bodley Head, London, 1985.

The Hillbilly Dictator, by Evan Whitton, ABC Enterprises for the Australian Broadcasting Commission, Crows Nest, New South Wales, 1989.

A History of Queensland, from 1915 to the 1980s, by Ross Fitzgerald, the University of Queensland Press, St Lucia, 1984.

In Place of Justice, by Peter James, Refulgence Publishers Pty Ltd, The Shield Press, Deception Bay, Queensland, 1974.

Inside the Brotherhood, Further Secrets of the Brotherhood, by Martin Short, Grafton Books, London, 1989.

Jigsaw, the biography of Johannes Bjelke-Petersen, Statesman not Politician, by Derek Townsend, Sneyd and Morley, Brisbane, 1983.

Joh, by Hugh Lunn, University of Queensland Press, St Lucia, 1978.

A Life of Crime, by Paul Wilson, Scribe Publications, Brunswick, 1990.

Masonic Grand Masters of Australia, by Kent Henderson, Ian Drakeford Publishing, Melbourne, 1988.

Murder! 25 true Australian crimes, by Alan Sharpe, Vivien Encel, Kingsclear Books, 1997.

The Premiers of Queensland, edited by Denis Murphy, Roger Joyce, Margaret Cribb and Rae Wear, University of Queensland Press, St Lucia, 2003

The Prince and the Premier, by David Hickie, Angus and Robertson, New South Wales, 1985.

Queensland Parliamentary Handbook, Queensland Parliamentary Library, annually.

Ray Whitrod, full interview transcript by Robin Hughes, Australian Biography project, Screen Australia Digital Learning, internet, 2000

The Road to Fitzgerald and Beyond, by Phil Dickie, University of Queensland Press, St Lucia, 1989.

Reminiscences of Charles Hopkins by Reuben Goldsworthy, South Australian Police Historical Society, 2009/10.

Return Your Verdict, by Eric Clegg, Angus and Robertson, Sydney, 1965.

Shadow of Shame, by Bob Bottom, Sun Books, Moray St, South Melbourne, 1988

The Sundown Murders, by Peter James, Boolarong Publications, Brisbane, 1990.

The Tangled Web, by Des Sturgess, Bedside Books, hotmail.com,

Three decades of Queensland Political History 1929-1960, compiled and edited by Clem Lack, the Queensland Government, Brisbane, 1961.

Trial and Error, by Don Lane, Boolarong Publications, Brisbane, 1993.

Working the System: Government in Queensland, by Peter Coaldrake, University of Queensland Press, St Lucia, 1989.

Official reports

First Report of the Parliamentary Judges Commission of Inquiry (on the behaviour of Justice Angelo Vasta), May 12, 1989.

The Fitzgerald Report (Report of a Commission of Inquiry Pursuant to Orders in Council), Queensland Government, July 3, 1989.

The Queensland Law Reporter, vol 53, no 18, Weekly Notes, Hallahan v Kryloff, ex parte Kryloff.

Queensland Reports of the Supreme Court 1964, Hallahan v Campbell, ex parte Campbell

Report by Arnold Bennett to the Queensland Minister for Justice and Attorney-General concerning the trial of Hendrikus Plomp on a charge of rape, August 30, 1962.

Reports on the Audits of The Department of the Arts, National Parks and Sport and the Queensland Film Corporation, dated February and April 1986 but not presented to Parliament and printed until 1988.

Report of the Australian Royal Commission of Inquiry into Drugs (the Williams Commission), presented on December 21, 1979 (Interim Report published November 6, 1979)

Report by the Honourable W J Carter on his Inquiry into the Selection of the Jury for the Trial of Sir Johannes Bjelke-Petersen, 1993.

Report of the Electoral and Administrative Review Commission on the history of the zonal system, 1990.

Report of the Lucas Inquiry (The Criminal Law Inquiry), May 30, 1977.

Report to the Queensland Government on Matters of Particular Relevance to the State of Queensland, presented by the Australian Royal Commission of Inquiry into Drugs, Commissioner: The Hon Mr Justice E S Williams, May 1980.

Report of the Royal Commission Appointed to Inquire into and Report on Certain Matters relating to Members of the Police Force and the National

Hotel, Petrie Bight, Brisbane. The Honourable Mr Justice H T Gibbs, Commissioner, April 10, 1964.

Report of the Stewart Royal Commission into Drug Trafficking (Mr Asia), 1983.

Report of the Woodward Royal Commission (NSW Royal Commission into Drugs), November 6, 1979.

Second Report of the Parliamentary Judges Commission of Inquiry (on the behaviour of Judge Eric Pratt), July 19, 1989.

The Sturgess Report: An Inquiry into Sexual Offences Involving Children and Related Matters by D G Sturgess, Brisbane, 1985.

Other sources

Australasian Criminal Register.

Back numbers of the Queensland Sunday Mail, Courier-Mail, Brisbane Telegraph, Brisbane Sun, Sydney Sunday Mirror, Australian, Adelaide Advertiser, Adelaide News, Mt Isa Mail, etc.

Cabinet memorandum no 528, Department of Business and Consumer Affairs Assessment of the Williams Interim Report, October 1979.

Cabinet Minute Decision no 10202 regarding the Interim Report of the Australian Royal Commission of Inquiry into Drugs, November 1979.

Collected papers of Percy Reginald 'Inky' Stephensen, State Library of New South Wales.

Collected papers of Sir Edward Stratten Williams, Queensland State Library

Contemporaneous notes written by Col Bennett August 7, 1969 to March 10, 1972.

Contemporaneous notes written by John Shobbrook, 1980.

Copy of breathalyser summons against Sir Edward Lyons, December 18, 1981.

Criminal record of John Edward Milligan.

Diaries of Terence Murray Lewis (tendered as exhibits at the Fitzgerald Inquiry).

Hansard, debates of the Queensland Legislative Assembly 1957-1987.

Interviews with Mike Ahern, Col Bennett, Ken Blanch, Bob Campbell, Senator Don Chipp, Norm Gulbransen, Bill Gunn MP, Kevin Hooper, Joe Moore (who knew Shirley Emerson at school), Arthur Pitts, Nigel Powell, Earl Rawlings, John Shobbrook, Gerald Stone, Des Sturgess, Terry White, Ray Whitrod, and other former honest police officers and politicians who prefer not to be named.

Letter from Col Bennet to Max Hodges July 5, 1971.

Letters written by Shirley Brifman.

Letters written by Bob Campbell to Parliamentarians 1976-1982.

Letters from Tony Murphy to Shirley Brifman.

Ministerial Statement by the Queensland Attorney-General on the tabling of the report by Arnold Bennett on his findings on an inquiry into certain questions raised by the Court of Criminal Appeal in connection with the trial of Hendrikus Plomp on a charge of rape, September 4, 1962.

Queensland State Archives - more than 50 statements and interviews from the Fitzgerald Inquiry.

Records of interviews between police and Shirley Brifman from July 2, 1971 to November 9, 1971, (and as tabled in South Australian Parliament in March, 1978).

Record of interview between John Shobbrook and John Milligan at Customs House, Sydney, on September 24, 1979.

Report by Sergeant First Class R K Carroll, dated October 11, 1971.

South Australia State Reports R v Bailey Criminal Appeal, June 3,4,9,1958.

Selected debates from the Federal Hansard.

Statement by Constable 1/c Brian Cook April 6, 1982.

Statement by Shirley Brifman June 15, 1971.

Statement by Sonny Brifman March 14, 1972.

Statements attached to Supreme Court Writs: 675 of 1982, Freier v Campbell and ABC; 848 of 1982, Lewis v Campbell; 849 of 1982, Lewis v Fancourt; 850 of 1982, Lewis v ABC; 851 of 1982, Murphy v ABC; 852 of 1982, Murphy v Fancourt; 853 of 1982, Murphy v Campbell.

Sunday Truth/Sunday Sun - 1957-1987.

Transcript of ABC Nationwide program for March 3, 1982.

Transcript of the findings of the Queensland Court of Appeal, in the case against Hendrikus Plomp, July 27, 1962.

Transcript of evidence to the National Hotel Inquiry, November 20, 1963 to February 24, 1964.

Transcript of evidence to the Williams Royal Commission (Queensland Police and Parliamentarians) January 3 to March 20, 1980.

Transcripts of evidence and certain exhibits from the Fitzgerald Inquiry, 1987-88.

Transcript of evidence at the inquest into the death of Robin Morton Corrie, 1971

Transcript of evidence at the inquest into the death of Cheryl Anne Mitchell, 1972.

Transcript of the evidence at the inquest into the death of Gary James Venamore, 1969.

Transcript of the trial of Glen Patrick Hallahan on a charge relating to Dorothy Edith Knight, August 1972.

Transcript of the committal and trial of Raymond Bailey, charged with murdering Thyra Bowman, 1958.

Transcript of judge's summary in the trial of Roy Clifford Hart, charged with wilfully and unlawfully setting fire to a dwelling house, September 25, 1962.

Transcript of the judge's remarks at the sentencing of Carl Markert May 11, 1970.

Transcript of the trial of Patrick John Creamer on charges of breaking and entering August 28, 1970.

Transcript of the trial of Roy Clifford Hart and Colin Roy Woodward on a charge of intent to defraud by burning down the Royal Hotel, Nambour, May 13, 1963.

Transcript of the trial of Denis Johnson and Michael Joseph Brennan on charges involving deception at a race track May 18, 1970

Transcript of the trial of Jack Herbert, Neil Freier and Paddy McIntyre, charged with official corruption; and conspiracy and attempting to obstruct the course of justice, May 18, to November 5, 1976.

Transcript of the sentencing of Donald Ross Kelly on a charge of bank robbery, April 17, 1972.

Transcript of the trial of Donald Maher, charged with the murder of Jack Cooper, April 26 to May 25, 1972.

Transcript of the trial of Hendrikus Plomp, charged with rape, April/May 1962.

Transcript of the trial of Jack Edward Wilson and Donald Frederick Flanders, charged with the Beerburrum Mailvan Robbery, February 4 to March 24, 1975.

8039538R00201

Printed in Great Britain
by Amazon.co.uk, Ltd.,
Marston Gate.